CISTERCIAN STUDIES SERIES: NUMBER ONE HUNDRED NINETY-EIGHT

JOAN E. BARCLAY LLOYD

Ss. Vincenzo e Anastasio at Tre Fontane near Rome:
History and Architecture of a Medieval Cistercian Abbey

CISTERCIAN STUDIES SERIES: NUMBER ONE HUNDRED NINETY-EIGHT

SS. VINCENZO E ANASTASIO AT TRE FONTANE NEAR ROME:
HISTORY AND ARCHITECTURE OF A MEDIEVAL CISTERCIAN ABBEY

by

JOAN E. BARCLAY LLOYD

Cistercian Publications
Kalamazoo, Michigan

*The work of Cistercian Publications is made possible in part
by support from Western Michigan University to
The Institute of Cistercian Studies.*

ISBN 13: 978 0 87907 698 6
ISBN 10: 0 87907 698 4

Library of Congress Cataloging-in-Publication Data

Lloyd, Joan Barclay.
    Ss. Vincenzo e Anastasio at Tre Fontane near Rome : history and architec-
ture of a medieval Cistercian abbey / by Joan E. Barclay Lloyd.
        p. cm. — (Cistercian studies series ; no. 198)
    Includes bibliographical references.
    ISBN: 0-87907-698-4 (hardcover : alk. paper)
    1. Santi Vincenzo e Anastasio (Church : Rome, Italy) 2. Cistercian
architecture—Italy—Rome. 3. Rome (Italy)—Buildings, structures, etc.
4. Santi Vincenzo e Anastasio (Church : Rome, Italy)—History. I. Title.
II. Series.

NA5620.V56L56 2005
726'.77094563—dc22

                                                                    2005027436

In loving memory of my mother
Rubi Margaret Barclay Lloyd

I said, Lord, be merciful unto me:
heal my soul; for I have sinned against thee.

Psalm 41:4

TABLE OF CONTENTS

ABBREVIATIONS

AA SS	*Acta Sanctorum*. I. Bollandus *et al.*, edd. Antwerp: Apud Ioannem Meursum, 1693 ff.
BAR	British Archæological Report
BAV	Biblioteca Vaticana Apostolica (Vatican Library)
Cistercian Art	*Cistercian Art and Architecture in the British Isles.* Christopher Norton-David Park, ed. Cambridge: Cambridge University Press, 1986.
CS	Cistercian Studies Series. Cistercian Publications.
LP	Le *Liber Pontificalis,* volumes 1 and 2. Ed. L. Duchesne. Paris: E. De Boccard, 1886–92; volume 3, with additions and corrections by C. Vogel, Paris: E. De Boccard, 1957. Three volumes reprinted 1981.
MGH	Monumenta Germaniae Historica. Munich-Hanover-Leipzig.
PL	*Patrologia cursus completus . . . series Latina.* Ed. Migne, J. P. Paris, 1844–1905.
RB	Rule of Saint Benedict / *Regula monachorum*
S. Bernardi Opera	*Sancti Bernardi Opera,* volumes 7–8. *Epistolae.* J. Leclercq and H. M. Rochais, edd. Rome: Editiones Cistercienses, 1977.
Statuta	*Statuta capitularum generalium Ordinis Cisterciensis.* 9 volumes. Bibliothèque de la Révue d'Histoire Ecclésiastique, 9–14B. Joseph-Marie Canivez, ed. Louvain: Bureaux de la Révue d'Histoire Ecclésiastique, 1933–1941.

PREFACE

ON THE FEAST OF SAINT PAUL, 25 January 1983 Pope John
Paul II beatified Sister Gabriella, a trappistine nun who died
in Italy in 1939 after dedicating her life to praying fervently
for christian unity. To mark the occasion, her mortal remains were
translated to the church of SS. Vincenzo e Anastasio at Tre Fontane
near Rome, where many visitors came to pay their respects. At the
time Jeremy Blake and I were working on the architectural survey presented in this volume. One day Abbot Angelo Buccitti OCSO introduced us to some of the visitors, telling them that while the trappist
community of SS. Vincenzo e Anastasio would happily replace their
old buildings with new ones, here were two people who had come
from as far away as Australia and England to study the medieval
monastery.

The abbey of Saint Anastasius—now SS. Vincenzo e Anastasio—at
Tre Fontane near Rome is a cistercian monastery, founded by Pope
Innocent II (1130–1143) during the lifetime of the great cistercian
saint, Bernard of Clairvaux. On the site of a much earlier, oriental-rite
monastic foundation, the medieval buildings were begun in the
twelfth century and extended during the thirteenth and fourteenth
centuries—and later. The abbey is an important example of medieval
cistercian architecture. It is particularly fascinating because of the
abbey's association with the papacy through its founder, Pope Innocent II, and its first abbot, Pietro Bernardo Paganelli, who became
Pope Eugenius III (1145–1153). Architecturally, the monastery shows a
combination of cistercian planning and medieval roman building
techniques. Being one of the great monasteries of Rome, it is an important example of roman medieval architecture.

This book is based on an architectural survey, an analysis of building techniques and historical research. It is divided into two parts. The first discusses the buildings and their history; the second sets out schematically the architectural, visual and historical data. The first chapter discusses the legends and history associated with Tre Fontane from ancient roman times to the present day. The next chapter outlines the early history of the Cistercians and the functions of the various parts of the monastery in the monks' way of life. This is followed in Chapter Three by a brief account of the origins and development of cistercian architecture. The fourth chapter describes the layout of the Tre Fontane buildings. Early images of the abbey, from the fifteenth century until today, illustrate how some of the major buildings have changed. The sixth chapter gives an overview of scholarly literature on the architecture of the abbey, including some important new data which came to light during the recent restoration of the church and from excavations. The buildings are then analysed afresh, and reconstructions of their original forms are proposed. The successive building phases are set out in chronological order and linked to historical evidence of building activity. The second part of the book sets out the various forms of documentation: the architectural data; early illustrations; and important dates and excerpts from historical documents, all given in chronological order.

The illustrations have been placed in the following order: after a site plan, there are photographs of the various parts of the complex, from the gatehouse, to the church, to the monastery. There follow images of inscriptions, then early prints, drawings and photographs. Images specific to Tre Fontane end with a reconstruction plan of the east wing. After all this there are illustrations of comparative material. Finally, the survey drawings, and a plan and an isometric reconstruction are included in fold-out format.

Professor Christopher Holdsworth introduced me to medieval history and the Cistercians when I was an undergraduate at University College London. Years later the late Professor Richard Krautheimer encouraged me to study the medieval monastic buildings of Rome, of which this cistercian abbey is an outstanding example. Most of the method of architectural analysis and history used in this book was learned from working as his research assistant in Rome.

Many people have made this study possible. I am particularly grateful to Jeremy Blake, who made the architectural survey and drew the isometric reconstruction of the abbey. Abbot Angelo Buccitti OCSO, gave Jeremy and me permission to enter the enclosed parts of the monastery to make all the measurements required for the survey. On several subsequent occasions he and his successors, Abbots José Ramón Sanchez and Giacomo (Jacques) de Brière, allowed me access to various parts of the buildings to take photographs, analyse masonry, and check my notes on windows, columns, capitals, and arches. To these abbots many thanks are due.

During work on this study Father Ansgar Christensen OCSO has been a helpful, patient friend. He assisted Jeremy and me when we were doing the survey and kept in touch afterwards. He made us feel very welcome at Tre Fontane. Fra Ansgar and Fra Giacomo sent us information on the renovations to the monastery made by Giovanni Belardi just prior to 2000. Other members of the community, like Father Emanuele and Fra Corrado, were always very hospitable.

Frequent visits to Rome from Australia have been expensive. I am very grateful for the generous financial assistance received from the Australian Research Council and La Trobe University in Melbourne, which made all this possible. I also wish to thank my colleagues in the Art History Program at La Trobe University for their moral support. In particular, I am grateful for the assistance of Susan Russell for reading the manuscript and making useful suggestions beyond those advocated by the three anonymous referees of the original text. I thank the staff of the Borchardt Library at La Trobe University, and especially the members of the Inter Library Loans division, for assistance in obtaining the literature I required.

The monks of Tarrawarra Abbey near Yarra Glen, not far from Melbourne, each year welcome a pilgrimage of staff and students from La Trobe University. I am grateful to Father Stephen List OCSO for a letter of introduction to the abbot of Tre Fontane; and to Father Michael Casey OCSO, for granting me access to books from the monastery library.

In Rome an Australian friend, Beth Hay, frequently put me up for several weeks at a time. She let me leave my measuring tapes, paper and other paraphernalia at her flat. I am grateful for her kindness and hospitality. Architect Giovanni Belardi showed me over the vault of the south transept in 1992. Karin Bull-Simonsen Einaudi has kindly furnished me with information from Rome when I have been unable to go there in person.

I thank E. Rozanne Elder for carefully editing the text and Elizabeth King for the photographic layout, as well as the other persons at Cistercian Publications who have brought this book to publication.

My family has been very supportive. My sister and my brother-in-law, Margaret and Colin Visser, my niece Emily and her husband Bernard, and my nephew Alexander have all been very helpful and encouraging, although we live far apart. This work is dedicated to the memory of my mother, Rubi Margaret Barclay Lloyd, who first introduced me to the history of art and continued over the years to encourage my study and writing.

Saint Benedict says that when one begins something good one should pray constantly to the Lord for the grace to bring it to completion (RB Prologue 4). As this study comes to an end, I pray a fervent *Deo gratias.*

Joan E. Barclay Lloyd

24 May 2004
La Trobe University
Bundoora
Melbourne
Australia

LIST OF ILLUSTRATIONS

TEXT ILLUSTRATIONS

PART I:
HISTORY AND ARCHITECTURE

I

TRE FONTANE IN
LEGEND AND HISTORY

T HE ABBEY OF SS. VINCENZO E ANASTASIO at Tre Fontane
near Rome is an outstanding example of medieval cistercian
architecture.[1] The monastery was founded by Pope Innocent II
c. 1140, as a daughter house of Clairvaux, during the lifetime of Saint
Bernard (1090–1153). From 1145–1153 its first abbot, Pietro Bernardo

---

1. For the architecture see: Oskar Mothes, *Die Baukunst des Mittelalters in Italien* (Jena: H. Costengoble, 1884) 97, 99–100; Giuseppe Tomassetti, 'Della Campagna Romana', *Archivio della Società Romana di Storia Patria* 19 (1896) 135–150; Arthur L. Frothingham, *The Monuments of Christian Rome* (New York: Macmillan, 1908) 105–106, 128–129, 187 and 197; Aristide Sartorio, 'L'abbazia cisterciense delle Tre Fontane', *Nuova Antologia* 167 (settembre, 1913) 50–65 (reprinted in Anonymous, *S. Paolo e la Tre Fontane* (Rome: L'Abbazia 'Nullius' dei Santi Vincenzo e Anastasio alle Acque Salvie, 1938) 113–121); Giovanni Battista Giovenale, 'Il chiostro medioevale di San Paolo fuori le Mura', *Bullettino della Commissione Archeologica Comunale di Roma* 45 (1917) 125–167, esp. 148–167; Renate Wagner-Rieger, *Die italienische Baukunst zu Gebinn der Gotik* (Graz-Koln: Verlag Hermann Böhlaus, 1956–1957) 2:27-30; Hanno Hahn, *Die frühe Kirchenbaukunst der Zistersienser* (Berlin: Verlag Gebr. Mann, 1957) 171–173; Cesare D'Onofrio and Carlo Pietrangeli, *Abbazie del Lazio* (Rome: Cassa di Risparmio, 1969) 184–188; Carlo Bertelli, 'L'enciclopedia delle Tre Fontane', *Paragone-Arte* 10 (1969) 24–49; Giuseppe Ruotolo, *L'abbazia delle Tre Fontane* (Rome: Abbazia delle Tre Fontane, 1972); Umberto Broccoli, *L'abbazia delle Tre Fontane. Fasi paleocristiane e altomedioevali del complesso 'ad Aquas Salvias' in Roma* (Trani: Vivere In, 1980); Angiola Maria Romanini, 'La storia architettonica dell'abbazia delle Tre Fontane a Roma. La fondazione cisterciense', *Mélanges à la Memoire du Anselme Dimier*, ed. Benoît Chauvin, vol. 3 (Pupillon, Arbois: 1982) 653–695; Germano Mulazzani, *L'abbazia delle Tre Fontane* (Milan: Tranchida Editori, 1988); Pio F. Pistilli, 'Architettura a Roma nella prima metà del Duecento (1198–1254)', *Roma nel Duecento*, ed. A. M. Romanini (Turin: Edizioni Seat, 1991) 16, 19, 21–23, 48–53; Pio F. Pistilli, 'Considerazioni sulla storia architettonica dell'abbazia romana delle Tre Fontane nel duecento', *Arte Medievale* serie 2, 6.1 (1992) 163–192; 'Ratio fecit diversum': *San Bernardo e le arte. Atti del congresso internazionale, Roma, 27–29 maggio 1991*, ed. A. M. Romanini, *Arte Medievale*, serie 2, 8, 1 (1994) 1–140; Giovanni Belardi, Jacques Brière et al., *Abbazia delle Tre Fontane: il complesso, la storia e il restauro* (Rome: Edilerica, 1995).

3

Paganelli, ruled the Church as Pope Eugenius III (1145–1153). This abbey, which had such important papal connections, was the only medieval Cistercian monastery built in the immediate vicinity of Rome. From the Middle Ages until 1812, when it was suppressed, there was a continuous cistercian presence. Since 1868 it has belonged to the Trappists.

The abbey of SS. Vincenzo e Anastasio alle Tre Fontane is located close to the Via Laurentina, about fourteen kilometres southeast of the Aurelian Walls which from the late third century encircled ancient Rome. The site is adjacent to the modern roman suburb of EUR, which was laid out in the 1940s. There are a number of buildings at Tre Fontane (fig 1): the medieval gatehouse, the so-called *Arco di Carlo Magno* or 'Arch of Charlemagne' (figs. 1–3); the medieval cistercian church of SS. Vincenzo e Anastasio (figs. 1 and 4–14); the monastic buildings, ranged around a cloister to the north of it (figs. 1 and 15–63); the sixteenth-century centrally planned church of S. Maria Scala Coeli, to the south (fig. 1, centre right); and some distance to the southeast the sixteenth-century sanctuary of S. Paolo alle Tre Fontane (fig. 1, top right), which commemorates the beheading of Saint Paul and contains the three fountains from which the place takes its name.

Tre Fontane has a long and fascinating history reaching back to roman antiquity. Different kinds of epigraphic and documentary evidence highlight important events, while pious traditions intertwine with historical facts associated with the place and its sanctuaries. It is often difficult to disentangle truth from legend and, what is more, legends have sometimes assumed an importance and a 'reality', which cannot be discounted in the subsequent history of Tre Fontane.

In antiquity the site was known as *Aquae Salviae,* the 'Salvian Waters'.[2] Salvius was a family name referring to an ancient roman gens, some of whose members rose to prominence in the second century

---

2. Anonymous (A. Barbiero OCSO), *S. Paola alle Tre Fontane,* 9. Mention of a nunnery of S. Maria and S. Nicola in '*Aqua Salvia*' in a document of 992 appears to refer to another location of similar name at the foot of the Aventine Hill, according to Giuseppe Gullota, 'Un antico ed unico documento sul monastero di S. Maria e S. Nicola in Acqua Salvia'. *Archivio della Società Romana di Storia Patria* 66 (1943) 185–195; and Guy Ferrari, *Early Roman Monasteries,* Studi di Antichità Cristiana, 23 (Vatican City: Pontificio Istituto di Archeologia Cristiana, 1957) 47–48, n. 34.

AD. The Salvian Waters probably formed part of their estates. As the name implies, the area has—until this century—been noted for water: fountains, a small river, and swampy marshes. Another expression used to describe it, *ad guttam iugiter manantem,* 'at the incessantly dripping drop' or 'at the perpetual fountain', has the same connotation.[3] In the past it was an unhealthy place whose inhabitants often contracted malaria. Today most of the water has been drained away, but there are still fresh springs and a rather damp atmosphere, especially in winter.

From late antiquity onwards the Salvian Waters were legally defined as a *massa,* a term used to denote a grouping of properties within the same geographical zone belonging to a great landowner, in this case probably the *gens Salvius.*[4] Since the Salvian Waters lay outside the city, the property may have included a villa or a farm.[5] Large blocks of tufa stone *(peperino)* that were excavated at Tre Fontane in 1897 now line the entry to the abbey and must have formed part of a roman building.[6] Roman law also permitted burials beyond the Walls of Rome.[7]

By far the most important religious tradition connected with the site concerned the martyrdom of Saint Paul. The apostle is believed to have been beheaded in Rome in 67 AD, during the persecution of Nero.[8] The Presbyter Gaius *c.* 200 referred to the trophies of the apostles in Rome: Peter at the Vatican and Paul along the Ostian Way.[9] Saint Paul's memorial was probably associated with his tomb, which from the fourth century was venerated under the high altar of the basilica

3. Richard A. Lipsius, *Die apokryphen Apostelgeschichten* (Brunswick: C. A. Schwetschke und Sohn, 1887) vol. 2, 399.

4. Pierre Toubert, *Les structures du Latium médiéval,* Bibliothèque française d'Athènes et de Rome, 221 (Rome: École Française de Rome, 1973) 328, 455–456, esp. 455 and n. 2.

5. At the time of Julian the Apostate, in 362, the wife of the Prefect Gordianus was condemned to work in the country villa at Aquas Salvias (see Anonymous [A. Barbiero ocso], *S. Paolo alle Tre Fontane,* 63–64, quoting from the life of blessed Gordianus: '*Acta Martyrum ex pervetustis variis mss. In codicibus . . . "uxorem autem ejus Marinam in quadam villa, quae vocatur ad Aquas Salvias, in servitio rusticorum opprimi".'*

6. Barbiero, following Grisar in *Civiltà Cattolica,* 10 (1897) 477, identifies the building as a roman temple, but without supporting evidence, Anonymous [Barbiero] *S. Paolo alle Tre Fontane,* 11.

7. Tradition has it that many christian martyrs were buried at the site, but their graves have never been discovered; see Anonymous [Barbiero] *S. Paolo alle Tre Fontane,* 53–65.

8. See below, C. DATES AND DOCUMENTS, 67.

9. See below, C. DATES AND DOCUMENTS, *c.* 200.

of S. Paolo fuori le Mura along the Via Ostiense.[10] In 258, however, the feast of Saints Peter and Paul (29 June) was celebrated *ad catacumbas,* at the catacomb of Saint Sebastian along the Via Appia, where remains of both the apostles appear to have been translated.[11] A little earlier, according to the *Liber Pontificalis,* Pope Cornelius (251–253), at the request of the roman matron Lucina, removed the bodies of Saints Peter and Paul from the catacomb by night; Lucina then laid the remains of Saint Paul in her land along the Via Ostiense, next to the place where he was beheaded.[12] Although it is not clear precisely where along the Ostian Way Lucina's property was located, nor exactly where the apostle suffered martyrdom, this account does not refer to the Salvian Waters, which are some distance from the Via Ostiense. It may refer to another site associated in early times with the martyrdom of Saint Paul and closer to the place of his burial.

Some early christian sarcophagi of the fourth century show Saint Paul going to his death in a swampy place characterized by marsh reeds and a boat.[13] This location may be somewhere along the River Tiber, which is close to the basilica of S. Paolo fuori le Mura and the Via Ostiense. Or it could be a place like the Salvian Waters. The poet Prudentius *c.* 413 described the River Tiber as flowing between the trophies of the apostles who through their martyrdom by cross (Saint Peter) and sword (Saint Paul) had irrigated either bank with their blood.[14]

---

10. Richard Krautheimer, *Corpus Basilicarum Christianarum Romae,* Monumenti di Antichità Cristiana, serie 2, 2 (Vatican City: Pontificio Istituto di Archeologia Cristiana, 1977) 5:97–164; see below, C. DATES AND DOCUMENTS, *c.* 650, 648–682.

11. Richard Krautheimer, *Rome: Profile of a City* (Princeton: Princeton University Press, 1980) 19.

12. *Le Liber Pontificalis.* ed. L. Duchesne (Paris: E. De Boccard, 1886–1892 and 1957, reprinted 1981) 1:150 and 152, n. 8. (The *Liber Pontificalis* was written *c.* 513, using much older material.) See also Johann Peter Kirsch, 'Der Ort des Martyriums des Hl. Paulus', *Römische Quartalschrift für christliche Altertumskunde und für Kirchengeschichte* 2 (1888) 235; see below, C. DATES AND DOCUMENTS, 251–253.

13. Kirsch, 'Der Ort', 235.

14. Prudentius, *Peristephanon* XII, 6–10, quoted in Kirsch, 'Der Ort', 234:
'Scit Tiberina palus quae flumine lambiter propinquo,
Binis dicatum caespitem trophaeis
Et crucis et gladii testis, quibus irrigans easdem
Bis fluxit imber sanguinis per herbas'.

By the mid-fifth century some apocryphal texts clearly referred to Saint Paul's martyrdom *ad Aquas Salvias*. The *Acts of Peter and Paul* by Pseudo-Marcellus mentioned his decapitation near a pine-tree there.[15] For centuries thereafter the site was venerated as the spot where the Apostle to the Gentiles suffered martyrdom. In 604 Pope Gregory the Great donated the estates, or *massa,* of the Salvian Waters to the basilica of S. Paolo fuori le Mura, precisely because they were associated with the martyrdom of Saint Paul.[16] Later, in the seventh century, oriental monks were given property *ad Aquas Salvias,* because they came from Cilicia—the region in Asia Minor in which Tarsus, the birthplace of Saint Paul, is situated.[17] Early guidebooks and regionary catalogues referred to the Salvian Waters as the place where Saint Paul was beheaded.[18] The tradition was continued in similar works of later times. By the seventeenth century it was said that at his execution the apostle's head bounced three times, on each occasion giving rise to a fountain, and to the name Tre Fontane.[19]

There seems quite early to have been a *martyrium,* a shrine commemorating the apostle's martyrdom, on the site of the present sixteenth-century church of S. Paolo alle Tre Fontane (fig. 1, upper righthand corner).[20] It marked the spot where the apostle was beheaded, and enclosed the three fountains which sprang up as his head hit the ground.[21] The date when the original building was erected is unknown. According to two inscriptions discovered in 1867 under the present church of S. Paolo alle Tre Fontane, Pope Sergius I in 688/9 restored the structure, which was described then as 'ancient', *prisca.*[22] It must have been built long before. Prior to its demolition in the late

---

15. See below, C. DATES AND DOCUMENTS, Fifth century.

16. See below, C. DATES AND DOCUMENTS, 604.

17. Ferrari, *Early Roman Monasteries,* 33.

18. See below, C. DATES AND DOCUMENTS, *c.* 650.

19. Giovanni Severano, *Memorie sacre delle sette chiese di Roma.* (Rome: Giacomo Mascardi, 1630) 418.

20. Anonymous [Barbiero], *S. Paolo alle Tre Fontane,* 42–49; Luca Maggi, *Giacomo della Porta: Il S. Paolo alle Tre Fontane* (Rome: Bonsignori Editore, 1996) 17–38.

21. From the Middle Ages, but at a date unknown to the present author, a stump of a column has been shown to pilgrims as the block on which the apostle laid his head at his execution.

22. See below, C. DATES AND DOCUMENTS, 688/9 and 1867.

sixteenth century, the building was described by Onofrio Panvinio, first in 1560 and then again in 1570.[23] There were two chapels, on different levels. In the higher chapel, which was covered with murals, there was one fountain, a pulpit decorated with mosaics, and an altar. The two remaining fountains were in the lower chapel, where an altar stood in an apse encrusted with marble; there were no murals. There was a small courtyard in front of both the chapels. Early maps show little sketches of this building (figs. 68 and 69).[24] The 1867 excavations brought to light remnants of a colonnaded portico, perhaps part of the small courtyard described by Panvinio. The same excavations also uncovered a mosaic pavement, some marble plaques, and inscriptions.[25] There are some capitals of sixth-century style at Tre Fontane— for example, one currently on a column supporting the statue of the Madonna and Child in the cloister (fig. 15). Federigo Guidobaldi has suggested that these formed part of a building of sixth-century date.[26] Perhaps the *martyrium* was connected with the cult of Saint Paul.

In addition to Saint Paul, Saint Zeno and 10,203 roman soldiers were thought to have been martyred *ad Aquas Salvias* in 299 under Diocletian and Maximian.[27] In the sixteenth century they were believed to be buried under the church of S. Maria Scala Coeli (fig. 1). In 1577 the commendatory abbot, Alexander Farnese, provided a reliquary for the head of Saint Zeno.[28] Although roman burials would have been legal at this extramural site, no archaeological evidence has been found for the graves of these early christian martyrs.

Basing themselves on Benedict of Soracte's *Chronicon*, which was written towards the end of the tenth century,[29] several scholars claimed

---

23. See below, C. DATES AND DOCUMENTS, 1560; 1570 and 1599.
24. See below, B. EARLY ILLUSTRATIONS, 1469, 1471, 1450–1500 and 1474.
25. See below, C. DATES AND DOCUMENTS, 1867. The mosaic of the Four Seasons now in the church of S. Paolo alle Tre Fontane is not that found on the site, but comes from Ostia Antica. Two of the inscriptions discovered in the excavations refer to the presence of armenian monks at Tre Fontane in 1267 and 1305; see below, C. DATES AND DOCUMENTS, 1267 and 1305.
26. Federigo Guidobaldi, Claudia Barsanti and Alessandra Guiglia Guidobaldi, *San Clemente: la scultura del VI secolo,* San Clemente Miscellany, 4.2 (Rome: San Clemente, 1992) 26, 241–245, 256, and figs. 382–384.
27. See below, C. DATES AND DOCUMENTS, 299.
28. See below, C. DATES AND DOCUMENTS, 1577.
29. See below, C. DATES AND DOCUMENTS, c. 1000.

that the first monastery *ad Aquas Salvias* was founded by the byzantine general Narses, who was in Italy from 552–574.[30] Yet, no earlier source mentions this, and Benedict was writing nearly five hundred years after the event. For this reason Ferrari, Sansterre and others have rejected his evidence.[31] On the other hand, Benedict correctly identified Narses as the builder of the Nomentana Bridge just outside Rome and he may have had access to some historical source, which no longer survives, for the general's building projects. Guidobaldi, as we noted above, has dated certain capitals on the site to the sixth century. It is not clear whether these were connected with the *martyrium* of Saint Paul or with a monastic establishment. From the fifth century onwards the popes founded monasteries at extramural shrines of the apostles and martyrs near Rome. For example: Pope Sixtus III (432–440) established a monastery beside S. Sebastiano, *ad catacumbas;* Pope Leo I (440–461) founded one at Saint Peter's; Pope Hilarus I (461–468) one at S. Lorenzo fuori le Mura.[32] If there was a memorial of the martyrdom of Saint Paul at Tre Fontane in the late sixth century, it is possible that Narses decided to set up such a monastic establishment.

The first clear reference to a monastery *ad Aquas Salvias* dates from 649, when George, abbot of the 'venerable monastery from Cilicia' in that place, signed a document at a synod held at the Lateran in Rome that year to condemn Monotheletism, the teaching that Christ has only one will, promoted by the byzantine emperor, Heraclius.[33] The monastery of these eastern cilician monks seems to have been established after 627 and before 649; probably it was founded shortly before 649.[34] Although there is a tradition that the monastery *ad Aquas Salvias*

---

30. See for example, Giovanni Battista De Rossi, 'Oratorio e monastero di S. Paolo apostolo alle Aque Salvie costruiti da Narsete patrizio', *Bullettino di Archeologia Cristiana* s. 4, 5 (1887) 79–81 and Tomassetti, 'Della Campagna Romana', 138.

31. Ferrari, *Early Roman Monasteries,* 35; Jean-Marie Sansterre, *Les moines grecs et orientaux à Rome aux epoques byzantine et carolingienne,* Académie Royale de Belgique, Mémoires de la Classe des Lettres, 46 (Brussels: Palais des Académies, 1983) 14.

32. *Le Liber Pontificalis,* vol. 1:234, 239, 245.

33. See below, C. DATES AND DOCUMENTS, 649; Ferdinando Antonelli, 'I primi monasteri di monaci orientali in Roma', *Rivista di Archeologia Cristiana* 5 (1928) 105–122, esp. 109–114; Ferrari, *Early Roman Monasteries,* 36–38; Sansterre, *Les moines grecs et orientaux,* 9 ff.; and Margaret Visser, *The Geometry of Love: Space, Time, Mystery, and Meaning in an Ordinary Church* (Toronto: Harper Flamingo Canada, 2000) 111–115.

34. Sansterre, *Les moines grecs et orientaux,* 14–16.

was founded during the pontificate of Honorius I (625–638), there is no historical evidence to confirm this.[35]

From the seventh century, an important relic at the monastery is mentioned—the head of Saint Anastasius, a persian monk who before his conversion to Christianity had lived in the area which now comprises Iraq and Iran. In 621 he had become a monk in Jerusalem, where he was martyred on 22 January 627 by Chosroes II.[36] It is probable that the monks from Cilicia brought this relic with them to Rome. The head of Saint Anastasius was credited with miraculous powers. A famous exorcism was effected with the aid of the relic in 713, when a syrian bishop brought to S. Anastasius his daughter, a nun from the nunnery of Saint Cassian at San Lorenzo fuori le Mura, to be delivered from evil spirits.[37] Since no woman was allowed within the monastic buildings, the bishop first brought his daughter to the oratory (or residence, *mansio*) of the holy Mother of God and then persuaded the hygumenarch, the head of the monastery, to bring the relic of Saint Anastasius into the basilica of Saint John the Baptist, where the woman was set free after long and arduous prayers of intercession. The written account of the miracle gives some important information about the buildings on the site. Apart from the shrine of S. Paolo alle Tre Fontane, there appear to have been two sanctuaries: the oratory of the Mother of God; and the basilica of Saint John the Baptist; in addition, there was the monastery itself.[38]

In 731 the Venerable Bede referred to 'the monastery of Saint Paul the apostle which is said to be *ad Aquas Salvias*'.[39] No doubt he derived the name of the monastery from the location of Saint Paul's martyrdom and its commemorative shrine. He claimed elsewhere to have re-translated the life of a Saint Anastasius, perhaps the patron of this monastery.[40]

---

35. Ferrari, *Early Roman Monasteries,* 38–39; Sansterre, *Les moines grecs et orientaux,* 5.
36. For his martyrdom, see below, C. DATES AND DOCUMENTS, 627; for the relic, C. DATES AND DOCUMENTS, 648–682.
37. See below, C. DATES AND DOCUMENTS, 713.
38. 'Miraculum S. Anastasii martyris', *Analecta Bollandiana* 11 (1892) 233–241.
39. See below, C. DATES AND DOCUMENTS, 731.
40. See below, C. DATES AND DOCUMENTS, 731.

In 723 or 739 the lombard king, Luitprand, visited the 'monastery of Saint Anastasius' in Rome. Probably as a result of this, he later founded a monastery dedicated to Saint Anastasius at Olonna.[41]

During the Second Council of Nicaea in 787, the roman delegates, Peter and Peter, referred to the head of Saint Anastasius and his icon, both of which were in his monastery in Rome.[42] The miraculous powers of the icon and the relic were cited as evidence in favour of venerating icons during the debates which brought iconoclasm to an end in the Eastern Church that same year.[43] The icon has now disappeared and only a fifteenth-century copy of it survives (fig. 64).[44] The famous relic of the head of Saint Anastasius was encased in an ornate silver reliquary in 1283.[45] In 1408 the saint's relics found their way to the roman church of S. Maria in Trastevere, from which they were returned to the monastery.[46] In 1810 the monastery's reliquaries disappeared, but some of the relics may have survived in different containers.[47]

The feast of Saint Anastasius of Persia was celebrated on 22 January, the anniversary of his martyrdom in 627. This was the same feast day as that of the spanish martyr, Saint Vincent, who was executed at Saragossa in 304. From the eighth century the feast of these two martyrs was celebrated in Spain on 22 January.[48] By the eleventh and twelfth centuries the two saints shared the same day in Rome. The relics of Saint Vincent are said to have been brought to the monastery of S. Anastasius *ad Aquas Salvias* in the thirteenth century.[49] Alexander Farnese, commendatory abbot of S. Anastasius, had a reliquary made for the head of Saint Vincent in 1577.[50] The present title of the medieval church, SS. Vincenzo e Anastasio, derives ultimately from the double

41. See below, C. DATES AND DOCUMENTS, 723 or 739; and *c*. 787.

42. See below, C. DATES AND DOCUMENTS, 787.

43. Iconoclasm began in the East in 726, ended in 787, but returned from 813–843. See Daniel J. Sahas, *Icon and Logos: Sources in Eighth-century Iconoclasm,* Toronto Medieval Texts and Translations, 4 (Toronto: University of Toronto Press, 1986) 3–44.

44. Carlo Bertelli, 'Caput Sancti Anastasii', *Paragone-Arte* 21: 247 (1970) 12–25.

45. See below, C. DATES AND DOCUMENTS, 1283.

46. See below, C. DATES AND DOCUMENTS, 14 June 1408.

47. See below, C. DATES AND DOCUMENTS, 1810.

48. See below, C. DATES AND DOCUMENTS, 8th century.

49. See below, C. DATES AND DOCUMENTS, 1225.

50. See below, C. DATES AND DOCUMENTS, 1577; it, too, disappeared in 1810.

feastday and the monastery's possession of relics of both martyrs. Saint Vincent precedes Saint Anastasius, probably because he was martyred over three hundred years before the persian saint. Yet it was only in 1294 that the Cistercian General Chapter agreed to the celebration of the joint feast of Saints Vincent and Anastasius at Tre Fontane in Rome.[51] In 1320 the Catalogue of Turin still called the monastery after Saint Anastasius alone[52] and throughout the fourteenth and fifteenth centuries this was its normal name.[53]

A fire at the monastery in 789–790 destroyed some of the buildings on the site.[54] The account of this disaster in the *Liber Pontificalis* refers to the basilica of the monastery of Saint Anastasius, the vestry, the hygumenarch's residence and other buildings, all of which burned to the ground. There was also a courtyard, in which a chest containing the precious relics of Saint Anastasius was lying once it had been saved from the flames. Pope Hadrian I (772–795) rebuilt, restored and adorned the buildings which had perished in the fire.

In the ninth century Popes Leo III, Gregory IV, Leo IV, Benedict III, and Nicholas I donated textiles, altar vessels, and lamps to the monastery of S. Anastasius the martyr.[55] These donations were among other extensive gifts bestowed by the popes on the various monasteries of Rome and listed in the papal biographies. From each list it is clear that S. Anastasius ranked high among the eastern monastic establishments of the city. Most of the gifts were given to the 'monastery of Saint Anastasius', but in 807 Pope Leo III specified that, while a silver crown should be donated to the monastery, a silver canister should be presented to 'the oratory of Saint Mary within the monastery *ad Aquas Salvias*'.[56] This oratory was probably none other than the *mansio* of Mary, the Holy Mother of God, mentioned in the account of the exorcism of 713.[57]

---

51. See below, C. DATES AND DOCUMENTS, 1294.
52. See below, C. DATES AND DOCUMENTS, 1320.
53. See below, C. DATES AND DOCUMENTS, 11 May 1358, 20 June 1372, 31 May 1373, 28 May 1378, 1 August 1389, August 1420.
54. See below, C. DATES AND DOCUMENTS, 789–790.
55. See below, C. DATES AND DOCUMENTS, 800–801; 807; 835–836; 847–855; 855–858; 858–867.
56. See below, C. DATES AND DOCUMENTS, 807.
57. See below, C. DATES AND DOCUMENTS, 713.

Towards the end of the tenth century the byzantine hermit, Saint Nilus, came to Rome from South Italy and was offered accommodation at S. Anastasius, 'which was situated far from the crowd and had always been served by greek monks . . .'.[58] He decided not to stay there. This account, however, attests to the oriental character of the monastery until 998. If it was deemed suitable for a hermit, the site was probably deserted at the end of the tenth century. That it was considered far from the city was to be significant, for, when Pope Innocent II wanted to found a cistercian abbey *c.* 1140, he needed to establish it in a place far from human habitation.[59] From 1059–1073 the *archipresbyter* of S. Anastasius, Suppus, was the spiritual father of Pope Nicholas II.[60] What status an archpriest had in medieval Rome is not certain. He was not necessarily a monk, although he might have been. Archpriests may also have been appointed to churches in Rome which were in need of renewal.

In 1081 the monastery of S. Anastasius was ceded to the monastery of S. Paolo fuori le Mura by Pope Gregory VII.[61] Latin monks who in the tenth century had been reformed by Saint Odo of Cluny then served the basilica of Saint Paul. Probably in 1081 a small community of benedictine monks went to live at S. Anastasius, which became a cell of the larger abbey. A medieval lectionary with collects, which has all the characteristics of a benedictine work of the late eleventh century, survives from this benedictine phase of the monastery's history.[62] It is not clear what buildings the latin monks lived in—they may have

---

58. See below, C. DATES AND DOCUMENTS, 998. It was about this time that the nunnery of S. Maria and S. Nicola in 'Aqua Salvia' was mentioned, but probably in another location, see Gullota, 'Un antico ed unico documento . . .', 185–195 and Ferrari, *Early Roman Monasteries,* 47–48.

59. Cistercian legislation makes this clear: Capitula IX.3: 'In civitatibus, castellis, villis, nulla nostra construenda sunt coenobia, sed in locis a conversatione hominum semotis', to which is added in Instituta 1.2: 'sed in locis a conversatione hominum semotis '. (Chrysogonus Waddell, *Twelfth-Century Statutes from the Cistercian General Chapter.* Studia et Documenta, 12 (Brecht: Cîteaux: Commentarii cistercienses, 2002) 512 and 537.

60. See below, C. DATES AND DOCUMENTS, 1059–1073.

61. See below, C. DATES AND DOCUMENTS, 1081.

62. See below, C. DATES AND DOCUMENTS, late eleventh century; Rome, Biblioteca Vallicelliana, MS C62; Pierre Jounel, *Le culte des saints dans les basiliques du Latran et du Vatican au douzième siècle,* Collection de l'École Française de Rome, 26 (Rome: École Française de Rome, 1977) 45–46, 57–61, 216–217.

been only a small community which took over or restored the existing structures.

In this way the monastery of S. Anastasius became officially linked to that of S. Paolo fuori le Mura. In 604, long before this association, the *massa* called the Salvian Waters had been ceded to the basilica of S. Paolo by Pope Gregory the Great.[63] When Pope Gregory VII in 1081 confirmed the possessions of S. Paolo fuori le Mura, he included among them the monastery of S. Anastasius *ad Aquas Salvias,* the *massa* mentioned in Gregory the Great's Bull, the church of Saint Phocas which belonged to S. Anastasius, and some towns in the Maremma in Tuscany.[64] These latter properties appear in later medieval literature and art among the most prized possessions of S. Anastasius.

Pope Leo III and Charlemagne were alleged to have donated to the monastery of Saint Anastasius in 805 twelve towns, *castra* or *castella,* and other property (mountains, fishponds, pastureland, woods, vineyards and the like) situated in the Maremma, the area around the modern town of Grosseto.[65] The donation was reputed to be a kind of *ex voto,* a thank-offering to the persian saint, who had guaranteed victory for the papal and imperial troops at Ansedonia when, on the advice of an angel in a vision, the saint's head was carried into battle. The events of the military campaign and the places ceded to the monastery were depicted in the thirteenth century on the walls of the abbey gatehouse, the 'Arch of Charlemagne'.[66] A silver reliquary made to contain the

---

63. See below, C. DATES AND DOCUMENTS, 25 January 604.

64. See below, C. DATES AND DOCUMENTS, March 1081.

65. See below, C. DATES AND DOCUMENTS, (805 ?). The terms *castrum* and *castellum* are commonly used in medieval Latium from the tenth to the thirteenth centuries; they are defined in Toubert, *Les structures,* 314, n. 1.

66. For these see Fernanda De Maffei, 'Riflessi dell'epopea carolingia nell'arte medievale: il ciclo di Ezechiele e non di Carlo a S. Maria in Cosmedin e l'arco di Carlo Magno a Roma', *Atti del Convegno Nazionale sul tema: la poesia epica e la sua formazione (1969).* (Rome: Accademia Nazionale dei Lincei, 1970) 351–386; Carlo Bertelli, 'Affreschi, miniature e oreficerie cistercensi in Toscana e in Lazio', *I Cistercensi e il Lazio: Atti delle giornate di studio dell'Istituto dell'Arte dell'Università di Roma (Roma 17–21 maggio 1977).* (Rome: Multigrafica Editrice, 1978) 71–81; Francesco Gandolfo, 'Aggiornamento scientifico e bibliografia', Guglielmo Matthiae, *Pittura romana del medioevo.* vol. 2 (Rome: Fratelli Palombi Editori, 1988) 283–284; Antonio Iacobini, 'La pittura e le arti suntuarie: da Innocenzo III a Innocenzo IV (1198–1254)', in Angiola Maria Romanini, ed., *Roma nel Duecento* (Rome: SEAT, 1991) 267–271; Stefania Quattrone, 'L'evoluzione storico-architettonica del complesso monumentale "oggi detto le Tre Fontane allore ad Aquas Salvias"', in Giovanni Belardi, Fra Jacques Brière, Liliana Pozzi, *et al., Abbazia delle Tre Fontane:*

head of Saint Anastasius was decorated in 1283 with images of the places in the Maremma.[67] In the narthex of the church of S. Anastasius there was a painting of them and an inscription, and in the sacristy there was a gilded bronze plaque inscribed with the deed of donation. This was copied in 1369 and again in the sixteenth century.[68]

Most modern scholars consider the story of the campaign to be legendary, the donation by Pope Leo and Charlemagne an eleventh or twelfth-century invention.[69] Some of the tuscan property was first mentioned in 1081 in the Bull of Pope Gregory VII which listed the possessions of the roman monastery of S. Paolo fuori le Mura.[70] The monastery of S. Anastasius also appears in the Bull as part of the patrimony of S. Paolo fuori le Mura. It is possible that the lands in the Maremma did then belong to S. Anastasius.[71] In 1130 Antipope Anacletus II confirmed the possessions of S. Paolo fuori le Mura, including the 'church of Saint Anastasius *ad Aquas Salvas*', as well as the unnamed *castella* belonging to the same church of Saint Anastasius.[72] It is not clear whether these *castella* were those in the Maremma, which were not mentioned by name in Anacletus' Bull. When Pope Innocent II founded the cistercian monastery of Saint Anastasius *c.* 1140, he endowed the abbey with property, but made no specific mention of holdings in the Maremma.[73] In 1152 Pope Eugenius III, formerly the founding abbot of the monastery, wrote to the Cistercian General Chapter requesting a dispensation from the Rule to allow the roman monastery to retain a certain *castrum* and other possessions which by an ancient law had belonged to it since the time of Innocent II.[74]

---

il complesso, la storia, il restauro. (Rome: Edilerica, s.r.l., 1995) 46–49; Joan E. Barclay Lloyd, 'The Medieval Murals in the Cistercian Abbey of SS. Vincenzo e Anastasio *ad Aquas Salvias* at Tre Fontane near Rome in their Architectural Setting', *Papers of the British School at Rome 65* (1997) 287–312.

67. See below, C. DATES AND DOCUMENTS, 1283.

68. See below, C. DATES AND DOCUMENTS, 1369.

69. Cf. Paul Fridolin Kehr, *Italia Pontificia* (Berlin: Weidmann, 1906) 1:173; De Maffei, 'Riflessi . . .', 351–386, esp. 368–378; Anthony Luttrell, 'The Medieval Ager Cosanus', in Mario Ascheri, ed., *Siena e Maremma nel Medioevo* (Siena: Betti Editrice, 2001) 27–58, but Tomassetti believed there was some truth in it, Tomassetti, 'Della Campagna Romana', 140–141.

70. See below, C. DATES AND DOCUMENTS, 1081.

71. See below, C. DATES AND DOCUMENTS, 1081.

72. See below, C. DATES AND DOCUMENTS, 1130.

73. See below, C. DATES AND DOCUMENTS, 1140 (3).

74. See below, C. DATES AND DOCUMENTS, August, 1152.

One wonders whether these 'possessions' were the property in the Maremma. Perhaps Innocent II took them from S. Paolo fuori le Mura and donated them—or restored them—to his new monastery at Tre Fontane, his cistercian foundation.[75] In 1153 Pope Eugenius III died.[76] At the request of Abbot Gozoinus and the Cistercian Chapter his successor, Pope Anastasius IV (1153–1154), granted a dispensation so that the monks of S. Anastasius could retain their (unnamed) property.[77] In 1161 Pope Alexander III (1159–1181) confirmed the monastery's possessions, including by name each of the places in the Maremma in Tuscany.[78] Alexander's Bull is the earliest surviving document to make specific reference to this property as belonging to the monastery of S. Anastasius. The abbey's possessions were re-confirmed in 1183 by Pope Lucius III (1181–1185); in 1191 by Pope Celestine III (1191–1198); and in 1255 by Pope Alexander IV (1254–1261).[79]

From 1216 the tuscan possessions, although still officially belonging to the abbey, were in the hands of the Aldobrandeschi family.[80] Pope Boniface VIII (1294–1303) confiscated the property briefly in 1302, but the monastery was still renewing its contract with the Aldobrandeschi in 1358.[81] In 1452 some of the property was ceded to Siena by the commendatory abbot of S. Anastasius.[82]

In all of this one thing seems clear: from 1161 to the mid-fifteenth century, the monastery of S. Anastasius *ad Aquas Salvias* owned vast estates in the Maremma. When the tuscan possessions were donated to S. Anastasius is not certain, nor do we know whether they previously belonged to the monastery of S. Paolo fuori le Mura. They may have belonged to the byzantine-rite monastery of S. Anastasius before 1081. The legend of Leo III, Charlemagne, and the siege of Ansedonia smacks of the *Chanson de Roland,* the imaginative poetry of the late eleventh and twelfth centuries, rather than seeming an historical

75. Eugenius III refers to the possessions of the monastery at the time of his predecessor Innocent II; see below, C. DATES AND DOCUMENTS August, 1152.

76. See below, C. DATES AND DOCUMENTS, 1153 (1).

77. See below, C. DATES AND DOCUMENTS, 1153 (2) and 1153–1154 (1).

78. See below, C. DATES AND DOCUMENTS, 10 July, 1161.

79. See below, C. DATES AND DOCUMENTS, April, 1183; July, 1191; and 1255.

80. See below, C. DATES AND DOCUMENTS, 1216 and 1269.

81. See below, C. DATES AND DOCUMENTS, 1302 and 11 May 1358.

82. See below, C. DATES AND DOCUMENTS, 12 Aug. 1452.

account. The story nonetheless authenticated the monastery's claims to the property, and the frescoes in the gatehouse and the narthex proclaimed this to the outside world.

In February 1130 two men were elected to the papacy.[83] They were Gregory Papareschi, Cardinal Deacon of S. Angelo, who took the name Innocent II, and Petrus Pierleone, Cardinal Priest of S. Maria in Trastevere, who took the name Anacletus II. The result was a very serious schism, which divided the Church throughout Christendom. Innocent was elected first by a small number of cardinals, brought together at the church S. Gregorio Magno on the Celian Hill by the papal chancellor, Haimeric. This election took place in secret immediately after Honorius II's death at the monastery of S. Andrea next to that church and a swiftly arranged burial there. Anacletus was elected shortly after Pope Honorius's death was made known, in a more normal procedure at the church of S. Marco at the foot of the Capitoline Hill by a larger number of cardinals and clergy, and he was acclaimed by the people of Rome. With two contenders for the See of Peter, people began taking sides. Fighting broke out in Rome, which Anacletus was able to retain. Later he also secured the support of Southern Italy and Roger of Sicily. Innocent went north, where he found strong allies, first in France, and then in Germany and England. He was aided by religious leaders like Saint Norbert of Xanten, founder of the Praemonstratensian Order of canons regular, and Saint Bernard of Clairvaux. The cistercian abbot travelled with Innocent from place to place, eloquently exhorting everyone to come over to his side. Indeed Saint Bernard's reputation and his persuasive diplomacy were crucial in Innocent's attaining recognition as the legitimate pope. Anacletus's detractors pointed out that his ancestors had been Jews, and they accused him of bribery, personal ambition, and sexual immorality.[84] Saint Bernard considered Innocent the candidate with the better character, but he was on the whole disillusioned by the power struggle, the

---

83. For this, see Pier Fausto Palumbo, *Lo Scismo del MCXXX*, Miscellanea della R. Deputazione Romana di Storia Patria, 13 (Rome: Presso la R. Deputazione alla Biblioteca Vallicelliana, 1942); and, with further bibliography, Mary Stroll, *The Jewish Pope: Ideology and Politics in the Papal Schism* (Leiden: E. J. Brill, 1987).

84. Stroll, *The Jewish Pope*, esp. 156–168.

worldly splendour of the papal court, and the venal attitudes he observed in Rome.[85] In Rome and South Italy Anacletus held sway until
25 January 1138, when he died. His supporters elected Victor IV to
succeed him, but they were subsequently won over to Innocent's side.
At Pentecost, in May 1138, the followers of Anaclete II and Victor IV
came to humble themselves at the feet of Innocent II and to swear
allegiance to him as pope, an event recorded with some satisfaction by
Saint Bernard.[86]

The monastery at Tre Fontane was caught up in the papal contest.
When Anaclete II reconfirmed the possessions of S. Paolo fuori le
Mura in 1130, he included among them the monastery of S. Anastasius
ad Aquas Salvias, as well as the churches in the *massa* at Nemi, a small
town overlooking the Specchio di Diana (Mirror of Diana), a volcanic
lake in the Alban Hills some forty kilometers from Rome, and the
castella belonging to S. Anastasius.[87] Since, from the time of Pope
Eugenius III, the monastery of S. Anastasius owned etates at Nemi,[88]
perhaps that *massa* had also been part of the property transferred with
S. Anastasius to S. Paolo fuori le Mura in 1081.

The monks of S. Paolo fuori le Mura likely supported Anacletus II
against Innocent II in the papal schism, for when Innocent was firmly
established as pope after Anacletus' death, he took the monastery of
S. Anastasius from S. Paolo fuori le Mura and ceded it to the Cistercians,
probably with its property—including that in the Maremma, Nemi, and
elsewhere. He wanted a cistercian abbey, a daughter house of Clairvaux,
close to Rome. His act can be seen as a kind of *ex-voto* or thank-offering
for the abbot of Clairvaux's support in the schism, and perhaps an
attempt to secure further spiritual help from the Cistercians.[89]

A few years later, in 1161, during another papal schism, Frederick
Barbarossa is said to have evicted the community of S. Anastasius and,

---

85. As pointed out by Stroll, Saint Bernard's reactions resulted in his criticism of Rome and
the papacy in his *De consideratione;* Stroll, *The Jewish Pope,* 120, 124, and 179.

86. See below, C. DATES AND DOCUMENTS, May 1138.

87. See below, C. DATES AND DOCUMENTS, 1130.

88. See below, C. DATES AND DOCUMENTS, 1145–1153 (1).

89. Stroll, *The Jewish Pope,* 133, calls the site of the monastery at Acquae Salviae 'a dreadful
place located in the swamps near Rome, where many of the monks contracted malaria'.

according to one account, 'the abbot of S. Paolo claimed that same place through the schismatic king', a claim possibly made through the Bulls of Gregory the Great, Gregory VII, and Anacletus II.[90] By 10 July 1161 the cistercian community had been reinstated at S. Anastasius by Pope Alexander III, who took the monastery under his protection and re-confirmed its possessions, specifically naming those in the Maremma and a summer residence at Nemi. Perhaps this was done as a precaution against further claims by the monks of S. Paolo fuori le Mura.

Pope Innocent II founded the cistercian monastery of S. Anastasius *ad Aquas Salvias c.* 1140.[91] A variety of sources refer to this. Shortly after he had securely established himself in Rome in 1138, Pope Innocent II wrote to Saint Bernard, requesting that he send monks to Rome for the new monastery. Innocent's letter does not survive, but a copy of Saint Bernard's reply does.[92] The abbot of Clairvaux seemed to treat the pope's request with little enthusiasm; he claimed he did not have enough monks to send to Rome;[93] in fact he put off till another time the possibility of setting up a cistercian house near the city.[94] Saint Bernard seems to have had a bad opinion of Rome, which he had visited during the schism, and may therefore not have wished to establish a roman foundation.[95] Normally there had to be an abbot and twelve monks to form a new monastery;[96] in the 1140s the Cistercians also ruled that no abbot should establish a new monastery unless he had sixty professed monks in his own community, and, moreover, he needed to have the permission of the General Chapter to make a

---

90. See below, C. DATES AND DOCUMENTS, 1161.

91. See below, C. DATES AND DOCUMENTS, *c.* 1140. We prefer this date to 1138, which is sometimes given.

92. See below, C. DATES AND DOCUMENTS, *c.* 1140, (1).

93. According to the cistercian statutes, an abbot and twelve monks were required to start a new foundation: 'Duodecim monachi cum abbate terciodecimo ad coenobia nova transmittantur'; *Statuta*, vol. 1:15.

94. See below, C. DATES AND DOCUMENTS, 1140 (1).

95. Paolo Brezzi, 'San Bernardo a Roma'. *Studi Romani* 1.4 (=36) (1953) 496–509; and Angiola Maria Romanini, 'La storia architettonica', 657–659. Saint Bernard, some years later, wrote very critically of Rome, that 'den of thieves'(*De consideratione;* PL 182:727–808).

96. According to the oldest version of the *Capitula* in Trento, Biblioteca Communale, MS 1711: Customary (dated *c.* 1136/40) there had to be an abbot and twelve monks to start a new foundation. *Instituta* xxxvii:2 (Waddell, *Twelfth-Century Statutes,* 546): 'Non mittendum esse abbatem novum in locum nocellum sine monachis ad minus XIIcim'.

new foundation.[97] The abbot of Clairvaux may simply not have had suitable men for this task when he wrote to the pope.

In the meantime, the abbot of Farfa, Adenolfo, had summoned a community of monks from Clairvaux to his abbey, intending to build them a monastery at Scandriglia. According to Geoffrey of Auxerre in the *Life of Saint Bernard,* the abbot of Farfa was prevented from fulfilling these plans because the pope in Rome—Innocent II—took the cistercian community away from Farfa and established it in another place—at S. Anastasius *ad Aquas Salvias.*[98]

Arnold (Ernaldus) of Bonneval, also in the *Life of Saint Bernard,* gives a more detailed account of Innocent II's foundation.[99] As part of the pontiff's restoration of the Church in Rome, he established the cistercian monastery of Saint Anastasius the martyr *ad Aquas Salvias.* There had been a monastery there before, yet at that time there was a church, but no one living there. According to Arnold, Innocent II constructed monastic buildings and renewed the church. He endowed the monastery with houses, fields, and vineyards. Then he requested and obtained from the abbot of Clairvaux, Saint Bernard, an abbot and a community of monks, the abbot being Bernardus—Pietro Bernardo Paganelli—formerly *vice-dominus,* or second-in-command, of the church in Pisa. The cistercian community came to serve the Lord in that place according to the Rule of Saint Benedict. Once the foundation had been established, men from that area joined them and their numbers increased.

This account is fascinating for several reasons. The author knew that there had previously been a monastery on the site. Whether he realized this had originally been a byzantine foundation, or whether he alluded to the previous benedictine community, is not known. It

97. In the Instituta of *c.* 1147 one finds that an abbot should have sixty professed monks before he could establish a new foundation, and he needed the permission of the General Chapter, 'Nullus de abbatibus nostris locum ad abbatiam faciendam accipiat, nisi prius sexaginta monachos professos habeat, et hoc licentia generalis capituli', Instituta XXXVII: 2 (Waddell, *Twelfth-Century Statutes,* 546).

98. See below, C. DATES AND DOCUMENTS, 1140 (2). For the *Life of Saint Bernard,* by Geoffrey of Auxerre, Arnold (Ernaldus) of Bonneval and William of Saint-Thierry, see Adriaan H. Bredero, *Bernard of Clairvaux: Between Cult and History* (Edinburgh: T & T Clark-Grand Rapids: Eerdmans, 1996) esp. 61–140.

99. See below, C. DATES AND DOCUMENTS, 1140 (3).

appears that there was no one living at Tre Fontane *c.* 1140. Arnold states that Innocent II constructed monastic buildings. The Cistercians probably lived a different style of community life from the earlier byzantine monks, who may have required more separated dwellings, as in a lavra; or, perhaps the monastic buildings had long fallen into decay. The Benedictines, who had succeeded the eastern monks, may have been very few in number, a small cell of S. Paolo fuori le Mura, and hence they may not have required extensive monastic structures. Or, the buildings may have been deemed unsuitable for the new foundation. It was cistercian custom to require of founding patrons enough suitable buildings that the first monks at any cistercian establishment could begin immediately to live in the new monastery according to the Rule.[100] Whatever monastic buildings had survived at Tre Fontane to the mid-twelfth century may have been considered inadequate or inappropriate for such a community. Like many contemporary patrons, Pope Innocent II appears to have laid out and built monastic structures for his new foundation. More than one building is mentioned; perhaps Innocent provided separate structures for the first monks and for the lay-brothers, the *conversi,* as cistercian custom required; or perhaps he built a large wing of the abbey.

Innocent also restored the church. In fact, more than one church then existed on the site (fig. 1). Earlier historical sources mention the sanctuary of S. Paolo alle Tre Fontane;[101] they speak of the oratory of Mary, the Holy Mother of God;[102] and they mention the basilica of Saint John the Baptist;[103] the basilica of the monastery of S. Anastasius;[104] or simply the basilica of S. Anastasius[105]—it is likely that these 'basilicas' were all the same building. Pope Innocent II may have merely restored or adapted one of these churches, possibly the basilica, for his new

---

100. Before monks went to live in a new monastery, there had to be an oratory, refectory, dormitory, guest room and gates so that the monks could begin immediately to serve God and live a regular life: Capitula IX.4 (Waddell, *Twelfth-Century Statutues,* 512): 'nec nisi prius extructis his officinis: oratio, refectorio, dormitorio, cella hospitium, et portarii, quatinus ibi statim et deo servire, et regulariter vivere possint'.

101. See below, C. DATES AND DOCUMENTS, 688/9.

102. See below, C. DATES AND DOCUMENTS, 713; 807.

103. See below, C. DATES AND DOCUMENTS, 713.

104. See below, C. DATES AND DOCUMENTS, 772–795.

105. See below, C. DATES AND DOCUMENTS, 856–867.

community. Later, the church was entirely rebuilt along cistercian lines.

The cistercian foundation was evidently the thirty-fourth daughter house of Clairvaux[106] and would have come under Saint Bernard's oversight. The abbot of Clairvaux or his delegate would have been required to make regular visitations,[107] and the new community would have been formed and subject to the decisions of the Cistercian General Chapter, which the abbot of S. Anastasius regularly attended.

The first cistercian abbot of S. Anastasius was Pietro Bernardo Paganelli. From some of his surviving correspondence with Saint Bernard,[108] it appears that the first group of monks moved rather unwillingly from Farfa to Rome. Abbot Paganelli was nostalgic about Clairvaux moreover and one senses that he found his new office and the location of the monastery difficult to accept. One of the difficulties of the site was probably its damp, humid atmosphere.

Sometime between *c.* 1140 and 1145 Saint Bernard wrote to the abbot and monks of the new monastery.[109] He apologized for not being able to visit them in Rome, but he rejoiced in what he heard about them from their abbot. He tried to encourage them in their cistercian way of life, urging them especially to seek unity in spirit and the bond of peace with humble charity, the seal of perfection.[110] Indeed, he stressed humility above all, and peace, so that they might enjoy the indwelling of the Holy Spirit. He realized that they lived in an unhealthy region and that some of them laboured with many infirmities; he sympathized with their bodily weakness, but he feared much more their vulnerability of soul. He did not think it appropriate for them to take medicines for their bodily ailments. It was not right for them, nor did it fit with honesty and purity, to seek advice from doctors or to receive medication. Instead he recommended the potion of humility and patience. The monks were to cry out to the Lord with

---

106. See below, C. DATES AND DOCUMENTS, 1140 (4).

107. See Waddell, *Twelfth-Century Statutes*, 41.

108. See below, C. DATES AND DOCUMENTS, 1140 (5).

109. See below, C. DATES AND DOCUMENTS, 1140–1145.

110. The concepts of unity in spirit, peace and humble charity were commonly alluded to in twelfth-century cistercian literature, as pointed out by Newman, *Boundaries of Charity, passim.*

all their heart, 'Heal my soul, Lord, for I have sinned against thee!' (Psalm 41:4).[111]

The monks likely suffered from ailments brought on by the humidity of the site. They may also have suffered from the deadly disease of malaria, the causes of which were little understood until the early twentieth century, when the female anopheles mosquito was identified as the carrier of the infected parasite.[112] The mosquito thrives in water and breeds in summer. Since blood is necessary in its breeding process, it takes a minute amount from its victims, whom it infects with the disease. The damp site of S. Anastasius at the Salvian Waters was an ideal place for the mosquito to spread the disease, especially during the summer months.

In 1145 Abbot Pietro Bernardo Paganelli was elected pope, taking the name Eugenius III.[113] Although Saint Bernard was against his assuming this high office, in which he would be obliged to deal with secular affairs and worldly princes, the abbot of Clairvaux eventually accepted it and wrote *De consideratione,* five books of fatherly advice.[114]

The new pope seems to have continued to look after his former abbey's material needs. He confirmed S. Anastasius as a cistercian foundation and requested a dispensation from the Cistercian General Chapter for the monastery to retain its possessions. S. Anastasius was to remain the abbey, but the monks were allowed to move in summertime to a residence at Nemi.[115] If the health problem were malaria, as

111. For medieval cistercian attitudes to sickness and health, see David N. Bell, 'The Siting and Size of Cistercian Infirmaries in England and Wales', in Meredith Parsons Lillich, ed., *Studies in Cistercian Art and Architecture 5,* CS 167 (Kalamazoo: Cistercian Publications, 1998) 211–237; and Peter Fergusson and Stuart Harrison, *Rievaulx Abbey: Community, Architecture, Memory* (New Haven and London: Yale University Press, 1999) 111–135.

112. The history of this scientific discovery is told by Angelo Celli, *Storia della Malaria* (Città di Castello, 1925); for malaria at Tre Fontane, see Anonymous (A. Barbiero OCSO), 'La malaria e gli eucalitti alle Tre Fontane', unpublished typescript, kindly lent to me by the monks of Tre Fontane; A. Calandro, 'Inizi di bonifica alle Tre Fontane', *L'Urbe* NS 37 (1974) 41–43; A. Calandro, 'Malaria alle Porte di Roma nel secolo scorso', *L'Urbe* NS 41(1978) 27–29; Joan Barclay Lloyd, 'SS. Vincenzo e Anastasio alle Tre Fontane near Rome: The Australian Connection', *Tjurunga* 46 (1994) 57–70.

113. See below, C. DATES AND DOCUMENTS, 1145.

114. Newman, *Boundaries of Charity,* 155–161. *De consideratione* has been translated into English by Elizabeth T. Kennan and John D. Anderson, *Five Books on Consideration. Advice to a Pope,* Cistercian Fathers Series, 37 (Kalamazoo: Cistercian Publications, 1976).

115. See below, C. DATES AND DOCUMENTS, 1145–1153 (1). A *'massa'* at Nemi, belonging to the monastery of S. Anastasius was mentioned in 1130, see below, C. DATES AND DOCUMENTS, 1130.

seems likely, this would have alleviated some of the monks' ills. In addition, Pope Eugenius presented the community with a book of Origen's *Homilies.*[116]

Eugenius may also have provided the abbey with new buildings. Elsewhere in Rome he initiated architectural projects: a papal palace at the Vatican, and a narthex for the basilica of S. Maria Maggiore.[117] At Tre Fontane he may have rebuilt the church, nostalgically looking back to the edifice he remembered at Clairvaux, before he left France for Italy; perhaps he extended Innocent II's monastic structures. Unfortunately, although such building activity seems likely, there is no documentary evidence to confirm it. On the other hand, attempts made by Eugenius III and his successors to have the Cistercian General Chapter allow Saint Anastasius to keep its tuscan possessions may point indirectly to building campaigns at Tre Fontane. Construction may have been financed by the income derived from the abbey's territory in the Maremma.

In the twelfth and thirteenth centuries several popes took the monastery of S. Anastasius under their protection; they continued to assert its status as the head of the abbey and they confirmed its possessions.[118] It is interesting to note that the Bull of Alexander III of 1161 still spoke of the 'monastery of S. Anastasius, the church of Saint John the Baptist and the church of Saint Mary, both next to the same monastery'.[119] These buildings were mentioned already in the account of the early eighth-century exorcism.[120]

116. See below, C. DATES AND DOCUMENTS, 1145–1153 (2).

117. Eugenius III's palace at the Vatican is mentioned, with another at Segni, by Boson, *Le Liber Pontificalis* 2:387: *Hic fecit unum palatium apud sanctum Petrum, et Signie alterum . . . ;* see also Katharina B. Steinke, *Die mittelalterliche Vatikanpaläste und ihre Kapellen.* Studi e Documenti per la Storia del Palazzo Apostolico Vaticano, 5 (Vatican City: Biblioteca Apostolica Vaticana, 1984) 32–34. At S. Maria Maggiore an inscription from the architrave records Eugenius III's rebuilding of the narthex: 'TERCIUS EUGENIUS ROMANUS PAPA BENIGNUS OBTULIT HOC MUNUS VIRGO SACRATA TIBI / QUE MATER XPISTI FIERI MERITO MERUISTI SALVA PERPETUA VIRGINITATE TIBI / ES VIA VITA SALUS TOTIUS GLORIA MUNDI DA VENIAM CULPIS VIRGINITATIS HONOR', quoted in Richard Krautheimer, *Corpus Basilicarum,* 3:7; and Vincenzo Forcella, *Iscrizioni delle chiese e d'altri edificii di Roma dal secolo XI fino al giorni nostri* (Rome, 1878) p. 9, no.1. See also Justo Fernández-Alonso, 'Cronologia della Basilica', in Carlo Pietrangeli, *S. Maria Maggiore* (Florence: Hardini, 1988) 26.

118. See below, C. DATES AND DOCUMENTS, 1161; 1183; 1191; 1255.

119. See below, C. DATES AND DOCUMENTS, 10 July 1161.

120. See below, C. DATES AND DOCUMENTS, 713.

On 1 April 1221, Pope Honorius III, assisted by seven cardinals, dedicated the monastic church at the abbey to the Mother of God and consecrated seven altars, in which relics were placed. The pope granted indulgences to pious visitors to the church. All this took place under an abbot named Nicholas. The event is commemorated in a long inscription still in the north aisle of the church (fig. 65).[121] It has generally been assumed that this church took the place of the earlier basilica dedicated to Saint John the Baptist.

The date of consecration marks a *terminus ante quem* for the building of the cistercian church, even though it may have occurred years after the church was completed. In twelfth and thirteenth-century Rome churches were often consecrated long after the building was completed–as happened at S. Clemente, for example, where the upper church was built by Cardinal Anastasius (*c.* 1099–*c.* 1125), but consecrated by Boniface VIII in 1295.[122] The dedication to the Mother of God was typically cistercian, for all churches of the Order were dedicated to Mary, queen of heaven and earth.[123] Indeed, it is a typically cistercian building and certainly does not appear to be an adaptation of a former late eighth-century basilica on the site. It was not dedicated to either Saint John the Baptist or Saint Anastasius, as that former basilica may have been, even though the relics of those and many other saints were deposited in its seven altars. There is no mention of the narthex in the inscription and one cannot use it to date that structure, which was certainly built after the church itself was completed.[124]

---

121. See below, C. DATES AND DOCUMENTS, 1 April 1221.

122. Joan E. Barclay Lloyd, *The Medieval Church and Canonry of S. Clemente in Rome,* San Clemente Miscellany, 3 (Rome: S. Clemente, 1989) 60–66.

123. Capitula IX.2: 'ordinatum est in honore regine celi et terre nostra omnia fundari debere cenobia'; and Instituta XVIII.3: '. . . omnes ecclesiae nostrae . . . in memoria eiusdem caeli et terrae reginae sanctae Mariae funduntur et dedicentur'. (Waddell, *Twelfth-Century Statutes,* 512 and 541).

124. Pistilli suggests that the narthex was built under Abbot Nicholas (1212–1230), but probably before 1221; Pistilli, 'Considerazioni', 170. It could, however, have been built several years earlier, though in a separate building campaign, than the church; it would not be dated *c.* 1140, as suggested in Ingo Herklotz, 'Der mittelalterliche Fassadenportikus der Lateranbasilika und seine Mosaiken', *Römisches Jahrbuch der Bibliotheca Hertziana* 25 (1989) 32–33, but it does appear to be a typical twelfth-century structure, as indicated in Romanini, 'La storia architettonica', 688.

An inscription now on the lintel of a window on the first floor of the north wing of the monastery (fig. 66) attributes the construction of 'this house', *hanc domum,* i.e. probably a part of the monastery, to Iacobus, penitentiary, *'POENITENTIARIUS',* and chaplain to Pope Honorius III (1216–1227), who built it for the salvation of his soul and that of his nephew, also called Iacobus.[125] It is not entirely clear what part of the buildings this refers to.

Another inscription on the lintel of the present sacristy doorway probably also dates from the thirteenth century, when the 'sacristy' was enlarged (fig. 67): FEC. FIERI. H: OP: ET: I: ET: L. It refers to two people, with the initials 'I' and 'L'.[126] It is not clear who they were, but the rest of the inscription, FEC. FIERI H. OP.. ('who had this work done'), suggests they were responsible for some important commission, probably this extension of the 'sacristy', which may, in fact, have functioned originally as the abbot's chapel.[127] Similarly, an inscription formerly above the chapter room doorway attributed work to Abbot Leonardus in 1306.[128] Again, it is not clear precisely what he did, but it is likely to have been located in the east wing of the monastery and probably included the chapter room itself. It has been suggested that

125. 'FATER IACOBUS DOMINI HONORIJ PP. POENITENTIARIUS AC CAPELLANUS, HANC DOMUM FIERI FECIT, PRO ANIMAM SUAM, ET JACOBI NEPOTIS'. There was in the early thirteenth century a Cardinal Giacomo de Pecorara (1231–44), who was a cistercian monk at Trois Fontaines in France, and who has been confused with the first Iacobus in this inscription. The chaplain and penitentiary of Pope Honorius III was instead a *magister* and Apostolic Legate in Ireland and Scotland; he was mentioned in the papal Register from 31 July 1220–9 May 1226, and he died before 3 July 1240, as explained by Agostino Paravicini-Bagliani, *Cardinali di Curia e 'familiariae' cardinalizie dal 1227 al 1254,* Italia Sacra: Studi e Documenti di Storia Ecclesiastica, 18 and 19 (Rome: Antenore, 1972) 112–123, esp. 118–119, n. 2; see also Ruotolo, *L'abbazia,* 86–91; and Pistilli, 'Considerazioni', 165 and nn. 13–15. There was evidently an abbot of S. Anastasius at Tre Fontane called Iacobus from 1230–1244, perhaps the second Iacobus of the inscription, Ruotolo, *L'abbazia,* 86–91.

126. See below, C. DATES AND DOCUMENTS, 13th century. Pistilli quotes A. Petrucci's opinion that the lettering could date from 1230–1270 and he would like to see the 'I' referring to Abbot Iacobus (1230–44), Pistilli, 'Considerazioni' 174 and 190, n. 56. I have suggested that the inscription dates after 1284, when the abbey received a bequest from Ildebrandino il Rosso Aldobrandeschi. The two members of the community signified by 'I' and 'L' may then be Abbots Iohannes (1302–6) and Leonardus (1306–29). See Barclay Lloyd, 'Medieval Murals', 330–331 and 342–343.

127. Barclay Lloyd, 'Medieval Murals', 334–336.

128. See below, C. DATES AND DOCUMENTS, 1306.

the inscription referred to the decoration of the upper floor of the eastern or monks' wing, which seems plausible.[129]

As Saint Bernard's *Apologia* made clear, the abbot of Clairvaux was violently opposed to adorning cistercian monasteries with distracting works of art, whether sumptuous ornamentation of the church or lively figural sculpture in the cloister.[130] To prevent the monks becoming absorbed in art to the neglect of their *lectio,* prayer, and monastic discipline, cistercian legislation of *c.* 1122–1135 prohibited sculpture and paintings, except for painted wooden crucifixes.[131] Yet, at Tre Fontane in the early thirteenth century *Christ blessing amid angels and the symbols of the Evangelists* and the *Siege of Ansedonia* were painted in the gatehouse, the 'Arco di Carlomagno', and *c.* 1270 a *Madonna and Child flanked by saints and donors* was added to the ensemble.[132] These murals greeted a visitor to the abbey, announcing Christ's blessing and portraying the history and geography of its possessions in the Maremma. Their location, in the outer bay of the gatehouse, may have been considered external enough not to infringe the cistercian prohibition of painted images within the monastery.

129. Melinda Mihályi, 'I Cistercensi a Roma e la decorazione pittorica dell'ala dei Monaci nell'abbazia delle Tre Fontane', *Arte Medievale,* 2 serie, 5.1 (1991) 175.

130. See Conrad Rudolph, 'Bernard of Clairvaux's *Apologia* as a Description of Cluny and the Controversy over Monastic Art', *Gesta* 27 (1988) 125–132; idem., *'Things of Greater Importance': Bernard of Clairvaux's Apologia and the Medieval Attitude toward Art.* (Philadelphia: University of Philadelphia Press, 1990).

131. *Capitula XXVI.2: 1Sculpturas nusquam, picturas tantum licet habere in crucibus, que et ipse nonnisi lignee habeantur';* and Instituta XX.2–3: 'Sculpturae vel picturae in ecclesiis nostris seu in officinis aliquibus monasterii ne fiant interdicimus, quia dum talibus intenditur, utilitas bonae meditationes vel disciplina religiosae gravitatis saepe negligitur. Cruces tamen pictas quae sunt ligneae habemus.' (Waddell, *Twelfth-Century Statutes,* 516 and 541). See also Christopher Norton, 'Table of Cistercian Legislation on Art and Architecture', in Christopher Norton and D. Park, edd., *Cistercian Art and Architecture in the British Isles* (Cambridge: Cambridge University Press, 1986) 324, 354 and 358, where it is noted that the legislation was repeated in 1213 and 1220. Waddell also publishes local references to the removal of art works at Signy, Vauclair, and Alcobaça (*Twelfth-Century Statutes,* 619: <30>, 631: <10>, and 681: <23>).

132. The murals were recorded by Antonio Eclissi in 1630; his copies are in the Biblioteca Apostolica Vaticana, Barb. Lat. 4402, fols 35r, 36r, 37r, and 40v–41r. Barclay Lloyd, 'Medieval Murals', 294–308, with further bibliography.

In the late thirteenth and fourteenth centuries these cistercian strictures on art appear to have been relaxed.[133] In 1272 a tomb was set up
in the narthex of S. Anastasius, and in it *Domina Thomae comitisse*—
probably Tomasia, wife of Guglielmo Aldobrandeschi—was buried.[134]
It is probably the tomb shown on the right in a seventeenth-century
view of the narthex by Eclissi (fig. 70), with the columns and a
'cosmatesque' canopy shaped like a cage, *a gabbia*. In other drawings
Eclissi shows murals which were in the narthex, but of which only the
faded figures of Saint James and Saint Leonard survive.[135] In 1283
Abbot Martin had a silver casing made for the head of Saint Anastasius.[136]
On the reliquary were images of the monastery's property in the
Maremma, reputedly donated by Pope Leo III and Charlemagne. In
lunettes above the extension to the sacristy, which may have formed
part of a late thirteenth-century abbot's chapel, there is a fresco of the
Coronation of the Virgin in the east and of the *Nativity of Christ* in the
west.[137] In the last years of the thirteenth or in the early fourteenth
century magnificent frescoes of birds and acanthus and allegorical
scenes related to everyday life were painted in the monks' dormitory
and on a wall that is now external, but was originally within two rooms
at the northeastern end of the monks' range.[138] Other murals included
a late thirteenth-century calendar in the east portico, and in the cloister
a series of standing saints, dated 1347.[139]

On 6 May 1284, during the reign of Abbot Martinus, Ildebrandino il
Rosso Aldobrandeschi made a will in which he left two hundred

133. Marcel Aubert, *L'architecture cistercienne en France,* 2nd ed., vol. 1 (Paris: Vanoest, 1947)
144.

134. See below, C. DATES AND DOCUMENTS, 1272.

135. Antonio Eclissi, drawings in Biblioteca Apostolica Vaticana, Barb. Lat. 4402, fols 42r
and 43r–51r. Barclay Lloyd, 'Medieval Murals', 309–323 with further bibliography.

136. See below, C. DATES AND DOCUMENTS, 1283.

137. Barclay Lloyd, 'Medieval Murals, 334–336 with further bibliography.

138. See below, A. ARCHITECTURAL DATA, 5. Medieval murals, (c) MURALS IN WING M. See also
Carlo Bertelli, 'L'enciclopedia', 155–189; Melinda Mihályi, 'I cistercensi a Roma', 155–189;
Barclay Lloyd, 'Medieval Murals', 336–344; Melinda Mihályi, 'Appunti sul tema iconografico
della cavea cum ave inclusa', in Antonio Cadei, ed. *Arte D"Occidente: temi e metodi: studi in onore
di Angiola Maria Romanini* (Rome: Sintesi informazione, 1999) 891–900.; Kristin Bliksrud
Aavitsland. *Florilegium. En undersökelse av billedspråket i Vita Humana-frisen, Abbazia delle Tre
Fontane, Roma.* Acta Humaniora 134, (Oslo:Unipub, 2002).

139. Barclay Lloyd, 'Medieval Murals', 332–334.

pounds to the monastery of S. Anastasius in Rome for the building of the place and for the provision of tasty dishes, or *pitances,* for the brethren—presumably the monks.[140] Ildebrandino died shortly afterwards, on 18 May 1284. It is possible that his bequest financed a part of the construction at the abbey that dates from the late thirteenth century.

As early as the late twelfth century the monastery began to acquire daughter houses: S. Maria Casanova at Civitella Casanova in 1191–1195; S. Maria d'Arabona in 1208; S. Maria de Caritate in 1211; S. Agostino di Montalto in 1234–1250; S. Maria in Palazzuolo in 1237; S. Maria de Insula Pontiana in 1243; S. Benedetto de Silva in 1250; S.Giusto di Tuscania in 1255.[141] In the fourteenth century the communes of Nemi and Genzano, in the Alban Hills southeast of Rome, became vassals of the abbey.[142] In the same century there is evidence that the monastery also held land in the territory of Leonessa in the Abruzzi and property in Rome.[143]

In 1320 the Catalogue of Turin recorded an abbot and fifteen monks resident at the monastery of S. Anastasius.[144] The position of the community must have changed from 1419 onwards, when commendatory abbots replaced elected superiors.[145] These men, who were not members of the community, were appointed by the pope and drew a private income from the abbey.[146] They seem to have disposed of some of its rich possessions—Nemi was given to the Colonna in

---

140. Gaspero Ciacci, *Gli Aldobrandeschi nella storia e nella 'Divina Commedia'.* (Rome: Multigrafica Editrice, 1980) vol. 2: Document DCVII: 'Item iudicavit et reliquit monasterio Sancti Anastasii de Urbe ducentas libras usualis monete pro fabrica loci et pietantiis fratrum.'

141. See below, C. DATES AND DOCUMENTS, 1191, 1208, 1211, 1234, 13 August 1237, July 1243, 1250 and 18 February 1255. Van der Meer tabulates the following houses affiliated to Tre Fontane and its daughters, with some different foundation dates: Casanova di Civitella (Penna), 1195; Ripalta (Civitate) 1201; Arabona (Chieti) 1209; Carità (Taranto) 1211; S. Pastore (Reate) 1218; S. Agostino in Montalto (Castro, Apulia) 1239; Palazzuolo (Albano) 1244; Ponzio (Gaeta) 1246; S. Spirito d'Ocre (Forconia) 1248; Stirpeto (Trani) 1259, Frédéric van der Meer, *Atlas de l'Ordre Cistercien* (Paris-Brussels: Editions Sequoia, 1965) Table III.

142. See below, C. DATES AND DOCUMENTS, 31 May 1373.

143. See below, C. DATES AND DOCUMENTS, 20 June 1372; 28 May 1378.

144. See below, C. DATES AND DOCUMENTS, c. 1320.

145. See below, C. DATES AND DOCUMENTS, 1419.

146. The position of the commendatory abbots is explained in Louis J. Lekai, O.Cist., *The Cistercians: Ideals and Reality* (Kent Ohio: Kent State University Press, 1977) 101–108.

1423, while some of the lands in the Maremma were ceded to Siena on 12 August 1452.[147]

Yet, some of the commendatory abbots were responsible for reforms and new building programmes. In the early sixteenth century the monastery was given a new Rule and submitted to the tuscan branch of the Cistercian Congregation in Italy.[148] In 1577 Alexander Farnese, commendatory abbot of Tre Fontane, had reliquaries made to encase the heads of Saints Vincent and Zeno.[149] In 1593 Pietro Cardinal Aldobrandini, also commendatory abbot, donated to the abbey a silver reliquary containing the head of Saint Felix.[150] The abbey built on the site of the beheading of Saint Paul and whose early basilica had been dedicated to Saint John the Baptist, another saint who had been decapitated, then possessed the heads of several saints: Anastasius, Vincent, Zeno, and Felix.

In 1582 the church of S. Maria Scala Coeli, but not its crypt, was blown down in a wind-storm.[151] It probably stood on the site of a former sanctuary of Our Lady, possibly the oratory of the Holy Mother of God, documented from 713 onwards.[152] From the late fourteenth century great indulgences could be gained there.[153] In 1412 John XXIII granted further indulgences to pious visitors to the church.[154] The sanctuary of Our Lady was well known because of a tradition that Saint Bernard of Clairvaux had once had a vision while saying Mass there of souls going up to heaven from purgatory on a ladder; for this reason the sanctuary was called *Scala Coeli,* and a significant indulgence was granted in order to free souls from purgatory when Mass was celebrated in the church.[155] Besides, S. Maria Scala Coeli was famed

---

147. See below, C. DATES AND DOCUMENTS, 1423; 12 August 1452.
148. See below, C. DATES AND DOCUMENTS, 1518–1523.
149. See below, C. DATES AND DOCUMENTS, 1577.
150. See below, C. DATES AND DOCUMENTS, 1593.
151. See below, C. DATES AND DOCUMENTS, 1582.
152. See below, C. DATES AND DOCUMENTS, 713; 807.
153. See below, C. DATES AND DOCUMENTS, 1364; 1362–1370 or 1370–1378.
154. See below, C. DATES AND DOCUMENTS, March 1412.
155. Kurt Schwager, 'Santa Maria Scala Coeli in Tre Fontane', in Bettina von Freytag gen. Löringhoff-Dietrich Mannsperger-Friedhelm Prays, edd., *Praestant interna: Festschrift für Ulrich Hausmann.*(Tubingen: Ernst Masmuth, 1982) 400; Anonymous, *S. Paolo e le Tre Fontane,* 111–112; Nigel J. Morgan, 'The Scala Coeli Indulgence and the Royal Chapels', *The Reign of Henry VII,* Proceedings of the Harlaxton Symposium (Stamford: Paul Watkins, 1995) 82–103

as the burial place of Saint Zeno and 10,203 roman soldiers who had helped to build the Baths of Diocletian and been martyred by that emperor in 299.[156] After the disaster of 1582, Alexander Farnese in 1583 had Giacomo della Porta rebuild the church of S. Maria Scala Coeli in its present form.[157]

The earlier building was drawn on fifteenth-century maps of Rome (figs. 68 and 69).[158] Sallustio Peruzzi drew a plan of it.[159] Onofrio Panvinio in 1560 and 1570 described it.[160] He said it was a round building with four chapels or apses, and two altars at either end; to the north there was an altar and in the east the main altar in an apse decorated with mosaics; there were four columns supporting the altar canopy (the ciborium), two of alabaster, one of granite, and one of marble.[161]

In 1599 Cardinal Aldobrandini commissioned Giacomo della Porta to rebuild the church of S. Paolo alle Tre Fontane.[162] In the process the venerable *martyrium* was destroyed and a new edifice constructed to a more up-to-date plan, with a square in front in which pilgrims could gather. This work was done swiftly in order to be ready for the Jubilee Year 1600.[163]

In 1608 Flavio Mathei, said to have repaired the monastery,[164] was buried in the church of SS. Vincenzo e Anastasio. He seems also to have had an inscription carved on the architrave of the narthex of the monastic church, naming Pope Innocent II, whom he counted among his ancestors, as the patron and restorer of the monastery.[165]

Shortly afterwards, in 1625, regular abbots were restored.[166] One of the most famous was Ferdinando Ughelli, author of *Italia Sacra*, who

---

is an account of the Scala Coeli Indulgence, as it affected the English and was transferred to various sanctuaries in England in the later Middle Ages.

156. See below, C. DATES AND DOCUMENTS, 299.

157. See below, C. DATES AND DOCUMENTS, 1583.

158. See below, B. EARLY ILLUSTRATIONS, 1469, 1471, 1450–1500, 1474.

159. See below, B. EARLY ILLUSTRATIONS, 1550–1567.

160. See below, C. DATES AND DOCUMENTS, 1560 and 1570; and see Schwager, 'Santa Maria Scala Coeli', 394–417.

161. Onofrio Panvinio, *Schedae de ecclesiis urbis Romae. c.* 1560, BAV, Vat. lat. 6780, 31v.

162. See below, C. DATES AND DOCUMENTS, 1599.

163. Maggi, *Giacomo della Porta* 45–120.

164. See below, C. DATES AND DOCUMENTS, 1608.

165. See below, C. DATES AND DOCUMENTS, 1608.

166. See below, C. DATES AND DOCUMENTS, 1625.

became abbot of Tre Fontane in 1640 and was buried in the church of SS. Vincenzo e Anastasio when he died.[167]

In 1810, during the Napoleonic Wars, a french emissary went through the accounts of the monastery. At this time the silver reliquaries disappeared,[168] and in 1812 the abbey was suppressed.[169]

In 1826 Pope Leo XII ceded the monastery to the Franciscan Friars Minor of the Observance, resident at S. Sebastiano on the Via Appia.[170] Evidently, a lay-brother from S. Sebastiano took visitors around the abbey during the day; otherwise the site was abandoned.

On the eighteenth centenary of the martyrdom of Saint Paul in 1867 the Comte de Maumigny paid for excavations and restorations in the church of S. Paolo alle Tre Fontane.[171] As we noted above, the excavations brought to light parts of a colonnaded portico, a mosaic pavement, fragments of marble, and some inscriptions, two probably referring to the restoration of the original *martyrium* by Pope Sergius I (687–701).

In 1868 Pope Pius IX ceded the monastery to the Trappists.[172] At first their community suffered terribly from malaria. To combat the disease they planted hundreds of eucalyptus trees, from seeds especially sent from Melbourne in Australia.[173] At the beginning of the twentieth century the true carrier of malaria was identified, and steps were taken to rid the site of stagnant water, the breeding ground for the female anopheles mosquito.

The early trappist community at Tre Fontane also had to clean up and restore the buildings.[174] Evidently, there was enough grass growing in the church of SS. Vincenzo e Anastasio to feed the cattle which for years had been kept in the basilica at night. The medieval church

---

167. See below, C. DATES AND DOCUMENTS, 1640.

168. See below, C. DATES AND DOCUMENTS, 1810.

169. See below, C. DATES AND DOCUMENTS, 1806; 1812.

170. See below, C. DATES AND DOCUMENTS, 1826.

171. See below, C. DATES AND DOCUMENTS, 1867.

172. See below, C. DATES AND DOCUMENTS, 1868.

173. Joan E. Barclay Lloyd, 'SS. Vincenzo e Anastasio alle Tre Fontane near Rome—the Australian connection', *Tjurunga: An Australasian Benedictine Review* 46 (1994) 57–70, with further bibliography.

174. Alessandro Calandro, 'Arrivo dei Trappisti alle Tre Fontane nel 1868'. *L'Urbe* N.S. 36.5 (1973) 34–38; Alessandro Calandro, 'Inizi di bonifica alle Tre Fontane', *L'Urbe* N.S. 37.3-4 (1974) 41–43.

and some of the other buildings were six feet deep in muck. The damp heaps of rubbish were the breeding ground of mosquitoes and flies. The cloister had to be cleared and a new garden planted. The garth was deep in water.

By 1878 the church of SS. Vincenzo e Anastasio had been cleaned and treated for damp. The floor had been raised and repaved (fig. 10).[175] An iron grill had been set up across the nave and aisles (visible in fig. 7) and the three existing altars had been repaired.[176]

In 1870 and 1942 the italian government expropriated land to construct housing close to the abbey.[177] To this day a trappist community lives at Tre Fontane. They have restored and modified the monastery buildings. The west range was refurbished and rebuilt in the 1950s.[178] Some repairs were also made to the roof of the church of SS. Vincenzo e Anastasio.

Between 1992 and 1994 architect Giovanni Belardi of the Soprintendenza dei Monumenti di Roma once again restored the medieval church of SS. Vincenzo e Anastasio.[179] The roof was renewed and new terracotta paving tiles were laid throughout the building, slightly raising the level of the floor. Belardi found important new evidence regarding the medieval construction of the cistercian church and some remains of the earlier building history of the site.[180] Belardi carried out extensive renovations to the monastery buildings in the two years prior to the Jubilee Year 2000.[181] Builders removed the ceiling of the thirteenth-century 'sacristy' extension north of the church (Plan I, S and Plan II, S1).[182] As a result, the room's original gothic ribbed vault and frescoes are now open to view. It is my opinion that this beautifully appointed space was originally built as the abbot's chapel shortly

---

175. See below, C. DATES AND DOCUMENTS, 1878.
176. See below, C. DATES AND DOCUMENTS, 1878.
177. See below, C. DATES AND DOCUMENTS, 1870; 1942; 1947–1948.
178. See below, C. DATES AND DOCUMENTS, 1950's.
179. See below, C. DATES AND DOCUMENTS, 1992–1994.
180. This will be discussed further in Chapter VI of this volume.
181. My information comes from Fra Giacomo and Br. Ansgar, members of the Tre Fontane monastic community, and Giovanni Belardi. We eagerly await the publication of Architect Belardi on this campaign at the monastery.
182. The thick ceiling is drawn in our Section CC'. It was most likely inserted in the nineteenth century.

after 1284.[183] Thanks to Belardi's restoration one can now appreciate the size and decoration of the medieval interior.[184]

In the monastery itself, Belardi's renovations included modern amenities like new offices in the business centre and new bathrooms throughout the complex. He also restored the chapter room, adding modern floor tiles. The architect repaved all four ambulatories of the cloister with rough brown tiles. In preparation for this repaving, the workmen dug down about two feet. At that level, near the entrance to the refectory in the north range and near the door leading into the slype in the east range, the original medieval paving was discovered. On the south, the threshold of a door was found and a colonette also came to light.

Upstairs in the monks' dormitory Belardi removed all the post-medieval cells (Plan II, Wing M, all subdivisions between walls 8, 23, 40, and 30). The arched windows along the east of the dormitory (Plan II, wall 8) were opened to reveal painted soffits. Some of the frescoes taken off the dormitory walls in the 1960s were hung in the dormitory.

The cells to the west of the dormitory were restored (Plan II, between walls 40 and 9). Directly above this, further renovations transformed the area into a suite of modern monastic cells, a storeroom, and a music room (Plan III, between walls 9 and 40).

In the north range the space over the refectory (Plan III) was converted into a novitiate, with a meeting room and renovated living quarters. The long room at right angles to the north range (Plan II, west of wall 14) was made into a wardrobe.

Beyond the medieval buildings, the structures beside the church of S. Paolo alle Tre Fontane have been transferred to a Secular Institute,

---

183. As explained in Barclay Lloyd, 'Medieval Murals', 334–336, and in Chapter VII, (b) *The east range (Wing M): 2)* WING M IN THE THIRTEENTH OR EARLY FOURTEENTH-CENTURY. The edifice is discussed by Pistilli, 'Considerazioni', 174–175, and dated in the 1240s. For other abbot's chapels in France, see Aubert, *l'Architecture*, 2:50. In Italy, a splendidly appointed octagonal chapel, with mid-fourteenth-century frescoes, was built east of the original sacristy at Chiaravalle della Colomba. This is discussed, as a new sacristy, in Valenzano, Guerrini and Gigli, *Chiaravalle della Colomba*, 68–70 and 95–121.

184. Besides removing the ceiling, Belardi has eliminated a nineteenth-century door and balcony in what used to be the vaulted room above the 'sacristy' (shown in our figs. 45, 46, and 47).

the Confraternity of the Blessed Sacrament and St. Trypho. There a day care centre now exists for children. The old cow stalls have been formed into the 'Casa San Bernardo', a tourist residence. Other outbuildings and the former residences of hired workers are in the process of being renewed as a centre for the care of older persons.

During the Jubilee Year 2000, an international exhibition of missionary activity was held at the abbey. Clearly, there are still transformations taking place at Tre Fontane and the abbey's architecture will continue to change and to fascinate visitors and scholars for many years to come.

II

THE CISTERCIAN ORDER
AND ITS ORGANIZATION

T O UNDERSTAND THE CISTERCIAN PHASE of S. Anastasius *ad Aquas Salvias,* we must first consider the history and customs of the Cistercian Order in the Middle Ages. Early in 1098 Robert, abbot of Molesme, and twenty companions, including Alberic and Stephen Harding, left their abbey to begin a 'New Monastery' at Cîteaux. Their intention was not so much to establish a new monastic Order as to return to the rigorous observance of the Rule of Saint Benedict, an observance free from the accretions of passing centuries and a life unhampered by feudal powers.[1] On the other hand, their interpretation of the Rule contained new features: they did not accept boys into the monastery; there were detailed prescriptions regarding vestments, altar vessels and crosses; and a conventual Mass and the Office of the

---

1. Marcel Aubert, *L'architecture cistercienne en France* (Paris: Vanoest, 1947, 2nd ed.) 1:4ff.; Anselme Dimier, *Les Moines bâtisseurs.* (Paris: Fayard, 1964) translated by Gilchrist Lavigne OCSO, *Stones Laid Before the Lord* (Kalamazoo: Cistercian Publications, 1999); Richard W. Southern, *Western Society and the Church in the Middle Ages* (Harmondsworth: Pelican, 1970) 250 ff.; Louis J. Lekai, *The Cistercians: Ideals and Reality* (Kent, Ohio: The Kent State University Press, 1977) 11–32; Clifford H. Lawrence, *Medieval Monasticism* (London: Longman, 1984) 146 ff.; Terryl Kinder, *Cistercian Europe* (Grand Rapids: Eerdmans-Kalamazoo: Cistercian Publications 2002) 31–34 (*L'Europe cistercienne* [Paris: Zodiaque, 1997] 29–32). Janet Burton, 'The Cistercian Adventure', *The Cistercian Abbeys of Britain: Far from the Concourse of men,* David Robinson, ed. (London: B.T. Batsford-Kalamazoo: Cistercian Publications, 1998) 7–14; Peter Fergusson and Stuart Harrison, *Rievaulx Abbey: Community, Architecture, Memory* (New Haven-London: Yale University Press, 1999) 2–4; Christopher N. L. Brooke, *The Age of the Cloister: The Story of Monastic Life in the Middle Ages* (Mahwah, New Jersey: HiddenSpring/Paulist Press, 2003) 166–194.

dead were to be celebrated every day.[2] In the autumn of 1099 the papal legate ordered Robert to resume his duties as abbot of Molesme. Alberic took over as abbot and governed Cîteaux until his death on 26 January 1109. During his tenure, in October 1100, the abbey was placed under papal protection. The first stone church and cloister were built in 1106. Instead of the black habit of the Benedictines, the monks of the new monastery adopted robes of undyed wool; from this they were sometimes called 'Grey', but more frequently 'White Monks'.[3]

When Alberic died, the english monk Stephen Harding became abbot and he governed Cîteaux until his death in 1133. To him are attributed the two documents which stand beside the Rule of Saint Benedict as the foundation of the cistercian way of life, the *Exordium coenobii cisterciensis* (the *Exordium parvum*) or 'Historical narrative of the beginnings of the Order', and the *Carta Caritatis,* the 'Charter of Love', its constitution.[4] The *Carta Caritatis* was confirmed by Pope Callixtus II in 1119, and again by Pope Eugenius III in 1152.[5] In addition, the *Ecclesiastica Officia* (the Customary for monks) and the *Usus Conversorum* (the Customary for lay-brothers) spelled out in detail the day to day observance of the Rule.[6] The Statutes of the annual General Chapters of the Order provided on-going legislation in practical matters.[7] In the

2. Goffredo Viti, *Architettura cistercense: Fontenay e le abbazie in Italia dal 1120 al 1160* (Casamari and Florence: Edizioni Casamari, 1995) 24. On lay-brothers, see James Donnelly, *The Decline of the Medieval Cistercian Lay Brotherhood* (New York: Fordham University Press, 1949); and Chrysogonus Waddell, *Cistercian Lay Brothers: Twelfth-Century Usages with Related Texts*, Studia et Documenta 10 (Cîteaux: Commentarii Cistercienses 2000).

3. See Kinder, *Cistercian Europe*, 59–63 (*L'Europe cistercienne*, 57–61) where the monks' cowl and the black scapular are also described.

4. In the edition of Chrysogonus Waddell, *Narrative and Legislative Texts from Early Cîteaux*, Studia et Documenta, 12 (Cîteaux: Commentarii Cistercienses 1999): *Exordium Parvum*, Introduction, 100–231, and Text, 232–259; *Carta caritatis:* Introduction, 261–272, and Text, 274–282.

5. Waddell, *Narrative and Legislative Texts*, 283–296, and below, C. DATES AND DOCUMENTS, 1 August 1152.

6. For the *Ecclesiastica officia*, see *Les* Ecclesiastica Officia. *Cisterciens du XIIème siècle,* Danièle Choisselet and Placide Vernet, edd., Le Documentation Cistercienne 22 (Reiningue: Abbaye d'Œlenberg, 1989); for the *Usus Conversorum*, see Waddell, *Cistercian Lay Brothers* (above, note 2). For a modern interpretation of the regulation and order of monastic spaces, see Megan Cassidy-Wells, *Monastic Spaces and their Meanings: Thirteenth-century English Monasteries* (Turnhout: Brepols, 2001).

7. J.-M. Canivez, ed., *Statuta capitularum generalium Ordinis Cisterciensis,* 9 volumes. Bibliothèque de la Révue d'Histoire Ecclésiastique 9–14B (Louvain: Bureaux de la Révue, 1933–1941). The first volume has now been largely superseded by Chrysogonus Waddell, *Twelfth-Century*

twelfth century it is possible that the abbots attending the General Chapter made notes or copies of the official version of the statutes, which they took home to their communities.[8]

From 1202 onwards the Statutes were copied more systematically into various collections. The General Chapter of 1204 commanded all abbots to possess a copy of this legislation, the *Libellus definitionem*. In 1265 the papal Bull *Clementina* demanded a revision, which was carried out by 1289. Shortly afterwards, the General Chapter of 1316 called for another revision, which was collated as the *Libellus antiquorum definitionum*. This was to be definitive, and earlier collections were to be suppressed. In 1350 an 'appendix' was added to it, the *Novellae definitiones*. All these documents provide information about the medieval Cistercians, their way of life, and their monasteries.[9]

In 1112 Saint Bernard and thirty companions joined Cîteaux. From then on the Cistercians became one of the most vibrant religious Orders of the Middle Ages. Numbers increased rapidly. Daughter houses of Cîteaux were established initially at La Ferté (18 May 1113), Pontigny (31 May 1114), Clairvaux (25 June 1115) and Morimond (end of June 1115).[10] The monks adopted a system of filiation, which was a new structure of monastic cohesion. Each of the daughter houses was related to Cîteaux as 'daughter' to 'mother' house. They then established their own affiliated monasteries, which related to them in the same way. At its foundation *c.* 1140, S. Anastasius *ad Aquas Salvias* was the thirty-fourth daughter house of Clairvaux, then governed by Saint Bernard.[11] By the time Saint Bernard died in August 1153, there were one hundred sixty-four abbeys in Clairvaux's filiation.[12]

Statutes from the Cistercian General Chapter. Studia et Documenta, 12 (Brecht: Cîteaux: Commentarii Cistercienses, 2002).

8. Waddell lists seven local collections of statutes, which may have resulted from such a practice. They include sets of Statutes found in manuscripts from Cîteaux-Igny, Signy, Alcobaça, Tre Fontane, Bujedo and Clairvaux, Waddell, *Twelfth-Century Statutes*, 26–27 and 607–750.

9. Christopher Holdsworth, 'The Chronology and Character of Early Cistercian Legislation on Art and Architecture', *Cistercian Art and Architecture in the British Isles*, Christopher Norton and David Parks, edd. (Cambridge: Cambridge University Press, 1986) 40–55; Lekai, *The Cistercians: Ideals and Reality*, 65–76; and Kinder, *Cistercian Europe*, 51–55 (*L'Europe cistercienne*, 49–52).

10. Archdale A. King, *Cîteaux and her Elder Daughters* (London: Burns and Oates, 1954).

11. See below, C. DATES AND DOCUMENTS, *c.* 1140 (4).

12. For the history of Clairvaux, King, *Cîteaux and her elder daughters*, 207–328.

It was characteristic of the Cistercians that the abbot of the parent house, or his delegate, made a visitation to the daughter abbeys once a year. Saint Bernard could not visit all the filiations of Clairvaux, but he did care for the well-being of the monks. He wrote to the community at S. Anastasius *ad Aquas Salvias* from Clairvaux. He apologised for not being able to come in person, but he wanted to encourage the monks; he was sympathetic about the unhealthy site of their monastery.[13]

When the abbots of all the filiations came together at the annual General Chapter at Cîteaux, various problems were discussed and corrections made. Although General Chapter legislation was binding on all cistercian houses, each abbey retained its autonomy. The Chapter maintained discipline and the observance of the Rule in a spirit of fraternal charity.[14] After he became Pope Eugenius III, Pietro Bernardo Paganelli, first abbot of S. Anastasius, attended the Cistercian General Chapter of 1147, as he would have done before ascending the papal throne.[15] The Chapter discussed matters specifically concerning the abbey of S. Anastasius *ad Aquas Salvias* in 1152, 1153, 1154 and 1294.[16]

A collection of Statutes from the General Chapter, dated 1160–1161, also survives in a manuscript from Tre Fontane which is now in Paris.[17] Thirty-one prescriptions are listed, covering a range of various matters, from details about the performance of liturgical offices to conditions that apply at the granges during harvest-time. Some of these statutes are unique to S. Anastasius, and may reflect some of the concerns or problems that had arisen at Tre Fontane. They state that lay brothers and novices may not read aloud to the community at the

---

13. See below, C. DATES AND DOCUMENTS, 1140–1145.

14. Kinder, *Cistercian Europe*, 51–55 (*L'Europe cistercienne*, 49–52). Dimier (*Moines bâtisseurs*, 40) makes the point that the Cistercian Order was more decentralised than that of Cluny; the autonomy of the abbeys was protected by the terms of the *Carta Caritatis*. The strong emphasis on the love of God and fraternal charity is discussed by W. Eugene Goodrich, 'Caritas and Cistercian Uniformity: An Ideological Connection?', CSQ 20 (1985) 31–43, and by Martha Newman, *The Boundaries of Charity: Cistercian Culture and Ecclesiastical Reform, 1098–1180* (Stanford University Press, 1996).

15. See below, C. DATES AND DOCUMENTS, 1147. He also wrote to the cistercian abbots in 1152 saying he would have liked to attend the General Chapter, but his papal duties prevented this; see below, C. DATES AND DOCUMENTS, 5 August 1152.

16. See below, C. DATES AND DOCUMENTS, August 1152; 1153 (1) and (2); 1153–1154 (1) and (2); and 1294.

17. Paris, Bibliothèque nationale de France, MS nouv. acqu. Latin 1402, f.5v, see Waddell, *Twelfth-Century Statutes*, 703–708.

'Collationes' before Compline.[18] The monks are not to stand surety or guarantor for seculars, nor to be constrained to give anything to powerful individuals.[19] Women are not allowed to spend the night in the monastery precinct, nor in a house outside the gate, even if this is beyond the enclosure. If a woman seems to be respectable, however, she may eat at the farm, and whatever is necessary may be administered to her. If she is unwilling to accept this, no more hospitality may be shown to her and she must be excluded even from the prayers of the community.[20] If a monk leaves or is sent away from the monastery and he contracts leprosy in the world outside, he should still be re-admitted up to three times.[21] When several abbots are present, only one may speak; in the refectory it is he who distributes the pittances, not the others.[22] When a priest serves as a deacon, he should wear his stole, not in the manner of a deacon, but around his neck as a priest.[23] When abbots arrive at the monastery, much talking by the monks is forbidden.[24]

There are in this manuscript also prayers to be said by monks and lay brothers for the peace of the Church, and for the kings of France and England and the bishop of Le Mans.[25] It is likely that the first of these prayers reflects cistercian support for Pope Alexander III (1159–1181) against Frederick Barbarossa and his antipopes.[26] The emperor took revenge on the monks of S. Anastasius, by evicting them from

18. Waddell, *Twelfth-Century Statutes,* 704, <7>.

19. Waddell, *Twelfth-Century Statutes,* 705–6, <23>.

20. Waddell, *Twelfth-Century Statutes,* 706, <24>.

21. Waddell, *Twelfth-Century Statutes,* 706, <25>. Waddell explains that RB 29.3 allowed a monk to be readmitted three times. He suggests that the example of someone contracting leprosy may refer to an actual case at Tre Fontane.

22. Waddell, *Twelfth-Century Statutes,* 706, <26>. Waddell suggests that the extra abbots may be visitors to the community. The abbot of the monastery would normally eat with the guests.

23. Waddell, *Twelfth-Century Statutes,* 706, <27>.

24. Waddell, *Twelfth-Century Statutes,* 706, <28>. Waddell adds, 'One can imagine the hubbub created by curious and news-hungry monks upon the arrival of a group of abbots, say, on their way back home from the General Chapter.'

25. Paris, Bibliothèque nationale de France, MS nouv. acqu. Latin 1402, f.78, Waddell, *Twelfth-Century Statutes,* 707–8, <32>, <33> and <34>.

26. Waddell, *Twelfth-Century Statutes,* 707, comments that the need for the prayers probably arose from this conflict, or from 'Henry II's anger over Cistercian support for Thomas Becket'.

their monastery, which was claimed by the monks of S. Paolo fuori le Mura in 1161.[27]

The *conversi,* or lay-brothers, were an important addition to the monastery.[28] From early in the eleventh century monasteries at Fonte Avellana, Camaldoli, and Vallombrosa in Italy, Hirsau in Germany, and Grandmont and Grande Chartreuse in France had received lay-brothers into their communities.[29] The early Cistercians adopted this practice and welcomed many conversi. Although their introduction was not a cistercian innovation, the Cistercians gave the *conversi* more importance than did any other Order. Instead of the Divine Office, they said such prayers as the *Pater Noster, Credo, Ave Maria,* and *Miserere.* They had different duties and living quarters, yet they and the monks formed a united community. By the end of the twelfth century, however, the lay-brothers in most religious Orders became discontented and their numbers declined, so that by the second half of the thirteenth century, very few were left.[30] Cistercian *conversi* sometimes rebelled against the monks, indulged in too much alcohol or committed other misdemeanours. In 1260 and 1261, the excesses of the lay-brothers of SS. Vincenzo e Anastasio at Tre Fontane were reported at the General Chapter at Cîteaux.[31]

Monks and lay-brothers alike had to do manual labour. This was mainly agricultural work, at first in rough, uncultivated terrain. Each community was supposed to be self-sufficient, producing its own food. Often the monks and *conversi* also built their churches, oratories, monasteries, granges and other buildings, with the help of local masons. When Saint Bernard's brother Gerard died in June 1138, the abbot of Clairvaux interrupted his commentary on the *Song of Songs* to praise Gerard's skill in all agricultural pursuits: building, working in the fields and orchards, or with water; instructing bricklayers, blacksmiths, cobblers, and weavers.[32] When Clairvaux was relocated and rebuilt

---

27. See above, Chapter I and DATES AND DOCUMENTS, 1161.

28. Kinder, *Cistercian Europe,* 305–311 (*L'Europe cistercienne,* 305–311).

29. Donnelly, *The Decline,* 1–14; Fergusson and Harrison, *Rievaulx,* 3.

30. Donnelly, *The Decline,* 22–37; Fergusson and Harrison, *Rievaulx,* 56–57.

31. Canivez, *Statuta* 2:466–467 (1260); 2:480 (1261). See also, Donnelly, *The Decline,* 76.

32. Bernardo di Chiaravalle, *Sermoni sul Cantico dei Cantici.* ed. and trans. Domenico Turco (Trani: Vivere In, 1982) 257–258; see also Viti, *Architettura Cistercense,* 36 and n. 37.

shortly after 1135, William of Saint-Thierry related in the *Life of Saint Bernard* that some monks chopped down trees, others cut stone, others built walls; yet others brought water from the River Aube in underground channels to the monastery buildings or to turn the mill.[33] Orderic Vitalis in the mid 1130s claimed that the Cistercians 'built monasteries with their own hands in lonely wooded places'.[34] The evidence of the buildings themselves suggests that outsiders also did some of the work; it is clear, however, that the cistercian insistence on manual labour may have caused lay-brothers and monks to participate in the construction of their buildings.

Like the Desert Fathers, the early monks of Cîteaux chose to settle in a solitary area far from human habitation. Such a location—a kind of desert—became a prerequisite for later cistercian abbeys. At Rome the cistercian monastery of S. Anastasius *ad Aquas Salvias* was located fourteen kilometres southeast of the third-century Aurelian Walls of the ancient city, at a site described in the late tenth century as '. . . situated far from the crowd . . .', '. . . *procul a turba positum* . . .'.[35] It was an ideal location for a cistercian abbey. Indeed, the Cistercian Statutes specified that no monasteries of the Order were to be constructed in towns, castles, or country-estates, but should be in places far from interaction with men.[36]

The remote site of S. Anastasius was described by Saint Bernard as 'unhealthy', although this did not seem to worry him unduly.[37] It was part of the radical nature of the cistercian calling to suffer the exigencies of the rough places where their abbeys were situated. They placed a

---

33. Quoted in Viti, *Architettura cistercense*, 36.

34. Orderic Vitalis, *The Ecclesiastical History,* ed. and trans. Marjorie Chibnall, (Oxford: Clarendon Press, 1969 ff.) 4:326–327.

35. See below, C. DATES AND DOCUMENTS, 998.

36. 'Quo in loco sint construenda coenobia. In civitatibus, castellis, villis, nulla nostra construenda sunt coenobis, sed in locis a conversatione hominum semotis.', *Statuta,* 1:13, with a date of 1134; cf. Christopher Norton, 'Table of Cistercian Legislation on Art and Architecture'. *Cistercian Art,* 318, giving a date of 1098–*c.* 1100. Norton here also refers to a passage in the *Exordium Parvum,* XV, which states that the holy men promised to imitate Saint Benedict, who did not build his monasteries in towns, castles or villas, but in places far from the concourse of people.

37. 'Scio . . . quod in regione habitatis infirma . . .', in the letter Saint Bernard wrote to the monks of S. Anastasius *ad Aquas Salvias, c.* 1140–1145; Ep. 345.2; *S. Bernardi Opera,* 8/I:286; PL 182: 550–551.

strong emphasis on poverty, and, as good soldiers of Christ, they could expect to suffer great austerities. Yet the first abbot of S. Anastasius, Pietro Bernardo Paganelli, was anxious to alleviate the illness of his monks—the problem was probably malaria in the summer months, when mosquitoes could thrive.[38] When he was elevated to the papacy as Eugenius III, Paganelli arranged for the community to spend the noxious summer months in Nemi, a small hill town south-east of Rome.[39] At the same time he specified that S. Anastasius *ad Aquas Salvias* should remain the 'head of the abbey',[40] perhaps because it was a papal foundation.

Cistercian abbeys were always located close to water. Often a stream or a river was diverted for the use of the monastic establishment. Usually the buildings were planned so that the stream passed along the side of the monastery furthest from the church. The fresh water was used for drinking, cooking, and washing; it also carried away waste from the kitchen, refectory, and latrines, all on that side of the complex, or it drove the mills and other devices in the monastic workshops.[41] At Tre Fontane water was plentiful. Early views of the abbey show a stream flowing past the monastery, which was approached over a bridge (figs. 68 and 69), and in his recent restoration campaign Belardi found sophisticated drainage systems in the medieval cistercian church.[42] Fifteenth-century views of Tre Fontane indicate hills around the abbey (figs. 68 and 69). True to cistercian practice, the monastery

38. This was certainly a problem in the nineteenth century, when the Trappists returned to Tre Fontane. It was not until the early twentieth century that the causes of malaria were scientifically investigated, as is explained by Angelo Celli, *Storia della malaria*. (Città di Castello: Società Anonima Tip. 'Leonardo da Vinci', 1925).

39. See below, C. DATES AND DOCUMENTS, 1145–1153 (1).

40. See below, C. DATES AND DOCUMENTS (1), 1145–1153. It is likely that the expression 'head of the abbey' means the chief location of the monastery; the Tre Fontane monks could not transfer that role to a monastery in a more salubrious place.

41. Meredith Parson Lillich, 'Cleanliness with Godliness: A Discussion of Medieval Monastic Plumbing', *Mélanges à la Mémoire du Anselme Dimier*, 3 (1982) 123–149. For medieval italian cistercian workshops, granges and other utilitarian buildings, Marina Righetti Tosti-Croce, *Architettura per il lavoro: dal caso cistercense a un caso cistercense: Chiaravalle di Fiastra* (Rome: Viella, 1993).

42. Giovanni Belardi, 'Considerazioni sui restauri in atto nell'abbazia delle Tre Fontane a Roma', *Arte Medievale*. 2 Serie, 7 (1993) 229–230; Giovanni Belardi, 'Il restauro dell'abbazia delle Tre Fontane' (seconda parte). *Arte Medievale*, 2 Serie, 8,1 (1994) 79–91 and Giovanni Belardi, 'Il restauro architettonico' in Giovanni Belardi, Fra Jacques Brière, Liliana Pozzi et al., *Abbazia delle Tre Fontane: il complesso, la storia, il restauro* (Rome: Edilerica s.r.l., 1995) 98–160.

of S. Anastasius was situated in the valley between them. According to a latin aphorism, 'Bernard loved valleys, Benedict hills, Francis towns, and Ignatius famous cities'.[43]

The cistercian Statutes stipulated that, whenever a new monastery was established, an abbot and twelve monks were required to begin the new foundation, and the new community should be able to begin to live according to their monastic Rule on arrival at the new site. This means that they had to have an oratory and the books, buildings, and everything else necessary for their way of life. Among the books there were to be Missals, the Rule of Saint Benedict, the Book of Customs, the Psalter, a Hymn-book, a book of Collects, a Lectionary, an Antiphonary and a Gradual. The buildings were to include an oratory, a refectory, a dormitory, guest cells, a porter's cell, and also temporal necessities.[44] When Saint Bernard wrote to Pope Innocent II saying he did not have enough men to send to Rome for his new monastery, he may indeed not have had a suitable group of twelve monks and an abbot for this purpose.[45] Instead, Pope Innocent II founded his new cistercian abbey at Tre Fontane with monks from Farfa.[46] The pope probably provided the monks with the books they required. Later, Pope Eugenius III added a volume of Homilies by Origen to their collection.[47] Arnold reported that Pope Innocent II constructed living quarters for the monks and restored the church.[48] In doing this, he

---

43. 'Bernardus valles, colles Benedictus amabat / Franciscus vicos, celebres Ignatius urbes', quoted from Dimier, *Moines bâtisseurs*, 36. Kinder has a slightly different version, which has Saint Dominic, instead of Ignatius, loving great cities: Kinder, *Cistercian Europe*, 81 (*L'Europe cistercienne*, 79).

44. Capitula IX: 4, Waddell, *Twelfth-Century Statutes*, 512: 'nec sine libris istis: psalterio, hymnario, collectane, antiphonario, gradali, regula, missali; nec nisi prius extructis his officinis: oratorio, refectorio, dormitorio, cella hospitum et portarii, quatinus ibi statim et deo servire, et regulariter vivere possint.', cf. Norton, 'Table', 318–321, with a date of 1098–c. 1100. See also the discussion on the installation of a new abbey in Kinder, *Cistercian Europe*, 105–130 (*L'Europe cistercienne*, 85–111).

45. See below, C. DATES AND DOCUMENTS, c. 1140 (1). Since Saint Bernard did not think highly of Rome, it is also possible that his response to Pope Innocent was a polite way of putting off the pope's request. However, by c. 1147, Instituta XXXVII demanded that abbots should have sixty professed monks and obtain permission of the General Chapter before establishing new monasteries; see Waddell, *Twelfth-Century Statutes*, 546, and *Instituta* XXXVII, 2.

46. See below, C. DATES AND DOCUMENTS, c. 1140 (2).

47. See below, C. DATES AND DOCUMENTS, 1145–1153 (2).

48. See below, C. DATES AND DOCUMENTS, c. 1140, (3).

made the preparations expected of a patron of a cistercian foundation. Probably Innocent II built the twelfth-century core of the east
range for the new community. The church he restored may have been
one of three sanctuaries known from documentary sources on the
site—the *martyrium* of S. Paolo alle Tre Fontane which marked the
spot where Saint Paul was said to have been beheaded; the oratory of
Our Lady; or the basilica of Saint John the Baptist, rebuilt by Pope
Hadrian I after a fire in the eighth century.[49] Not long after the Cistercians arrived at Tre Fontane, they built a new church laid out according to a typical early cistercian plan. This church was consecrated by
Pope Honorius III in 1221[50] and dedicated in the first instance to the
Mother of God, as was typical of cistercian practice.[51]

Although some early images of the church S. Anastasius show a
bell-tower beside it (e.g. fig. 69), there is no architectural evidence for
such an elaborate structure. It would, moreover, have contravened the
cistercian Statutes, which proscribed stone towers for bells.[52] At Tre
Fontane the monastic buildings stand to the north of the church (Plan I,
fig. 1). It was more usual in cistercian monasteries for them to be
located to the south, but their position was in the end dictated by the
topography of the site and the location of the stream or river that provided water for the monks' needs.[53] At the monastery of S. Anastasius
ad Aquas Salvias, the location of the claustral buildings may have been
complicated by the existence of previously erected structures south of
the monastery church.

It was one of the aims of the Order to be united in all things—to
have the same customs and the same chant; to use the same books for
the day and night offices and for Mass as those used at the 'New Mon-

---

49. See below, C. DATES AND DOCUMENTS, 789–790.

50. See below, C. DATES AND DOCUMENTS, 1 April 1221.

51. Capitula IX: 2:, 'Ordinatum est in honore regine celi et terre nostra omnia fundari
debere cenobia'; and Instituta XVIII: 3: '. . . omnes ecclesiae nostrae . . . in memoria eiusdem
caeli et terrae reginae Sanctae mariae fundentur ac dedicentur' (Waddell, *Twelfth-Century
Statutes,* 512 and 541); cf. 'Ordinatum est in honore reginae coeli et terrae nostra omnia
debere coenobia . . .', Norton, 'Table', 318, dated 1098–*c.* 1100.

52. 'Turres lapidee ad campanas non fiant', I. B. Annual Statuta, 1158; Waddell, *Twelfth-
Century Statutes,* 70, <13>; cf. 'Lapidee turres non fiant in ordine nostro', Norton, 'Table', 328
and 330, with dates of 1157 and ?1182–1183.

53. Anselme Dimier, *L'art cistercien: France,* La Nuit des Temps, 16 (Paris: Zodiaque, 1982)
39; Lillich, 'Cleanliness with Godliness', 41.

astery' at Cîteaux; so that everything might be done without discord, and the monks might be one in love, living by the same customs, according to one Rule.[54] It is not surprising, then, that the layout of the various buildings comprising a cistercian monastery should reflect this desire for unity within the Order. In spite of considerable variations in style and building materials, it has been possible to draw up a typical plan for a cistercian monastery.[55] The abbey of S. Anastasius *ad Aquas Salvias* reflects this practice.

On one side stood the church, the largest and most important edifice in the abbey. It was there that the community prayed.[56] The monks attended the conventual Mass at the high altar, or Mass was said by the priests privately at side altars, as in the four chapels which open off the transept at Tre Fontane. The monks chanted the Hours seven times a day, beginning with Vigils in the middle of the night— when they came down from the dormitory by the night stairs into the transept—through Prime, Terce, Sext, None, and Vespers, and ending with Compline, the last office of the day. The monks' choir extended about halfway down the nave of the church, after which there was a space for sick members of the community. Behind them, to the west of the monks' choir, was a choir for the *conversi*, who did not chant the Divine Office at the prescribed times, but said numerous prayers learned by heart. Their part of the church had its own door in the western half of the nave.

---

54. *Carta Caritatis Prior,* III, 1098–c. 1100, quoted by Norton, 'Table', 319: '. . . et hoc etiam volumus, ut mores et cantum, et omnes libros ad horas diurnas et nocturnas et ad missas necessarios secundum formam morum et librorum novi monasterii possideant, quatinus in actibus nostris nulla sit discordia, sed una caritate, una regula similibusque vivamus moribus'. See also Instituta: '*De unitate conversationis in divinis et humanis.* II (Waddell, *Twelfth-century Statues,* 537): Ut autem inter abbatias unitas indissolubilis perpetuo perseveret, stabilitatem est primo qui ab omnibus *regula* beati benedicti uno modo intelligatur, uno modo teneatur; dehinc ut hiidem libri quantum dumtaxat ad divinum officium pertinet; idem victus, idem vestitus, iidem denique per omnia mores inveniantur.'

55. Aubert, *L'architecture cistercienne,* 1:107 ff.; Wolfgang Braunfels, *Monasteries of Western Europe* (London: Thames and Hudson, 1972) 74–75, 2:1–144; Carolyn Malone and Walter Horn, 'Layout of the Cistercian Monastery in the twelfth and thirteenth centuries', in Walter Horn and Ernest Born, *The Plan of St. Gall* (Berkeley: University of California Press, 1979) 2:315–356, esp. 349–356; Dimier, *L'art cistercien,* 39–41; for variations in style and building materials, Kinder, *Cistercian Europe,* 364–365 (*L'Europe cistercienne,* 386).

56. Cassidy-Welch, *Monastic Spaces,* 73–103.

The various monastic buildings were ranged around a cloister, as was the case at S. Anastasius *ad Aquas Salvias*.[57] The east range abutted the transept of the church and was reserved for the monks. The chapter room was on the ground floor; the dormitory was upstairs.[58] On the side opposite the church was the monks' refectory, which was flanked by the warming-room and the kitchen.

On the western side of the cloister, and separated from it by the *conversi* corridor, was the lay-brothers' accommodation, including their refectory and dormitory, as well as the monastery cellar.[59] They were clearly separated from the monks, in the church and in the monastery. Although the monastic buildings seemed to house two distinct religious groups—the monks and lay-brothers—they in fact formed one community.

The cloister was at the heart of the monks' quarters. They would frequently pass through it, or walk or process around it.[60] Seated within it they would read, meditate, and at the end of the day sit and listen to extracts from the works of the Church Fathers.

The cloister walk built against the church's aisle was a special place for reading. At Tre Fontane the walk is a modern reconstruction, but it was probably preceded by a medieval portico in the same place. There the monks listened to and commented upon Scripture, the writings of the Fathers and the lives of the saints after Compline each evening. This practice was called the *collationes,* after the *Conferences* of John Cassian, which had been recommended by Saint Benedict.[61] The monastery books were kept in an *armarium,* a cupboard next to the sacristy or under the night stairs. The cloister walk closest to the church may have been provided with benches, as at Tre Fontane when the Trappists rebuilt it in the twentieth century (fig. 88). In the same cloister walk

---

57. Cassidy-Welch, *Monastic Spaces,* 47–71.

58. Virginia Jansen, 'Architecture and Community in Medieval Monastic Dormitories', in *Studies in Cistercian Art and Architecture,* 5, ed. Meredith Parsons Lillich (Kalamazoo: Cistercian Publications, 1998) 59–94.

59. For an account of how the lay-brothers' wing functioned in danish medieval cistercian monasteries, see James France, 'The Cellarer's Domain' in *Cistercian Art and Architecture 5*, CS 167 (Kalamazoo: Cistercian Publications, 1999) 1–39.

60. For the cloister, Kinder, *Cistercian Europe,* 131–140 (*L'Europe cistercienne,* 129–138). On Palm Sunday the monks processed around the cloister.

61. RB 42.5.

the monks also received the *mandatum,* the washing of their feet every Saturday, by those appointed to serve at meals for the week past and the week to come. This cistercian practice recalled how Christ washed his disciples' feet at the Last Supper and was a sign of humble service. From these two practices, the cloister walk beside the church aisle was called the 'Collation' or 'Mandatum' cloister.[62]

The eastern wing of the monastery was where the monks lived. Next to the church were the book-cupboard or *armarium* and the sacristy, both of which were relatively small. The Cistercians spent six or seven hours a day at prayer; several hours doing manual work, often in the fields; and part of their time reading. Their monastic library was not always very large. Similarly, cistercian sacristies contained only simple liturgical objects; often vestments and liturgical vessels were kept in the chapels of the church for immediate use. Hence the monks did not at first require large or elaborate sacristies. On the other hand, from the late thirteenth century onwards, when the Cistercians relaxed some of their strictures against sacred art, larger sacristies—and sometimes a private chapel for the abbot, were built beside their churches. At S. Anastasius the *armarium* and the old sacristy seem originally to have been one small room. In the late thirteenth century, Abbot Martinus (1283–1302) donated a costly silver reliquary to the abbey.[63] In the same century, perhaps in 1284, a new sacristy—or the abbot's private chapel—was laid out with a high, ribbed vaulted ceiling (figs. 45–48).[64] It was adorned with murals of the *Coronation of the Virgin* and the *Nativity* (fig. 87). In the twelfth century such paintings would have been unthinkable, for the Statutes expressly forbade them, allowing only painted wooden crosses.[65] Saint Bernard was not in

---

62. Aubert, *L'architecture cistercienne,* 2:2; Dimier, *L'art cistercien,* 39–41; Kinder, *Cistercian Europe,* 135–137 (*L'Europe cistercienne,* 134–135).

63. See below, C. DATES AND DOCUMENTS, 1283.

64. Joan E. Barclay Lloyd, 'The Medieval Murals in the Cistercian Abbey of SS. Vincenzo e Anastasio *ad Aquas Salvias* at Tre Fontane, near Rome in their Architectural Setting', *Papers of the British School at Rome,* 65 (1997) 323–344.

65. Capitula XXVI: 2: 'Sculpturas nusquam, picturas tantum licet habere in crucibus, que et ipse nonnisi lignee habeantur'; and Instituta XX: 2–3: 'Sculpturae vel picturae in ecclesiis nostris seu in officinis aliquibus monasterii ne fiant interdicimus, quia dum talibus intenditur, utilitas bonae meditationis vel disciplina religiosae gravitatis saepe negligitur. Cruces tamen pictas quae sunt ligneae habemus.' (Waddell, *Twelfth-Century Statutes,* 516 and 541) ; cf. 'Sculpturas nusquam, picturas tantum licet habere in crucibus quae et ispae lignaeae habeantur',

favour of any figural art in the cloister, as his *Apologia* makes abundantly clear.[66] In the early thirteenth century the General Chapter reiterated the prohibition of paintings, except for an image of the Saviour.[67] Several abbots were disciplined for allowing figural art, as happened in 1242, when the General Chapter rebuked the abbot of Valparaiso in Spain for decorating with frescoes the cloister and various rooms of his abbey.[68] In the later thirteenth and in the fourteenth century it became more common for cistercian monasteries to be adorned with murals.[69] A vast campaign to decorate the monks' wing at S. Anastasius in the late thirteenth or early fourteenth century would fit in with this trend.[70]

Beyond the sacristy was the chapter room. After Prime each day the monks gathered there for the reading of the martyrology, other readings, and prayers to bless the work of the day. A chapter of the Rule of Saint Benedict was read and the abbot usually gave a short commentary. The duties of the day were outlined. In the chapter room the monks held their 'chapter of faults' in which they accused themselves or each other of various misdemeanours and received appropriate

---

quoted in Norton, 'Table', 324 and dated *c.* 1122–1135; see also David Park, 'Cistercian Wall Painting and Panel Painting' in *Cistercian Art,* 181–210. See also Aubert, *L'architecture cistercienne,* 1:142. For early cistercian attitudes to art, Conrad Rudolph, *'Things of Greater Importance': Bernard of Clairvaux's Apologia and the Medieval Attitude toward Art* (Philadelphia: University of Pennsylvania Press, 1990).

66. *St. Bernard's Apologia to Abbot William,* trans. Michael Casey, OCSO, *Bernard of Clairvaux: Treaties, I,* Cistercian Fathers Series 1 (Spencer, MA: Cistercian Publications, 1970); reissued as *Cistercians and Cluniacs: The Case for Cîteaux. The* Apologia *of Abbot Bernard of Clairvaux,* CF 1A (Kalamazoo: Cistercian Publications); Conrad Rudolph, 'Bernard of Clairvaux's *Apologia* as a Description of Cluny and the Controversy over Monastic Art', *Gesta* 27 (1988) 125–132; Rudolph, *'Things of Greater Importance'.*

67. 'Auctoritate Capituli generalis inhibetur ne de cetero fiant in Ordine picturae, sculpturae, praeter imaginem Salvatoris . . .' in 1213; cf. 'De sculpturis et picturis ne fiant. Sculpture vel picture notabiles in ecclesiis nostris seu in officinis aliquibus monasterii vel grangiarum ne fiant interdicimus preter ymaginem salvatoris . . .' in 1220; quoted in Norton, 'Table', 354 and 358.

68. Aubert, *L'architecture cistercienne,* 1:144 gives the example of the abbot of Valparaiso, while Norton, 'Table', gives several other examples.

69. Aubert, *L'architecture cistercienne,* 1:144.

70. Carlo Bertelli, 'L'enciclopedia delle Tre Fontane', *Paragone-Arte* 20.235 (1969) 24–49; Melinda Mihályi, 'I Cistercensi a Roma e la decorazione pittorica dei Monaci, nell'abbazia delle Tre Fontane', *Arte Medievale,* 2 serie, 5,1 (1991) 155–189; Barclay Lloyd, 'The Medieval Murals', 323–344; Kristin Bliksrud Aavitsland, *Florilegium: En undersøkelse av billed-språket Vita humana-frisen, Abbazia delle Tre Fontane, Roma.* Acta Humaniora 134 (Oslo: Unipub, 2002).

penances from the abbot.[71] The abbot might also discuss with the monks important matters affecting the life of the community. The abbot's throne was set against the east wall of the chapter room and the monks sat around the north, east and south walls, probably on the kind of stepped 'benches' shown in a drawing of Tre Fontane by Seroux d'Agincourt.[72] On certain important occasions the *conversi* also attended chapter; often they would remain in the cloister walk, listening to the abbot through the arched openings in the west wall of the chapter room (fig. 30).[73] In winter the monks could read in the chapter room, rather than in the drafty corridors of the cloister.[74] When the abbot died—or, as at S. Anastasius in 1145, became pope—the new abbot was elected in the chapter room.

Beyond the chapter room there was often a passageway leading from the cloister to the eastern side of the monks' wing. This was the case at S. Anastasius. (Plan I, fig. 1). Beyond that there was often a staircase, the 'day stairs', from the cloister to the dormitory above. Most monasteries had a parlour, an *auditorium,* where the prior, the abbot's second-in-command, would see the monks. For two months after their profession the newly professed monks would continue to meet the master of novices there.

Beyond the cloister on the ground floor of the eastern wing there was usually a large room, the monks' room. In some monasteries it also served as a novices' room; in others there was another room with that function at this end or at right angles to this end of the monks' wing. At Tre Fontane, there is now a large room at the northern end of the east range, whose interior has been remodelled in modern times.

At the very end of the monks' wing, furthest from the church, there was often a narrow toilet block for the monastery latrines.[75] Often the latrines were upstairs and the stream or river at ground level washed away the waste.

---

71. Cassidy-Welch, *Monastic Spaces,* 105–132, with comments on the monastic custom of accusation, confession, and receiving punishment in the chapter room.

72. This is illustrated in Romanini, '"Ratio fecit diversum"', 34, fig. 61.

73. Aubert, *L'architecture cistercienne,* 1:52; Kinder, *Cistercian Europe,* 265–266 (*L'Europe cistercienne,* 247).

74. Aubert, *L'architecture cistercienne,* 1:117–118.

75. Lillich discusses monastic latrines in 'Cleanliness with Godliness', 129–131, 135–137.

Above the eastern wing of the monastery was the monks' dormitory, one large room. Although the abbot was advised to sleep in the dormitory with the monks, in some early cistercian abbeys the abbot had a private cell next to the church and near the night stairs.[76] Saint Bernard himself had a small cell at Clairvaux;[77] and an abbot's cell still exists beside the night stairs at Le Thoronet.[78] The sacristan, who had to wake up the community for the midnight office, may have occupied a separate cell near the stairs in some monasteries; the infirmarian also had his own cell.[79] Often the novices were accommodated at the end of the dorter furthest from the church. Sometimes, however, a separate novitiate building stood beside that end of the monks' wing. On the eastern side of the monks' range, often also in a separate building, was the infirmary.[80]

The range of the cloister opposite the church contained the warming-room or calefactory, the refectory, and the kitchen. The calefactory, the only heated room in the monastery, was a place for monks to read and for the scribes to prepare their ink and parchment. The monks also cleaned and greased their shoes there. Tonsures were cut in the warming-room, and four times a year the monks were bled. After the blood-letting, they usually went upstairs to rest in a room located above the calefactory and entered through the dorter or by its own staircase.[81]

After *c.* 1150 the refectory in cistercian monasteries was often at right angles to the cloister ambulatory opposite the church,[82] as is the

---

76. Aubert, *L'architecture cistercienne,* 1:35; 2:91–92; and Jansen, 'Architecture and Community', 59–94 (dormitories) and 76 (abbot's or abbess's, room).

77. Aubert, *L'architecture cistercienne,* 1:13.

78. Aubert, *L'architecture cistercienne,* 2:91–92. Aubert mentions other examples at Chaalis, Mortemer, Noirlac, Senanque, Silvacane and Beaulieu (Tarn-et-Garonne). He says that in the fourteenth century cistercian abbots often abandoned this cell and constructed other, more spacious accommodation for themselves. For le Thoronet, see also Yves Esquieu, *L'abbaye du Thoronet* (Ouest France: Ministère de la Culture, 1985) 20.

79. Kinder, *Cistercian Europe (L'Europe cistercienne),* 271–272.

80. [68] David N. Bell, 'The Siting and Size of Cistercian Infirmaries in England and Wales', *Studies in Cistercian Art and Architecture,* 5 (CS 167) 211–237; Fergusson and Harrison, *Rievaulx,* 111–135.

81. Aubert, *L'architecture cistercienne,* 2:114–116; Kinder, *Cistercian Europe (L'Europe cistercienne),* 278–280.

82. Peter Fergusson, 'The Twelfth-century Refectories at Rievaulx and Byland Abbeys', *Cistercian Art,* 160–180; Anne Claire Rochet, 'The Refectory Wing of the Cistercian Abbey of Vaux-de-Cernay', *Studies in Cistercian Art and Architecture* 5:187–210.

case in the abbey of Tre Fontane. Many cistercian refectories have a lectern on one side, since it was monastic custom to listen to readings during meals. Opposite the refectory in the cloister there was often a fountain, so that the monks could wash their hands before meals.[83] No such fountain survives at S. Anastasius; instead, there may have been a wash basin or trough, a *lavatorium*. Beyond the refectory was the kitchen, which served both monks and *conversi,* who had their own dining room.

West of the cloister, and separated from it by the *conversi* corridor, was the lay-brothers' wing.[84] This was usually divided into two parts, with a passageway between them leading into the cloister. Closest to the church on the ground floor was the Great Cellar; beyond the passageway was the *conversi* refectory. Above was the lay-brothers' dormitory.

Pope Eugenius III petitioned the Cistercian General Chapter to allow the monks at S. Anastasius to retain property belonging to the monastery.[85] This was an unusual request, since the Statutes forbade the monks to derive income from churches, altars, tombs, tithes of work or food, country-estates, villeins, property in land, or income from ovens, mills, or other similar sources.[86] Yet from at least the time of Pope Alexander III, if not before, the Cistercians at S. Anastasius claimed the rich property in the Maremma associated with the legend of Pope Leo III and Charlemagne.[87] In the late thirteenth century, the tomb of a benefactress was erected in the narthex of the monastery church of S. Anastasius.[88] Eclissi, in the seventeenth century, drew this and another, probably medieval, arcosolium tomb, in the narthex (fig. 70). Magnificent tombs of lay patrons were not usual in early

---

83. Such fountain pavilions still exist at Le Thoronet and at Fossanova. For fountains at other monasteries, see Lillich, 'Cleanliness with Godliness', 131–141.

84. France, 'The Cellarer's Domain', 1–39.

85. See below, C. DATES AND DOCUMENTS, August 1152.

86. Instituta IX: 1–2 ; Waddell, *Twelfth-century Statutes, 539*: 'Quod redditus non habeamus. IX. Ecclesias, altaria, sepulturas, decimas alieni laboris vel nutrimenti, villas, villanos, terrarum census, furnorum et molendinorum redditus, et cetera his similia monastice puritati adversantia, nostri et nominis et ordinis excludit institutio.'

87. See below, C. DATES AND DOCUMENTS, (805?), 1081, 10 July 1161. One wonders whether the legend was made up to support the monks' claim to the lands in the Maremma, precisely because of the cistercian proscriptions against such ownership.

88. See below, C. DATES AND DOCUMENTS, 1272.

cistercian churches or abbeys, but rules regarding them were relaxed in the early thirteenth century.[89]

When a new cistercian foundation was made, provision had to be made for receiving guests by providing a guest cell.[90] At S. Anastasius it is probable that the wing west of the *conversi* building was built for guests, and it has that function still to-day.

Like most cistercian abbeys, S. Anastasius *ad Aquas Salvias* was encircled by an enclosing wall entered through a major gateway.[91] Seventeenth-century and later prints show these elements (figs. 71, 72, 75, 76 and 77).

S. Anastasius *ad Aquas Salvias* is a fine example of a medieval cistercian monastery. Although remodelled in the late-nineteenth and twentieth centuries, much of the medieval structure survives. From the buildings one can imagine some aspects of the life-style of the cistercian monks and lay-brothers at that far distant time.

89. A prohibition of 1134 was relaxed in 1217, according to Aubert, *L'architecture cistercienne*, 1:329ff.

90. This may have been because the Rule of Saint Benedict strongly recommended hospitality; see also Kinder, *Cistercian Europe*, 368–368 (*L'Europe cistercienne*, 372–373).

91. The precinct wall, which 'acted as a symbolic barrier between the spiritual world of the monks and the secular world beyond, as well as a necessary physical demarcation' is discussed by France, 'The Cellarer's Domain', 13–14. For the lay-out of early cistercian gatehouses in England, see Peter Fergusson, '"Porta Patens Esto": Notes on Early Cistercian Gatehouses in the North of England', *Medieval Architecture and its Intellectual Context. Studies in Honour of Peter Kidson*. (London: The Hambledon Press, 1990) 47–59. See also Kinder, *Cistercian Europe*, 367–371 (*L'Europe cistercienne*, 371–375).

III

MEDIEVAL CISTERCIAN ARCHITECTURE

T HE CHURCH AND MONASTERY BUILDINGS at S. Anastasius *ad Aquas Salvias* must be seen in the context of medieval cistercian architecture elsewhere in Europe. As the Order spread rapidly in the twelfth century, hundreds of monasteries were built.[1] Extensive remains can be found in France, Belgium, England, Ireland, Germany, Switzerland, Scandinavia, Italy, Spain, Portugal, and even in Poland and Greece.[2] All these were affiliated to older

1. By 1153 there were 339, by the end of the twelfth century 525; and in the seventeenth century there were 740, according to Peter Fergusson, *Architecture of Solitude: Cistercian Abbeys in twelfth-century England*. (Princeton: Princeton University Press, 1984) 4–5; and Peter Fergusson and Stuart Harrison, *Rievaulx Abbey: Community, Architecture, Memory* (New Haven-London: Yale University Press, 1999) 2, who provide the following figures: 330 abbeys by 1150; 525 by 1200; 738 by 1500, as well as 654 women's monasteries.

2. General studies of cistercian architecture include Frédéric van der Meer, *Atlas de l'Ordre Cistercien* (Paris-Brussels: Editions Sequoia, 1965); Kenneth Conant, *Carolingian and Romanesque Architecture,* The Pelican History of Art (Harmondsworth: Penguin Books, 1966) 223–237; Whitney S. Stoddard, *Art and Architecture of Medieval France* (New York: Icon Editions, Harper and Row, 1972) 21–29; Wolfgang Braunfels, *Monasteries of Western Europe* (London: Thames and Hudson, 1972) 67–110; Carolyn Malone and Walter Horn, 'Layout of the Cistercian Monastery in the Twelfth and Thirteenth Centuries', Walter Horn and Ernest Born, *The Plan of St. Gall* (Berkeley: University of California Press, 1979) 2:315–356, and Terryl Kinder, *Cistercian Europe* (Grand Rapids-Kalamazoo: Eerdmans-Cistercian Publications, 2002; originally published as *L'Europe cistercienne* [Paris: Zodiaque, 1997]). For some examples from Germany, Switzerland, Austria, Italy, Spain, England, Ireland, and Scandinavia, see Hanno Hahn, *Die frühe Kirchenbaukunst der Zisterzienser* (Berlin: Verlag Gebr. Mann, 1957) 128–258. For cistercian architecture in France, see Marcel Aubert, *L'Architecture cistercienne en France*, 2 vols. (Paris: Vanoest, 1947); and Anselme Dimier, *L'Art cistercien: France* (Paris: Zodiaque, 1982). For England, see Peter Fergusson, *Architecture of Solitude* (above, n. 1); Christopher Norton and David Park, edd., *Cistercian Art and Architecture in the British Isles.* edd. (Cambridge: Cambridge University Press, 1986); David Robinson, ed., *The Cistercian Abbeys of Britain: Far from the Concourse of Men* (London: B. T. Batsford-Kalamazoo: Cistercian Publications, 1998). For Ireland, see Roger Stalley, *The Cistercian Monasteries of Ireland* (London and

monasteries and ultimately to Cîteaux and its first four 'daughters', La
Ferté, Pontigny, Clairvaux and Morimond.[3]

Medieval cistercian buildings were austere, compared with contemporary benedictine monastic houses, not to mention the great
pilgrimage churches and cathedrals of the late eleventh, twelfth and
thirteenth centuries.[4] At first the White Monks had very small oratories, often built of wood,[5] but later larger structures of stone were
erected for their growing communities. At Cîteaux there was first a
small church which was replaced in 1106 by a rectangular church with
a chancel flanked by a chapel on either side, at Pontigny the monks
originally had a plain rectangular stone church.[6] In England, early
cistercian churches, like that at Waverley, begun 1129–1132, had a
single nave, short transept arms and a rectangular chancel flanked by a
chapel on either side (fig. 98).[7] At the time of the Order's greatest ex-

---

New Haven: Yale University Press, 1987). For Italy, see Renate Wagner-Rieger, *Die italienische Baukunst zu Beginn der Gotik*, 2 vols. (Graz-Koln: Verlag Hermann Böhlaus, 1956–57); Lelia Fraccaro Longhi, *L'architettura delle chiese cistercensi italiane* (Milan: Casa Editrice Ceschina, 1958); Cesare D'Onofrio and Carlo Pietrangeli, *Abbazie del Lazio* (Rome: Cassa del Risparmio, 1969); Angiola Maria Romanini, 'Le abbazie fondate da San Bernardo in Italia e l'architettura cistercense "primitiva"' in *Studi su s. Bernardo di Chiaravalle nell'ottavo centenario della canoniz-zazione: convegno internazionale, Certosa di Firenze (6–9 novembre 1974)*, Bibliotheca Cisterciensis, 6 (Rome: Certosa di Firenze, 1975) 281–305; *I cistercensi e il Lazio*. (Rome: Multigrafica Editrice, 1978); Daniele Negri, *Abbazie Cistercensi in Italia* (Pistoia: Libreria Editrice Tellini, 1981); and Goffredo Viti, *Architettura cistercense* (Casamari and Florence: Edizioni Casamari, 1995). For Greece, see Beata K. Panagopoulos, *Cistercian and Mendicant Monasteries in Medieval Greece* (Chicago and London: The University of Chicago Press, 1979).

3. The history of Cîteaux and the first four affiliated monasteries is recounted in A. Archdale King, *Cîteaux and her Elder Daughters* (London: Burns and Oates, 1954).

4. Buildings like Ste Foy at Conques, St. Sernin at Toulouse, or Santiago at Compostela, or the abbey church of Cluny III are briefly discussed by Conant, *Carolingian and Romanesque Architecture*, 157–175 and 185–221.

5. Jean Owens Schaeffer, 'The Earliest Churches of the Cistercian Order', in Meredith P. Lillich, ed. *Studies in Cistercian Art and Architecture* 1, CSS 66 (Kalamazoo, 1982) 1–12; rpt E. R. Elder, ed., *The New Monastery*, Cistercian Fathers Series 60 (Kalamazoo 1998); Nicola Cold-stream, 'The Mark of Eternity: The Cistercians as Builders–The First Wooden Buildings', *Cistercian Abbeys of Britain*, 37–41.

6. For Cîteaux, see Martine Plouvier, 'L'Abbaye de Cîteaux', *Congrès Archéologique de France* 152 (1994) 66–68; and *Pour une Histoire monumentale de l'Abbaye de Cîteaux 1098–1998*, Martine Plouvier and Alain Saint-Denis, edd., Studia et Documenta, 8. (Cîteaux: Commentarii Cister-cienses, 1998) 123–130. For the early church at Pontigny, Terryl N. Kinder, 'A Note on the Plan of the First Church at Pontigny', *Mélanges à la Mémoire du Père Anselme Dimier, Benoit Chauvin*, ed. (Pupillon, Arbois: B. Chauvin, 1982–87) 6: 601–608.

7. Fergusson, *Architecture of Solitude*, 22–28; Richard Halsey, 'The Earliest Architecture of the Cistercians in England', *Cistercian Art*, 65–85; Coldstream, 'The Mark of Eternity', 40,

pansion in the mid-twelfth century larger stone churches were built, with nave and aisles, transepts, subsidiary chapels, and sanctuary. After the death of Saint Bernard in 1153, the typically plain east end of cistercian churches was extended to accommodate extra chapels, often linked by an ambulatory.

Like the churches, the monastic buildings also changed over time.[8] While a simple configuration of dormitory, refectory, chapter room, kitchen and subsidiary spaces was possible in the early days, a more clearly defined 'standard' cistercian plan was followed in many of the later monasteries.[9] In this there were two important innovations—the lay brothers' wing, built west of the cloister and often separated from it by the *conversi* lane or corridor;[10] and the refectory, laid out at right angles to the range opposite the church.[11]

The earliest small and simple buildings of the Cistercian Order in Burgundy were often related to still earlier hermit cells and oratories. They embodied the cistercian ideals of poverty, simplicity and solitude and were strikingly different from contemporary french benedictine and cluniac buildings.[12] At Cîteaux in 1098 there was already a church,[13]

---

notes that similar plans have been found through excavation at Tintern, Rievaulx, and Sawley in Britain, and at Lyse, a daughter of Fountains, in Norway.

8. Ferguson, *Architecture of Solitude*; Fergusson and Harrison, *Rievaulx Abbey.*

9. Aubert, *L'architecture cistercienne*, 107ff.; Carolyn Malone and Walter Horn, 'Layout of the Cistercian Monastery in the Twelfth and Thirteenth Centuries', in Walter Horn and Ernest Born, *The Plan of St. Gall* (Berkeley: University of California Press, 1979) 2:315–356, esp. 349–356; and Dimier, *L'Art Cistercien*, 39–41.

10. The characteristics of the *conversi* wing in danish monasteries are discussed in James France, 'The Cellarer's Domain: Evidence from Denmark', in Meredith Parsons Lillich, ed., *Studies in Cistercian Art and Architecture* 5, CS 167 (Kalamazoo, 1998) 1–38.

11. Fergusson, 'The Twelfth-century Refectories at Rievaulx and Byland Abbeys,', *Cistercian Art*, 160–180; Anne Claire Rochet, 'The Refectory Wing of the Cistercian Abbey of Vaux-de-Cernay', *Studies in Cistercian Art and Architecture* 5:187–210, esp. 190–195.

12. Benedictine and cluniac buildings are discussed briefly in Conant, *Carolingian and Romanesque Architecture*, 139–175 and 185–221; Stoddard, *Art and Architecture in Medieval France*, 3–68, and Braunfels, *Monasteries of Western Europe*, 47–66.

13. A church is mentioned in a notice of around 1100 reporting the initial donation of land at Citeaux for the foundation of the monastery: 'Et quia ejusdem loci ecclesiam quam illuc usque tenerat . . . dimisit eam atque ab omnimoda ejus ulterius possessione renuntians, predictis fratribus ad Dei servitium dereliquit' (J. Marilier, ed., *Chartes et documents concernant l'Abbaye de Citeaux, 1098–1182*, Bibliotheca Cisterciensis 1 [Rome 1961], item 23, pp. 49–51); E. R. Elder has translated this as 'And to the aforesaid brothers he turns over for the worship of God the church at the site which he has owned until now, . . . he relinquishes and utterly renounces any further ownership of any kind' (*The New Monastery*, Cistercian Fathers Series, 60 [Kalamazoo: Cistercian Publications, 1998] 11).

but the first monks began to erect a wooden monastery which Odo, Duke of Burgundy, delighted by their holy fervour, completed at his own expense, in addition, generously endowing the monastery with land and flocks of sheep.[14] The early church and wooden monastic structures were soon replaced by a stone cloister and a church which was consecrated in 1106.[15] This church apparently survived into the early eighteenth century, when it was described as, '. . . not . . . more than fifteen feet wide; the length is proportionate; the choir could be thirty feet. It is vaulted and very pretty. There are three windows in the sanctuary and two in the nave'.[16] A barrel vault probably covered this small building.

Nothing is known of the first church at La Ferté, founded from Cîteaux in May 1113, but at Pontigny in May 1114 the monks apparently took over a hermit's oratory, and an early church is depicted on eighteenth-century plans as rectangular in shape. According to Terryl Kinder, it was approximately 6–7 meters wide and 7–10 meters long.[17]

The early church at Clairvaux was described in 1517 as, '. . . a chapel of wood, into which Saint Bernard could see through a window which was in his room . . .'.[18] In 1642 Manrique referred to it as, 'a humble chapel . . . about twenty feet long and fourteen wide dedicated to the blessed Virgin. It was built in a few days . . .';[19] and Dom

---

14. *Exordium Parvum*, III; in Chrysogonus Waddell, *Narrative and Legislative Texts from early Cîteaux* (Cîteaux: Commentarii Cistercienses, 1999) 238: 'Tunc domnus Odo dux burgundie, sancto fervore eorum delectatus, sancteque romane ecclesie prescripti legati litteris rogatus, monasterium ligneum quod inceperunt de suis totum consummavit, illosque inibi in omnibus necessarius diu procuravit, et terris ac pecoribus habunde sublevavit'. See also Jean Owens Schaeffer, 'The Earliest Churches', 1–12, esp. 2 and n. 7 (CF 60 195–207, esp. 197); Anselme Dimier, *Receuil de Plans d'églises cisterciennes* (Paris: Vincent Fréal, 1949 ff.) 1: 99 and 2: pl. 78; Viti, *Architettura Cistercense*, 21 and n. 10, and 32–33.

15. Dimier, *Plans*, 1: 99 and 2: pl. 79; Fergusson, *Architecture of Solitude*, 3.

16. Edmond Martène, *Voyage littéraire de deux religieux bénédictins de la congrégation de saint-Maur.* . . . (Amsterdam, 1717) 223–224—quoted and translated by Schaeffer, 'The Earliest Churches', 3 (CF 60:198).

17. Schaeffer, 'The Earliest Churches', 3–4 (CF 60:200); Terryl Kinder, 'Some Observations on the Origins of Pontigny and its First Church', *Citeaux, Commentarii Cistercienses*, 31 (1980) 9–19; and Terryl Kinder, 'A Note of the Plan of the First Church at Pontigny', 601–608.

18. From a letter from the queen of Sicily, quoted and translated by Schaeffer, 'The Earliest Churches', 5 (CF 60:202), from Didron, 'Un Grand Monastère au XVIe siècle', *Annales archéologiques* 3 (1845) 236–237.

19. Angelo Manrique, *Cisterciensium seu verius ecclesiasticorum annalium a conditio cistercio* (Lyon, 1642) p. 80, quoted and translated by Schaeffer, 'The Earliest Churches', 4 and 11, note 20 (CF 60:197 and 201, n. 20).

Joseph Meglinger in 1667 described the church as a 'very temple of poverty', with a bare high altar and two altars flanking the entrance to the choir.[20] Despite the dimensions given by Manrique, Dom Milley, c. 1708, illustrated the early oratory in the old monastery at Clairvaux as roughly square in plan, with a raised square central space with a high roof, surrounded by a lower aisle on all four sides, all constructed of wood (figs. 93–96); in plan and elevation it seems to have been something like a scandinavian stave church.[21]

At Morimond, all that is known of the original buildings is that the Cistercians in 1115 took over a hermitage belonging to a hermit named Johannis.[22]

Monastic buildings in this primitive phase were correspondingly simple. At Clairvaux in 1517 the queen of Sicily mentioned a small, low room built of wood near the entry gate, where Pope Eugenius III (the former abbot of S. Anastasius *ad Aquas Salvias*) was welcomed.[23] She also noted: 'After it comes the refectory, the length of which is between eighteen and twenty paces; it is very low and panelled . . . Above is the dormitory of equal size. At the top of the stairs is the chamber of Saint Bernard, which is very small.'[24] According to Meglinger, the early chapel and the monks' living quarters were all under the same roof; the dormitory was located directly above the refectory, which had a bare earth floor; the kitchen was next to the refectory and was 'very small but sufficient'; near the stairs was the cell of Saint Bernard, 'more like a dungeon than a room'.[25] Milley's plan showed a long room in the old monastic complex which was

---

20. The description was published in Henri Chabeuf. 'Voyage d'un délégue au chapitre générale de Cîteaux en 1667', *Mémoires de l'académie des sciences, arts et belles-lettres de Dijon* (1883–84) 314–317, and quoted and translated by Schaeffer, 'The Earliest Churches', 5 (CF 60:203); see also the version of Meglinger's journey and description of Clairvaux in PL 185:1565 ff., especially cols. 1598–1609.

21. Details of Milley's drawings are reproduced in Schaeffer, 'The Earliest Churches', 6 and 7 (CF 60:204–205), Figs. 3 and 4. Milley's plans are in Paris, Bibliothèque Nationale, Estampes (Topographie de al France, Aube, Arrondissement Bar-sur-Aube, folios 27, 28 and 29). A clear plan based on Milley is also given in Viti, *Architettura cistercense*, 33. See also Dimier, *Plans*, 1: 100.

22. Schaeffer, 'The Earliest Churches', 7–8 (CF 60:203–204).

23. Quoted and translated by Schaeffer, 'The Earliest Churches', 5 (CF 60:202).

24. Quoted and translated by Schaeffer, 'The Earliest Churches', 5 (202).

25. Quoted and translated by Schaeffer, 'The Earliest Churches', 5 (202); see also PL 185, 1598–1609.

probably the early refectory, over which stood the dormitory; there were smaller rooms at either end (figs. 95 and 96).[26]

As the Order grew, the earliest small buildings gave way to more complex stone structures. It is likely that churches of the second generation of cistercian oratories in France were influenced by small burgundian romanesque churches.[27] The first cistercian monastery outside France was in Italy, founded from La Ferté in 1120 at Tiglietto, where the twelfth-century church can be reconstructed (fig. 97).[28] It had a nave and two aisles separated by rectangular piers, sustaining arches, and a clerestory wall pierced by roundheaded windows; similar openings illuminated the aisles. The easternmost bay was much longer than the rest, forming a transept, which did not project beyond the aisle walls; there was no real crossing. Excavations have revealed that the church ended in a rectangular presbytery, flanked by one rectangular chapel on either side. The church was built of brick. While in many ways this 'basilical' building can be compared with other north italian churches, its design is also close to the primitive, 'reduced' version of the so-called 'bernardine' plan. For stylistic reasons, Pistilli dates the twelfth-century part of the church to the 1140s and 1150s, but one wonders whether it is earlier, closer in time to the monastic foundation.

At Waverley Abbey in England, which was founded from l'Aumône in Normandy in 1128, the first stone church was begun between 1129 and 1131/1132.[29] It is one of the earliest cistercian churches to survive in any significant measure (fig. 98). The long rectangular nave, covered with a wooden roof, had no aisles. A transept extended north and south, communicating with a rectangular presbytery. At the crossing there were arches on the north, south and east, but not on the west, so

---

26. Schaeffer, 'The Earliest Churches', 6 and 7 (204–205), Figs. 3 and 4.

27. Fergusson, *Architecture of Solitude*, 28; Elie Lambert, 'Remarques sur les plans d'églises dits cisterciens', *Deutsch-Französiche Kunsthistoriker-Tagung. L'architecture monastique. Actes et travaux de la Rencontre Franco-Allemande des Historiens de l'art (1951)* (Mayence, 1951) 7–12.

28. The cistercian east end of the church was excavated by Pacini for the Soprintendenza per la Liguria. A large part of the twelfth-century structure survives; it was extended in the thirteenth century, much repaired in the fourteenth century and remodelled in the seventeenth century, as explained by Pio F. Pistilli, 'Santa Maria di Tiglietto: prima fondazione cistercense in Italia (1120)'. *Arte Medievale*, 2 serie, 4,1 (1990) 117–149.

29. Fergusson, *Architecture of Solitude*, 22–28; Dimier, *Plans*, 1: 179 and 2: pl. 327.

that the nave led straight to the presbytery. The transept arms were probably lower than the nave and each opened in a single chapel to the east. These chapels were barrel vaulted and apparently closed off from the transept by a western wall and were entered through a doorway. The church was simple and rectangular in design, and clearly preceded later cistercian plans. Tintern (founded 1130), Fountains (1135 and 1148) and Sawley (*c.* 1150) in Britain, and Lyse in Norway (1146) all had similar churches.

Some of the earliest cistercian monastic buildings in Britain are known from medieval written sources.[30] Often the lay patron provided temporary wooden accommodation, which was replaced at a later date by stone buildings constructed by the monks, lay brothers and hired builders, sometimes in a different, more suitable, location. While patrons were obliged to provide the new community with all the buildings necessary for the monks to fulfil their duties from the start, there seems often to have been an 'experimental' phase in which the community lived in 'temporary' accommodation on the site, so as to be able to assess the suitability of the place. Peter Fergusson has shown how at Meaux in England the monks were originally installed in a pre-existing house built of wattle and daub, where they had their dormitory on the ground floor and their oratory on the floor above; this must have suited them, because they retained this unusual arrangement when they built a new monastery.[31]

From the mid-1130s much larger churches and monasteries replaced the existing buildings, probably in order to cater to the constantly increasing size of the communities. Most significant were the new structures at Clairvaux, where most of the medieval buildings were demolished during the French Revolution. Of the church, only a part of the gable end of the south transept survives, incorporated in a contiguous eighteenth-century building. The lay-brothers' building of thirteen and a half bays still stands and has been partially restored; remnants of the early monastery remain west of the former abbey entrance, and part of the medieval guest wing and gatehouse are now

---

30. Fergusson, *Architecture of Solitude*, 22–25.

31. Peter Fergusson, 'The first architecture of the Cistercians in England and the work of Abbot Adam of Meaux', *Journal of the British Archaeological Association* 136 (1983) 74–86. See also Fergusson, *Architecture of Solitude*, 24.

enveloped in a maximum security prison.[32] The demolished medieval buildings are known chiefly from Joseph Meglinger's description written in 1667[33] and from Milley's plan and view of 1708 (figs. 93 and 94). The building campaign of *c.* 1135–1145 was, moreover, mentioned in the twelfth century in the *Exordium Magnum* and the *Life of Saint Bernard*.

> The bishops of the region, noblemen and merchants of the land heard of it and joyfully offered rich aid in God's work. Supplies were abundant, workmen quickly hired, the brothers themselves joined in the work in every way: some cut timbers, others shaped stones, others built walls, others divided the river, set it in new channels and lifted the leaping waters to the mill-wheels; fullers and bakers and tanners and smiths and other artificers prepared suitable machines for their tasks, that the river might flow fast and do good wherever it was needed in every building, flowing freely in underground conduits; the streams performed tasks in every office and cleansed the abbey and at length returned to the main course and restored to the river what it had lost. The walls which gave the abbey a spacious enclosure were finished with unlooked-for-speed. The abbey rose; the newborn church, as if it had a living, moving soul, quickly developed and grew.[34]

Planning for the new monastery began in 1135, while Saint Bernard was in Rome and his cousin, Geoffrey de la Rochetaille was prior, and Achard, known for his architectural work, was novice-master. They made plans to rebuild the monastery along the banks of the River

---

32. This information has been kindly communicated by Terryl Kinder, who is currently preparing a detailed paper on the subject. We eagerly await that communication. See also Peter Fergusson, 'Programmatic Factors in the East Extension of Clairvaux', *Arte Medievale*, 1 (1994) 87–102; and the very brief discussion in Jean-Michel Musso, 'L'Abbaye de Clairvaux', *Forme et Sens. La Formation à la Dimension religieuse du Patrimoine culturel*. Actes du Colloque Ecole du Louvre (Paris: Louvre, 1996) 48–51.

33. PL 185:1598–1609.

34. *Vita Prima*, 2.5, by Arnold/Ernaldus; PL 185/1:285. The translation is from Christopher Brooke, 'St. Bernard, The Patrons and Monastic Planning', *Cistercian Art*, 21–22. Brooke believes this is a true account of the 1135 rebuilding of Clairvaux. While he notes that it stresses the importance of the work done by the lay-brothers, he finds the role of Saint Bernard to be ambivalent in the planning and construction of the new buildings.

Aube. Geoffroi d'Ainai, who had experience in advising new communities on how to establish and build new monasteries, was also involved in the project.[35] The new church at Clairvaux (fig. 99) had a nave flanked on either side by a single aisle which extended in eleven bays to a square crossing, east of which originally was a rectangular presbytery which gave way after 1154 to the chevet seen in the plan. The transept arms were three bays deep and each opened in three chapels in the east and two in the west. The church was preceded by a narthex as wide as the church and subdivided to correspond with the nave and aisles. The new church was consecrated in 1145. It has been suggested that the plan of Clairvaux was worked out by using the dimensions of the crossing and transept as modules.[36]

Pontigny is the only one of the five cistercian proto-abbeys where most of the large twelfth-century church still stands (fig. 100).[37] It was probably begun in the late 1130s or in 1140. A seven-bay nave, flanked by a single aisle on either side, led to a square crossing and, originally, a rectangular presbytery. The transept arms were three bays deep and opened in three chapels in each arm to the east, two to the north, two to the south, and two in each arm to the west. Preceding the nave was a low porch, subdivided into three separate spaces, corresponding to the nave and aisles. The nave and transept arms had a two-storey elevation, with pointed arcades and transverse arches separating the vaulted bays.

At Cîteaux a new church was built *c.* 1140–1150, but it did not survive the Revolution.[38] Views of the church and monastery from the pre-Revolutionary period provide evidence of its appearance. The medieval plan (fig. 101) can be reconstructed from sixteenth, seventeenth,

35. Geoffrey helped the communities of Rievaulx and Vauclair plan and erect their building; see Fergusson and Harrison, *Rievaulx Abbey*, 55,

36. Francois Bucher, 'Cistercian Architectural Purism', *Comparative Studies in Society and History 3* (1960–61) 89–105, and Hahn, *Kirchenbaukunst*, 117–122.

37. Terryl Nancy Kinder, *Architecture of the Cistercian Abbey of Pontigny: The Twelfth Century Church*. unpublished Ph.D. thesis., Indiana University, 1982; Dimier, *Plans*, 1: 148–149; 2: pl. 235 and 236; and 3: pl. 237.

38. Pierre Gras, 'Vues et plans de l'ancien Cîteaux', *Mélanges à la Mémoire du Père Anselme Dimier*, 6:549–575. See also Martine Plouvier, 'L'Abbaye Médiévale: Histoire et Analyse Critique'; and Martine Plouvier and Placide Vernet, 'Plans et vues de l'abbaye de Cîteaux', *Pour une Histoire de l'Abbaye de Cîteaux*, 122–152 and 380–396.

and eighteenth-century drawings and prints,[39] and from descriptions of it written down by Joseph Meglinger (1667), and Edmond Martène and Urbain Durand (1717).[40] The nave was flanked by one aisle on either side and extended in nine bays to the square crossing, beyond which was a rectangular presbytery. (Again, the east end was extended at a later time.) Chapels opened east and west off the north arm of the transept, and three to the east only off the south arm. The church was preceded by a narthex.

Excavations at Morimond, where the medieval church has been destroyed, have revealed a seven-bay nave, with one aisle on either side, a transept and an east end, which may have been remodelled at a later time (fig. 102). The abbey church at La Ferté, which was rebuilt between 1210–1220, was destroyed during the French Revolution, but its plan can be reconstructed from a drawing done in 1680. There was a seven-bay nave, flanked by single aisles, and preceded by a narthex. The transept arms had four bays and four chapels to the east. The presbytery was rectangular.

In 1154–1174, shortly after Saint Bernard's death, the original rectangular presbytery of Clairvaux was replaced by a polygonal east end with an ambulatory and nine radiating chapels (fig. 99).[41] Probably in imitation of these developments at Clairvaux, the rectangular presbytery of Pontigny also gave way in the late twelfth and early thirteenth century to a chevet with ambulatory and radiating chapels (fig. 100). In the later twelfth century the small flat-ended presbytery of Cîteaux was enlarged to include twelve chapels in a rectangular east end (fig. 101).[42] At Morimond there was a rectangular east end with twelve chapels, very like the later presbytery at Cîteaux (fig. 102). When this arrangement was made is not clear. These extended east

39. For example the 'Plan géométral de Cisteaux 1717' (Dijon, AD Côte-d'Or, 11H209) and a site plan of 1755 (Dijon, AD Côte-d'Or, C4415) illustrated in Pour une Histoire . . . de . . . l'Abbaye de Cîteaux, 15 and 52.

40. J. Meglinger, Iter cisterciense. Migne, PL 185, cc. 1598–1609 and Edmond Martène and Urbain Durand, Voyage littéraire de deux bénédictins de la Congrégation de Saint-Maur (Paris, 1767) 1:198–224. These texts are discussed in Plouvier, 'L'Abbaye Médiévale', 122–152.

41. This kind of architecture was more typical of pilgrim churches, like St. Sernin in Toulouse, and Benedictine or Cluniac buildings, such as Cluny III and Paray-le-Monial. For this phase of Clairvaux, see Fergusson, 'Programmatic Factors'.

42. Dimier, Plans, 1: 99; 3: pl. 80; Hahn, Die frühe Kirchenbaukunst, 122.

ends, with several more chapels, are typical of later twelfth and thirteenth-century cistercian churches. Probably the chapels were built to provide for the need for separate altars to accommodate the numerous priests in the cistercian communities.

Despite the later addition of a chevet, it is clear that medieval cistercian architects worked with a square, modular plan[43] with a long nave, single aisles, transepts with chapels opening off both arms and usually a rectangular, flat-ended presbytery. This architectural planning is reflected in Villard de Honnecourt's drawing of a church made of squares to be built for the Order of Cîteaux; it is particularly close of the design of Citeaux.[44] There were, however, churches with semi-circular or polygonal apses, and apsed chapels, as at Sénanque (begun in 1160), Léoncel (1188), Obazine (begun in 1156), Le Thoronet (begun c. 1160) (fig. 103), Fontfroide (late twelfth century) and Flaran (1180–1210).[45]

The various phases in church architecture—seen at Cîteaux, La Ferté, Pontigny, Clairvaux and Morimond—are also typical of some smaller cistercian foundations. The abbey at Ourscamp in France (fig. 104) was founded in 1129 and the first stone church built in 1134. This was greatly extended in 1154, consecrated in 1201, and then an apse, ambulatory and radiating chapels, were added in 1232.[46]

The style of east end with apse, ambulatory, and radiating chapels was probably first taken up by the Cistercians after the rebuilding at Clairvaux in 1154–1174. It has been suggested that this arrangement at Clairvaux may have been designed initially to form a kind of *martyrium* or shrine at the tomb of Saint Bernard.[47] Well-known examples, beyond the scope of this study, existed at Longpont (consecrated in 1227),[48]

43. With one or two rows of columns or piers sustaining cross vaults, such as at Clairvaux (fig. 93) and Fontenay (fig. 106).

44. Villard de Honnecourt labelled his design, 'Vesci un glize desquarie, di fu esgardee a faire en l'ordene d Cistiaus'. This drawing is frequently illustrated, see for example, Kinder, *Cistercian Europe*, 171 (*L'Europe cistercienne*, 169).

45. Dimier, *L'art cistercien*, 132–140; 150–156; 158–182; 184–191; 228–252; and 306–312.

46. Caroline Bruzelius, 'The Twelfth-century Church at Ourscamp', *Speculum* 56:4 (1981) 28–40; Dimier, *Plans*, 1: 143–144 and 2: pl. 218, 219 and 220.

47. An idea which has been put forward by Peter Fergusson, 'Programmatic Factors'.

48. Caroline Bruzelius, 'Cistercian High Gothic: The Abbey Church of Longpont and the Architecture of the Cistercians in the Early Thirteenth Century', *Analecta Cisterciensia 35* (1979) 1–204.

Royaumont (1229–1235), Alcobaça (consecrated 1252) (fig. 105),[49] Altenberg (after 1255) and Doberan (1294–1365). In the late thirteenth century there were other variants in the design of the east end, like the 'hall-choir' at Heiligenkreuz (1288–1295) in Austria.[50]

The church of S. Anastasius *ad Aquas Salvias* was laid out in the manner of the second church of Clairvaux, but its east end was never extended into a chevet. As the thirty-fourth daughter of Clairvaux, the architecture of the abbey resembles that of other monasteries of the same filiation. Built of brick, with rectangular piers and roundheaded windows in the clerestory and aisles, it was in some ways similar to early italian cistercian churches, like that at Tiglietto.

The church was probably planned by a cistercian architect or master builder. That men with such skills planned other cistercian buildings is evident from historical sources. At Clairvaux enlarged stone buildings were erected shortly after 1135 by monks like Achard and Geoffrey d'Ainai.[51] Two years previously, the same Geoffrey d'Ainai had been in England, where he taught the monks at Fountains how to order their lives and build houses in the cistercian manner. He probably trained some of the english monks—Robert, Alexander and Adam—in architecture, so that they could help plan and build other english cistercian monasteries. Geoffrey is also thought to have supervised the building of Clairmarais in Flanders in 1140.[52] Similarly, shortly after 1135 Saint Bernard sent Achard to Himmerod, not only as novice master for the new abbey, but also to draw up a plan and erect the church and monastery buildings.[53] In 1142 a monk named Robert was sent to Mellifont in Ireland to supervise the building of the abbey.[54] In 1207 the monas-

---

49. Gusmao, *A real abadia de Alcobaça: estudo histórico-arqueológico* (Lisbon: Editora Ulisseia, 1948) 120.

50. Braunfels, *Monasteries of Western Europe,* 91.

51. The circumstances of this rebuilding are recorded in the *Vita Prima* (PL 185:285), and discussed by Peter Fergusson, *Architecture of Solitude,* 166; see also Anselme Dimier, *Les Moines bâtisseurs* (Paris: Fayard, 1964) 108.

52. Fergusson, *Architecture of Solitude,* 169.

53. Esser, 'Über den Kirchenbau . . . Himmerod' 195–221; Esser, 'Les fouilles à Himmerod', 311–312 (below, n. 56); see also Braunfels, *Monasteries of Western Europe,* 91.

54. Fergusson, *Architecture of Solitude,* 169–170; Dimier, *Moines bâtisseurs,* 110; Roger Stalley, 'The Architecture of the Cistercian Churches of Ireland, 1142–1272', in *Cistercian Art,* 120–124.

tery of Walkenreid was laid out and built under the guidance of two monks, Jordan and Berthold.[55]

Many cistercian churches followed the 'bernardine' plan of Clairvaux II of *c.* 1133–1145.[56] Fontenay, founded in 1119 from Clairvaux, is one of the most complete examples of such a 'bernardine' church (fig. 106).[57] The surviving buildings were erected after the valley had been drained in 1130. The church was begun in 1139 and completed in 1147, when it was consecrated by Pope Eugenius III. In it, the founding abbot, William, was buried in 1149. The church has an eight-bay nave, flanked by a single aisle on either side; the transept has two chapels opening off each arm and the presbytery is rectangular. The nave is separated from the aisles by piers with engaged half-columns, which sustain pointed arcades, and pilasters with engaged half-columns above them towards the nave, which sustain transverse ribs across the nave's pointed barrel vault (fig. 92). Barrel vaults at right angles to the nave cover each bay of the aisles. There are pointed barrel vaults over both arms of the transept, and over the eastern chapels. There is a similar covering over the presbytery. The crossing is illuminated by five roundheaded splayed windows in the east wall; two rows of three windows open in the presbytery. There are no clerestory windows in the nave, but each bay of the aisles is lit by a window.

The church at Fossanova in Lazio is very similar to that of Fontenay.[58] While S. Anastasius at Tre Fontane is often seen as following Fontenay's design, and while the plan is similar, there are some pronounced differences in elevation. The roman church does not have multiple piers; the plain rectangular brick piers at Tiglietto are closer to those

---

55. Fergusson, *Architecture of Solitude,* 170; Dimier, *Moines bâtisseurs,* 110.

56. For the 'bernardine' plan, see Karl Heinz Esser, 'Über den Kirchenbau des Hl. Berhard von Clairvaux', *Archiv für Mittelrheinische Kirchengeschichte* 5 (1953) 195–222, and Karl Heinz Esser, 'Les fouilles à Himmerod et le plan Bernardin', *Mélanges Saint Bernard: congrès de l'association bourguignonne des sociétés savantes, 8 centennaire de la Mort de Saint Bernard, 1953.* (Dijon: Association des Amis de Saint Bernard, 1954) 311–315. Saint Bernard must certainly have assented to the plan, but he cannot in my view be held responsible for designing it.

57. Dimier, *Plans,* 1: 110–111 and 2: pl. 117; Dimier, *L'art cistercien,* 66–72; Pierre Bourgeois, *Abbaye Notre Dame de Fontenay: Monument de Patrimoine mondial–Architecture et Histoire* (Bégrolles en Mauge: Bellefontaine, 2000) 1:37–72, with numerous architectural and analytical drawings in volume 2.

58. Dimier, *Plans,* 1: 112 and 2: pl. 120.

at Tre Fontane. As Belardi's recent restoration campaign has shown, the nave in the roman abbey was originally vaulted, with a pointed barrel vault, but there were no transverse ribs, as at Fontenay and Fossanova, and S. Anastasius was illuminated by large roundheaded splayed windows in the clerestory in each bay of the nave. The vaulting of the aisles of the roman church is made up of cross-vaults, not barrel vaults placed at right angles to the nave. The east wall of the crossing at Tre Fontane is similar to Fontenay in being pierced by an array of windows, which in the roman church echo those on a lower level in the presbytery. These windows would have illuminated the choir and gradually filled the eastern end of the church with light early in the morning.[59]

Sartorio believed the roman abbey was much influenced by Chiaravalle di Milano, founded from Clairvaux in 1135 and also consecrated in 1221.[60] The east end has a rectangular presbytery, flanked on either side by three eastern chapels which open off the transept. The two easternmost bays of the nave are separated from the aisles by rectangular piers, but the rest are round. The ribbed cross vaults are very different from what is known of the vaulting at Tre Fontane. The fourteenth-century tower over the crossing was not copied in the roman church.

At Fontenay part of the monastic buildings survive (fig. 106).[61] They stand to the south of the church, with the cloister in the centre. The east range, or monks' wing, has a sacristy, chapter room, parlour, passage-

---

59. Fergusson, *Rievaulx Abbey*, 73, describes this beautifully: 'Such windows provided light for the monks' stalls as well as dramatising the entry of dawn light at two levels (the sanctuary entry wall and the terminal wall) to announce the end of Vigils'. See Fergusson and Harrison, *Rievaulx Abbey*, 73.

60. Aristide Sartorio, 'L'abbazia cisterciense delle Tre Fontane', *Nuova Antologia* 167 (settembre 1913) 50–65; Hahn, *Kirchenbaukunst*, 149–155, who dates the begining of construction to the mid-twelfth century. See also Wagner-Rieger, *Die italienische Baukunst*, 1:41–48 and *Chiaravalle: Arte e storia di un'abbazia cistercense*, Paolo Tomea, ed. (Milan: Electa, 1992). A daughter of this monastery, Chiaravalle di Fiastra, also survives and has a 'bernardine' plan; see the important study by Antonio Cadei, 'Chiaravalle di Fiastra', *Storia dell'Arte*, 34 (1978) 247–288; and Daniele Negri, *Abbazie Cistercensi in Italia* (Pistoia: Libreria Editrice Tellini, 1981) 85–93. Recent excavations and renovations at Fossanova have brought to light new evidence on the site and buildings of that monastery, as noted in Stefano Coccia et al., 'Abbazia di Fossanova: Indagini archeologiche nel refettorio', *Archeologia Medievale* 24 (1997) 55–86.

61. Bourgeois, *Abbaye Notre Dame de Fontenay*, 1:73–98 (monks' building), 99–109 (calefactory), 111–120 (monks' refectory), and 119–121 (kitchen).

way, and monks' room. In the south range there are two rooms east of the refectory. One would have been the warming room or calefactory. The refectory itself was reconstructed at a later date. The *conversi* wing to the west has been demolished, but the foundations have come to light since 1990.[62]

The plan of Fontenay was probably based on that at Clairvaux (figs. 93 and 94). The monks' quarters at Clairvaux, situated south of the church around a cloister, were most likely built between 1133–1145. The *conversi* were evidently accommodated in the old monastery to begin with, although it is clear that the location of their buildings west of the cloister was part of the original project. When Milley drew his plan in 1708, the ground floor of the eastern wing consisted of the suite of rooms (fig. 93) which became standard in most cistercian monasteries: the *armarium* and sacristy next to the south transept, the chapter room, a narrow passageway, stairs to the first floor, and a long monks' room. The monks' dormitory would have oversailed all this. It is also possible that, prior to the building of a separate novitiate in 1186–1191, the monks' room was reserved for novices. In the south range of the cloister stood the *calefactorium*, the refectory at right angles to the cloister walk, and the kitchen. Probably there was a chamber over the *calefactorium*. Projecting into the garth was a fountain house, where the monks washed their hands before meals. The cloister was separated from the lay-brothers' building by the *conversi* lane. In the *conversi* block were the cellar and the lay-brothers' refectory, divided by a covered passageway. The *conversi* dormitory would have been located above these structures.

Many cistercian church plans make clear that the monastic structures were laid out in modular fashion, with one or two rows of columns or piers sustaining cross vaults. This can be seen at Clairvaux (fig. 93) and Fontenay (fig. 106). It can also be discerned at Tre Fontane in the chapter room and in the *conversi* building. At Casamari in Lazio a similar modular arrangement can still be seen.[63]

62. Bourgeois, *Abbaye Notre Dame de Fontenay*. 1:121–123.

63. The architecture of this cistercian abbey is discussed in Federico Farina, *L'Abbazia di Casamari nella Storia dell'architettura e della spiritualità cisterciensi* (Casamari: Edizioni Casamari, 1990) 16–46.

Early monasteries had usually located the refectory in the range opposite the church and parallel to the cloister walk. The cistercian custom of placing the refectory at right angles to the cloister probably began at Clairvaux, *c.* 1150.[64] From there it spread to many other abbeys. In some english houses—for example, at Rievaulx, Fountains and Kirkstall—the refectory was first built parallel to the cloister walk, but then, in the 1160s, 1170s and 1180s, it was rebuilt at right angles to it. In most abbeys at which construction began after 1160, the refectory was built in a north-south direction—for example at Waverley and Furness (between 1160 and 1180), and at Byland, Roche, Jervaulx, and Sawley (begun in the 1170s). In some small monasteries, however, the old disposition of the refectory parallel to the cloister walk was retained, as at Boxley (*c.* 1160) and Sibton (*c.* 1180). At Tre Fontane the present refectory incorporates some twelfth-century walls, but is largely a nineteenth-century reconstruction.

In his plan and view of Clairvaux, Milley shows many other structures (figs. 93 and 94). These included the novitiate, infirmary, guest wing and gatehouse. In addition, cistercian abbeys often had other functional buildings such as a mill, forge, bakehouse, and grange.[65] Although Millay's plan was drawn in 1708, it is likely that many of these features belonged to the 1135–1145 building campaign. Cistercian monasteries from *c.* 1135 onwards tended to follow a standard plan, although methods of construction, materials, and architectural style varied considerably from one monastery to another. Clairvaux probably served as a model for many later houses of the Order and the plan of S. Anastasius at Tre Fontane, a daughter house of Clairvaux, was likely based upon it. Although the monastery is north of the church and roman materials like brick, tufa, and ancient roman columns and capitals were used, the basic layout was remarkably similar to that of the french mother house.

---

64. For an excellent discussion of the development of the cistercian refectory especially in England, Peter Fergusson, 'The Twelfth-century Refectories at Rievaulx and Byland Abbeys' in *Cistercian Art,* 160–180.

65. For a study of these buildings in Italy, particularly at Chiaravalle de Fiastra, see Marina Righetti Tosti-Croce, *Architettura per il Lavoro: dal caso cistercense a un caso cisterciense: Chiaravalle de Fiastro* (Rome: Villa, 1993).

The abbey of SS. Vincenzo e Anastasio at Tre Fontane represents an almost complete set of cistercian monastic buildings. Despite the arduous task of distinguishing several different phases of construction—including the restoration and remodelling of the late nineteenth and twentieth centuries—it remains one of the most fascinating and important examples of medieval cistercian architecture to survive.

IV

THE LAYOUT OF THE
TRE FONTANE BUILDINGS

G RASPING THE LAYOUT of the Tre Fontane buildings requires a brief introduction. Since there is still a monastic community in residence, not every visitor may be admitted to many areas in the complex, not even to the parts of the medieval church reserved for the monks. It is therefore important to describe the church and monastic buildings briefly.

A thorough architectural analysis of the cistercian buildings appears further on in this volume.[1] It is based on a survey, carried out in 1983 by architect Jeremy Blake and the author, which resulted in the measured drawings in plan and section that are reproduced here (Plans I, II and III; Sections AA', BB' and CC'; and Gatehouse, Plans and Section). Reference will be made to these drawings in this description. On these drawings various parts of the complex have been given names or letters, and the major walls of the church and monastery have been numbered to facilitate their identification by the reader.

From Via Laurentina a modern visitor to Tre Fontane walks down a sombre avenue, past a statue of Saint Benedict erected in 1948,[2] to a double-storeyed gatehouse which gives access to the monastery grounds (figs. 1, 2 and 3). On the groundfloor of this edifice there is a passageway divided into two bays covered by cross-vaults on either side of the actual gateway into the monastery (Gatehouse, Plans and

---

1. See below, Chapter VII.
2. Giorgio Datseris, *L'abbazia delle Tre Fontane in Roma: Guida.* (Rome-Trani: Vivere In, 1989) 16–17.

Section: Plan A and Section).[3] North and south of the passage stand modern structures and there is a small apartment above the vaults. On the upper floor a six-light opening faces northwest (fig. 2), while a triple-light window looks towards the abbey church (fig. 3).

Traces of medieval frescoes dating from the thirteenth century survive on the outer vault and its corresponding lunettes.[4] Although little survives of these paintings today, their subject matter is known from drawings made by Antonio Eclissi in 1630.[5] On the ceiling, there was a fragmentary bust of Christ, surrounded by angels and symbols of the evangelists; in the eastern lunette was depicted a *Madonna and Child with Saints,* including Saints Paul and Benedict, and other smaller figures, wearing cistercian habits; to north and south there were scenes of the campaign against Ansedonia, in which Charlemagne and Pope Leo III were victorious thanks to the relics of Saint Anastasius of Persia, the patron saint of the monastery. While the story was probably legendary, it helped authenticate the abbey's claims to its possessions in the Maremma in Tuscany, which were depicted in the southern lunette.[6] From the subject matter of these frescoes, the medieval gatehouse is often called 'the arch of Charlemagne'.

Beyond the gatehouse an irregular space opens in front of the medieval cistercian church of SS. Vincenzo e Anastasio (fig. 1). To the south on a high mound stands S. Maria Scala Coeli, rebuilt in 1583 by Giacomo della Porta over an earlier sanctuary for Alexander Cardinal Farnese, then commendatory abbot of Tre Fontane.[7] It is now a cen-

---

3. The original gate no longer survives, but the medieval threshold and jambs are in place.

4. For these frescoes see De Maffei, 'Riflessi dell'epopea carolingia nell'arte medievale', 351–386; Bertelli, 'Affreschi, miniature e orefecerie cistercensi in Toscana e in Lazio', 71–81; Gandolfo, 'Aggiornamento scientifico e bibliografia', 283–284; Iacobini, 'La pittura e le arti suntuarie', 267–271; Quattrone, 'L'evoluzione storico-architettonica del complesso monumentale', 46–49; Barclay Lloyd, 'The Medieval Murals in the Cistercian Abbey of SS. Vincenzo e Anastasio' (above, Chapter 1, note 66) 287–348. See also below, A. ARCHITECTURAL DATA, 5. *Medieval Murals,* (b) MURALS IN THE GATEHOUSE. For the decoration of medieval gates, Julian Gardner, 'An Introduction to the Iconography of the Medieval Italian City Gate', *Dumbarton Oaks Papers* 41 (1987) 199–213; and Aavitsland, *Florilegium* (above, Chapter 2, note 70).

5. The drawings are now in the Bibliotheca Apostolica Vaticana, Barb. lat. 4402, fols. 35r–37r and 40v–41r. In Barclay Lloyd, 'The Medieval Murals', 298–311, I published them and compared them with what remains of the medieval murals.

6. See below, C. DATES AND DOCUMENTS, (805?).

7. See below, C. DATES AND DOCUMENTS, 1583; for a description of the church before it was blown down by the wind, C. DATES AND DOCUMENTS, 1560; for an interesting study of this

trally planned, domed church with three apsed chapels. A medieval colonnade survives in the crypt, where there are some fragments of a marble pavement in medieval 'cosmatesque' designs as well as some medieval liturgical furniture.[8] Traditionally Saint Bernard's vision of souls going to heaven occurred while he was saying Mass in the crypt.[9] In addition, this sanctuary was formerly thought to house the mortal remains of the roman martyr, Saint Zeno, and his 10,203 companions.[10]

Further to the southeast, at the end of an avenue of trees, is the church of S. Paolo alle Tre Fontane (fig. 1). The present church was built in 1599 by Giacomo della Porta for Pietro Cardinal Aldobrandini, commendatory abbot of Tre Fontane.[11] It has an entrance vestibule, a rectangular central space with an apse at the northern and southern ends, and an apsed chancel in the east. Along the eastern wall, on either side of the chancel, are three aedicules, which mark the location of the three fountains which reputedly sprang up when Saint Paul was beheaded.[12] This building took the place of the earlier *martyrium*, which had two chapels on different levels containing the three fountains and a portico in front.

The medieval cistercian church of SS. Vincenzo e Anastasio is by far the largest of the three sanctuaries on the site (fig. 1; Plan I). It is preceded by a colonnaded narthex of a type common in Rome in the twelfth and thirteenth centuries (figs. 4–6). From the southern side of

---

church and its antecedent structures, Klaus Schwager, 'Santa Maria Scala Coeli in Tre Fontane', *Praestant interna: Festschrift für Ulrich Hausmann,* ed. Bettina von Freytag gen. Löringhoff *et al.* (Tübingen: Ernst Wasmuth, 1982) 394–417; see also Clare Robertson, '*Il gran cardinale': Alessandro Farnese, Patron of the Arts* (New Haven and London: Yale University Press, 1992) 197–200.

8. Dorothy Glass, *Studies on Cosmatesque Pavements* (Oxford: BAR, 1980) 115.

9. This legend was widely diffused from the fifteenth century onwards; see, for example, Onofrio Panvinio, *De praecipuis Urbis Romae sanctioribusque basilicis, quas Septem Ecclesiae vulgo vocantur* (Rome: Apud Haeredes Antonii Bladii, 1570) 89, or Giovanni Severano, *Memorie sacre delle sette chiese di Roma* (Rome: Per Giacomo Mascardi, 1630) 416–417.

10. For Saint Zeno and his companions, Cesare Baronio, *Annales Ecclesiastici.* (Lucca: Typ. Leonardi Venturi, 1738) 2:290.

11. See below, C. DATES AND DOCUMENTS, 1599.

12. For descriptions of the previous building, see below, C. DATES AND DOCUMENTS, 1560; for a small vignette of the building, see below, B. EARLY ILLUSTRATIONS, 1469 Pietro del Massaio, *miniature of Rome;* 1471 *Copy* of Pietro del Massaio's miniature of Rome and 1474 Alessandro Strozzi, *Map of Rome,* detail, and our figs. 68 and 69; for the excavation of this building in the nineteenth century, see below, C. DATES AND DOCUMENTS, 1867.

the portico, it is clear that this structure was built against the pre-existing fabric of the church (fig. 5).[13] An inscription on the narthex architrave, attributing the medieval restoration of the monastery to Pope Innocent II in 1140, appears to date from the early seventeenth century.[14]

The medieval church is now entered from the west through three doorways, which lead into a central nave and two aisles (Plan I, fig. 7). East of the nave is a transept which extends north and south beyond the aisles. Two rectangular chapels open eastwards from each transept arm. In the centre, and extending further east, there is a rectangular chancel (Plan I). The nave and aisles are divided into nine bays by rectangular brick-faced piers which support semi-circular arches and high clerestory walls (fig. 7). Externally the clerestory walls are strengthened by narrow brick pilasters, one above each pier (fig. 8). From within the nave the beginnings of a pointed barrel vault are visible, but the vessel is in fact covered with wooden beams (fig. 7) and a terracotta tile roof. The aisles are groin-vaulted (fig. 9). The nave and aisles are illuminated by roundheaded windows. Two tiers of windows open in the church facade (fig. 4); they are all roundheaded, except for the top central one, which is a circular oculus.

A semi-circular arch frames the sanctuary (fig. 10). Similar arches stand north and south of the crossing and connect the sanctuary to the nave arcades. The chancel has a straight east wall which opens in three roundheaded windows and an oculus with quatrefoil tracery (figs. 10 and 11). A similar sequence of windows opens above the western arch framing the chancel (fig. 7). The chancel and the transept arms are covered with slightly pointed barrel vaults, but the roof at the crossing is a continuation of that in the nave. The chapels which open off the transept are entered through semi-circular arched openings and are all covered with pointed barrel vaults (fig. 12); the windows are roundheaded, except for that south of the chancel, which is circular. Above the chapels two roundheaded splayed windows light each transept arm (fig. 10). The south wall of the transept opens in three roundheaded splayed windows (fig. 13), but in the north wall of the transept there are no windows (fig. 14).

13. This was pointed out by Pio F. Pistilli, 'Considerazioni sulla storia architettonica romana delle Tre Fontane nel duecento', Arte Medievale, serie 2, 6.1(1992) 168–170.
14. See below, C. DATES AND DOCUMENTS, 1608.

The monastery buildings, ranged around a cloister (figs. 15–24), stand north of the church. Normally cistercian claustral buildings lay south of the church, unless the geography of the site did not allow this, and south of the church of Saint Anastasius is a hill. As was usual in cistercian monasteries, the east range provided accommodation for the monks (figs. 17–50); for this reason, it has been labelled 'Wing M' on the architectural drawings (see, for example, Plan I). The north range, opposite the church, was where the refectory was located, at right angles to the cloister walk (figs. 15, 16, 23, 24 and 51–58); this has been called 'Wing R' on the survey drawings. To the west of the cloister, and separated from the cloister by a 'lane' or corridor, was a building where the lay-brothers, or *conversi*, lived (figs. 16 and 59); it is denoted 'Wing C' on the plans and sections. The cloister walk just north of and parallel to the church (figs. 8, 17, 88) has been labelled 'Wing A'. Jutting out to the west and at an angle to the *'conversi* wing' is a block which now serves as a guest house (figs. 60–63); this has been labelled 'Wing O', from the italian word for guest, *ospite*.

The cloister walk beside the church is single-storeyed while the rest of the monastic buildings are double-storeyed, except for parts of the east range, which rises in three levels, and the 'tower' at the northern end of the *'conversi* wing' which has an extra floor.

On the groundfloor of the east range north of the church (Plan I), Wing M, are the present sacristy (figs. 25–28)—labelled 'S' on the architectural drawings—, the chapter room—'CR' (figs. 29–31)—, and an adjacent vaulted passage which connects the cloister with a covered space (figs. 32 and 33) which opens on its eastern side in three wide arches of different height and span (figs. 34 and 35). North of this passage is a modern toilet block, within which is a column which formerly supported a medieval staircase to the upper floor, the monastic 'day stairs' (fig. 36; Section AA'). To the north there is a large room with a modern vaulted ceiling, modern storerooms, and a passage beyond.

On the groundfloor of the east range, the cloister walk is accessible from the church (fig. 37). On either side of a wide arched opening in the middle of the cloister colonnade and between brickwork piers stand four sets of three ancient roman column shafts, cut down to about one third of their original height; they have ancient bases and medieval 'impost blocks', but no capitals (figs. 18, 21 and 22). The short columns support an arcade, which is surmounted by the western wall of Wing M. Above the arcade large relieving arches strengthen the wall (fig. 20); diaphragm arches also span the ambulatory, which is vaulted (fig. 19).

The monks' wing is double-storeyed (figs. 17, 18, 34, 35 and 38–40). Upstairs (Plan II and Section AA') was the medieval monks' dormitory, 'D', a long room until recently subdivided by narrow, modern partitions. From the dormitory a medieval staircase—the 'night stairs' —leads down to the north arm of the transept of the church. Another set of steps—the 'day stairs'—gave access to the cloister. West of the dormitory there is a row of smaller rooms, likewise subdivided, and a modern staircase. In the southern corner is a vaulted chamber, which from at least the fifteenth century was the abbey prison (figs. 42–44); it is labelled 'P' on the plans. East of the dormitory a corridor connects a rectangular room in the northern corner with a row of six cells. Before Belardi's restoration in 1998–2000, there was also a room immediately above the present sacristy, S (Section CC'); this upper chamber is labelled 'SI' on the architectural drawings (figs. 45–48). Directly over the two chapels east of the northern arm of the transept (Plan II), there was a post-medieval sick-bay, with windows opening on the north transept; through them infirm members of the community could follow the services below. This sick-bay was closed off by Belardi, and 'S' and 'SI' were transformed into a single room by the removal of a nineteenth-century floor and ceiling between them.

While the ceiling of the dormitory, D, reaches to the full height of the monks' wing, there is a mezzanine level west and east of it (Sections BB' and CC'). To the west (Plan III) there are two large rooms and a corridor with some smaller rooms opening off it. A narrow walkway crosses the northern end of the building. This gives access to an external terrace to the east, where a row of modern pillars support a lean-to roof (figs. 40, 49 and 50). The dormitory roof and eastern terrace were restored by Belardi.

In the north range, Wing R, at groundfloor level (Plan I) there are, opening off the cloister walk (figs. 15, 16, 23, 24, 51 and 52): a room with modern vaulting; two smaller cross-vaulted interleading rooms (figs. 53 and 54); the refectory, R (figs. 55–58); a kitchen, with an internal stair to a storeroom above; and a passageway. In Wing R the cloister colonnade consists of a large central arched doorway and five sets of three slender medieval colonnettes (fig. 15) standing on medieval bases and sustaining medieval impost blocks; the groups of colonnettes alternate with brickwork piers (fig. 23, right). The ambulatory is spanned by diaphragm arches and covered by medieval vaulting. Above the cloister ambulatory (Plan II), a corridor which formerly gave access to two rooms east and west of the refectory, above which is a loft (Plan III), was remodelled by Belardi as a new novitiate.[15]

The western, lay brothers', range, Wing C (fig. 59), has been renovated and refaced in modern times. A modern colonnaded portico runs along its western and northern ends at the base of a kind of 'tower'. At groundfloor level to the east is the *conversi* corridor or lane, which is covered with a barrel vault (Plan I). West of this there are, from south to north: two parlours and a passageway; the guest refectory; a library; a hallway, with a flight of stairs leading to the floor above; a row of three small rooms on the west, opening into a long storeroom on the east; two small rooms; and a square room, a staircase and a small rectangular room. Upstairs (Plan II) a central corridor runs from a large room in the south to the 'tower' in the north. Opening off this corridor are rooms facing east and west. On the south, four of the rooms have been extended eastwards over the *conversi* lane and the western cloister walk. The large room on the south has also been extended over the cloister ambulatory.

The uppermost floor of the tower is divided into two rooms, one on either side of the stairwell (Plan III). The larger room is lit on the west by a triple-arched window, divided by colonnettes. Three modern rooms stand between the 'tower' in Wing C (Plan I) and the refectory. They flank one side of a small courtyard between the northern end of the conversi range, the refectory, and the kitchen.

West of Wing C, and at a marked angle to it, is the modern guest house, Wing O (figs. 60–63). At its western end on the ground floor (Plan I) is a large room spanned by two arches. East of that there are two small rooms, a passage, and a larger parlour. Further east is a

---

15. On Plan II we show the upper level of the refectory, which is higher than any of the other rooms in this wing.

staircase, with a small room beneath it, a passage, and an irregularly-shaped parlour. Upstairs (Plan II) a central corridor gives access to rooms on either side.

The monastic buildings were built, extended, and modified at various times. An attempt has been made to reconstruct their successive building phases in the fuller, architectural analysis.[16] It is clear, however, that, after the Trappists took over the abbey in 1868, thorough restorations were made, a fact which complicates the study of the medieval buildings.

16. See below, Chapter VII.

V

IMAGES OF TRE FONTANE

EARLY DRAWINGS, PRINTS and photographs sometimes show features of the Tre Fontane buildings which no longer survive.[1] These representations can therefore be a useful source of information for the architectural history of the medieval abbey.

The earliest images of the buildings at Tre Fontane occur on fifteenth- and sixteenth-century maps and views of Rome.[2] Since the site was some distance from the Aurelian Walls, not all maps of the city included it. On the other hand, its sanctuaries placed it on the pilgrim route, for it was believed that S. Paolo alle Tre Fontane was where the apostle Paul had been beheaded, while S. Maria Scala Coeli had been endowed with the Scala Coeli indulgence after the vision of Saint Bernard, and was thought to contain the relics of over ten thousand martyrs.[3] During a Holy Year (Jubilee) there were traditionally seven important churches to visit in Rome: St. Peter's, S. Paolo fuori le Mura, the Lateran basilica, S. Sebastiano, S. Maria Maggiore, S. Croce in Gerusalemme and S. Lorenzo fuori le Mura. By the end of the sixteenth century two more were added: S. Maria Annunziata and the sanctuaries at Tre Fontane.[4] The site then ranked among the nine most visited by pilgrims to Rome.

---

1. Those known to us are listed below in B. EARLY ILLUSTRATIONS.

2. See below, B. EARLY ILLUSTRATIONS, 1469, 1471, 1450–1500, 1474 and 1561.

3. See below, C. DATES AND DOCUMENTS, 1362–70 or 1370–78; March 1412; and see Kurt Schwager, 'Santa Maria Scala Coeli in Tre Fontane', *Praestant interna: Festschrift für Ulrich Hausmann,* ed. Bettina von Freytag gen. Löringhoff *et al.* (Tübingen: Ernst Wasmuth, 1982) 398 and n. 25.

4. For this reason Tre Fontane was one of the places mentioned in 1639 by Baglione, see Giovanni Baglione, *Le Nove Chiese di Roma,* ed. L. Barroero *et al.* (Rome: Archivio Guido Izzi, 1990) 85–94.

Pietro del Massaio, in his miniature of Rome of 1469, shows three small buildings at Tre Fontane. These represent the churches of the beheading of Saint Paul, S. Maria Scala Coeli, and S. Anastasius. The location, bounded by a hill, has a river runnning through it.[5] This miniature was copied with slight variations in 1471 (fig. 68), and again sometime between 1450 and 1500.[6] On the 1469 and 1450–1500 versions the site is labelled *Hic decollatio S. Petri et Pauli,* 'Here the beheading of Saint Peter [sic] and Paul [took place]'—the reference to Saint Peter's beheading was obviously a mistake. On the 1471 drawing (fig. 68) only Saint Paul is mentioned and reference is made to the fountains, which indicates their importance in the tradition of the apostle's martyrdom. The drawings of this sanctuary show two small rectangular buildings running parallel to each other and joined together.[7] This corresponds with Panvinio's description of S. Paolo alle Tre Fontane in 1560, where two chapels were said to house the three fountains;[8] there is, however, no view of the courtyard mentioned by Panvinio, nor is there one of the colonnaded portico discovered in the 1867 excavations.[9]

In the 1469 and 1471 representations, S. Maria Scala Coeli is shown as a polygonal building with a small rectangular room jutting out from one side (fig. 68). Pointed gables crown the main part of the edifice, suggesting that it was originally vaulted or domed. They provide no indication that the church had four chapels or apses, as described by Panvinio in 1560.[10] The abbey church of S. Anastasius is named *Sci. anastasij,* or *S. nastasii.* It is shown as a basilica with a nave and two aisles, and it is partially hidden by a hill in the 1469 and 1471 images (fig. 68). In the drawing of 1450–1500 the church is viewed from the east and shown with a nave, two aisles, a semi-circular apse, and a medieval bell-tower. While this was typical of most medieval churches in Rome, neither the apse nor the campanile were part of the cistercian

---

5. See below, B. EARLY ILLUSTRATIONS, 1469.

6. See below, B. EARLY ILLUSTRATIONS, 1471 and 1450–1500; the latter had only two churches, S. Anastasio and S. Maria Scala Coeli.

7. See below, B. EARLY ILLUSTRATIONS, 1469 and 1471; there is no drawing of this sanctuary on the 1450–1500 version, but its presence is noted in writing.

8. See below, C. DATES AND DOCUMENTS, 1560.

9. See below, C. DATES AND DOCUMENTS, 1867.

10. See below, C. DATES AND DOCUMENTS, 1560.

building.[11] The 1450–1500 drawing has a bridge over the river in front of the abbey church, while the 1471 version (fig. 68) merely shows the river encircling the church and hill, but there is no bridge close to the abbey.

Alessandro Strozzi's *Map of Rome* of 1474 shows the bridge across the river at the entrance to the site (fig. 69). Behind it stand the three churches named, from left to right, *le fonti*—'the fountains'; *S. Nastasa*—S. Anastasius, and *Scala Celi*—S. Maria Scala Coeli. As in Pietro del Massaio's view, S. Paolo alle Tre Fontane consists of two contiguous buildings, one of them having an apse. Beside this sanctuary rises a bell-tower, although none has been recorded elsewhere. S. Maria Scala Coeli is polygonal, with a small rectangular room adjoining one side. The roof of the main body of this church looks like a broken dome. S. Anastasius is a basilica, with a nave, two aisles, a semi-circular apse, and a romanesque bell-tower.[12]

These small fifteenth-century sketches show S. Paolo alle Tre Fontane and S. Maria Scala Coeli before they were rebuilt in the late sixteenth century.[13] Although in some details they may depend on each other,[14] they provide important evidence for the original appearance of these buildings.[15] While the basilica of Saint Anastasius is included, the cistercian monastery is not. Dosio's *Map of Rome,* made in 1561, shows several buildings at the site named *Tre Fontane.*[16] In the middle is a church which is a basilica with a nave, two aisles, and a

11. For twelfth-century roman churches, see Richard Krautheimer, *Rome: Profile of a City, 312–1308* (Princeton: Princeton University Press, 1980) 161–192; and Peter C. Claussen, 'Renovatio Romae. Erneuerungsphasen römischer Architektur im 11. und 12. Jahrhundert', *Rom in hohen Mittelalter,* ed. B. Schimmelpfennig and L. Schmugge (Sigmaringen: Jan Thorbecke Verlag, 1992) 87–125; and Claussen, *Die Kirchen der Stadt Rom im Mittelalter, 1050–1300, A-F* (Stuttgart: Franz Steiner Verlag, 2002). The Cistercian Chapter of 1157 expressly forbade stone bell-towers: see Chrysogonus Waddell, ed., *Twelfth-Century Statutes from the Cistercian General Chapter.* Studia et Documenta, 12. (Brecht: Cîteaux: Commentarii Cistercienses, 2002) 70 <13>, 579 <16>, 618 <25>, 631 <6>, and 681 <19>). There is no evidence of there ever being such a belfry at Tre Fontane. On medieval belltowers in Rome, see Ann E. Priester, *The Belltowers of Medieval Rome and the Architecture of Renovatio* (dissertation. Princeton University, 1990); *idem,* 'The Belltowers and Building Workshops in Medieval Rome', *Journal of the Society of Architectural Historians* 52 (1993) 199–220.

12. Again, this is a mistake. It is possible this drawing depends on the previous one.

13. See below, C. DATES AND DOCUMENTS, 1582, 7 April 1582, 1583, 29 January 1584, 1599 and 1600.

14. For example, the drawing of S. Anastasius in the Strozzi and 1450–1500 Pietro del Massaio vignettes are possibly related.

15. For S. Maria Scala Coeli, Schwager, 'Santa Maria Scala Coeli', 394–417 and fig. 83.4.

16. See below, B. EARLY ILLUSTRATIONS, 1561.

romanesque bell-tower. What the other structures are is not clear; they do not resemble the earlier images of S. Paolo alle Tre Fontane or S. Maria Scala Coeli. They may in a general way stand for the cistercian monastery, but the representation is a mere pictogram, not a precise rendering of the actual buildings.

A more accurate plan of S. Maria Scala Coeli by Sallustio Peruzzi survives from 1550–1567.[17] In it the church appears cross-shaped, having a semi-circular, colonnaded porch and a staircase at its entrance. At the crossing, the arms of the cross are connected by walls at an angle. Opposite the entrance a double-staircase leads to the crypt. The plan in part fits Panvinio's description of the edifice as having four chapels or 'apses' opening off a central core.[18] On the other hand, the arm of the cross through which one entered would not have been a chapel. As Schwager pointed out, the shape of the building resembles that of late antique pavilions or the chapel of the Holy Cross which formerly stood beside the Lateran Baptistery.[19] According to Schwager, S. Maria Scala Coeli may originally have been a late roman structure, which was remodelled as an oratory; like many early sanctuaries dedicated to the Blessed Virgin Mary, it was a centrally planned building.[20] Only the crypt has survived from the Middle Ages, but there are also traces of earlier walls, indicating that this is a building that would merit more thorough archaeological investigation.

One of the finest views of Tre Fontane is by Giovanni Maggi (fig. 71).[21] It is one in a series of engravings of the *Nine Churches of Rome* which Maggi prepared for the Holy Year 1600. The view is surrounded on three sides by smaller images. On the left there are three images connected with the legend of Saint Bernard and S. Maria Scala Coeli: at the lowest level, two paintings represent Saint Bernard and his

17. See below, B. EARLY ILLUSTRATIONS,1550–1567; Schwager, 'Santa Maria Scala Coeli', Tafel 83,1.

18. See below, C. DATES AND DOCUMENTS, 1560 and 1570.

19. Schwager, 'Santa Maria Scala Coeli', 403–4.

20. As such its history may have resembled that of the Pantheon, which in 610 became the marian church of S. Maria ad Martyres, Schwager, 'Santa Maria Scala Coeli', 404 and 405, referring to the ideas put forth in Richard Krautheimer 'Sancta Maria Rotunda', in Richard Krautheimer, *Studies in Early Christian, Medieval and Renaissance Art* (New York: New York University Press, 1969) 107–114.

21. See below, B. EARLY ILLUSTRATIONS, 1600.

vision of Our Lady;[22] in the middle there is an image of the altar in S. Maria Scala Coeli, with an inscription recording the relics of Saint Zeno and 10,203 martyrs; and at the top lefthand corner there is a painting of Saint Bernard saying Mass, having a vision of souls going up a ladder from purgatory to heaven. To the right of *Saint Bernard's Vision* appears Guido Reni's *Crucifixion of Saint Peter,*[23] which is followed by a representation of the high altar in the church of S. Anastasius,[24] and then the *Beheading of Saint Paul* by Bernardino Passarotto.[25] On the far right are depicted the three *aediculae* which after 1599 housed the three fountains in S. Paolo alle Tre Fontane. Maggi's view of the site shows the church of S. Paolo alle Tre Fontane in the background and S. Maria Scala Coeli on the right; both are the recently completed, late sixteenth-century buildings. In the centre is the medieval church of SS. Vincenzo e Anastasio, preceded by its colonnaded narthex. Maggi shows the facade windows of the church arranged as they are today, but the roundheaded openings have double-light tracery (compare figs. 71 and 4). At the northeastern end of the nave roof stands a simple structure housing the monastery bells: this single wall with bells attached was probably a sixteenth-century addition. To the left of the medieval church stands the monastery, its four wings ranged around the cloister garden. The west range, the *conversi* wing, extends further north than the others and ends in a tower. The roof-line of this wing is at two different levels. This is no longer the case today (compare figs. 59 and 71). On the groundfloor in the Maggi print three doors open into its west facade, while upstairs there are small rectangular windows in the northern section, and in the southern two larger square windows. Prominent in Maggi's view is the present guest-house, northwest of the church and west of the *conversi* building. There are four rectangular openings in its western facade, in front of which there is a walled garden which no

22. The latter is probably the altarpiece, painted by Giovanni de' Vecchi in 1592 for Cardinal Aldobrandini for the high altar of S. Maria Scala Coeli, as explained by Clare Robertson, *'Il gran cardinale': Alessandro Farnese, Patron of the Arts* (New Haven and London: Yale University Press, 1992) 200.

23. Now in the Pinacoteca of the Vatican Museums, but formerly at S. Paolo alle Tre Fontane.

24. This was probably a fifteenth- or sixteenth-century arrangement.

25. Baglione, *Nove Chiese,* 93.

longer exists (compare figs. 60 and 71). The whole Tre Fontane complex is surrounded by a wall and entered through a plain gateway on
the left and the more elaborate 'Arch of Charlemagne' on the right,
visible between the churches of SS. Vincenzo e Anastasio and S. Maria
Scala Coeli. The medieval gatehouse has an arched entrance on the
groundfloor and a six-light opening on the upper floor. To its left there
appears to be part of a wall in a bad state of repair, or perhaps a
stepped buttress.

There are a few anomalies in this view. There is no sign of the
refectory, which now stands at right angles to the north range; a place
where instead the artist shows a number of trees. The refectory may
be hidden by the northern extension of the *conversi* block. If so, it
must have been a very low building, not visible to Giovanni Maggi
when he viewed the monastery from the northwest. Conversely, the
trees depicted in that place may indicate that by 1600 the medieval
refectory was in ruins.

The tower at the northern end of the west range in Maggi's view is
proportionately higher than the present tower and there are no colonnaded porticoes around it as there are today (compare figs. 59 and 71).
Behind the tower Maggi shows a small building which seems not to be
attached to the monastery complex; it may be an outhouse.

Nicholas van Aelst made an engraving c. 1600 of the nearby pilgrim
church of S. Maria Annunziata and *Santi Vincentio et Anastasio alle Tre
Fontane o vero all'Aqua Salvia*.[26] This shows the monastery and the three
churches on the site, with the sixteenth-century church of S. Paolo
alle Tre Fontane not yet completed.

Van Aelst's image is very similar to a view made by Giacomo Lauro
in 1612, and published in 1630 (fig. 72).[27] The two prints are either
derived from a common source or else Lauro copied that of van Aelst;
the main difference is that in the later view the church of S. Paolo alle
Tre Fontane is complete. Both images show the three churches on
the site and the monastery, as well as the nearby pilgrim church of
S. Maria Annunziata. The church of SS. Vincenzo e Anastasio is depicted

26. This is illustrated in Robertson, *'Il gran cardinale'*, 198, fig. 188.

27. B. EARLY ILLUSTRATIONS, 1612 (30); Mulazzani claims it was published in 1628, see
Germano Mulazzani, *L'abbazia delle Tre Fontane.* (Milan: Tranchida Editori, 1988) 18.

with a high nave, no visible aisles, and a fine narthex, incorrectly drawn with six—not four—columns, and showing those in the centre more widely spaced than the others.[28] Above the architrave there are low arches. The facade of the church has five double-light round-headed windows and a rose window. To the northeast of the nave rises a wall supporting the bells (with a cross and weather vein atop in Lauro's view). There is a sloping buttress nearby. To the left of the church are the monastic buildings. One can make out the east, north, and west ranges and the present guest-house west of the lay-brothers' wing. The *conversi* range abuts a tall tower at the far left. It is clear that the west range had been built in two different phases and that the tower was apparently a later addition. In van Aelst's engraving the tower has only two windows, while Lauro shows eight. A narrow partition with two windows, one above the other, appear in van Aelst's work at the northern end of the *conversi* block next to the tower; this does not appear in Lauro's illustration. In both views three doorways and a number of roundheaded and rectangular windows open in the western facade of the *conversi* wing. There is no sign of the refectory in either view, and in both the roof of the north range is higher than that of the west and the east ranges. East of the monks' wing in both views there is a dilapidated structure without a roof. The precinct wall surrounding the monastery has two gateways, the more elaborate being the 'Arch of Charlemagne', pictured with its arched entrance on the groundfloor and a four-light opening on the first floor in Lauro's print, but with six lights in the same place in van Aelst's engraving.

In 1630 Antonio Eclissi made a number of pen and wash drawings of the frescoes in the 'Arch of Charlemagne' and in the narthex.[29] Although most of these show murals, there are three architectural

---

28. The 'column' at the southern end 'replaces' the brickwork pier now at that corner.

29. See below, B. EARLY ILLUSTRATIONS, 1630 (1), 1630 (2), 1630 (3), 1630 (4) and 1630 (5). The murals and Eclissi's drawings of them are discussed in Fernanda De Maffei, 'Riflessi dell'epopea carolingia nell'arte medievale: il ciclo di Ezechiele e none di Carlo a S. Maria in Cosmedin e l'arco di Carlo Magno a Roma', *Atti del Convegno Nazionale sul tema: la poesia epica e la sua formazione (1969)*. (Rome: Accademia Nazionale dei Lincei, 1970) 351–386; Joan E. Barclay Lloyd, 'The Medieval Murals in the Cistercian Abbey of Santi Vincenzo e Anastasio *ad Aquas Salvias* at Tre Fontane near Rome in their Architectural Setting', *Papers of the British School at Rome* 65 (1997) 287–323.

drawings: one of the narthex (fig. 70)[30] and two of the gatehouse (figs. 73 and 74).[31]

The view of the narthex—*Portico*—shows its east, north, and south walls in elevation and its western colonnade in plan (fig. 70). This no doubt suited the purpose of the drawing, which was to show the location of the murals—indicated by letters of the alphabet. Eclissi indicates the position of the four columns and the piers at 'T' and 'V' in the foreground. In the facade wall of the church he shows only one central doorway. Against this wall stand two tombs: one, on the left, consists of an ancient sarcophagus with an arched canopy above it; the other is an elaborate 'cosmateque' construction—four columns with corinthian capitals supporting a canopy with colonnettes—typical of roman funerary monuments of the second half of the thirteenth century.[32] The righthand tomb was probably that of Tomasia, wife of Guglielmo Aldobrandeschi, who was buried in the narthex in 1272.[33] To the right of the tomb Eclissi shows four steps leading southwards out of the portico. The southeastern pier is represented, with its bracket and architrave. On the northern side of the narthex is merely a plain wall, part of the west wing of the monastery. Eclissi shows the roof beams of the narthex in the upper part of his drawing. The first of Eclissi's two architectural drawings of the gatehouse is a plan of the structure, *Pianta dell'Arco avanti la Chiesa de SS. Vincenzo et Anastasio* (fig. 73) showing the division of the passageway into two bays. Three arches are indicated by dotted lines; that near the centre marks where the medieval gate stood. The murals which interested Eclissi were in the vault and lunettes of the bay represented in the lower part of his plan. The other architectural drawing—a view of the gatehouse facade, *Facciata dell'Arco* (fig. 74)—pictures the building from the northwest. On either side of a semi-circular arch thick lower walls, topped by a plain marble cornice, rise in a narrower form to the upper floor, which has an opening of seven lights with small arches sustained by colonnettes. No subsidiary structures are shown beside the gatehouse.

30. BAV, Barb. lat. 4402, fol. 42 r.

31. BAV, Barb. lat. 4402, fols. 38r and 39r.

32. Ingo Herklotz, 'Sepulcra' e 'Monumenta' del medioevo. Studi sull'arte sepolcrale in Italia (Rome: Edizioni Rari Nantes, 2nd ed., 1990) 162–163, nn. 63 and 64.

33. See below, C. DATES AND DOCUMENTS, 1272.

Eclissi's other drawings of the 'Arch of Charlemagne' are all connected with its medieval mural decoration.

An engraving by Israel Silvestre, made between 1641 and 1646, provides a view of the buildings at Tre Fontane from the northwest (fig. 75).[34] S. Maria Scala Coeli is visible on the right, but only the curved pediment of the facade of S. Paolo alle Tre Fontane appears above the nave roof of SS. Vincenzo e Anastasio. Silvestre shows the cistercian church with its tall clerestory articulated by pilasters. Its facade is pierced by two rows of windows, but the upper ones seem proportionately too small and the lower ones too large. The narthex is partly hidden by the 'Arch of Charlemagne' and the present guest-house. At the northeastern end of the nave, instead of the plain bell-wall seen in earlier views, there is an elaborate onion-topped steeple—probably a fantastic addition by the artist. Of the monastery itself one can clearly see the west facade of the *conversi* wing, the roof and northern gable of the monks' wing, and the present guest-house. The west range, complete with tower, is divided into two main parts. A horizontal line across the northern part seems to mark its lower and upper floors. The roof of the monks' wing extends as far north as the *conversi* tower. Its northern facade has a high, stepped gable.[35] Further north there are some indistinct, small structures which may correspond to the small structures behind the tower in the west range in Maggi's view of 1600 (compare figs. 71 and 75). Silvestre does not show the refectory. The guest-house has four windows in its western facade; on the northern two doorways at ground floor level and five small windows in the upper floor. An enclosing wall runs around the Tre Fontane complex, which is entered through a plain rectangular entrance and the 'Arch of Charlemagne', which is shown as a double-storeyed structure, with a semi-circular arched entrance on the ground floor and a six-light opening above.

---

34. See below, B. EARLY ILLUSTRATIONS, 1641–1646.

35. Pistilli makes much of the stepped gable facade, seeing it as typical of late thirteenth-century buildings in Rome associated with the Cistercians and the Caetani family: Pio F. Pistilli, 'Considerazioni sulla storia architettonica dell'abbazia romana delle Tre Fontane nel duecento', *Arte Medievale*, serie 2, 6.1 (1992) 182–192. This view of the monastery by Silvestre is the only one which shows this feature, of which nothing remains in the fabric of the building.

Filippo De Rossi's *View of Tre Fontane,* published in 1652 (fig. 76),[36] has a view of the buildings behind a depiction—at A—of the beheading of Saint Paul. In the distance—at E—is the nearby church of S. Maria Annunziata. At B, De Rossi shows S. Paolo alle Tre Fontane; at D, S. Maria Scala Coeli; and at C, the church and monastery of SS. Vincenzo e Anastasio. The monastery church is preceded by a huge narthex, with six tall columns, a straight architrave, flat relieving arches and a sloping roof. The church facade has only four windows. Beside the high nave is a bell support, perhaps a slender tower. The monastery buildings extend northwards, with the present guest-house pointing in a more northwesterly direction. The roof of the monks' wing is visible, but does not reach as far as the north range, which is higher than the *conversi* wing, clearly divided into two parts, with tower added. There are three doorways in the west range, in which a variety of windows open on two levels. In many ways this rendering of the church and monastery resembles the depictations of van Aelst and Lauro, on which it probably depends (compare figs. 72 and 76).

Giuseppe Vasi's engraved *View of Tre Fontane,* published in 1753 (fig. 77),[37] shows the sixteenth-century churches of S. Maria Scala Coeli and S. Paolo alle Tre Fontane on the right, with the medieval church of SS. Vincenzo e Anastasio in the centre. Its facade opens in six windows filled with tracery. Four columns and the southern pier of the narthex are visible behind the gatehouse and enclosing wall. The 'Arch of Charlemagne' is depicted with its arched entrance and a six-light opening on the upper floor. The wall enclosing the complex is delapidated, particularly to the left of the gatehouse. Of the monastery buildings only the west range is clearly shown. On its groundfloor there are three doorways, above which are roundheaded and rectangular windows. The roof-line at the northern end of this wing is lower than the rest and there is no tower.

Towards the end of the eighteenth century, *c.* 1789, Seroux d'Agincourt commissioned a series of measured drawings in ink and light wash of the church and monastery of SS. Vincenzo e Anastasio (figs.

---

36. See below, B. EARLY ILLUSTRATIONS, 1652.
37. See below, B. EARLY ILLUSTRATIONS, 1753.

78 and 79).[38] Important dimensions were later scribbled over them. In one the facade and narthex were portrayed from the west. Great care was taken to show the correct disposition of the windows, and reveal that the round centre window was blocked. There was a ledge between all but the two central columns of the narthex. Two accompanying details illustrate the form of the splayed roundheaded windows in the facade, and a capital, architrave, relieving arch, decorative roundel, and brick and marble cornice of the narthex colonnade. Among Seroux d'Agincourt's drawings there is one showing the plan, two sections, and a detail of one of the triple-light windows of the chapter room.[39] In the sections and in the plan the central supports are piers. In a fairly recent restoration one pier was found to encase a column, which was freed of surrounding masonry; a second column was substituted for the other pier.[40] The vaulting, as the drawings illustrate, rested on the central piers and on corresponding simple supports on the walls. The two sections show a stepped floor, designed presumably to facilitate community seating around the room.[41] As Romanini has pointed out, the doorway was then a rather low, arched opening, which has since been changed (fig. 29).[42] In the south-north view a small rectangular window opens in the east wall, where now there are large roundheaded windows (fig. 31).

In his book on the history of art, published in French in 1823 and in Italian in 1825, Seroux d'Agincourt included several illustrations of

38. BAV, Vat. lat. 13479, fols. 47, 178, 184, 185 and 186. These are referred to by Angiola Maria Romanini, '"Ratio fecit diversum": la riscoperta delle Tre Fontane a Roma chiave di lettura dell'arte bernardina', *Arte medievale*, serie 2, 8 (1994) 76, n. 38. She also refers to Melinda Mihályi, 'L'abbazia delle Tre Fontane a Roma nei disegni antichi e nelle fotografie,' in press, which I have not yet been able to read.

39. This drawing has been reproduced in Romanini, '"Ratio fecit diversum"', 34, fig. 61, with a reference 'BAV, Vat. lat. 13479, fol. 303', but I have not found this drawing in that place. The drawing is also illustrated in Stefania Quattrone, 'L'evoluzione storico-architecttonica del complesso monumentale "oggi detto le Tre Fontane allora detto ad aquas salvias"' in Giovanni Belardi, Fra Jacques Brière *et al.*, *Abbazia delle Tre Fontane: il complesso, la storia, il restauro* (Rome: Edilerica s.r.l., 1995) 39, with reference solely to 'B.A.V.'.

40. This is recounted in Cesare D'Onofrio and Carlo Pietrangeli, *Abbazie del Lazio* (Rome: Cassa di Risparmio, 1969) 188.

41. The floor level of the chapter room has since been raised, about 0.50 m., as pointed out by Romanini, '"Ratio fecit diversum"', 36.

42. Romanini, '"Ratio fecit diversum"', 36.

the church of SS. Vincenzo e Anastasio. Among these were a plan, a longitudinal section, and an elevation (fig. 80), as well as a view of the facade, a detail of one bay of the nave arcade, and some brickwork.[43] The plates for the book are obviously based on the earlier drawings, but the drawings are livelier, more detailed, and more accurate than the book illustrations. The drawings, for example, provide a longitudinal view of the church from the south (fig. 79) showing the narthex, nave, aisles, south transept, and presbytery. The proportions of one part to another are evident. In the clerestory there is a brick pilaster over every pier in the nave. There are no chapels east of the south transept. Details are given of the nave and aisle windows and of the brick and marble cornice. When this drawing is compared with the plate in d'Agincourt's book (fig. 80, number 3), one notes that the elevation has been reversed. Normally this would be permissible, but at Tre Fontane the north transept does not open in three windows as does the southern, and the narthex is attached to the monastery on the north. The drawing undoubtedly provides the more accurate view. The printed plan (fig. 80, number 5) clearly shows the narthex, with its four columns and two outer piers, and the steps at its south entrance. The church as shown is entered through three doorways, one in the nave and one in each of the aisles. In the first two bays of the aisles there appear to be two small chapels. Seroux D'Agincourt does not indicate any of the four chapels east of the transept. Perhaps they had been blocked up by the time the book was published. The published section is clearly related to the earlier drawing (compare fig. 80, number 4 and fig. 78). The printed version indicates that the ground level west of the narthex had risen to almost half the height of the columns.

An anonymous engraving published in Paris in 1804 concentrates on the 'Arch of Charlemagne', which stands prominently in the centre foreground.[44] The groundfloor of the west facade is strengthened by two buttresses, while a taller buttress shores up the northeast corner of the edifice. Upstairs there is an elegant six-light opening above a

---

43. Seroux d'Agincourt, *Storia dell'Arte*. (Milan: Per Ranieri Fanfani, 1825) vol. 2, Tavv. XXV, 3, 4, 5; LXV, 15 and LXXI, 21; see below, B. EARLY ILLUSTRATIONS, 1825.

44. See below, B. EARLY ILLUSTRATIONS, 1804; it is illustrated in Mulazzani, *L'abbazia*, 21.

marble stringcourse, which divides the lower and upper levels of the building. On the north facade is a rectangular doorway and some openings beneath the roof. The artist shows part of the facade and narthex of SS. Vincenzo e Anastasio behind the enclosing wall. There is also a partial view of the guest-house, which has a covered, external staircase attached to its western facade. This is the only record of such a stair. The main focus of the print is the gatehouse, which stands out against the landscape, with a rough, winding road and a pool of water in the foreground. Luigi Rossini's *View of the Remains of the Arch of Charlemagne* also concentrates on the gatehouse.[45] This engraving shows that by 1818 the upper storey no longer existed to its full height.

Olivier's sketch of the Tre Fontane buildings made in July 1820 shows part of S. Maria Scala Coeli on the right, the gatehouse in silhouette, SS. Vincenzo e Anastasio with its narthex, and the main blocks of the monastery buildings.[46] The upper floor of the gatehouse is visible, but no details of the six-light opening are provided; like the rest of the sketch, this portion may be unfinished. Conversely, the upper floor may have been in a delapidated state by that time.[47] The church of SS. Vincenzo e Anastasio is shown with a central rose window in its facade, and two small windows on either side. The tall nave has pilasters along its clerestory wall. Olivier shows the main blocks of the monastery: the guest house is in the foreground; the west range is depicted with no tower; and the east range, or monks' wing, runs parallel to it and ends in a high gable. The bell-wall is above the roof of the monks' wing, not attached to the northern nave wall, as is usually the case. Between the *conversi* and monks' wings a low building juts out—perhaps it is the refectory.[48] In these structures Olivier shows few windows; he seems merely to have sketched the solid mass of the various parts of the complex, giving very few details.

Paul Letarouilly in 1853 published plans of the three churches at Tre Fontane, a section through S. Maria Scala Coeli, and a general view

45. See below, B. EARLY ILLUSTRATIONS, 1818.

46. See below, B. EARLY ILLUSTRATIONS, July 1820; illustrated in Schwager, 'Santa Maria Scala Coeli', Tafel 82,1.

47. Compare with Rossini's *View* of 1818, mentioned above.

48. If so, this would be the first time it appears in views of the monastery.

(fig. 81).[49] His plan of SS. Vincenzo e Anastasio in many ways resembles that of Seroux d'Agincourt—the narthex with its four columns, two piers, and southern entrance; the three entrances to the church, those on the north and south giving access to two 'chapels' which fill the first two bays of the aisles; the nave and the aisles, with their cross-vaulting marked; the transept, with no chapels opening off it to the east, and the rectangular sanctuary. Letarouilly added some of the basic dimensions of the church—depth of narthex, 6.430 metres; length of narthex colonnade, pier to pier, 17.700 m.; length of nave, 43.300 m.; width of nave, 9.180 m.; width of nave and aisles, 20.750 m.; width of transept, 29.300 m. Letarouilly's general view shows the church of S. Maria Scala Coeli in the foreground, with S. Paolo alle Tre Fontane further back. On the left is SS. Vincenzo e Anastasio with part of the attached monastery. There is no indication of the 'Arch of Charlemagne'. The narthex of SS. Vincenzo e Anastasio has four rather low columns between two piers. Letarouilly shows ionic capitals above the columns—ancient spoils used as brackets over the piers—and flat relieving arches in the architrave. The tiled roof of the narthex slopes down from the church facade, which is shown with its four double-light roundheaded windows and rose window, as well as its brick and marble cornice. The church's three doors appear behind the narthex colonnade. The roof of the two transept arms is visible behind the portico. To the left of the church one can see part of the conversi building, rising higher than the narthex. A horizontal line close to the roof may indicate that it had previously been raised. The present guest-house seems then to have been in a sorry state, lacking a proper roof and shored up by two thick buttresses.

In 1884 Oskar Mothes published some architectural drawings of the church and monastery.[50] The plan he provides of the site is dominated, however, by Mothes' theories about its development from the eighth century onwards.[51] Nonetheless he shows the four chapels east of the transept—none of which had appeared on Seroux d'Agincourt

---

49. Paul Letarouilly, *Edifices de Rome modern* (Liège: D'Avanzo et C'e., 1853) 3: pl. 339; see below, B. EARLY ILLUSTRATIONS, 1853.

50. Oskar Mothes, *Die Baukunst des mittelalters in Italien* (Jena: H. Costgenoble, 1884) 97, figs. 19–25.

51. This is discussed more fully below in Chapter Six.

or Letarouilly's plans.[52] The northern cloister ambulatory appears in Mothes' illustration, but by the early twentieth century it had disappeared.[53]

In 1913 Aristide Sartorio illustrated an article on the cistercian abbey at Tre Fontane with a sketch-plan of the buildings (fig. 82).[54] This shows the church of SS. Vincenzo e Anastasio and its narthex. Three doors lead from the entrance porch into the church. There are two chapels on either side of the sanctuary, as there are today.[55] A line indicates the position of the wrought iron grill which from the late nineteenth century has stood between the monks' eastern end of the nave and the rest of the church. In the monastery Sartorio shows only the cloister, refectory, and chapter room. There are cloister colonnades on only two sides—on the east and on the north; that on the east was connected with the north aisle of the church. Parallel to the north aisle, Sartorio marked in dotted lines the position of a third colonnade—where there is now a modern, restored portico, our Wing A. On the western side of the cloister Sartorio indicated the *conversi* passageway and he showed it opening east into the northern cloister walk, but he drew no cloister colonnade along the western side of the cloister garth, where there is now a modern, restored ambulatory.[56]

An early twentieth-century site plan (fig. 1)[57] includes S. Paolo alle Tre Fontane, S. Maria Scala Coeli, SS. Vincenzo e Anastasio, the ground-floor of the monastery, and the 'Arch of Charlemagne', as well as two sections—one, AB, provides a cutaway view of the north range, the cloister, and the church; the other, CD, a cutaway view of the monks' wing, the cloister, and the *conversi* wing. Undoubtedly an important drawing, this presents the buildings very much as they are today (compare our Plan I). Cloister ambulatories stand south and west of the garth. There are, however, some variations: one of the arches in the

---

52. Mothes does, however, appear to distinguish between the chapels on the north and south, the hatching showing they may have been built at different times.

53. It is shown only in dotted lines by Aristide Sartorio in 1913, see our fig. 82.

54. See below, B. EARLY ILLUSTRATIONS, 1913.

55. These are not drawn on Seroux D'Agincourt or Letarouilly's plans, see our figs. 80 and 81.

56. Mothes in 1884 drew the southern cloister ambulatory in plan and elevation. One wonders about the accuracy of Mothes' drawings.

57. See below, B. EARLY ILLUSTRATIONS, before 1938.

eastern portico of the monks' wing appears to be filled in; the northern end of the east range consists of only two rooms; in the rooms east of the refectory in the north range there are some partitions, which no longer exist; the present guests' dining room in the *conversi* building does not appear; the colonnaded porticoes north and west of the 'tower' at the northern end of Wing C are not shown.

A number of early photographs show the Tre Fontane buildings in the late nineteenth and first half of the twentieth century, after the monastery had been entrusted to the Trappists in 1868.[58] The growth of eucalyptus trees among and around the buildings enables one to place four of these images in chronological order. The first (fig. 83), *c.* 1870, has no trees;[59] in 1880–90 a few planted in the cloister garden appear above the roof of the *conversi* wing (fig. 84);[60] in the two early twentieth-century views the gum-trees tower above the roof of the *conversi* wing and surround the sanctuaries to such an extent that S. Paolo alle Tre Fontane is completely hidden (*e.g.* fig. 85).[61]

In all these photographs the 'Arch of Charlemagne' is shown with a low upper storey, without the characteristic multiple-light opening illustrated in earlier views (see figs. 71, 72, 74, 75, 76). Rossini in 1818 was the first to represent the gatehouse without an upper storey. Clearly, it was rebuilt in the twentieth century as part of the extensive restoration of the Tre Fontane buildings. Beside the arch in all early photographs there is a small building on two floors (figs. 83, 84 and 85). This probably forms the nucleus of the present structure in that place (see our Plan and Sections of the Gatehouse; and figs. 2 and 3).

The church and narthex of SS. Vincenzo e Anastasio are most clearly shown in the earliest of the photographs (fig. 83), and the facade can be seen in that of 1880–90 (fig. 84). The roof of the nave looks a little lower than its east and west walls; the pilasters are visible along the north clerestory wall; the lower three facade windows have been blocked.

---

58. See below, B. EARLY ILLUSTRATIONS, 1870 (1), 1870 (2), *c.* 1870 (1), *c.* 1870 (2), 1870s, 1879, 1880–1890, late 19th century (1), late 19th century (2), late 19th century (3), early 20th century, early 20th century, early 20th century, mid-20th century (?), *c.* 1945–1949 and *c.* 1960 (?).

59. ICCD, E 70095.

60. ICCD E 70105; this has the date '1880–1890' written on it.

61. ICCD E 70104; and E 70088. We only illustrate the first of these. Other early photographs are ICCD E 70095, E 70105, E 70104, E 70088; see below, B. EARLY ILLUSTRATIONS, *c.* 1870, 1880–1890, early 20th century, early 20th century.

The narthex is clearly visible in the photograph of *c.* 1870 (fig. 83).
Already by then the columns stood on high supports, as they do today.
This had clearly been different earlier in the nineteenth century, when
Seroux d'Agincourt and Letarouilly made their drawings of the building, for they showed the columns immersed in the surrounding earth
(compare figs. 80 and 81). The early Trappists raised the columns,
lowered the floor level, and cleaned up the narthex shortly after their
arrival.[62]

The present guest house is partly visible in the early photographs.
There appears to be an oval window in the apex of its west facade, with
one or two rectangular openings beneath it (figs. 83–85). The roof of
the monks' wing is also visible; it does not end in a stepped gable, as
had been shown in the view by Israel Silvestre in 1641–46 (fig. 75).

The early photographs provide important evidence regarding the
conversi wing and its adjacent tower. That part of the monastery was
entirely refaced and partly rebuilt by the 1940s and 1950s.[63] Its present
appearance (fig. 59) is very different from what has been recorded in
these photographs (figs. 83–85). That taken in 1880–1890 (fig. 84) and
one of the early twentieth century prints (fig. 85) show the whole
western facade of the west range. The corner tower recorded in
earlier representations (see, for example, figs 71, 72, 75, 76) is gone,
but in its place there is a single-storey lean-to structure, which may be
a remnant of it or may have been built over its foundations. The
present 'tower', with its colonnaded portico on two sides (fig. 59), is
almost entirely a work of the 1940s and can be seen in a photograph of
1945–1949 (fig. 86).[64]

In the early photographs the *conversi* wing can clearly be seen to
have been built in several different phases. Masonry changes and various openings are visible. From the 1880–1890 view (fig. 84), it is clear
that there was a double-storeyed block which stretched northwards
from the church and narthex to a point beyond the first arched doorway and a rectangular doorway and window on the groundfloor.
Beyond that the masonry appears to be laid in four broad stripes of
differently coloured material. All the early photographic views of the

---

62. See below, C. DATES AND DOCUMENTS, 1878.
63. Below, C. DATES AND DOCUMENTS, 1950s.
64. ICCD, E 70110; see below, B. EARLY ILLUSTRATIONS, *c.* 1945–1949.

conversi wing show these changes of masonry in the northern part of the block. Yet, even in this northern part of the building, there is a further vertical division close to the second, lower, arched doorway on the groundfloor. All this seems to indicate that an original low, single storey was raised in two or three campaigns to its late nineteenth-century height. Earlier views show a clear change in roof-line (figs. 71, 72, 76, 77); they also indicate that the *conversi* wing was made up of two, sometimes three, parts (figs. 72, 76). On the groundfloor the early photographs show a variety of arched and rectangular doorways. All mark a tall arched entrance on the far right (figs. 83, 84). Near this, in the 1880–1890 photograph, there is a rectangular doorway with a window above it. In the northern part of the *conversi* wing, very close to the second vertical line, there is a much lower arched doorway—most clearly visible in fig. 84. North of that is a wider, somewhat higher, opening, and near the northern end of the wing there is a small rectangular door. In the upper floor there are rectangular and roundheaded windows: two large roundheaded openings in the southern part of the upper floor; a similar opening directly above the low arched doorway; and one large and three small rectangular windows in the northern part of the *conversi* wing. A close-up of the masonry low down at the northern end of this block (fig. 86) shows: a band of brickwork, rows of fairly large tufelli, perhaps alternating with one row of bricks (perhaps medieval *opus listatum*); a kind of irregular *opus saracinescum* with mortar smeared around the small tufa blocks; and tufa masonry with less mortar visible. When this was built is not very clear, but the lowest band may be twelfth-century, and the upper parts may have been constructed much later.

In the late 1960s, when late medieval frescoes were discovered in the monks' wing, Carlo Bertelli had a number of photographs taken of them and of other features of the building.[65] Most are now in the Istituto Centrale per il Catalogo e la Documentazione in Rome. They offer important evidence regarding the original position of the murals (see, for example, our figs. 49, 50).[66] There are also photographs of the

---

65. See below, B. EARLY ILLUSTRATIONS, Late 1960s.
66. I have written about the location of these frescoes in Barclay Lloyd, 'The Medieval Murals', 323–344.

monastic prison (figs. 42–44), showing that the room south of the monks' dormitory had that function, at least in the fifteenth century.

During the 1992–1994 restorations, new architectural drawings were made to illustrate the discoveries made by Giovanni Belardi and his associates.[67] Drawings and new colour photographs also illustrate the work of Angiola Maria Romanini and her colleagues.[68]

67. Illustrated in Belardi, Brière *et al.*, *Abbazia delle Tre Fontane*. This work is discussed further below, in Chapter Six.

68. A. M. Romanini *et al.*, 'Ratio fecit diversum': San Bernardo e le arti. Atti del congresso internazionale, Roma, 27–29 maggio 1991, Arte medievale, serie 2, 8 (1994) 1–140. This work is discussed further below, in Chapter Six.

VI

THE ARCHITECTURE OF THE MEDIEVAL ABBEY OF S. ANASTASIUS IN SCHOLARLY LITERATURE

IMPORTANT DISCUSSIONS OF THE BUILDING HISTORY of the medieval abbey of S. Anastasius *ad Aquas Salvias* have been published in German and Italian, but very few English-speaking scholars have written about it. A brief, critical overview of this literature seems therefore appropriate before presenting a new analysis.

In 1884 Oskar Mothes included the church in his study of medieval italian buildings.[1] After claiming that the initial foundation had been made by Pope Honorius I in 625, he suggested that the present structure was largely the result of rebuilding begun by Pope Hadrian I after the fire of 772 and completed by Leo III in 796.[2] Mothes provided architectural drawings of the church and wrote a description of what he thought was its eighth-century appearance: a basilica with an apse, nave, two aisles, and the inner narthex—the nave and aisles separated by colonnades with columns 4.275 m. high sustaining arches 3.45 m. wide.[3] This reconstruction is no longer accepted, although Angiola Maria Romanini at one time suggested that the present church was merely a cistercian extension of the eighth-century building.[4] Not

---

1. Oskar Mothes, *Die Baukunst des Mittelalters in Italien* (Jena: H. Costengoble, 1884) 97, 99–100.

2. Mothes, *Die Baukunst,* 99. The precise date of 625 is no longer accepted. Nothing survives from the intervention of Hadrian I and Leo III.

3. Mothes, *Die Baukunst,* 97 and Figs. 19–25; 99–100.

4. Angiola Maria Romanini, 'La storia architettonica dell'abbazia delle Tre Fontane a Roma. La fondazione cisterciense', *Mélanges à la Memoire du Anselme Dimier,* ed. B. Chauvin (Pupillon, Arbois: B. Chauvin, 1982) 3:675.

enough is known about the previous structures on the site to make such assumptions.

In 1896, when Giuseppe Tomassetti wrote about Tre Fontane, only two cloister walks were standing.[5] He considered this the oldest cloister in Rome but thought it had not been built before the medieval church, which he dated to the twelfth century.

Arthur Frothingham in 1908 thought that the gatehouse with its frescoes survived from the eighth century, and that the eastern side of the cloister had been built in carolingian times.[6] But neither the types of masonry in those parts of the buildings nor the styles of painting in the gatehouse are typical of work of such an early date. He attributed the church of SS. Vincenzo e Anastasio, with its piers and 'severe simplicity' to the cistercian monks. He noted the differences between the northern and eastern sides of the cloister, and pointed out that the eastern wall of the cloister was constructed with a system of piers, small arcades, and large relieving arches, 'a blind arcade' (see fig. 20), so that structurally it could take the weight of the upper floor of that wing of the monastery. That is to say, he believed the east range had been built originally as a double-storeyed block.

In 1913 Aristide Sartorio published a penetrating architectural analysis of the church and monastery at Tre Fontane.[7] The abbey was entirely medieval, he noted, and suggested that it had all been planned by a cistercian architect. Unusually for Rome there were pointed barrel vaults in the choir and transepts and in the four chapels flanking the chancel. The nave, too, was to have been covered by a pointed barrel vault, but this, he thought, was never built. The narthex, which Sartorio believed dated from the first decades of the thirteenth century, he considered different from most nartheces in Rome, except that of S. Lorenzo fuori le Mura. The wooden brackets of the roof he thought were gothic in design.[8]

5. Giuseppe Tomassetti, 'Della Campagna Romana', Archivio della Società Romana di Storia Patria 19 (1896) 135–150.

6. Arthur L. Frothingham, The Monuments of Christian Rome (New York: Macmillan, 1908) 105–106, 128–129, 187 and 197.

7. Aristide Sartorio, 'L'abbazia cisterciense delle Tre Fontane', Nuova Antologia 167 (settembre, 1913) 50–65; reprinted in Anonymous, S. Paolo e le Tre Fontane. XXII secoli di storia messi in luce da un monaco cisterciense (Trappista). (Rome: L'Abbazia 'Nullius' dei Santi Vincenzo e Anastasio alle Acque Salvie, 1938) 113–121.

8. It is possible that the roof has been restored.

According to Sartorio, there were originally only two cloister walks, those on the east and on the north.[9] He drew them in a sketch-plan on which he also traced the position of the south ambulatory (fig. 82). Sartorio thought the modern guest house (our Plans I and II, Wing O and figs. 60–63) was the abbot's residence[10] and could not understand why it led east to the *conversi* corridor and not into the cloister proper.[11] While he noted its tufa masonry, he did not recognize this as typical of thirteenth- and fourteenth-century construction in Rome.[12] Consequently, he did not realize that this wing was a late extension of the monastery buildings. He thought the original refectory had been preserved in its entirety, whereas it has been heavily restored.[13]

Sartorio believed that the church and monastery had been built by lombard and roman masons. The connection with the Lombards, for which there is no evidence, may have stemmed from his conviction that SS. Vincenzo e Anastasio at Tre Fontane was the direct successor in Italy of the cistercian abbey of Chiaravalle in Milan, founded 1131.[14] He thought that the bricks used in the church had been made specifically for this building by lombard masons, and that they were not roman spoils, as was more normal in medieval Rome.[15] In fact, the bricks—which have now been measured all over the buildings—are of different sizes and colours; certainly they and the long voussoirs around the arches in the church are roman spoils.

Giovanni Battista Giovenale in 1917 was particularly interested in the medieval cloister.[16] He noted the differences between the east and north colonnades—the thick pieces of roman column and reused bases in the east (figs. 21–22); and the thin colonnettes made specifically for this building in the north (fig. 23).[17] He suggested that the

9. Sartorio, 'L'abbazia', 50, 60 and fig. 2, our fig. 82; reprinted in Anonymous, *Tre Fontane*, 113, 117 and 118, without the drawing; this agrees with Tomassetti's evidence noted above.

10. Sartorio, 'L'abbazia', 57; while we do not think Wing O had that function in the Middle Ages, the later commendatory abbots may have used it so.

11. Sartorio, 'L'abbazia', 57; Anonymous, *Tre Fontane*, 117.

12. On this type of masonry and its dates, see Joan E. Barclay Lloyd, 'Masonry Techniques in Medieval Rome', *Papers of the British School at Rome* 53 (1985) 241–244; 275–276.

13. Sartorio, 'L'abbazia', 58, Anonymous, *Tre Fontane*, 118.

14. Sartorio, 'L'abbazia', 50, 54, 55, Anonymous, *Tre Fontane*, 113–115.

15. Sartorio, 'L'abbazia', 53, Anonymous, *Tre Fontane*, 114–115.

16. Battista Giovenale, 'Il chiostro medioevale di San Paolo fuori le Mura', *Bullettino della Commissione Archeologica Comunale di Roma* 45 (1917) 125–167, esp. 148–167.

17. Giovenale, 'Il chiostro', 149–150.

eastern wing of the cloister had been built by lombard masons in the last decades of the eleventh century for the cluniac monks from S. Paolo fuori le Mura. Pope Innocent II, he thought, had subsequently restored the monastery before the Cistercians arrived. He too believed this was one of the earliest cloisters in Rome.

A history of the abbey written by A. Barbiero ocso—but published anonymously in 1938—discussed many aspects of the sanctuaries and the monastic buildings.[18] Barbiero first referred to the ancient names of the area and explained the topography of the site.[19] He outlined the life of Saint Paul and his martyrdom, which according to tradition took place at Tre Fontane, and he recounted the stories of other early christian martyrs associated with the site.[20] Using a variety of sources, Barbiero discussed the history of the site until the foundation of the cistercian abbey in the twelfth century. With its quotations from historical documents, its epigraphic records and its illustrations, Barbieri's work remains a fundamental study of the early history of Tre Fontane. Since the section on architecture was merely a transcription of Sartorio's earlier analysis,[21] however, it will not be discussed here.

In 1956–1957 Renate Wagner-Rieger published a two volume work on medieval italian architecture in which she discussed the cistercian churches of north, central, and southern Italy.[22] With regard to SS. Vincenzo e Anastasio alle Tre Fontane, the earliest cistercian church in Southern Italy, she pointed out the nave's 'basilical' layout, the square piers, semi-circular arches, the windows, the traces of the nave vault which she thought had never been built, and the aisles covered with cross vaults.[23] The transept was considerably lower than the nave and aisles, but linked to the nave arcades by arches that were wider and higher than those in the nave. On account of these arches, the

18. Anonymous, *Tre Fontane*. I am grateful to the monks at Tre Fontane, who let me peruse a typed manuscript which formed part of the planned, but never published, second volume telling the history of the abbey from the late twelfth century until the present time.

19. Anonymous, *Tre Fontane*, 9–21.

20. Anonymous, *Tre Fontane*, 22–33.

21. Anonymous, *Tre Fontane*, 113–121.

22. Renate Wagner-Rieger, *Die italienische Baukunst zu Beginn der Gotik,* 2 vols. (Graz-Koln: Verlag Hermann Böhlaus, 1956–1957).

23. Wagner-Rieger, *Die italienische Baukunst,* 2:27–30.

nave seemed to continue into the transept, rather than form a separate entity. The arms of the transept were covered with barrel vaults, and each opened in two eastern chapels, similarly vaulted, as was the low central 'apse' beyond the nave. The high wall at the west end of the apse opened in four windows.

Wagner-Rieger considered this church planning unique in Rome and compared it with burgundian cistercian architecture. The east end was typically 'bernardine', she thought; the barrel-vaulted transept arms were reminiscent of Fontenay, as the nave vault would also have been, and so too was the arrangement of windows in the wall west of the apse. On the other hand the form of the nave piers at Tre Fontane differed from those at Fontenay, and so too did the aisle vaults, which in the burgundian church were transverse barrel vaults. The proportions of the two churches were also different. Whereas in burgundian churches the height of the nave and aisles did not differ very much, that was not the case at SS. Vincenzo e Anastasio, where the proportions of nave to aisles were more like those of a roman basilica. (Yet, one may note that, compared with other twelfth-century churches in Rome, the cistercian building has a very high nave.)

In 1957 Hanno Hahn included the abbey church of SS. Vincenzo e Anastasio alle Tre Fontane in his book on cistercian architecture.[24] In it he discussed the proportions of the 'bernardine' plan.[25] He applied his general observations in the first instance to the abbey church at Eberbach, in Germany, and then in short notices to one hundred fifty-six other cistercian churches, including SS Vincenzo e Anastasio at Tre Fontane. Hahn demonstrated a system of modular proportions in variants of the 'bernardine' plan. The system relied on two significant measurements, which we shall refer to as 'M1' and 'M2'. M1 was the overall width of the nave and aisles. M2 was the width of the transept from its west wall to the east wall of the transept chapels.

From these basic dimensions Hahn devised four 'laws'. Law I stated that M1 was equal to the length of the presbytery and crossing. According to law Ia, M1 was also the dimension of the crossing and one

---

24. Hanno Hahn, *Die frühe Kirchenbaukunst der Zistersienser* (Berlin: Verlag Gebr. Mann, 1957) 171–173. Hahn does not apply his system of cistercian proportions to Tre Fontane.

25. Hahn, *Die frühe Kirchenbaukunst*, 66–82 and 314–339.

transept arm, measured along the north-south axis. Law II asserted that M2 was the same as the distance from the east wall of the presbytery to the centre point of the crossing. Law IIa stated that M2 was half the total length of the transept, i.e. from the centre point of the crossing to the north or the south wall. The ratio of M2 to the north-south length of both transept arms and the crossing was 1:2.

Hahn also concluded that the ratio of M2 to M1 was 3:4. This gave him another important dimension, M3, which was three times M2 or four times M1. Law IV stated that M3 was equal to the length of the church from the west façade to the east wall of the transept chapels, but did not include the eastern extension of the presbytery beyond the transept chapels. Hahn's system of proportions has been criticized by both Antonio Cadei and David Walsh.[26] When Cadei applied Hahn's schema to his plan of Chiaravalle di Fiastra, he found notable discrepancies.[27] Cadei attributed this to Hahn's use of small plans for many of the churches he analysed; in the case of Chiaravalle di Fiastra Hahn's figures were not as accurate as those from Cadei's 1:100 survey.[28] Walsh also found discrepancies in measurements when he applied Hahn's system to the excavated walls of Bordesley Abbey,[29] and he pointed out that, in working out the proportions of cistercian churches, architectural historians often used small or inaccurate plans. It was not always clear whether dimensions were taken from foundations or rising walls; or from the inner or outer face, or the mid-point, of walls. Meters, Walsh also found, were not a good measure for analyzing medieval dimensions. He calculated that twelfth-century cistercian architects in France and England regularly used the roman foot equal to 29.5 cm.[30] Walsh therefore recommended that, in working out the proportions of medieval cistercian buildings, measurements be converted into roman feet. Walsh wondered as well whether

26. Antonio Cadei, 'Chiaravalle di Fiastra', *Storia dell'Arte* 34 (1978) 265–269; David A. Walsh, 'Measurement and Proportion at Bordesley Abbey', *Gesta* 91/2 (1980) 109–113; and David A. Walsh, 'An Architectural Study of the Church', *Bordesley Abbey* II, British Series III, edd. S. M. Hirst and S. M. Wright (Oxford: British Archæological Reports, 1983) 222–225.

27. Cadei, 'Chiaravalle', 265–269.

28. Cadei, 'Chiaravalle', 268.

29. Walsh, 'An architectural study', 222–225.

30. In Rome the measure for one roman foot is usually 29.56 cm.

medieval cistercian architects would have found the crossing space or the center point of the crossing meaningful in their measurements. He did agree with Hahn that the proportion 3:4 was very important in cistercian churches.

Hahn divided the one hundred fifty-six churches on his list into six types, according to variations in their plan.[31] First there was the small four-chapel type, as at Fontenay, to which Laws I–IV could be applied. Secondly there was the small six-chapel type, as at Clermont. The third type included medium to large churches with four, six, or more chapels, like Eberbach. Churches of the fourth type had eight chapels and large choirs, and were designed after the later additions to Clairvaux and Cîteaux. The sixth type comprised churches with single choir apses.

Hahn classified SS. Vincenzo e Anastasio at Tre Fontane among the churches of his first type, but he did not give a detailed analysis of its dimensions and proportions according to the system he had devised.[32] He noted that the buildings—both church and monastery—were much restored, but well-preserved. He dated the church to the years 1140–1150. To Hahn, the church seemed not so much a roman building as an example of early burgundian cistercian architecture, close to Fontenay in type. He noted the pointed vaults in the presbytery, transept arms, and four eastern chapels, as well as that begun—but, he thought, never finished—over the nave, and the simple cross-vaults over the aisles. He observed the nave crossing, the rather low transept, and the low, projecting chancel. He thought the interior of the church plain, but monumental; the walls hardly articulated. The plain squarish piers that separate the nave and aisles seemed to him typical of early cistercian churches, like some in Switzerland and Scandinavia. He mentioned the flat pilasters that articulate the exterior of the nave clerestory, and noted that there was no tower. The windows in the choir, in the eastern crossing wall, and in the west wall of the nave were simple in form. The semi-circular arches between nave and presbytery—and opening into the transept arms and eastern chapels—contrasted rather incongruously with the pointed vaulting. He thought the nave was more brightly lit than that at Fontenay.

---

31. Hahn, *Die frühe Kirchenbaukunst,* 318–339.
32. Hahn, *Die frühe Kirchenbaukunst,* 171–173.

In all this Hahn found a strong influence stemming from local roman customs. The church seemed in some ways to resemble a roman basilica. On the other hand, vaulting the nave–a little over 20 m. high—was beyond the technical expertise of medieval roman builders. Hahn did not follow Sartorio's theory that the church of SS. Vincenzo e Anastasio was influenced by Chiaravalle in Milan. The 'basilical' layout, the masonry, and several other features seemed to him to be typically roman. As he put it, when in Rome one built as the Romans built, 'in Rom baute man römisch'.[33]

Cesare D'Onofrio and Carlo Pietrangeli suggested c. 1969 that the 'Arch of Charlemagne' rose over the oratory of Saint John the Baptist, recorded in early documents.[34] This is unproven, although the remains of an apse near the gatehouse did come to light in excavations made in 1938/39.[35] The authors also thought the church had been begun by Pope Innocent II, who built the nave and presbytery, and completed by Pope Honorius III, who built the parts of the edifice in *opera listata*.[36] On the other hand, they mentioned that the aisle walls— in the same masonry—had been built at a much earlier time.[37] D'Onofrio and Pietrangeli gave a consecration date of 1244.[38] Yet they admitted that the church was a precious example of cistercian architecture of the 'bernardine' period, and that its simplicity was due to its early date.

D'Onofrio and Pietrangeli found the monastery buildings so over-restored as to make it difficult to distinguish between medieval and modern parts.[39] The cloister was, in their opinion, the oldest of those surviving in Rome.[40] They mentioned that the vaulted ceiling of the chapter room was sustained in the centre by two piers, one containing

33. Hahn, *Die frühe Kirchenbaukunst*, 173, quoting Leo Bruhns, *Die Kunst der Stadt Rom* (Vienna, 1951) 211.

34. Cesare D'Onofrio and Carlo Pietrangeli, *Abbazie del Lazio* (Rome: Cassa di Risparmio, 1969) 184.

35. See below, C. DATES AND DOCUMENTS, 1938/39.

36. D'Onofrio and Pietrangeli, *Abbazie*, 184–185.

37. D'Onofrio and Pietrangeli, *Abbazie*, 185–186.

38. D'Onofrio and Pietrangeli, *Abbazie*, 184; the same mistake was made by Vincenzo Forcella, *Iscrizioni delle chiese e d'altri edifici di Roma dal secolo XI fino ai giorni nostri* (Rome: Ludovico Cecchini, 1878) 12:322.

39. D'Onofrio and Pietrangeli, *Abbazie*, 188.

40. D'Onofrio and Pietrangeli, *Abbazie*, 188.

a column; they believed the other pier took the place of a column.[41] They noted that the sacristy and the room above it had been added in the thirteenth century.[42] They also observed that the refectory is today completely restored. Yet its east wall is built of twelfth-century *opus listatum* to a level just above the present windows.[43]

In 1969 and 1970 two studies of wall-paintings at Tre Fontane included scholarly opinions about the date of the medieval buildings.[44] Carlo Bertelli discussed the late thirteenth or early fourteenth-century frescoes in the east range of the monastery (our Plans II and III, Wing M) in the roof-space of the dormitory, on what is now an external wall (our Plan III, wall 8; and figs. 49 and 50), and in the room which was then above the sacristy (our Plan II, 'SI'; and fig. 87).[45] He thought most of the east range and the north range were built contemporaneously with the medieval church, with an upward extension of tufelli— i.e. *opus saracinescum*—added to both wings early in the thirteenth century.[46] He noted, besides, two double-light windows in the eastern wall of the chapter room, where there are now two large, modern, roundheaded openings (fig. 31).[47] The three arches along the eastern side of the monks' wing (figs. 34 and 35; our Plan I, wall 7), reminded Bertelli of the early thirteenth-century blind arcade along the aisle of S. Lorenzo fuori le Mura, and he gave them a similar date in the early thirteenth century. Above the arches he saw part of a small blocked

41. D'Onofrio and Pietrangeli, *Abbazie,* 188; the present restoration of the room has two central columns and no piers; we believe this was the original arrangement.

42. D'Onofrio and Pietrangeli, *Abbazie,* 188; we agree with this assertion and the date.

43. D'Onofrio and Pietrangeli, *Abbazie,* 188; and see below, A. ARCHITECTURAL DATA, Wall 10. The twelfth-century masonry was covered with plaster in Giovanni Belardi's restoration of 1998–2000.

44. Carlo Bertelli, 'L'enciclopedia delle Tre Fontane', *Paragone-Arte* 20.235 (1969) 24–49 and Fernanda De Maffei, 'Riflessi dell'epopea carolingia nell'arte medievale: il ciclo di Ezechiele e non di Carlo a S. Maria in Cosmedin e l'arco di Carlo Magno a Roma', *Atti del Convegno Nazionale sul tema: la poesia epica e la sua formazione (1969).* (Rome: Accademia Nazionale dei Lincei, 1970) 351–386.

45. Bertelli, 'L'enciclopedia', 24–49; see below, A. ARCHITECTURAL DATA, 5. Medieval Murals, (c) MURALS IN WING M. The floor between the sacristy and the vaulted room above it was removed by architect Giovanni Belardi in 1998–2000, as we noted above, at the end of Chapter One.

46. Bertelli, 'L'enciclopedia', 42.

47. Bertelli, 'L'enciclopedia', 42; see below, A. ARCHITECTURAL DATA, Wall 7; the double-light windows mentioned by Bertelli are clearly visible in D'Onofrio and Pietrangeli, *Abbazie,* fig. 194.

window which is no longer visible.[48] The northward continuation of the east wall of the chapter room and the eastward extension of the north wall of the monks' wing (our Plans I and II, walls 7 and 30; and fig. 89) added further living space. Bertelli thought the upper floor in this part of the east range had been restructured, perhaps in the seventeenth century, then again in 1868, as well as more recently. Around 1868 two large windows were opened at the northern end of the dormitory, and four in the east, (our Plan II, wall 30 and wall 7; fig. 38). This necessitated some changes in the roofing over the east wing.[49] In a much more recent campaign, a terrace was constructed over the rooms above the chapter room and the three groundfloor arches (figs. 49 and 50; our Plans II and III, Section BB'). It was then that the frescoes on the eastern side of wall 8 were discovered.[50]

With regard to the sacristy and the frescoed room which was above it (our Plans I and II, Section CC', figs. 45–48 and 87),[51] Bertelli noted that they were built against the older structures of the church, and out of the same tufa masonry found elsewhere in the east and in the north range of the monastery.[52] He dated all this *opus saracinescum* to the early thirteenth century.[53] In the sacristy he noted the mysterious inscription on the lintel of the doorway: FEC . . . FIERI: H: OP: ET: I: ET L (fig. 67), but did not attempt to explain it.[54] Although Bertelli assigned it an early thirteenth-century date and connected it with the inscription of IACOBUS, now in the north range (fig. 66),[55] he was convinced on stylistic grounds that the frescoes were much later, made between the time of Cimabue and Giotto, close in time to the mosaics of S. Maria Maggiore in Rome, executed by Jacopo Torriti in 1296.[56]

---

48. Bertelli, 'L'enciclopedia', 42.

49. Bertelli, 'L'enciclopedia', 42–43.

50. Bertelli, 'L'enciclopedia', 43.

51. In the latest renovations architect Giovanni Belardi has restored the rooms that were previously above one another (Plans I and II, S and S') to their original form of being a single room; see above, the end of Chapter One.

52. Bertelli, 'L'enciclopedia', 46.

53. It is found in medieval roman buildings securely dated from 1208–1368, see Barclay Lloyd, 'Masonry techniques', 241–242, 244, and 275–276.

54. Bertelli, 'L'enciclopedia', 46. The lintel is over the entrance to the room with the gothic ribbed vault and frescos.

55. See below, C. DATES AND DOCUMENTS, 1216–1227, for this inscription.

56. Bertelli, 'L'enciclopedia', 34–40.

Fernanda De Maffei, discussing the frescoes in the 'Arch of Charlemagne' suggested that they had been painted in two campaigns: the first in 1153–1161; the second *c.* 1221, since Seroux d'Agincourt had recognized in the lunette with the *Madonna and Child* the portrait of Pope Honorius III, who consecrated the church of SS. Venanzio e Anastasio, dedicating it to the Blessed Virgin Mary in that year.[57] Most later scholars date all the murals to the thirteenth century.[58]

In 1972 Giuseppe Ruotolo published a history of the cistercian abbey at Tre Fontane, based mostly on surviving documents and earlier historical works, with occasional comments on the buildings.[59] Over the door of the chapter room, for instance, Ruotolo reported an inscription, recorded by the seventeenth-century writer Gaspar Jongelinus, stating that Abbot Leonardus had had work done in 1306.[60] Ruotolo claimed that Abbot Leonardus' building campaign was difficult because it required that the whole monastery be demolished and then restructured.[61] This claim seems to stretch the evidence given in the inscription. According to Ruotolo, instead of rebuilding the entire monastery, the abbot had merely renovated the chapter room and reinforced the cloister ambulatory with piers and arches. Ruotolo's theory about the piers and arches in the cloister is incorrect, for while it is probable that Abbot Leonardus had had work done in the chapter room, the piers are built of twelfth-century masonry and so date from long before 1306.

57. De Maffei, 'Riflessi', 372–378.

58. Carlo Bertelli, 'Affreschi, miniature e oreficie cistercensi in Toscana e in Lazio', *I Cistercensi e il Lazio.* (Rome: Multigrafica Editrice, 1978) 74–77; Francesco Gandolfo, 'Aggiornamento scientifico e bibliografia' in Guglielmo Matthiae, *Pittura romana del medioevo* (Rome: Fratelli Palombi Editori, 1988) 2:283–284; Antonio Iacobini, 'La pittura . . .', *Roma nel Duecento*, ed. Angiola Maria Romanini (Rome: SEAT, 1991) 267–271; Stefania Quattrone, 'L'evoluzione storico-architettonica del complesso monumentale "oggi detto le Tre Fontane allore ad Aquas Salvias"', in Giovanni Belardi, Fra Jacques Brière, Liliana Pozzi, *et al.*, *Abbazia delle Tre Fontane: il complesso, la storia, il restauro* (Rome: Edilerica, s.r.l., 1995) 46–49; Joan E. Barclay Lloyd, 'The Medieval Murals in the Cistercian Abbey of SS. Vincenzo e Anastasio ad Aquas Salvias at Tre Fontane near Rome in their Architectural Setting', *Papers of the British School at Rome* 65 (1997) 287–308.

59. Giuseppe Ruotolo, *L'abbazia delle Tre Fontane* (Rome: Abbazia delle Tre Fontane, 1972).

60. The wording of the inscription, 'Dominus Leonardus abba fecit fieri hoc opus, Anno Domini M.CCCVI', was noted by Gaspar Jongelinus, *Notitia Abbatiarum Ordinis Cisterciensis per orbem universum* (Cologne: Apud Joannes Henningium Bibliopolam, 1640) 7:7.

61. 'L'impresa era difficile perchè bisognava demolire l'intero monastero e poi ricostruirlo', Ruotolo, *L'abbazia*, 175.

In 1980 Umberto Broccoli published a study of the abbey at Tre Fontane, which was concerned mostly with its early history and with the early medieval sculpture on the site.[62] He claimed that the gatehouse was a medieval tower which had formerly been part of a fortified surrounding wall which had transformed the monastery into a castellated city, like the *Civitas Leonina* around the Vatican.[63] This vision is imaginative, but not founded on any historical evidence. The 'Arch of Charlemagne' was not so much a defensive tower, as the usual gateway to a monastery, and the former enclosing walls were nothing other than those that usually surround an abbey's precinct.

In 1982 Angiola Maria Romanini published a detailed study of the monastery and church.[64] She admitted that the plan of the buildings in general outline was typical of early cistercian architecture—in particular, the church resembled the 'small type' of 'bernardine' structure identified by Hahn, with its nave and aisles separated by square piers, its wide rectangular transept arms and square crossing, and its rectangular choir flanked by two chapels on either side.[65]

In the east end of the church and in the adjoining east range of the monastery, however, Romanini found some unusual features, even 'errors', in the classic 'cistercian' layout.[66] She based her conclusions partly on anomalies in the plan of the buildings and partly on the use of various kinds of masonry in the complex. The plan she referred to was small and not very accurate. Yet Romanini deduced from it that the walls of the chapter room and its adjacent structures were strangely off axis to the church and the perpendicular lines of the cloister.[67] Like other scholars, Romanini believed that only the east and north ambulatories of the cloister were medieval, and that of these the eastern

---

62. Umberto Broccoli, *L'abbazia delle Tre Fontane. Fasi paleocristiane e altomedioevali del complesso 'ad Aquas Salvias' in Roma* (Trani: Vivere In, 1980).

63. Broccoli, *L'Abbazia*, 32–33. For the *Civitas Leoninia*, see Richard Frautheimer, *Rome: Profile of a City, 312–1308* (Princeton: Princeton University Press, 1980) 117–120.

64. In the first part of her study, 'La storia architettonica', 653–671, Romanini discusses in detail the history of the cistercian monastery from contemporary documents; she then (pp. 671–695) turns to a subtle and searching analysis of the buildings.

65. Romanini, 'La storia architettonica', 671, referring to Hahn, *Die frühe Kirchenbaukunst*, 171–173.

66. Romanini, 'La storia architettonica', 672; when discussing 'errors' in plan, however, she relied on drawings which she admitted were inaccurate.

67. Romanini, 'La storia architettonica', 672, 673 and 679.

was the older.[68] She claimed, moreover, that the east range seemed to have no dimensional or structural connections with either the church or the north range.[69] A more detailed study was necessary, she asserted, to make clear the building phases within the eastern wing.[70]

Three main types of masonry in the buildings were distinguished by Romanini: brickwork; *opus mixtum* (her term in this publication for what is here called *opus listatum*); and tufa masonry *(opus saracinescum)*.[71] Within these types, she identified variants. Following Sartorio, she thought some of the brickwork had been made of newly fired bricks,[72] whereas elsewhere roman spoils were employed. With regard to *opus mixtum,* she claimed that there were significant changes in the regularity of the rows of tufa blocks and bricks, the size of the brick fragments and tufelli, and the height of the plaster between them.[73] Tufa masonry she mentioned only in passing.[74]

Romanini recalled that several scholars thought the rougher variants of *opus mixtum* represented parts of earlier structures, perhaps parts of the rebuilding of the church and monastery by Popes Hadrian I (772–95) and Leo III (795–816).[75] Two main theories had been enunciated: that the parts of the buildings in brickwork were erected by the Cistercians and the parts in *opus mixtum* remained from earlier structures of the cilician monastery;[76] or, the Cistercians built the parts in brickwork and medieval roman masons the parts in *opus mixtum*.[77] Yet

---

68. Romanini, 'La storia architettonica', 673. Cf. Tomassetti, 'Della Campagna Romana', 135–150; Sartorio, 'L'abbazia', 50–65 and Anonymous, *Tre Fontane,* 113–121; and Giovenale, 'Il chiostro', 125–167, esp. 148–167.

69. Romanini, 'La storia architettonica', 673.

70. *Ibid.*

71. *Opus listatum* and *opus mixtum* are two terms used for the same kind of masonry, which consists of alternating rows of bricks and tufa blocks; *opus saracinescum* is made of small tufa blocks only. In medieval Rome the tufa blocks in *opus saracinescum* are usually smaller than those in *opus listatum.*

72. Romanini, 'La storia architettonica', 675; we do not agree with her, or with Sartorio.

73. Romanini, 'La storia architettonica', 673 and 675.

74. Romanini, 'La storia architettonica', 673, where she described the masonry made of small tufa blocks but did not use the term, *opus saracinescum.*

75. Romanini, 'La storia architettonica', 675, with further bibliography. Their theories have been refuted by Maria Avagnina in Maria E. Avagnina *et al.,* 'Strutture murarie degli edifici religiose di Rome nel XII secolo', *Rivista dell'Istituto Nazionale d'Archeologia e Storia dell'Arte* 23–24 (1976–77) 239–241.

76. Romanini, 'La storia architettonica', 677.

77. *Ibid.*

comparison with other medieval buildings in Rome shows that this kind of *opus mixtum/listatum* occurs frequently in the late eleventh and twelfth century—in the piers of the lower church of S. Clemente, *c.* 1080; in the gatehouse of the upper church of S. Clemente in the early twelfth century; in the left aisle wall of S. Prisca, in 1105; in the left transept wall of S. Bartolomeo in Isola, variously dated 1113 or 1159–1181; in the blockings of the outer colonnade of Sto. Stefano Rotondo, in 1130–1143; in the cloister of S. Lorenzo fuori le Mura, 1187–1191.[78] This type of *opus listatum* is in fact typical of late eleventh and twelfth-century building in Rome, and it is often combined with plain brickwork in the same pier, wall or building.[79]

One place where brickwork and *opus mixtum / listatum* were used in an unusual way at Tre Fontane occurs in the north wall of the transept (fig. 14). For Romanini the reworking or patching in that wall indicated that the church itself had been restuctured.[80] She suggested that the 'bernardine' east end had been added to an earlier building and patched up during construction. This led her to speculate about the relation between the present cistercian church and the earlier basilica of Saint John the Baptist which had formed part of the cilician monastery *ad Aquas Salvias* and which had been rebuilt after a fire by Pope Hadrian I (772–795). She thought the present church might have been moulded on to the earlier basilica, and its plan influenced by the former building. Or it might have contained some walls dating from that earlier time. Yet one notes that the plan of the present church is very cistercian. Although it is built of two distinct types of masonry—brickwork and *opus listatum*—they do not necessarily indicate separate phases of construction.

78. Barclay Lloyd, 'Masonry techniques', 239–241, 273–274; for S. Lorenzo fuori le Mura, Joan E. Barclay Lloyd, 'The Architecture of the Medieval Monastery of S. Lorenzo fuori le Mura, Rome', *Architectural Studies in Memory of Richard Krautheimer,* ed. Cecil L. Striker (Mainz: Verlag Philipp von Zabern, 1996) 99–102.

79. For example, in the gatehouse of the medieval church of S. Clemente, in the monastery of S. Lorenzo fuori le Mura, or in the building next to SS. Nereo ed Achilleo, see Barclay Lloyd, 'Masonry Techniques', 239–241; 243–244; 273–274; and Joan E. Barclay Lloyd, *The Medieval Church and Canonry of S. Clemente in Rome,* San Clemente Miscellany III (Rome: San Clemente, 1989) 110.

80. Romanini, 'La storia architettonica', 689–694.

In 1991 Pio Pistilli referred briefly to the medieval buildings at Tre Fontane and in 1992 he wrote an article about the thirteenth-century additions to the church and monastery.[81] He was of the opinion that the narthex had been added to the abbey church just prior to its consecration in 1221 by Pope Honorius III, when Nicholas was abbot (1212–1230).[82] While the narthex was certainly added to the nave in a separate building campaign, a thirteenth-century date is not certain, as the brickwork of its piers has a *modulus* normal in Rome in the twelfth century.[83] If the church were begun around the middle of the twelfth century, there remained in that century nearly fifty years during which the narthex could have been constructed.

Pistilli also distinguished three thirteenth-century building phases in the east range of the monastery. First, he discussed the work in the pontificate of Honorius III of a certain Iacobus, who was a *poenitentiarius,* a penitentiary and chaplain to Pope Honorius III (1216–1227), and who is mentioned in the inscription in the frame of a window now in the north range (our Plan II, Wing R, wall 29; fig. 66), as having built 'this house, for [the good of] his soul and [that] of his nephew Jacobus'.[84] In fact, Pistilli proposed a more precise date of 1222–1227 for this building campaign.[85] He suggested that the inscription referred to the upper floor of the north range between the monks' dormitory and the refectory. The new rooms were built as a residence, which Pistilli called the *'palazzetto di "frater Iacobus"'* the little palace of Fra Giacomo.[86] He commented on the symmetrical disposition of the windows and the tufa masonry in the wall above them (fig. 54). On his plan he marked this part of the north wing as having been built in twelfth-century masonry *(opus listatum)*, but raised about 2 m. in

81. Pio F. Pistilli, 'Architettura a Roma nella prima metà del Duecento', *Roma nel Duecento (1198–1254),* ed. A. M. Romanini (Turin: Edizioni Seat, 1991) 16, 19, 21–23, 48–53; and Pio F. Pistilli, 'Considerazioni sulla storia architettonica dell'abbazia romana delle Tre Fontane nel duecento', *Arte Medievale* serie 2, 6.1 (1992) 163–192.

82. Pistilli, 'Architettura', 49–51; Pistilli, 'Considerazioni', 168–170; he disagreed with Herklotz, who proposed a date *c.* 1140, Ingo Herklotz, 'Der mittelalterliche Fassadenportikus der Lateranbasilika und seine Mosaiken', *Römisches Jahrbuch der Bibliotheca Hertziana* 25 (1989) 32 and 33.

83. See below, A. ARCHITECTURAL DATA, Walls 6, 19 and 22.

84. See below, C. DATES AND DOCUMENTS, 1216–1227.

85. Pistilli, 'Architettura', 53; Pistilli, 'Considerazioni', 170–174.

86. Pistilli, 'Architettura', 53; Pistilli, 'Considerazioni', 170.

thirteenth-century *opus saracinescum*. It is not clear what this campaign entailed, apart from the raising of the walls and the addition of a new roof. Nor does Pistilli give any details about the layout of this residence.[87]

Pistilli's second phase included the sacristy (our Plan I, S, Plan II, SI and Section CC'; and figs. 45–48), which he labelled *sagrestia duecentesca* on his plan. The position is correct, but the date he proposed, *c.* 1240, is conjectural.[88] He gave a detailed and appreciative analysis of the building and an interesting interpretation of the enigmatic inscription over the door (fig. 67): FEC. FIERI. H: OP: ET: I: ET L, suggesting that 'I' and 'L' were the initials of two members of the monastic community. He thought the sacristy and the guest house might have been built in the same campaign, although there is no evidence for this.[89]

Pistilli's third phase was a far-reaching restructuring of the east range.[90] This he dated to the end of the thirteenth or the beginning of the fourteenth century. It included the portico of three arches along the east face of the monks' wing (figs. 34 and 35), an external staircase, and an upper floor which communicated with the dormitory, creating a huge space. It is not clear how Pistilli envisaged the interconnection of these new and old rooms. He gave no plan of the upper floor. Certainly the eastern wall of the original block continued to rise to nearly its full height (see our Plans II and III, wall 8; Sections BB' and CC'). The walls of the dormitory were raised and a new roof was added. According to Pistilli, the northern facade was crowned with a stepped gable.[91] Apart from the print by Israel Silvestre of 1641–1646 (fig. 75), a detail of which was published by Pistilli, there is no evidence for such a gable. Other earlier views, like that of Giovanni Maggi in 1600 (fig. 71), do not show it and there is no trace of it in the surviving structure (see fig. 38). The interior walls of the monks' wing were decorated with frescoes. According to Pistilli, this lavishly appointed building resembled italian palace architecture of the later thirteenth or early

---

87. Pistilli, 'Architettura', plan on p. 21; Pistilli, 'Considerazioni', 170–174, and plan in tav. 2.

88. Pistilli, 'Architettura', 21; Pistilli, 'Considerazioni', 173–175.

89. Pistilli, 'Considerazioni', 174.

90. Pistilli, 'Considerazioni', 175–192.

91. Pistilli, 'Considerazioni', 182 and tav. 43.

fourteenth century; in particular it was similar to the Rocca Caetani outside Rome at Capo di Bove, dated 1302–1303.[92] Pistilli suggested that the cistercian monks moved into the *conversi* building, while the east range became a sumptuous *edificio di rappresentanza,* 'a building for receiving distinguished visitors', worthy of papal Rome on the eve of the first Jubilee in 1300.[93] Such a transformation of a medieval cistercian monks' building into magnificent reception rooms seems rather unlikely.

Two important volumes were published in 1995. One contains the proceedings of an international conference on 'Saint Bernard and the Arts', held in Rome in 1991; the other the results of Giovanni Belardi's restoration of the church of SS. Vincenzo e Anastasio between 1992–1994.[94] In the first, Romanini revised her earlier study and provided a more detailed analysis of the church and the twelfth-century parts of the east range;[95] Belardi presented some new data, mainly on the vaulting, drainage, and floor of the church;[96] Maria Letizia Mancinelli, Laura Saladino, and Maria Carla Somma studied the various types of masonry used in the buildings and summarised information from five small excavations beneath the floor of the church;[97] Roberta Caglianone and Roberto Iazeolla made a geometric and architectonic analysis of the relationship of the church to the southern end of the east range;[98] and Paola Rossi discussed the restoration of the medieval

92. Pistilli, 'Considerazioni', 179–187; this building had stepped gables.

93. Pistilli, 'Considerazioni', 187 and n. 93.

94. *'Ratio fecit diversum': San Bernardo e le arte. Atti del congresso internazionale, Roma, 27–29 maggio 1991,* ed. Angiola Maria Romanini, *Arte medievale,* serie 2, 8.1, vol. 1 (1994), and Giovanni Belardi, Fra Jacques Brière, Liliana Pozzi, *et al., Abbazia delle Tre Fontane: il complesso, la storia, il restauro* (Rome: Edilerica, 1995).

95. Angiola Maria Romanini, '"Ratio fecit diversum": la riscoperta delle Tre Fontane a Roma chiave di lettura dell'arte bernardina', *Arte medievale,* serie 2, 8 (1994) 1–78.

96. Giovanni Belardi, 'Il restauro dell'abbazia delle Tre Fontane (seconda parte)', *Arte medievale,* serie 2, 8 (1994) 79–91. In 1993 Belardi had presented some details of the drainage and roofing in Giovanni Belardi, 'Considerazioni sui restauri in atto nell'abbazia delle Tre Fontane a Roma', *Arte Medievale,* serie 2, 7 (1993) 229–230.

97. Maria Letizia Mancinelli, Laura Saladino and Maria Carla Somma, 'Abbazia delle Tre Fontane. Analisi delle strutture murarie', *Arte medievale,* serie 2, 8 (1994) 93–105; and Maria Letizia Mancinelli, Laura Saladino and Maria Carla Somma, 'Indagini all'interno della chiesa dei SS. Vincenzo e Anastasio', *Arte medievale,* serie 2, 8 (1994) 107–120.

98. Roberta Caglianone and Alessandro Iazeolla, 'Prime osservazioni dal rilievo architettonico del complesso delle Tre Fontane', *Arte medievale,* serie 2, 8 (1994) 121–132.

transennae in the church windows.[99] The volume is profusely illustrated with beautiful colour photographs, some taken from the scaffolding erected by Belardi and his restoration team, which made
possible new views of the higher parts of the buildings. There are also
new architectural drawings by Belardi and by Caglianone and Iazeolla.
In *Abbazia delle Tre Fontane: il complesso, la storia, il restauro* Stefania
Quattrone discussed the history of the complex; Fra Jacques Brière
OCSO, gave a short history of the Cistercian Order, with some remarks
about cistercian architecture; Belardi reported more fully on the discoveries made during the restoration; Liliana Pozzi analysed the types
of masonry; and Claudia Tempesta gave an account of the restoration
of the frescoes.

While not all of this material can be discussed in detail here, the
most important new discoveries by Belardi will be noted; then the
results of the excavations. Next the architectonic analysis of Caglianone
and Iazeolla will be examined, especially in relation to the importance
of the north transept and the relative proportions of the church,
worked out according to the schema of Hahn. Finally, some comments
will be made on the important study by Romanini.

Belardi's work on the church was mainly connected with the roof
and the floor, but in the course of the restoration he uncovered important evidence about the overall structure and the building-history
of SS. Vincenzo e Anastasio.[100] With experience in restoring other
medieval monastic buildings at Valvisciolo and Fossanova, Belardi was
well qualified to undertake the project at Tre Fontane. He also had
access to the reports of two earlier twentieth-century restoration
campaigns at SS. Vincenzo e Anastasio, those in 1940 and in 1957–
1961, and he could identify some of the work carried out then.[101]

Belardi found differences in the way the two side aisles were constructed, perhaps suggesting that they had been built in separate
building campaigns. The roofing over the aisle vaults was fairly recent

99. Paola Rossi, 'Le transenne di finestra alle Tre Fontane. Appunti per una ricerca', *Arte Medievale*, serie 2, 8 (1994) 133–140.

100. Giovanni Belardi, 'Il restauro', *Arte Medievale*, serie 2, 8 (1994) 79–91; Giovanni Belardi, 'Il restauro architettonico', in Giovanni Belardi, Jacques Brière, Liliana Pozzi *et al.*, *Abbazia delle Tre Fontane*, 97–164.

101. See below, C. DATES AND DOCUMENTS, 1940 and 1957–1961.

and the fill inserted between the vaulting and the roof cover had caused long cracks in the vaults.

From high up on the scaffolding, Belardi could see that the walls of the south arm of the transept did not bond with those of the nave and south aisle. The south arm of the transept is still covered by a fine medieval pointed barrel vault, but the restorers uncovered a huge crack, which they repaired. Above the vault they found traces of channels in peperino stone; these led to a system of drainage and water spouts to remove rainwater from the building. This showed that the original roofing over the vault was different from the more modern terracotta tiled roof which covered the cistercian water-drainage system. From this and from traces of brick on top of the vaulting Belardi deduced that a bricked-over *extrados* originally covered the vault. In the church it was evident that the vault in the south transept sprang from a point 70 cm. higher than the springing of the corresponding vault in the north transept.[102]

In restoring the nave roof, Belardi found evidence that the nave vault had actually been built, whereas until then most architectural historians had believed that the vault had only been planned and never constructed. In the roof of the nave there was a system for removing rainwater similar to that in the transept, with channels carved in peperino connected to receptacles which emptied into external stone spouts that projected from the clerestory walls. This hydraulic mechanism was designed to work within the framework of a barrel vault, with extrados, covering the nave. The modern terracotta tiled roof above wooden beams oversailed what was left of the hydraulic system and vault. In the highest reaches of the nave walls, which—to take account of the vaulting—were 1.40 m. wide, abundant traces were found of the structural material of which the medieval vault was made. Cut bricks also revealed its outline on the inner east and west facades. From this, Belardi was able to reconstruct the height and profile of the medieval barrel vault. High up on the nave walls there were also traces of the holes used to set in place the centering on which the vault was constructed, and the associated scaffolding. It is likely that it

---

102. Belardi accounted for this in relation to the floor levels. His theories about them are discussed below.

was built in the twelfth century, fell down fairly soon after construction, and was then replaced by roofing with wooden beams. The beams now in place date from later restorations, from the eighteenth-century onwards. A beam originally close to the inner facade has now been removed because it obscured the windows; it was certainly not part of the original architectural structure of the nave. Belardi did not, of course, reconstruct the vault, but he renewed the supports for the beams on the nave walls, using modern materials and techniques.

The vaulting over the chancel and north transept arm survives. The use of the same materials show that the covering of the north arm was contemporaneous with the vaulting of the south arm of the transept. Unlike the south arm, the north arm was joined to the nave wall, but this join was, Belardi thought, part of a later reconstruction.

Belardi pointed out that the two southeastern chapels appeared to be of modern construction. They do not appear in a plan of the church until as late as 1957. (The plan, however, seems to show only the upper level of the south transept wall, with its two windows, and not the groundfloor entrances to the chapels, nor the chapels themselves. One may note that the chapels' arched openings in the east wall of the south transept are certainly medieval; it is possible that the chapels' other walls were rebuilt on the old foundations in the 1950s.)

In discussing his repaving of the church, Belardi pointed out that the floor originally sloped down to the north, towards the cloister. This resembles the planning of the abbey of Fossanova, where the slope allowed water to be drained into a cistern in the cloister. This was probably a cistercian hydraulic measure to collect water for the use of the community. At Tre Fontane Belardi also found evidence for water drainage and a system of airing the level below the floor. At some time after the Middle Ages—possibly in the nineteenth century—the church was re-paved, and the slope was 'corrected' by lowering the level of the floor on the south. A perceptible difference in height of the springing of the vault in the south and north arms of the transept may be accounted for by this 'correction' in the slope of the floor. One can also observe that the blocked 'cemetery' or 'death door' in the south wall of the south transept—which was highlighted in the restoration—had its threshold above the nineteenth-century floor level. In the south arm of the transept the foundations are visible below the rising walls, but not in the north arm. Externally, the foundations are also visible on the south side of the building. (In the restoration Belardi resurfaced the floor with terracotta paving tiles, and inserted an under-floor heating system in the presbytery, which is now the monks' choir.)

While the floor was being prepared for restoration, five small excavations were made beneath it under the direction of Professor Letizia Pani Ermini. The results of these investigations have been published by members of the excavation team: Mancinelli, Saladino, and Somma.[103] The first excavation was made in the north aisle, against the north aisle wall in the fifth bay *c.* 20 m. from the facade. Digging to a depth of 1.432 m. below the pre-restoration paving, the excavators found an airing and drainage system which they thought was part of the nineteenth-century restoration of the church floor. This system included bricks placed in pointed ridges, *a cappuccina,* rectangular brick channels, and a hole piercing the aisle wall. The excavators also found the foundations of the north aisle wall, which rises above a thicker base. The original depth at which the foundation was laid was not uncovered.

The second excavation was along the east and part of the north and south sides of the northeastern pier which divides the nave from the north aisle and transept. It uncovered a system of airing and drainage similar to that found in the first excavation. The excavators also uncovered parts of a foundation wall which seemed to underpin and link the nave piers to the eastern wall of the transept. Under the brickwork of the northeastern pier was a foundation of tufa blocks standing on a base 20–22 cm. wider on either side, of less regularly laid material.

The third excavation examined the northern and eastern sides of the first pier on the southeast, which divides the nave from the south aisle and transept. There were features similar to what had been found under the northeast pier: an analogous system of ventilation and drainage; and the underlying east-west foundation wall linking all the piers on the south, probably to the facade and the eastern wall of the transept. The pre-restoration floor was lower down, which is consistent with Belardi's understanding of the slope in the original floor of the church from south to north, towards the cloister.

103. Mancinelli, Saladino and Somma, 'Indagini all'interno della chiesa', 107–120.

The fourth excavation took place in the interior of the southwest corner of the south transept. A similar airing and draining system under the pre-restoration floor came to light, with holes in one of the outer walls of the transept. The excavation demonstrated that the nineteenth-century restorers made apertures in the external walls of the church for ventilation and drainage. The foundation of the medieval south transept walls had been laid in two parts: a lower level of roughly shaped tufa blocks, with more regular rows of tufa above an offset of *c.* 15–20 cm.

The fifth excavation, at the corner of the north transept and the north aisle wall,—after uncovering the usual system of airing and draining, at a level of 39.2 cm. below the pre-restoration floor—uncovered a wall 1.22 m. wide and going in a north-south direction. This wall, which stands beneath the western part of the west wall of the transept and part of the north aisle wall (see Plan I, wall 4), was made up of a nucleus of tufa with an accurately laid form of *opus listatum* on either side. The latter masonry, with tufa blocks of 14 x 14 cm. alternating with only one row of bricks, is typical of sixth and seventh-century construction in Rome. At a depth of 1.04 cm. the foundation of this early wall came to light, as did part of the preparation for a floor, with a small fragment of a marble paving *in situ*. The wall and the marble-encrusted floor would have belonged to a building of some importance which pre-dated the cistercian church and monastery.

Several conclusions were drawn from the data obtained in the excavations. The system of ventilation and drainage was part of the nineteenth-century attempt to deal with humidity in the church. The excavators noted slight differences in the techniques of laying the medieval foundations in the north and south of the building. The levels of the rising walls in each excavation provided evidence for the slope of the floor in the cistercian church. The wall discovered in the fifth excavation showed a connection between the present complex and an earlier, pre-existing building with a marble-encrusted floor. The wall follows the same direction, and has the same width, as the eastern wall of the cloister (Plan I, wall 4). The *opus listatum* of the lower wall is unique among the masonry types in the church of SS. Vincenzo e Anastasio. Because it may date from the sixth or seventh century, the excavators thought it could be part of the building complex of the former cilician monastery.

In a study based on an architectural survey of the church and the east range of the monastery, Roberta Caglianone and Alessandro Iazeolla concentrate on the area closest to the north arm of the transept and on the relation of the church to the monks' wing.[104] They list the major *internal* dimensions of the church:

- total length   64.22 m.
- width of nave and aisles: 20.74–20.89 m.
- height of the nave at the inner facade
  and at its connection to the transept   20.74 m.
- length of nave   43.32 m.
- width of nave   9.28 m.
- length of south aisle   42.72 m.
- width of south aisle   4.60 m.
- height of south aisle   6.65 m.
- length of north aisle   42.81 m.
- width of north aisle   4.14 m.
- height of north aisle   6.12 m.
- all piers except   1.42 m. x 1.42 m.,
  - the first from the west   1.31 m. x 1.43 m.
  - and the easternmost piers   1.90 m. x 1.42 m.
- width of the entire transept, from north to south   29.08 m.
- depth of south arm   9.40 m.
- height of south arm   11.81 m.
- depth of north arm   9.31 m.
- height of north arm   10.79 m.
- depth of northeastern chapels   4.71 m.
- width of NE chapel on north   3.27 m.
- width of NE chapel on south   4.35 m.

The authors found that no walls they examined were perfectly orthogonal. The closest approximation to a right angle was found at the northwestern corner of the north arm of the transept, which they

---

104. Caglianone and Iazeolla, 'Prime osservazioni', 121–132.

identified as a pivotal point in the plan. Most of the east-west walls of the east range of the monastery differed slightly in alignment from those in the transept of the church. Moreover, in elevation the walls are not straight, but slight variations were found at different levels. Caglianone and Iazeolla stressed that the north wall of the transept was a key element in understanding the development of the building.

Caglianone and Iazeolla discussed the dimensions of the church according to Hahn's schema of relative proportions.[105] They found the measurements according to Hahn's system fitted the facts, but with some notable discrepancies. That they included the thicknesses of the walls means that their measurements in this part of the study are larger than the internal dimensions given above.

The first major dimension (M1, the width of nave and aisles) was 22.49 m. The second measurement (M2, the depth of the transept arms and the eastern chapels) was 16.65 m. on the north and 17.10 m. on the south. These dimensions multiplied by 3 and 4 respectively should give the third major dimension, M3, the total length of the church: in the first case, M1, 22.49 m. x 3 = 67.47 m. In the second, M2, 16.65 m. x 4 = 66.60 m. on the north, and 17.10 m. x 4 = 68.40 m. on the south. (The actual *external* length was measured as 66.45 m.)

The first dimension, M1 (22.49 m.), by Hahn's system is supposed to equal the distance from the choir to the west end of the crossing, which at Tre Fontane is in fact 22.02 m., showing a discrepancy of 0.47 m. M1 (22.49 m.) is also supposed to equal the width of one transept arm plus the crossing, which here is 21.65 m. (a discrepancy of 0.84 m.) on the north, and 21.73 m. (with a discrepancy of 0.76 m.) on the south.

The second dimension, M2 (16.65 m. on the north, or 17.10 m. on the south) is meant to equal the depth of the sanctuary measured from the centre of the crossing, which at Tre Fontane is 17.76 m., a discrepancy of 1.11 m. on the north, or 0.66 m. on the south. M2, in Hahn's system, is also supposed to equal half the total width of the transept measured from the center of the crossing. Here, there are slight differences in the north and south arms—the northern measurement is 15.50 m. (with a discrepancy of 1.15 m.), the southern

105. Hahn, *Die frühe Kirchenbaukunst*, 66–82 and 314–339, and see our discussion of Hahn's theories above.

15.83 (with a discrepancy of 1.27 m.). The second dimension, M2, is also meant to equal the width of the nave plus one aisle, here 16.93 m. on the north (a discrepancy of 0.28 m.) and 17.60 m. on the south (a discrepancy of 0.50 m.).

Within Hahn's system the first and second dimensions are proportionate to each other, at 4:3. Since there are variations in the second dimension, the authors calculated an ideal measure by taking the first dimension as given and then working out algebraically what the second should be, which equals 16.87 m. This is close to the depth of the north transept and chapels (16.60 m.). In fact, the total external length of the church is 66.45 m., which when divided by 3 = 22.15 m. (which is close to the combined width of the nave and aisles (22.49 m.), with a discrepancy of only 0.34 m.) and when divided by 4 = 16.61 m. (which is almost exactly the depth of the north transept arm and the northeastern chapels).

By analysing the proportions in this way, one can identify the north transept arm again as the key element in understanding the building. This concurs with Belardi's discovery that the south arm of the transept does not bond with the crossing and south aisle, and that the southeastern chapels have been rebuilt.

Romanini revised and extended her earlier study, especially with regard to the church building and the parts of the east range erected prior to 1221.[106] Her revised discussion is more detailed and more comprehensive than that in her earlier work and in it she takes into consideration the new evidence from Belardi's restoration of the church and the exploratory excavations under the floor. She also provides an evaluation of the sculptural decoration and the use of ancient roman spolia, some previously unpublished drawings,[107] and some comparative material from other cistercian buildings. Romanini concludes the revised study with a new discussion of various rooms, such as the old sacristy, and features, such as the night and day stairs.

As in her earlier work, Romanini begins by looking at anomalies in the plan and the use made of the three types of masonry—brickwork,

---

106. Romanini, '"Ratio fecit diversum"', 1–78.

107. Some are by Seroux d'Agincourt, see Romanini, '"Ratio fecit diversum"', tavv. 61, 117, 127 and 128.

opus listatum (the term she uses in this publication), and tufelli. She admits that the bricks are mostly re-used, with only very few newly fired.[108] She still finds some walls in the monastery obliquely aligned to the church, seeing them as evidence for pre-existing buildings on the site and sometimes claiming that the *opus listatum* masonry remains from those earlier structures.[109] In her analysis, she identifies successive 'blocks' of construction, with subsidiary phases which she dates within fairly narrow margins.

The first constructional 'block' she divides into two phases. While the foundations of the church were probably outlined in their entirety at the outset, the first phase started at the crossing and included the choir, the north arm of the transept to just above the arches leading into the chapels east of it (which abut the choir), and the south arm of the transept to the same height.[110] At that time the door for transporting the dead from the church was opened in the south wall of the transept, but subsequently it was blocked. The date she assigned to this first phase is *c.* 1140–1147, from the arrival of the cistercian monks to the election of their abbot as Pope Eugenius III.[111]

The second phase of the first 'block' included construction in the east range of the monastery. The builders, however, had to take into account some pre-existing walls in *opus listatum*. Romanini identified as the 'old sacristy', *sacrestia antica,* the room west of the present sacristy—which dates from the thirteenth century. As was common in early cistercian monasteries, the twelfth-century sacristy was fairly small and probably contained the book-cupboard. This *armarium,* she suggested, could have been located under the stairs or inserted into the west wall of the sacristy. The second phase of this first construction block included the old sacristy and *armarium* just north of the northern arm of the transept, the night stairs, the western side of the chapter room, the passage, the parlour, the day stairs, and a large part

108. Romanini, '"Ratio fecit diversum"', 8.

109. For example, Romanini, '"Ratio fecit diversum"', 13–14.

110. Romanini, '"Ratio fecit diversum"', 18.

111. She gives 1147 as a cut-off date on the grounds that Bernardo Paganelli became Pope Eugenius III in that year; most authorities give 1145 as the beginning of his pontificate, e.g. Richard Krautheimer, *Rome Profile of a City, 312–1308* (Princeton: Princeton University Press, 1980) 328; Richard P. McBrian, *Lives of the Popes* (HarperSanFrancisco, 1997) 200.

of the dormitory. This section was begun around 1147 and completed by 1153, during the pontificate of Eugenius III. Between the first and second 'block', around 1153, the cloister colonnade was constructed.

In the second 'block', the crossing was completed; the north aisle of the church was constructed; the nave piers, clerestory, and pointed barrel vault were built—but the vault soon fell and was replaced by wooden roofing.[112] At the same time, the walls and vault of the north arm of the transept were completed; and the walls of the south arm were built.[113] Romanini sees this second 'block' as 'post-bernardine' architecture, dated between 1153 and 1161.[114]

In the third construction 'block', the south arm of the transept was completed;[115] the south aisle was built from the foundations and vaulted—and at the same time the north aisle was vaulted; the north range of the monastery was built; in the monks' wing the chapter room and dormitory were enlarged; and transverse arches were built across the cloister colonnade, which was then vaulted. All this was done from 1185/1191 to 1221.

Romanini proposes two new hypotheses regarding the building of the east range of the monastery. Initially, she suggests, the chapter room was only half its present size (on Plan I, the area surrounded by walls 4, 8, and half of walls 24 and 25).[116] The eastern limit of the chapter room then would have been where the columns now stand. As her reason, Romanini points out that upstairs a wall stands above the colonnade, which reaches to the highest level of the building (Plans II and III, wall 8). Romanini's hypothesis is not convincing. Walls often stand above colonnades. At the highest levels of the building there are no upward extensions of the eastern half of walls 24 and 25, nor of

112. Romanini, '"Ratio fecit diversum"', 22 and 28. Belardi's restoration work, as we noted above, has clarified the situation of the nave vault, which was certainly built, but fell down. Previously it was thought that the vault was begun, but never completed.

113. Romanini, '"Ratio fecit diversum"', 26, 25 and 31. As we noted above, the recent restoration campaign showed that the higher reaches of the north transept and the north wall of the crossing bond, which indicates that they were built at the same time; on the contrary, the vault over the south transept was added later.

114. Romanini, '"Ratio fecit diversum"', 29. She gives no evidence, however, for this clear dating.

115. Romanini, '"Ratio fecit diversum"', 25. The chapels east of the south transept are so heavily restored that it was not possible to include them in her discussion.

116. Romanini, '"Ratio fecit diversum"', 36–37 and fig. 62.

wall 7 (our Plan III). These walls, however, do extend upwards to the middle level (our Plan II). Moreover, on the groundfloor there is no clear fissure, no neat joining of the masonry where the western half of walls 24 and 25 would have been joined to the eastern half.

As her second hypothesis, Romanini proposes that the dormitory was originally only half its present width. (On our Plans I and II, its perimeter was between walls 8 and 23, and also an upward extension of wall 4 and a northern wall, which no longer exist.[117]) Again, one may express some reservations about Romanini's theory. While the recent excavations show that wall 4 stands directly above a much earlier wall, they provide no evidence that it formerly rose to the height of the dormitory. The west wall of the present dormitory is compara- tively narrow at that level and built above the vaulting of the cloister ambulatory and not above wall 4 (Plan II and Sections BB' and CC', wall 40). If Romanini's hypothesis were correct, it would have been necessary first to build an upper level of wall 4, and then subsequently to demolish it in order to widen the dormitory. This seems unneces- sarily complicated. Nor is there any evidence for such a procedure. Moreover, blocked rectangular medieval windows framed by marble slabs, visible high up in the west wall of the east range, wall 9, resemble those in the higher reaches of the east wall of the dormitory, wall 8, which were recently unblocked by Belardi to reveal painted decora- tion.[118] It is likely that these similar windows opened in the east and west sides of the medieval dormitory. Besides this, there is no reason why the dormitory could not originally have been built from wall 8 to wall 9 on our Plan II and Section CC'. The sturdy nature of the cloister colonnade, the relieving arches, and the vaulting of the ambulatory were in all probability intended to support the western side of the dormitory on the floor above.[119] It seems probable that only the diaphragm arches across the ambulatory were added in a subsequent phase. Later still, the rather thin wall 40 was built upstairs, resting on the vaulting.

117. Romanini, '"Ratio fecit diversum"', 37–42.

118. The windows in wall 9 are visible in our figs. 17, 18 and 39, while one unblocked win- dow in wall 8 is illustrated in our fig. 41. For these windows see below, A. ARCHITECTURAL DATA, wall 8 and wall 9. Belardi's campaign is discussed briefly at the end of Chapter One.

119. As pointed out by Frothingham, The Monuments of Christian Rome, 105–6, 128–129, 187 and 197.

Romanini suggests that when the dormitory was extended westwards, it was also enlarged to the north.[120] She proposes that the east range originally ended at the northern limit of the present cloister walk, but that subsequently the monks' wing was prolonged beyond that to the present north wall of the dormitory (our Plans I and II, wall 30). Although there are some variations in the thickness and direction of walls 8 and 9 north of the cloister, there are no other indications in the fabric of the building to support this hypothesis. There is no thick medieval wall surviving at the northern limit of Romanini's original reconstruction. Moreover, wall 9 is very similar in construction both north and south of the north range, except for the part of the cloister colonnade with relieving arches.

The upward extension of the highest reaches of the dormitory in tufa masonry, Romanini thinks, was part of a campaign to raise the roof of the east range, which may have coincided with the mural decoration in that part of the building.[121] This seems likely.

Romanini proposes that, when the east range was extended northwards, the north range was built. It is clear, as several authors have pointed out, that the refectory wing was built later than the monks' building.[122] There is, however, no evidence as to the date when it was added, except that, to judge by the masonry, it must have been during the twelfth century.

My study, published in 1997, considers the medieval murals at Tre Fontane which survive in fragmentary condition in the gatehouse, the narthex, and the monks' range, and their relation to the layout of the buildings.[123] The subject matter of the murals in the gatehouse and narthex was reconstructed with the help of Antonio Eclissi's drawings of 1630.[124] In the gatehouse there were early thirteenth-century paintings: Christ blessing and surrounded by the symbols of the evangelists; scenes from the siege of Ansedonia under Pope Leo III and Charlemagne, in which victory was assured by the presence of the

120. Romanini, '"Ratio fecit diversum"', 37–42.
121. *Ibid.*
122. *Ibid.*
123. Barclay Lloyd, 'The Medieval Murals', 287–348.
124. BAV, Barb. Lat. 35r–51r.

head of Saint Anastasius; a depiction of the pope and the emperor donating the property in the Maremma to the abbey; and images of the various towns ceded to S. Anastasius. Directly above the doorway leading to the abbey was a later thirteenth-century image of the Madonna and Child flanked by Saints Benedict, Paul, Bernard, and possibly Anastasius, and two smaller figures of cistercian monks. In the narthex there were images of the lives of Saints Vincent of Saragossa and Anastasius of Persia, as well as further allusions to the siege of Ansedonia and the donation of land in the Maremma. Also depicted were Saints Leonard, James, and two crowned female saints. A figure in a cistercian habit and a red cloak was probably Eugenius III, the founding abbot of the monastery and pope from 1145–1153. The date of these murals is unknown, but they were likely painted in the later thirteenth century.

Murals discovered in the monks' range in the 1960s were in three locations: the medieval monks' dormitory; along an outside wall; and in lunettes above the sacristy. All these date from the late thirteenth or early fourteenth century. By setting these murals within an architectural analysis of the building one could assert that the dormitory murals were most likely painted after the roof of the dormitory had been raised. The frescoes found on an outside wall consisted of a series of scenes, which Carlo Bertelli connected with the illuminations in a medieval Encyclopedia,[125] as well as a design including horizontal stripes. From the layout of the upper floors of the monks' wing, it was argued that the paintings were originally in two rooms, which flanked the northern end of the dormitory. These rooms may have formed part of the abbot's residence in the thirteenth century. The murals in the sacristy were originally part of the large late-thirteenth-century room that opened off the twelfth-century sacristy, and which has been restored by Belardi.[126] I suggested that that room was the abbot's chapel and had been built in the late thirteenth century.

125. Carlo Bertelli, 'L'Enciclopedia delle Tre Fontane', Paragone-Arte 20 .235 (1969) 24–49; and Aavitsland, Florilegium (above, Chapter 2, note 70).

126. Architect Giovanni Belardi has now restored this room to its original shape by removing the floor that was built between the two levels, probably in the nineteenth century.

Melinda Mihályi in 1999 published a study of the Encyclopedia, or *Vita umana,* murals, especially two that include birds and cages.[127] Literary works from the fourth to the fourteenth century help to explain the meaning of these images. The caged birds might signify souls imprisoned in the flesh, or monks in their monasteries. Mihályi compared the Tre Fontane depictions with birds in early christian and medieval mosaics, medieval french manuscripts, and with the bird imagery in the murals of the papal palace at Avignon.

Marina Righetti Tosti-Croce compared the reuse of ancient pieces of sculpture at Tre Fontane with a similar recycling of ancient carving at other cistercian churches in Italy (for example, at S. Maria di Castagnola in Chiaravalle and S. Maria in Morimondo).[128] Her study further elaborated the meaning that can be given to the use of *spolia.*

Paola Rossi looked at the medieval liturgical furnishings in the church of S. Anastasius.[129] There are now ancient capitals supporting the altar tops of the altars in the transept chapels, but they were most likely placed there in modern times. The high altar is more clearly medieval, decorated with thirteenth-century 'cosmatesque' patterns typical of twelfth and thirteenth-century work.[130] It was probably installed at SS. Vincenzo e Anastasio in 1878, when Prior Giuseppe Franchino repaved the floor.[131] The provenance of the altar is unknown and a date of 1230–1240 is assigned to it.[132]

In his study of Rievaulx abbey, Peter Fergusson refers several times to the buildings at Tre Fontane.[133] When Aelred of Rievaulx went to Rome in the spring of 1142, he likely stayed at the roman cistercian

127. Melinda Mihályi, 'Appunti sul tema iconografico della cavea cum ave inclusa', in Antonio Cadei *et al.,* edd., *Arte D'Occidente: temi e metodi: studi in onore di Angiola Maria Romanini* (Rome: Sintesi informazione, 1999) 2:891–900.

128. Marina Righetti Tosti-Croce, 'Tra spolia e modelli altomeioevali: note su alcuni episodi di scultura cistercense', *Arte d'Occidente,* 1:381–389.

129. Paola Rossi, 'Breve nota sulle problematiche relative agli arredi liturgici nella chiesa abbaziale delle Tre Fontane a Roma', *Arte d'Occidente,* 1:405–423.

130. As shown in Dorothy Glass, *Studies in Cosmatesque Pavements,* (Oxford, British Archaeological Reports, 1980) 142, n. 8.

131. The work of Prior Giuseppe Franchino is reported in Vincenzo Forcella, *Iscrizioni,* 12:319.

132. Rossi, 'Breve nota', 419.

133. Peter Fergusson and Paul Harrison, *Rievaulx Abbey: Community, Architecture, Memory* (New Haven-London: Yale University Press, 1999) 63, 73, 79, 81.

abbey, but building there would not by then have progressed very far.[134] Fergusson also saw the church at Tre Fontane as one of a series of cistercian churches in France, Sweden, Switzerland, Italy, and Germany, in which there was practically no articulation of the interior, which had a horizontal rather than a vertical emphasis.[135] Such churches possibly belong to a particular type of cistercian church building.

In the 1140s and 1150s there were two ways in which the heights of the presbytery and transept were related to the nave in cistercian churches. In one, the height of the nave, transept arms, and presbytery was the same.[136] In the other, used at Fontenay, some irish abbeys, and Tre Fontane, the presbytery and transept arms were lower than the nave.[137] At Tre Fontane this design allowed the builders to pierce the east wall of the crossing with three roundheaded windows and a circular window, in the same disposition as the windows in the east wall of the presbytery (see our figs. 7, 10, and 11). These crossing windows and the splayed windows in the clerestory of the nave illuminated the monks' choir. The two sets of windows—in the presbytery and the crossing—allowed the dawn light to enter dramatically at two levels (the sanctuary wall and the terminal wall) at the end of Vigils.[138]

Square piers, vaulted transept chapels, and splayed clerestory windows, moreover, distinguish the church of S. Anastasius. The design contrasts with that of the roman basilica of S. Maria in Trastevere, built at nearly the same time in 1138–1143. The austere simplicity at Tre Fontane may be seen as adhering to Saint Bernard's aesthetic ideals and as a criticism of papal imperialism.[139] Fergusson further suggests that, 'Tre Fontane represented the Order's adherence to the *primitiva ecclesia* of Peter rather than the *renovatio imperii romani* of S. Maria in Trastevere.'[140] This theory is attractive, for it echoes the ideals of the early Cistercians. Yet, architecturally, in plan, elevation, and decoration,

134. Fergusson and Harrison, *Rievaulx Abbey*, 63.

135. Fergusson and Harrison, *Rievaulx Abbey*, 79.

136. Fergusson gives examples of this at Preuilly (Seine-en-Marne) and Kirkstall: Fergusson and Harrison, *Rievaulx Abbey*, 73.

137. Fergusson and Harrison, *Rievaulx Abbey*, 73; for the Irish examples, R. Stalley, *The Cistercian Monasteries of Ireland* (London-New Haven: Yale University Press, 1987) 79–92.

138. Fergusson and Harrison, *Rievaulx Abbey*, 73.

139. Fergusson and Harrison, *Rievaulx Abbey*, 81, with reference to earlier literature.

140. Fergusson and Harrison, *Rievaulx Abbey*, 81.

S. Maria in Trastevere resembles the early christian basilicas of Old Saint Peter's and S. Paolo fuori le Mura in Rome, while SS. Vincenzo e Anastasio at Tre Fontane represents a break with the roman early christian tradition in favour of burgundian cistercian architecture.[141]

141. For the early christian revival in twelfth-century roman churches like S. Maria in Trastevere, see Krautheimer, *Rome,* 161–202, especially 176–178.

VII

AN ARCHITECTURAL ANALYSIS
OF THE MEDIEVAL STRUCTURES

RECENT STUDIES of SS. Vincenzo e Anastasio at Tre Fontane, Letizia Pani Ermini's excavations, and Giovanni Belardi's restoration campaigns have clarified some of the structural features of the church and monastery.[1] Architect Jeremy Blake has made survey drawings of the complex at 1:100 (Plans I, II, and III, Sections AA, BB, CC, and DD, Gatehouse: plans and section) which make possible a new architectural analysis of the buildings. On these drawings, the walls have been numbered to facilitate discussion, and the types of masonry that are accessible have been entered.[2] While building materials and masonry techniques are typical of medieval Rome, the layout of both church and monastery are almost 'classically' cistercian. In this analysis, the constituent parts of the complex will be discussed in the following order:

A. the church;

B. the east range (Wing M);

C. the north range (Wing R);

---

1. Discussed above, Chapter Six. Giovanni Belardi has not published the results of his most recent restoration of the monastery, S. Maria Scala Coeli and S. Paolo alle Tre Fontane. The main features of this campaign are outlined in Chapters One and Four. The accounts, based on a conversation with Belardi, rely on information provided by Abbot Jacques de Brière and Father Ansgar Christensen, and a visit to Tre Fontane in November, 2002.

2. The types of masonry follow those in Joan E. Barclay Lloyd, 'Masonry Techniques in Medieval Rome, c. 1080–c. 1300', *Papers of the British School at Rome* 53 (1985) 225–277.

D. the west range (Wing C);

E. the guest house (Wing O);

F. the narthex; and

G. the Gatehouse.

A. THE CHURCH

The church of SS. Vincenzo e Anastasio presents a fascinating mixture of early cistercian planning and roman medieval masonry techniques. The layout (Plan I) is typical of cistercian architecture.[3] The nave is flanked by one aisle on either side; the transept extends beyond the aisles; two rectangular chapels open off each transept arm; and the sanctuary is rectangular. This layout, typical of a small version of the 'bernardine' plan with four transept chapels, was followed by several cistercian monasteries after the rebuilding of the church at Clairvaux around 1135–1145.[4]

The church was probably planned in its entirety, but built in successive phases.[5] The recent excavations reveal that one wall of the complex (Plan I, wall 4, close to its juncture with wall 23) rises above a wall from a pre-existing structure dating from the sixth or seventh century.[6] Apart from that, the church and monastery appear to date from the twelfth century onwards.[7]

3. As outlined in Marcel Aubert, *L'architecture cistercienne en France* (Paris: Vanoest, 1947); Hanno Hahn, *Die frühe Kirchbaukunst der Zisterzienser* (Berlin: Verlag Gebr. Mann, 1957); Carolyn Malone and Walter Horn, 'Layout of the Cistercian Monastery in the Twelfth and Thirteenth Centuries', in Walter Horn and Ernest Born, *The Plan of St. Gall.* (Berkeley: University of California Press, 1979) 2:315–319 and 349–356; and Peter Fergusson, *Architecture of Solitude: Cistercian Abbeys in Twelfth-century England* (Princeton: Princeton University Press, 1984).

4. Hahn, *Die frühe Kirchenbaukunst,* 171–173, 324.

5. Angiola Maria Romanini, 'Ratio fecit diversum': la riscoperta delle Tre Fontane a Roma chiave di lettura dell'arte bernardina', *Arte Medievale,* serie 2, 8 (1994) 1–78.

6. Maria Letizia Mancinelli, Laura Saladino, and Maria Carla Somma, 'Indagini all'interno della chiesa dei SS. Vincenzo e Anastasio', *Arte Medievale,* serie 2, 8 (1994) 111–118.

7. In this we agree with Giuseppe Tomassetti, 'Della Campagna Romana', *Archivio della Società Romana di Storia Patria* 19 (1896) 148; Aristide Sartorio, 'L'abbazia cisterciense delle Tre Fontane', *Nuova Antologia* 167, settembre (1913) 50; Hahn, *Die frühe Kirchbaukunst,* 171–3 and Carlo Bertelli, 'L'enciclopedia delle Tre Fontane', *Paragone-Arte* 20.235 (1969) 42; but disagree with Arthur L. Frothingham, *The Monuments of Christian Rome* (New York: Macmillan, 1908)

The restoration of the church in 1992–1994 by Giovanni Belardi showed that the upper level of the walls of the north transept bond with the nave and north aisle, whereas those of the south transept, nave, and south aisle do not.[8] The chapels on the north are as they were built in the twelfth century, but those on the south were rebuilt in the 1950s, possibly over earlier foundations. The nave was originally vaulted, but the vault subsequently collapsed. The floor of the church appears originally to have sloped downwards from south to north towards the cloister.[9]

As it stands today, one rectangular and eight square brickwork piers separate the nave and aisles on either side. The piers sustain semi-circular arcades and high clerestory walls pierced by roundheaded splayed windows (figs. 7 and 9). The windows were located rather low down, to accommodate the pointed barrel vault which has not survived. The nave is continuous from the west front to the high east wall of the crossing (Plan I, wall 3, fig. 7). The shape of the nave vault is clear from the upper curves in the clerestory walls (Plan I, walls 20 and 21; figs. 7 and 9). Five roundheaded splayed windows and a rose window open in the west façade (Plan I, wall 5; fig. 4). At the east end of the crossing there are three round-headed splayed windows and an oculus above the arch leading into the presbytery. The aisles are low, cross-vaulted, and lit by small roundheaded splayed windows (Plan I, figs. 7 and 9).

The transept arms which extend north and south beyond the nave and aisles are lower than the nave and are covered with pointed barrel vaults (figs. 10, 11, 13 and 14). In the south transept wall (Plan I, wall 18), the cemetery door has been blocked. While in the south transept wall (Plan II, wall 18; fig. 13) there are three roundheaded splayed

105–6; 128–129; 187 and 197; Giovanni Battista Giovenale, 'Il chiostro medioevale di San Paolo fuori le Mura', *Bullettino della Commissione Archeologica Comunale di Roma* 45 (1917) 148–167; and Angiola Maria Romanini, 'La storia architettonica dell'abbazia delle Tre Fontane a Roma. La fondazione cisterciense', *Mélanges à la Memoire du Anselme Dimier* (Arbois: 1982) 3: 671–695, esp. 679–681.

8. Giovanni Belardi, Jacques Brière, Liliana Pozzi, *et al.*, *Abbazia delle Tre Fontane: il complesso, la storia, il restauro* (Rome: Edilerica s.r.l., 1995) 98–160; Giovanni Belardi, 'Considerazioni sui restauri in atto nell'abbazia delle Tre Fontane a Roma', *Arte Medievale* 2,7 (1993) 229–230; and idem., 'Il restauro dell'abbazia delle Tre Fontane', *Arte Medievale*, seroe 2,8 (1994) 79–91.

9. See the works cited in note 8.

windows, with the central one stepped above the other two, there are no windows in the north transept wall (Plan I, wall 23; fig. 14). Two roundheaded splayed windows open in the east wall of each transept arm, above the entrances to the chapels (fig. 10).

The rectangular presbytery is covered with a pointed barrel vault and has a straight east wall. Three roundheaded windows and an oculus with quatrefoil tracery (fig. 10) illuminate the sanctuary. The shapes and arrangement of these windows are repeated higher up in the east wall of the crossing (figs. 7, 10 and 11).

Four low, rectangular chapels now open east of the transept arms (figs. 10, 11 and 12). Semi-circular arches frame their entrances and the chapels are covered with pointed barrel vaults (figs. 10, 12, 14). Those on the north are each lit by a single roundheaded splayed window. Those on the south probably had similar openings. An oculus in the chapel south of the presbytery is part of a modern reconstruction.

While SS. Vincenzo e Anastasio appears to be typically cistercian, some authors have noted its roman 'basilical' layout.[10] Yet the church is very different from other twelfth-century basilicas in Rome—like SS. Quattro Coronati (1099–1116), S. Clemente (1099–*c.* 1119), S. Crisogono (1127), or S. Bartolomeo in Isola (1113 or 1163)[11]—with their colonnades and semi-circular apses. In particular it differs from S. Maria in Trastevere, erected between 1130–1143 by the founder of the cistercian abbey at Tre Fontane, Pope Innocent II (fig. 91).[12] That church was built to an early christian plan based on that of Old Saint Peter's and S. Paola fuori le Mura, but on a smaller scale.[13] A wide, low nave was flanked by one aisle on either side; these led into a transept

10. Renate Wagner-Rieger, *Die italienische Baukunst zu Beginn der Gotik* (Graz-Köln: Verlag Hermann Böhlaus, 1956–57) 2:27–30; Hahn, *Die frühe Kirchenbaukunst,* 172–173.

11. For twelfth-century churches in Rome, see Richard Krautheimer, *Rome: Profile of a City, 312–1308* (Princeton: Princeton University Press, 1980) 161–178; Peter C. Claussen, 'Renovatio Romae. Erneuerungsphasen römischer Architektur im 11. und 12. Jahrhundert', in *Rom in hohen Mittelalter,* ed. B. Schimmelpfennig and L. Schmugge (Sigmaringen: Jan Thorbecke Verlag, 1992) 87–125; Peter C. Claussen, *Die Kircken der Stadt Rome im Mittelalter, 1050–1300, A-F.* (Stuttgart: Franz Steiner Verlag, 2002).

12. For S. Maria in Trastevere, Dale Kinney, *S. Maria in Trastevere from its Founding to 1215,* unpublished Ph. D. thesis, (New York: Institute of Fine Arts: 1975). Both Tre Fontane and S. Maria in Trastevere were built by Pope Innocent II, as pointed out by Mary Stroll, *The Jewish Pope: Ideology and Politics in the Papal Schism* (Leiden: E.J. Brill, 1987) 125–126.

13. Krautheimer, *Rome,* 161–178, esp. 176–177.

no wider than the rest of the church, and a central semi-circular apse. Eleven ancient roman column shafts, with ancient bases and capitals —some taken from the Baths of Caracalla—separated the nave and aisles.[14] Two enormous granite columns with corinthian capitals and ornate impost blocks supported the triumphal arch leading from the nave to the transept, while pairs of smaller columns originally stood between the transept and the aisles. The apse, which was decorated with a blind arcade on the outside, sheltered a magnificent mosaic depicting Christ and the Blessed Virgin Mary enthroned in glory between saints and the donor pope, all set against a shimmering gold background. Around the apsidal arch, the mosaic decoration continued with huge standing figures of the prophets Isaiah and Jeremiah and the symbols of the evangelists flanking a cross in a roundel. The planning, the proportions, the roman spoils, and the figural mosaics were all very different from the design of the SS. Vincenzo e Anastasio alle Tre Fontane.

In elevation the monastery church has other features common in cistercian architecture, but virtually unknown in medieval Rome: pointed barrel vaults covered the chancel (fig. 10), the transept arms (figs. 13 and 14), and the chapels (fig. 12),[15] and originally the nave (figs. 7 and 9). This vaulting was common in early cistercian churches, but unique in roman architecture of the twelfth century. It was furthermore unusual to have groin vaulting in the aisles of a medieval roman church, although this became common later, in the fifteenth century.[16] In some early cistercian churches—like that at Fontenay which was consecrated by Eugenius III in 1147—the aisles were covered with transverse barrel vaults (fig. 92), but this was not the case at Tre Fontane.[17] The recent restoration campaign has shown that the extrados of the vaults of SS. Vincenzo e Anastasio incorporated a sophisticated system of drainage.[18] This again was different from normal practice in Rome.

14. Dale Kinney, 'Spolia from the Baths of Caracalla', *The Art Bulletin* 68.3 (1986) 379–397.
15. Sartorio, 'L'abbazia', 55.
16. This was pointed out by Gunther Urban, 'Die Kirchenbaukunst des Quattrocento in Rom', *Römisches Jarhbuch für Kunstgeschichte* 9/10 (1961/2) 73–287.
17. One wonders whether the lack of transverse barrel vaults in the aisles meant that the nave vault at Tre Fontane was not sufficiently supported.
18. Belardi, Brière, Pozzi et al., *Abbazia delle Tre Fontane*, 127–133.

The transept arms and the rectangular presbytery were built lower than the nave. Although there was a 'crossing' at Tre Fontane where the nave met the transept, there was no tower, and the roof of the nave extended straight through to the wall east of the crossing, as at Fontenay and some other cistercian churches.[19]

The exterior of the clerestory of the nave was articulated by a row of pilasters, 0.93 m. wide, one above every nave pier (fig. 8). These were in most instances connected with the drainage system discovered by Belardi;[20] they would also have strengthened the high clerestory walls, perhaps acting as narrow 'buttresses'. These 'buttresses' find some comparison in medieval Rome in the pilasters in the clerestory walls at S. Clemente and S. Maria in Trastevere in the twelfth century.[21] At S. Clemente two external 'buttresses', one on either side of the nave, rose above the central pier in each colonnade, on the lower level forming part of those piers. At S. Maria in Trastevere, a central clerestory pilaster-buttress rose directly above the nave colonnade.

Brickwork piers in the nave were unusual In Rome, where colonnades were the norm.[22] The theory that at Tre Fontane the piers enclosed columns of an earlier basilica[23] is precluded by the length of the inter-columniations, 4.60–4.90 m. centre to centre. There were no capitals at Tre Fontane, only a thin marble cornice on each pier at the springing of the arcade (figs. 7 and 9). The arches were outlined with brick voussoirs.

Although some twelfth-century churches in Rome had narrow roundheaded splayed windows in their aisles,[24] it was unusual to have them in the clerestory, as is the case at SS. Vincenzo e Anastasio. At the

19. Peter Fergusson and Stuart Harrison, *Rievaulx Abbey. Community, Architecture and Memory* (New Haven: Yale University Press, 1999) 73.

20. Belardi, Brière, Pozzi *et al., Abbazia delle Tre Fontane,* 127–133.

21. Joan E. Barclay Lloyd, *The Medieval Church and Canonry of S. Clemente in Rome,* San Clemente Miscellany, 3 (Rome: San Clemente, 1989) 38 and 107.

22. There were, however, piers in S. Lorenzo in Lucina, rebuilt in 1130, see Richard Krautheimer, *Corpus Basilicarum Christianarum Romae,* Monumenti di Antichità Cristiana, 2 Serie, 2 (Vatican City: Pontificio Istituto di Archeologia Cristiana and the Institute of Fine Arts, New York University, 1959) 2:159–184, esp. 181.

23. A suggestion hinted at by Romanini, 'La storia architettonica', 688.

24. I found these at S. Clemente, built *c.* 1118, and they can still be seen at S. Crisogono, dated 1127; see Barclay Lloyd, *S. Clemente,* 26, 38, 108, and 120. They seem narrower than those at Tre Fontane, but in all three churches the apex of their arches is very close to the eaves' line of the aisle roofs.

cistercian abbey the disposition of the windows in the facade, sanctuary, and south transept—with central openings stepped above the others (figs. 4, 7, 9, 10, 11 and 13)—is also characteristic of medieval architecture outside Rome. As was typical of early cistercian church architecture, the windows at the east end of the nave echo those in the chancel.

The proportions of the church are un-roman. The nave at its apex is 20.74 m. high, its width (between the inner faces of the piers) is only *c.* 9.20 m.; it is little more than twice as high as it is wide. Such steep proportions are most unlike the wide, low naves of roman basilicas, even those of the Middle Ages.[25] The highest point of the nave is approximately equal to the total internal width of the nave and aisles.[26]

Masonry

While the church of SS. Vincenzo e Anastasio exhibits many cistercian features, most of the masonry techniques used in the building are typical of medieval Rome. The church is built of three types of masonry, all of them common in the city in the twelfth century.

Because the medieval slope in the church's floor was evened out in the late nineteenth century, it is possible to see the foundation walls in the south transept.[27] In the recent excavations directed by Letizia Pani Ermini, moreover, some of the foundation walls were uncovered.[28] Their masonry is a kind of *opus caementicium,* made up of uneven rows of roughly cut stone. This resembles the foundations of the twelfth-century basilica of S. Clemente, visible today in the excavations under the church.[29]

---

25. At S. Clemente the proportions of height to width of the nave of the early christian basilica were 13:15 (or nearly 4:5); of the medieval church 14.5:11 (or nearly 3:2), Barclay Lloyd, *S. Clemente,* 125, n. 2.

26. Further information on the dimensions of the church is given below under the heading *Setting Out.*

27. The floor was lowered 55–65 cm. beside the facade (Plan I, wall 5) and in the south transept, walls 4 and 18; see A. ARCHITECTURAL DATA, Walls 4, 5 and 18. According to Forcella the floor was raised in 1878, but he may have meant only the pavement of the sanctuary, see below, C. DATES AND DOCUMENTS, 1878.

28. Mancinelli, Saladino, and Somma, 'Indagini all'interno della chiesa', 107–120.

29. Barclay Lloyd, 'Masonry Techniques in Medieval Rome', *Papers of the British School at Rome* 53 (1985) 243 and 276 and Barclay Lloyd, *S. Clemente,* 16–17.

The rising walls of the cistercian church are constructed either of medieval *opus listatum*—rows of tufa blocks alternating with one, two, or three courses of bricks—or of twelfth-century brickwork with no *falsa cortina* pointing except between the voussoirs of arches.[30] These two types of masonry were common in late eleventh and twelfth-century Rome and they were often used together in the same building, or even in the same wall.[31] One cannot distinguish different phases of construction at SS. Vincenzo e Anastasio by the use of *opus listatum* and brickwork.[32] The whole fabric appears to date from the twelfth century.

One feature of the masonry is unusual—the corners of the church are reinforced with tufa quoins, e.g. in walls 1, 4, and 19.[33] This can be seen in cistercian architecture in France, for example at Le Thoronet,[34] but SS. Vincenzo e Anastasio is the only building in medieval Rome I know where this element is found.

The bricks used in the construction of SS. Vincenzo e Anastasio vary in length, height, and colour. As in most other medieval roman buildings, it is likely that they are all ancient spoils. This is particularly true of the long voussoirs which frame the arches of the crossing and which are mostly roman *bipedales* or *sesquipedales*, i.e. bricks *c.* 60 or *c.* 45 cm. long, although often two bricks make up one voussoir (figs. 7, 9, 10, 13 and 14). Similarly the shorter voussoirs in the nave arcades appear to be re-used ancient roman bricks (figs. 7 and 9). It is possible that the brickwork in the choir, transepts, chapels, and nave was intended to give the interior of the sanctuary a more 'finished' appearance. This might explain why the south and west walls of the south arm of the transept were constructed of *opus listatum* externally, but faced with brickwork inside.[35]

---

30. For the dating of this masonry, Barclay Lloyd, 'Masonry', 225–244.

31. Barclay Lloyd, 'Masonry', 239–241 and 273–274.

32. Such theories are summed up in Romanini, 'La storia architettonica', 675–679.

33. A. ARCHITECTURAL DATA, Walls 1, 4 and 19. This was pointed out by Pio F. Pistilli, 'Considerazioni sulla storia architettonica dell'abbazia romana delle Tre Fontane nel duecento'. *Arte Medievale* 2 serie, 6, 1 (1992) 170.

34. François Cali, *L'Ordre Cistercien*. (Paris: Arthaud, 1972) figs. 5 and 6.

35. Often walls in medieval Rome were built of brickwork on one side and *opus saracinescum* on the other, see Barclay Lloyd, 'Masonry', 231 and 244. This is a rare case of brickwork on one side and *opus listatum* on the other.

As Romanini has pointed out, there are some anomalies in the walls of the transept.[36] The masonry of the north and south walls of the transept is different (compare figs. 13 and 14). The south wall (Plan I, wall 18) is built of medieval *opus listatum* outside, twelfth-century brickword with no *falsa cortina* pointing inside, and with tufa quoins in the corners. In the north transept wall (Plan I, wall 23) there are significant changes of masonry (fig. 14).[37] The western part of this wall is constructed of *opus listatum,* which—approximately 3 m. from wall 3 —seems to stop in almost a straight line from the vault of the transept down to about a third of the height of the wall, where it broadens in a rough diagonal. Between wall 3 and this line, wall 23 is built of twelfth-century brickwork with no *falsa cortina* pointing. Romanini saw this as an indication that the wall in *opus listatum* existed before the brickwork part of the wall was built,[38] which is a fair assumption. Furthermore, a short distance east of the stairs leading from the transept into the monastery, within the stretch of *opus listatum* masonry, there was another brickwork 'patch' or 'fill'. From all this Romanini originally concluded that the church was constructed in different phases, with the cistercian east end having been added to part of an earlier wall, perhaps from the eighth-century.[39] While the western wall of the north arm of the transept stands on part of a sixth or seventh-century wall,[40] the layout of the pre-existing building did not shape the almost classically cistercian plan of the church. The anomalies may be more clearly explained if one considers wall 23 as part of the east range of the monastery.

Blake's architectural survey drawings of the church and monastery help to clarify the changes of masonry in the north wall of the transept (Plans I and II, wall 23; and fig. 14). The fill near the night stairs is clearly the blocking of a doorway, the rest of which survives as a deep niche or cupboard in the old sacristy (Plan I). Plans I and II also show that the change of masonry in wall 23 occurs at the eastern

36. Romanini, 'La storia architettonica', 671–695.

37. Romanini, 'La storia architettonica', 689–694.

38. Romanini, 'La storia architettonica', 691–694.

39. Romanini published a clear black and white photograph, which shows the masonry, her fig. 545, and discussed the masonry in Romanini, 'La storia architettonica', 689–694; there is a colour illustration, in Romanini, '"Ratio fecit diversum"', fig. 11 (compare our fig. 14).

40. Mancinelli, Saladino, and Somma, 'Indagini all'interno della chiesa', 111–118.

limit of wall 8, which is one of the major walls of the east range of the monastery. One may conclude from this that the twelfth-century core of Wing M was already standing when the Cistercians began setting out their church. The east end of the church was added, not to a pre-existing basilica, but to the existing east range of the monastery. This would agree with the claim by Arnold that Pope Innocent II (1138–43) constructed monastic buildings but merely restored a church at Tre Fontane when he founded the cistercian monastery.[41]

Setting out

The Cistercians were famous for their modular planning and their use of square and rectangular spaces. In the mid thirteenth-century, Villard de Honnecourt characterized the layout of cistercian churches as 'ad quadratum', 'made up of squares'.[42] His drawing of a cistercian church shows a grid of lines, forming squares and rectangles in a cross-shaped plan.[43] In explaining how the Cistercians set out their buildings, David Walsh noted, furthermore, that in France and England they seem to have made their measurements in roman feet,[44] and it is very likely that at the abbey of S. Anastasius they used this roman measure.[45]

Twelfth-century builders seem not to have used carefully measured, scaled architectural drawings, but relied for the most part on the practical experience of a master builder.[46] The medieval plans that have

41. See below, C. DATES AND DOCUMENTS, c. 1140 (3).

42. Paris, Bibliotèque Nationale, MS fr. 19.093, fol. 14v.

43. It is often illustrated; see for example, Terryl N. Kinder, Cistercian Europe (Grand Rapids: Eerdmans-Kalamazoo: Cistercian Publications, 2002) 171 (L'Europe Cistercienne [Paris: Zodiaque, 1997] 169.)

44. David A. Walsh, 'Measurement and Proportion at Bordesley Abbey'. Gesta 19.2 (1980) 109–113; and idem., 'An Architectural Study of the Church'. Bordesley Abbey II. British Series 3. edd. S. M. Hirst and S. M. Wright (Oxford: British Archaeological Reports, 1983) 222–225. See also Eric Fernie, 'Historical Metrology and Architectural History'. Art History 1.4 (1978) 383–399, for various measures used in the Middle Ages.

45. In Rome the roman foot is usually calculated at 29.56 cm.

46. Robert Branner, 'Villard de Honnecourt, Reims, and the Origin of Gothic architectural Drawing', in The Engineering of Medieval Cathedrals, Studies in the History of Civil Engineering 1, ed. Lynn T. Courtenay (Aldershot: Ashgate, 1997) 63–80, at 64. The same is claimed for Middle Byzantine Master Builders by Robert Ousterhout, Master Builders of Byzantium (Princeton: Princeton University Press, 1999) 58–85.

survived date from the late thirteenth-century onwards.[47] When a new cistercian monastery was to be built in the first half of the twelfth century, we note that Saint Bernard did not provide a plan, but he sent a monk with expertise in laying out churches and monasteries, like Achard or Geoffrey d'Ainai. Such a monk may have carried a drawing with him, and probably some notes, but no such documentation has survived. What is evident is the similarity in layout of many 'bernardine' churches. They seem to be variants on a 'standard plan' whose basic form and proportions were known to cistercian master builders.

Medieval churches were usually set out on site using ropes, a measuring rod, large compasses, stones or pegs.[48] Dimensions could be painted on the rope and possibly on the ground as well. Stones or pegs were used to mark important points, such as the location of corners, walls, piers, or columns. Using this method the builders could set out the plan of the building on site. The ropes could be stretched out straight, or placed diagonally, or used to draw a circle.[49]

The measuring rod was useful for measuring smaller dimensions. Medieval masons also used an L-square, though only for squaring stone, rather than securing right angles in the plan of the building. For these a system of geometry was needed. Indeed, it is clear that medieval master builders set out churches using quite complex geometry, with modular proportions, the golden section, and quadrature (geometrical relationships, based on inscribed and rotated squares and their diagonals).[50]

---

47. See for example the discussion of medieval architectural drawings in Wolfgang Schöller, 'Le Dessin d'Architecture à l'époque gothique'; Werner Müller, 'Le dessin technique à l'époque gothique'; and Valerio Ascani, 'Le dessin d'Architecture medieval en Italie' in *Les Batisseurs des Cathedrales Gothiques,* ed. Roland Recht (Strasbourg: Editions des Musées de Strasbourg, 1989), 227–235; 237–254; and 255–277; and in Nigel Hiscock, *The Wise Master Builder: Platonic Geometry in Plans of Medieval Abbeys and Cathedrals* (Aldershot: Ashgate, 2000) 171–203. For drawings of smaller parts of cistercian buildings, see, however, Peter J. Ferguson, 'Notes on two Cistercian engraved designs', *Speculum* 54 (1979) 1–17.

48. Branner, 'Villard de Honnecourt', 64; Ousterhout, *Master Builders,* 58–62.

49. The use of ropes to set out the monastic church, Cluny Three, begun in 1088, is shown in Paris, Bibliothèque Nationale MS lat. 17716, fol. 43, where two miniatures illustrate the dream of Gunzo: see Kenneth John Conant, 'Mediaeval Academy Excavations at Cluny, IX: Systematic Dimensions in the Buildings', *Speculum* 38 (1963) 1–45 and plate IX; and Carolyn M. Carty, 'The Role of Gunzo's Dream in the Building of Cluny III'. *Gesta* 27 (1988) 113–123.

50. In early medieval churches in England the chancel was often in the form of a square, the diagonal of which was rotated forty-five degrees to produce the width of the nave, which

In antiquity Pythagoras demonstrated that in a right-angled triangle the square on the hypotenuse (diagonal) is equal to the sum of the squares on the other two sides. When both shorter sides are equal, as in a square, the squared proportions are $1 + 1 = 2$, or $1:\sqrt{2}$, the $\sqrt{2}$ being 1.4142.[51] The roman architect, Vitruvius, further pointed out, following Plato, that when the diagonal of one square was used to create the sides of a second square, the latter would be double the area of the first. He also noted that to set out right-angled triangles, the ratio of 3:4:5 could be used.[52] While medieval architects frequently employed the ratios $1:\sqrt{2}$ and 3:4:5 in their buildings, they probably relied in all of this more on practical experience and training than on knowledge of ancient geometry.

It is my belief that the setting out of the cistercian church of S. Anastasius began in the corner made by walls 23 and 4 (Plan I), since wall 23 was already standing. The lower part of wall 4, built in the sixth or seventh century, may also have survived south of the east range in the foundations, where its center may have been accessible to the medieval builders. The builders probably stretched their rope

---

was then often tripled to give its length. For this see Eric Fernie, 'A beginner's guide to the study of architectural proportions and sytems of length'. *Medieval Architecture and its Intellectual Context: Studies in Honour of Peter Kidson.* Eric Fernie and Paul Crossley edd. (London and Ronceverte: The Hambledon Press, 1990) 229–237; Nicola Coldstream, *Medieval Craftsmen: Masons and Sculptors* (London: British Museum Press, 1991), 24–39; Jean Gimpel, *The Cathedral Builders* (Salisbury: Michael Russell, 1983) 75–97; Thomas W. Lyman, 'Opus ad triangulum versus opus ad quadratum in medieval five-aisled churches' in Xavier Barral I Altet, ed., *Artistes, Artisans et Production artistique au moyen Age* (Paris: Picard, 1987) 2:203–219; Lon R. Shelby, 'The geometrical knowledge of mediaeval master masons'; Lon R. Shelby and Robert Mark, 'Late Gothic Structural Designs in the "instructions" of Lorenz Lechler' and Eric Fernie, 'The Ground Plan of Norwich Cathedral' in *The Engineering of Medieval Cathedrals,* 27–53; 87–105; and 107–116. For more complex underlying systems of quadrature and triangulation, as well as the use of polygons, concentric circles and the golden section in cistercian church plans in Wolfgang Wiemer, 'Die computergestützte Proportionsanalyse am Beispiel con Planaufnahmen und Entwürfen von Kirchgrundrissen'. *Architectura* 28.2 (1998) 107–155. For an analysis of the underlying geometry and its meaning from antiquity to the Middle Ages, see Hiscock, *The Wise Master Builder,* especially 3–22 and 171–203. For more complex ways of setting out medieval churches, see Hiscock, *The Wise Master Builder,* especially 3–22 and 171–203, with an analysis of the underlying geometry and its meaning from antiquity to the Middle Ages.

51. Fernie, 'A beginner's guide', 230, points out that the proportions are related to the ratio of a side of a square to its diagonal, or 1:1.4142.

52. Vitruvius, *The Ten Books on Architecture,* Book IX. 5–7, translated by Morris Hicky Morgan (New York: Dover Publications, 1960), 252–253.

along wall 4 from the centre of wall 23 to the center of wall 18 (the south wall of the transept). This measures 30.01 m., or 101.82 roman feet.[53]

With the rope in place, the builders could mark the location of the center of the transept, as well as the center of walls 22, 21, 20, 19 and 18 along wall 4. From the centre of wall 23 to the center of wall 22 measures 4.55 m. (15.4 roman feet). From there to the center of wall 21 is 5.35 m. (18.09 roman feet). From there to the center of wall 20 measures 10.65 m. (36.03 roman feet). From there to the center of wall 19 is 5.70 m. (19.28 roman feet); and from there to the center of wall 18 is 3.8 m. (12.85 roman feet). There are some discrepancies in the distances between walls 20 and 18. When the measurement is taken from the center of wall 20 to the south face and not the center of wall 19, the result is 5.35 m. (18.09 roman feet). If the final dimension is taken from the north face and not from the center of wall 19, it measures 4.3 m. (14.5 roman feet). These dimensions are closer to those between walls 21 and 22, and 22 and 23, but the south aisle is about 0.30 m. wider than the north aisle.

Despite the discrepancies, the dimensions from wall 23 to wall 18, expressed to the nearest roman foot, shows that these divisions of wall 4, follow the sequence: 13.50, 18, 36, 18 and 13.50. Now 18 is half of 36, which means that each aisle to the nave is ideally in the ratio of 1:2. The internal width of the nave and aisles is *c.* 72 roman feet. The ratio of this dimention to the full length of the transept, which is 101.82 roman feet, is $1:\sqrt{2}$.

Moreover, from the corner of walls 23 and 4 to the centre of the corner between walls 1 and 20 is 30.01 m., or 101.82 roman feet. Similarly, from the corner of walls 4 and 18 to the corner of walls 1 and 21 measures 30.1 m. or 101.82 roman feet. These measurements are equal to the length of the transept, measured along wall 4. The diagonals

---

53. The dimensions given in metric figures have been scaled from our 1:100 survey drawings and they may therefore have some slight discrepancies. The centers are those of the rising walls, not the foundations, which were wider. This too may result in inaccuracies, as the recent excavations demonstrated that the rising walls were built with a setback of between 15 and 22 cm. from the outer faces of the foundations, as pointed out by Mancinelli, Saladino, and Somma, 'Indagini all'interno della chiesa', 107–120.

cross in the presbytery at a point that is level with the east face of wall 2, the eastern wall of the transept chapels. Perhaps they were used to locate that wall and the depth of the presbytery. From the point where they intersect to the center of the façade, wall 5, measures 60 m., or 202.98 roman feet. This is almost exactly double the length of the transept, which is 101.82 roman feet.

The crossing is almost square, with sides approximately 10.65 m. or 36 roman feet long. The diagonal is very close to 50.9 roman feet, which stands in relation to the internal width of the nave and aisles (*c.* 72 roman feet) in the ratio of 1:√2.

In all this it seems the Cistercian plan was based on three related squares: one with a side of 36 and a diagonal of 50.9; the next with a side of 50.9 and a diagonal of 72 and the third with a side of 72 and a diagonal of 101.82. Each square doubles the area of the next and the principal dimensions are in the ratio of 1:√2.

The depth of the north transept arm from the middle of wall 4 to the center of wall 3 is 10.50 m. (35.52 roman feet). The total depth of the transept including the chapel is 16.10 m. (54.47 roman feet), or approximately three times 18.09 roman feet.[54] The dimensions of the southern transept arm are a little different from those of the northern transept arm. This may be due to the fact that the southern transept was built last, as is shown by the fact that its wall 4 does not bond in its upper reaches with wall 20.[55]

The length of the nave from the center of wall 4 to the center of wall 5 is 43.6 m. (147.5 roman feet), i.e. exactly twice as long as the width of the nave and aisles, when one includes half of each outer wall. The width of the nave and aisles is in the ratio of 1:2 to the length of the nave.

54. This means that the transept arm is approximately 4.5 roman feet wider than the length from the center of the crossing to the centre of wall 23. Hahn, *Die frühe Kirchenbaukunst*, 66–78 proposed that these measurements formed a square, which is not the case at Tre Fontane.

55. Belardi, Brière, Pozzi *et al.*, *Abbazia delle Tre Fontane*, 98–160; Belardi, 'Considerazioni sui restauri', 229–230; and a longer article, Belardi, 'Il restauro dell'abbazia delle Tre Fontane', 79–91. Discrepancies in the southern transept arm were also noted by Roberta Caglianone and Alessandro Iazeolla, 'Prime osservazioni dal rilievo architettonico del complesso delle Tre Fontane'. *Arte Medievale*, serie 2, 8 (1994) 121–132.

Most of the piers are 1.40 m. (4.73 roman feet) square. The excavations have shown, however, that the piers stood on foundation walls 30–44 cm. (1.01–1.49 roman feet) wider than this.[56] Only at the east and west ends of the nave do the piers vary in size. Those at the crossing are 1.4 m. by 1.95 m. (4.73 by 6.6 roman feet). The difference in length was needed to support the large arches, which span the crossing in a west-east direction. The bays vary in length from 4–4.9 m. (13.53–16.58 roman feet).

In the Middle Ages profound meanings were given to the various shapes and key dimensions of a building.[57] While the higher forms of medieval geometry and numerology are beyond the scope of this study, the scaled dimensions discussed here confirm the fact that the cistercian builders did use geometric systems and modular proportions in roman feet for setting out the church of SS. Vincenzo e Anastasio. The result was a harmoniously proportioned building which facilitated prayer and contemplation.

B. THE EAST RANGE (WING M)

The Twelfth Century

The core of the east range of the monastery, as we noted above, appears to have been built in the twelfth century, before the church was begun.[58] When the night stairs were constructed, it was modified to connect the dormitory with the church. At the same time a small cell was perhaps built for the abbot. The monastery buildings were then extended in the thirteenth or early fourteenth century. One can trace the building phases on the survey drawings (Plans I, II, and III, Sections AA', BB', CC', and DD') and through changes of masonry.

The part of wall 23 built in *opus listatum* between walls 4 and 8 seems to have been standing when the church was set out.[59] Although

---

56. Mancinelli, Saladino and Somma, 'Indagini all'interno della chiese', 107–120.
57. As explained by Hiscock, *The Wise Master Builder.*
58. Discussed under *Masonry* above.
59. This is explained above in the discussion of the masonry of the church.

its masonry in the old sacristy is not open to view, wall 8, north of wall 25, is all built of medieval *opus listatum,* datable to the twelfth century (figs. 32 and 33; and Plan I). Indeed, it is clear that wall 8 was the original eastern limit of Wing M—except for the stretch where it crosses the chapter room—CR—over two columns. There the building originally extended eastwards to wall 7 (Plans I and II, walls 24, 7 and 25).[60] Walls 2 and 7 north of walls 23 and 25, and walls 24 and 28, east of walls 7 and 8 respectively, were built of *opus saracinescum,* and hence at a later date, in the thirteenth or fourteenth century.

The monks' wing at its northern end (Plan I and Section AA') is strengthened by two sloping buttresses, extensions of walls 8 and 9 (figs. 38 and 39).[61] Moreover, from the east, an arched buttress, an extension of wall 30 and 3.20 m. long, further strengthens the northeast corner. At the other end of the east range another sloping buttress is visible high up in the centre of wall 23 (fig. 17).[62] It is likely, then, that the roughly diagonal lower part of the *opus listatum* at the original eastern edge of wall 23 (fig. 14) is another buttress, built to reinforce that corner of the eastern wing of the monastery. From this, one may conclude that the east end of the church was added to the earliest part of *Wing M,* which was already standing.

This would agree moreover with the documentary evidence, which claims that Pope Innocent II constructed monastic buildings and restored the church *c.* 1140.[63] The east range appears to be very cistercian in plan and was probably newly built at that time. The church Pope Innocent restored may have been any of the three already on the site.[64] Later, the cistercian monks added a typically cistercian church to the monastic buildings provided by the medieval pope.

60. In this we disagree with Angiola Maria Romanini, '"Ratio fecit diversum", 36–37.

61. The buttress for wall 9 was later reinforced, as can be seen in our fig. 39.

62. It is well illustrated in Romanini, '"Ratio fecit diversum"', 27, fig. 45. Romanini, '"Ratio fecit diversum"', 41, believed this buttress had the function of covering a join between the original south wall of the dormitory and its later westward extension, but, like the buttresses at the northern end of the east range, it seems more likely this buttress was built to support the high structure.

63. See below, C. DATES AND DOCUMENTS, *c.* 1140 (3).

64. Besides the martyrium of Saint Paul, there was the oratory of S. Maria and the basilica of Saint John the Baptist, mentioned in the earlier documents, see below, C. DATES AND DOCUMENTS, 713 and 807.

A few other details seem to confirm that the east range was constructed in a different phase from the east end of the church. Wall 4, where it crosses Wing M, is thicker than it is in the north transept of the church—1.22 m. in the old sacristy, but only 0.85 m. in the north transept. This is the wall which was found in recent excavations to stand upon an earlier one, 1.22 m. wide.[65] The portion of wall 4 in the old sacristy has the same width as the earlier wall, which suggests that it was built directly above it. In the church—where the excavation took place—the rising wall is narrower by 37 cm. This may indicate a different phase of construction. It is also possible that the change is so great because the western edge of the staircase was built against the west wall of the transept and the earlier structure formed part of its footing. In his 1998–2000 restoration Giovanni Belardi discovered under the arches of the night stairs a door and some steps which gave access from the eastern cloister walk to the old sacristy. The door may have been the original entrance to Wing M before the church was built.

Brickwork in the east range—in wall 9, for example—is often marked with *falsa cortina* pointing, but in the church this only occurs between voussoirs and around arches. Moreover, in Wing M there are no quoins to reinforce the corners of the building, as there are in the church. These variations in masonry may indicate that two different gangs of twelfth-century masons constructed the monks' wing of the monastery and the medieval church.

It seems, then, that the earliest phase of the east range—datable to the twelfth century—is the oldest part of the monastic complex as it stands today,[66] and pre-dates the east end of the church. As originally built, wall 8 was its eastern limit, except for the chapter room, where the building extended eastwards to wall 7, which was also constructed in medieval *opus listatum*—as were walls 24 and 25 to the north and south of that room.[67] The original western limit of Wing M was wall 9,

65. Mancinelli, Saladino and Somma, 'Indagini all'interno della chiesa dei SS. Vincenzo e Anastasio', 111–118.

66. This was clearly seen with regard to the cloister by Frothingham, *The Monuments*, 105–106, 128–129, 187 and 197, and Giovenale, 'Il chiostro', 148–167.

67. As we noted above, there is no indication in walls 24 and 25 of more than one phase of construction, as was suggested by Romanini, '"Ratio fecit diversum"', 36 and 37.

also built of *opus listatum,* except for the cloister colonnade with its spoils of ancient roman column shafts (figs. 21 and 22) and its piers, relieving arches, and intervening wall, all of which were constructed in twelfth-century brickwork often marked with *falsa cortina* pointing (fig. 20). Frothingham pointed out that this part of the wall was made especially strong—with heavy pieces of column and its 'blind arcade' —to support an upper storey.[68] Romanini, on the other hand, thought that the cloister colonnade was originally single-storeyed and that at first the dormitory was a long narrow room laid out between our walls 4, 8, 23 and a point corresponding to the northern end of the cloister ambulatory; in a later phase of construction, she thought, the dormitory was extended westwards to our wall 9 and northwards to our wall 30.[69] This extension would have been possible only after the demolition of the upper level of wall 4 and Romanini's suggested northern wall. Since there is simply no evidence for this, it seems more likely that the cloister ambulatory was not just a portico built against the rest of the building, but an integral part of the double-storeyed structure.

The east range was originally delimited to the south by wall 23, with two buttresses. At the northern end stood wall 30, reinforced by three buttresses on the north and east. On the groundfloor beyond that, wall 31, judging by its thickness, could have been medieval.[70]

Upstairs was the dormitory (Plan II, D), which Belardi has restored by clearing the upper floor of its narrow, modern partitions between walls 8, 23, 40 and 30.[71] Wall 40 is clearly narrower than walls 8 and 9, and it rests, not on wall 4, but on the vaulting of the cloister ambulatory (Sections BB' and CC'). It appears to be a later partition. One must also exclude the row of cells and other rooms built on a higher level along the east of wall 9 (Plan III and Sections BB' and CC'). It seems likely that walls 8, 23, 9 and 30 originally delimited the dormitory (fig. 89).

68. Frothingham, *The Monuments,* 197.

69. Romanini, '"Ratio fecit diversum"', 21, 37–42.

70. We have not been able to examine its masonry. Wall 32, further north, was built in the late nineteenth or early twentieth century.

71. Belardi's latest restoration has been described briefly at the end of Chapter I. The partitions he removed appear on our Plan II.

East of the dormitory was a much smaller rectangular room (fig. 89 and Plan II, X) surrounded by walls 8, 25, 7, and 24. Structurally this room stood over the eastern part of the chapter room (Section BB'). Probably it communicated with the dormitory through one or two doors, possibly where there are now two deep niches in wall 8. The function of this room is unknown; perhaps it served as an infirmary.

The original dormitory windows can be seen in wall 9 from the cloister garth (fig. 18). There is a row of small medieval rectangular openings, each having a marble lintel and brick voussoirs above; these were formerly blocked, but were reopened by Belardi in 1998–2000. Higher still there are two larger rectangular medieval marble-framed windows with voussoirs in a flat relieving arch on top. A third, marble-framed window of the same type can be seen high up in wall 9 from north of the refectory range, Wing R (fig. 39). Lower down to the left is another small, blocked window of the type seen from the garth. Other rectangular dormitory windows survive in wall 8 (Plan II and fig. 41); they were recently opened by Belardi to reveal traces of fresco decoration.[72] From the modern terrace along the east of Wing M (Plan III and figs. 49 and 50), one can make out traces of two of these blocked medieval openings, one on either side of the buttress.[73]

From the cloister garth and from the terrace, it is clear that the dormitory walls were raised in height—approximately 1.30–1.80 m.—in the thirteenth or fourteenth century, since the *opus listatum* masonry changes to *opus saracinescum* (see Sections AA', BB', and CC' and fig. 18).[74] The original dormitory walls would have been 6.00–6.50 m. high on the east and west.

On the groundfloor (Plan I), wall 4 forms the eastern side of the cloister walk in Wing M. From south to north doorways open into the old sacristy, the chapter room, and the vaulted passageway. The first two openings were originally somewhat further north.[75] The chapter

72. They were referred to above at the end of Chapter One.
73. See below, A. ARCHITECTURAL DATA, Wall 8. They are clearly visible in Romanini, '"Ratio fecit diversum"', figs. 65 and 68.
74. See below, A. ARCHITECTURAL DATA, Wall 8.
75. For the exact location of the original openings, see A. ARCHITECTURAL DATA, Wall 4. Romanini, referring to a drawing of Seroux d'Agincourt, showed that the chapter room door has changed in shape and size; and Romanini *et al.* have reconstructed the location and form

room has two triple-light windows opening onto the cloister. Their arcades are 1.335 m. high and they are each subdivided by two pairs of twin colonnettes with medieval ionic capitals and bases (fig. 30). Their arcades are surrounded by brick voussoirs and there is some brick-work with *falsa cortina* pointing above and beside the windows. While Romanini thinks the brickwork was a later insertion, it is just as plausible to think that it was part of the original structure.[76]

Against wall 4 in the cloister piers were built which partly blocked the chapter room windows and the original doorway into the old sac-risty (Plan I and figs. 25 and 30). They must be part of a later building phase, although at least three of them—the second, third, and fourth from the church—are clearly medieval.[77] The piers may have been inserted to strengthen this part of the building shortly after its con-struction. Romanini thought these piers were built when the cloister ambulatory was vaulted and the dormitory enlarged.[78] If the piers and vaults were built at the same time, it is hard to see why the eastern piers obstruct the door to the old sacristy and the windows of the chapter room. The vaulting could surely have been built in a way that avoided this. If, on the other hand, the piers were built to sustain the diaphragm arches, which were inserted after the ambulatory vaulting was already in place, then their awkward position can be explained, because it would have been necessary to take into account the form of the pre-existing vaults. At its northern end wall 4 now crosses a vaulted space to wall 30. Since this part of the interior has been modernised, it is not clear what the layout was in the Middle Ages.

Most of the groundfloor of the east range was vaulted in the Middle Ages (Plan I, Wing M). In the old sacristy, the vaulting has a strange zig-zag effect, but is clearly medieval. The chapter room is covered with six medieval cross vaults. The passageway north of the chapter room is covered with a groin vault which could be medieval. The four cross-vaults in the large northern room are modern, but they may

---

of the door to the old sacristy, and give two alternative reconstructions of it, Romanini, '"Ratio fecit diversum"', 36; and 55–58.

76. Romanini, 'La storia architettonica', 682–3; and Romanini, '"Ratio fecit diversum"', 10–12.

77. See below, A. ARCHITECTURAL DATA, Wall 4.

78. Romanini, '"Ratio fecit diversum"', 37–38 and fig. 62.

have replaced medieval vaulting. This vaulting was probably considered a suitable support for the upper storey.[79]

The old sacristy stood beside the church. The deep niche in wall 23 marked a doorway into the transept. In wall 24 there are also two small niches (fig. 26). As Romanini has noted, this little room probably served as a sacristy before the new sacristy was built further east in the thirteenth century. It may also have held a cupboard, or *armarium,* to contain the monastery's collection of books.[80]

In the chapter room the system of six vaults is now supported by two ancient columns sustaining ancient ionic capitals, one of which is partly recut. The impost over the southern column and some of the brickwork above it are part of a modern repair.[81] The large windows in wall 7 are modern substitutes for two smaller double-light openings.[82] Nonetheless, the plan of the chapter room is typically cistercian.[83] So is its position within the overall layout of the monastery. It is likely to have had broad steps for seating set out against the north, east and south walls. Seroux d'Agincourt's sketch of the room shows a low arched doorway, which preceded the present over-restored one (fig. 29).

A vaulted corridor or slype next to the chapter room—like the one at Tre Fontane—was a feature of most medieval cistercian houses. It was usually followed by a parlour, the day stairs, and the monks' room and/or novitiate. At the end of the monks' building and furthest away from the church was often the monks' latrine. At SS. Vincenzo e Anastasio the northern part of the east range has been modernised and the layout has probably been changed.

---

79. At S. Clemente parts of the building, which had an upper storey, were often vaulted on the lower floors, Barclay Lloyd, *S. Clemente,* 22–24.

80. In many cistercian monasteries it was customary to have the *armarium* in a small room near the cloister. Often the books were kept in a cupboard under the night stairs.

81. Romanini, 'La storia architettonica', 684, n. 82, says that this column and its capital were placed there in modern times, in which case this would be a modern restoration of the original arrangement, in our opinion. She also suggests that the vaulting of this room is post-medieval, but there are clear traces of the imprint of woven matting on the vaults, which we deem to be an indication that it is medieval.

82. These are mentioned by Bertelli, 'L'enciclopedia', 42 and illustrated in Cesare D'Onofrio and Carlo Pietrangeli, *Abbazie del Lazio* (Rome: Cassa di Risparmio, 1969) fig. 194.

83. The chapter rooms at Fossanova and Casamari have a similar plan (Sartorio, 'L'abbazia', 58).

Against the eastern side of wall 4 two medieval staircases were built (see Section AA'). Each was supported by two arches, one semi-circular, the other parabolic; between them was an ancient column sustaining a late antique composite capital (figs. 27, 28 and 36). Beneath the stairs are medieval vaults clearly showing the imprint of woven matting. The southern staircase is in part built against the west wall of the north arm of the transept. In the old sacristy, one can see that this staircase was attached to wall 4, after the latter was built. This staircase may date from the building campaign in which the north arm of the transept was erected. In the Middle Ages these staircases gave access to the dormitory, 'D' (Plan II). By the stairs on the south—the classic cistercian 'night stairs'—the monks descended from the dormitory to the church for the night Office of Vigils; by that on the north, the 'day stairs', they went up from the area north of the cloister (Plan I and Section AA').

The church of SS. Vincenzo e Anastasio is clearly connected to the east range of the monastery (Plan I).[84] The night stairs led from the dormitory to the transept. Moreover, as we pointed out above, a door led from the north transept into the old sacristy. In the southern corner of the cloister ambulatory, Sartorio drew another bay of the colonnade linking wall 9 to the north aisle wall of the church (fig. 82).[85] This may have been a later addition. The last pier in the present ambulatory of the east range was L-shaped when it was built in the Middle Ages, indicating that another ambulatory was planned—and probably built—along the north aisle of the church, where the modern Wing A now stands.[86] This ambulatory, however, is narrower than that in the east range—3.90 m. as against 5.60 m.—which may be another indication that the church was laid out after the first phase of Wing M had been built.

Above the bay connecting the eastern cloister ambulatory to the church, on the level of the dormitory, was built a small, groin-vaulted room which later became the monastic prison (Plan II, P; figs. 17 and

84. Romanini, 'La storia architettonica', 673, claims that the monastic buildings, and in particular the eastern wing, were not related to the layout of the church. We disagree with her conclusion.
85. Sartorio, 'L'abbazia', 52, fig. 2 and 60.
86. Sartorio drew it in dotted lines, Sartorio, 'L'abbazia', 52, fig. 2; our fig.82.

42–44). Its walls were comparatively thin and low. From the interior it is clear that they were built of twelfth-century *opus listatum*. There is an arched niche in its eastern wall (fig. 43) and a window and a medieval door in wall 9 (fig. 17).[87] Where this room is attached to the dormitory there is a notable setback in wall 9. Originally the room communicated with the dormitory through a semi-circular arch in wall 23 (partly visible in figs. 42 and 43). This room seems to have been added, after the dormitory was built, over the bay in the cloister ambulatory which connected the cloister to the north aisle of the church. It was probably built at the time the north arm of the transept was constructed. A separate alcove, or cell, it later served as a place for a monk who was sick, physically or spiritually, and hence in need of some seclusion from the rest of the community. On the other hand, there were twelfth-century cistercian monasteries where the abbot or the sacristan had just such a cell, close to the night stairs and beside the church.[88] It is possible that this small room, which later became the monastery prison, was initially the abbot's cell.

Wing M In The Thirteenth or Early Fourteenth Century

The east range was extended in three places in the thirteenth or early fourteenth century, when the present sacristy was built, the portico along the eastern side of the monks' building was erected, the dormitory walls were raised, and a new roof was provided.[89] The modifications can be clearly distinguished by their construction in *opus saracinescum*, a type of masonry made up of small tufa blocks and used in Rome in the thirteenth and fourteenth centuries.

Wall 2 was extended north of the church to meet wall 24, which was prolonged east of the chapter room (CR). The resulting rectangular space between the east end of the church, the old sacristy, and the chapter room, was the present 'sacristy' (Plan I, S). The floor, which once divided the 'sacristy' from the vaulted room above it (Plan II, SI),

---

87. See below, A. ARCHITECTURAL DATA, Wall 4.

88. Kinder, *Cistercian Europe*, 55–56 (*L'Europe cistercienne*, 271–272); Saint Bernard himself is said to have had a small cell and an abbot's cell still exists at Le Thoronet, see Aubert, *L'architecture cistercienne*, 1:13, 35; 2:23, 91–92.

89. Pistilli, 'Considerazioni', 163–192.

was probably a nineteenth-century insertion (Section CC', S and SI). There is no doubt that these two superimposed rooms originally formed one elegant space covered by a ribbed groin vault (figs. 45–48), so Belardi has now removed the later floor.[90] This vaulted room, at 4.50 m. high, was higher than the rooms beside it on the groundfloor of the east range, but lower than the church and dormitory. Walls 2 and 24 were extended in *opus saracinescum*—and hence in the thirteenth or fourteenth century. The eastern corners were reinforced with pilasters. The large roundheaded window and door in the eastern wall are modern, but small medieval windows survive in the northern wall.[91] Inside, there are in the present upper level two medieval murals—*The Nativity* (fig. 87) in the lunette of wall 8; and *The Coronation of the Virgin Mary* in the lunette of wall 2.[92] These were probably painted in the final years of the thirteenth or the first years of the fourteenth century.[93] An enigmatic inscription on the lintel over the present sacristy doorway, FEC. FIERI. H : OP : ET : I : ET : L—'I and L had this work done'—may allude to the construction or the decoration of this room, but it is impossible to say with certainty who 'I' and 'L' were; or to arrive at a precise date. Pistilli has suggested that 'I' stands for 'Iacobus', abbot of S. Anastasius from 1230–1244, who may have built the sacristy *c.* 1240, but the identity of 'L' remains a mystery.[94] Another possibility is that 'I' stands for Abbot Iohannis (1302–1306) and 'L' for Abbot Leonardus (1306–1329).[95] If that were so, the room may have been added late in the thirteenth or early in the fourteenth century, which is the date normally given for the fresco decoration. This vaulted room is normally called the sacristy, and that is

90. See above, at the end of Chapter I. The architectural survey drawings in this volume still show it.

91. These are discussed in detail by Pistilli, 'Considerazioni', 174–175.

92. Bertelli, 'L'enciclopedia', 34–36; Melinda Mihályi, 'I Cisterciensi a Roma e la decorazione pittorica dell'ala dei Monaci nell'abbazia delle Tre Fontane', *Arte Medievale* 2 serie, 5,1 (1991) 155–161; Joan E. Barclay Lloyd, 'The Medieval Murals in the Cistercian Abbey of SS. Vincenzo e Anastasio *ad Aquas Salvias* at Tre Fontane, Rome in their Architectural Settings', *Papers of the British School at Rome* 65 (1997) 323–336.

93. Bertelli, 'L'enciclopedia', 34–36; Mihályi, 'I Cisterciensi', 155–161; Barclay Loyd, 'The medieval murals', 334–336 and 342–344.

94. Pistilli, 'Considerazioni', 173–175.

95. Barclay Lloyd, 'Medieval Murals', 343–344.

indeed its present function. In the late thirteenth or early fourteenth century, however, several cistercian abbots built a lavishly appointed private chapel for their own use, next to the church and east of the sacristy and *armarium*[96]—precisely the location of this room. Moreover, in the south wall there are traces of a small niche of the type often found near an altar. If this were an abbot's chapel, the altar would have stood under the painting of *The Coronation of the Virgin*, and *The Nativity* would have been visible to anyone leaving the chapel.

Along the northeast side of east range was built a portico with three arches of unequal span along its eastern side in wall 7, one arch in wall 30, and another in wall 28 on the groundfloor (Plan I, and figs. 33–35). The piers and arches were built of *opus saracinescum,* and the western side of the southernmost pier was faced with brickwork, with a variable 5 x 5 modulus of 24.5–27 cm.—often 26 cm.—which points to a date in the first half of the thirteenth century.[97] A combination of *opus saracinescum* and brickwork is known elsewhere in Rome in the thirteenth century.[98] From the east, the change of masonry in wall 7 is clearly visible just north of the buttress at the corner of the chapter room (fig. 31). The arches have grey tufa or *peperino* voussoirs. Below the present, modern windows the *opus saracinescum* masonry has been disturbed.[99] At the northeastern end there is a horizontal marble slab, perhaps the threshold of a doorway, which may originally have opened at the top of an external staircase.[100] On the other hand, Van Aelst and Lauro's early seventeenth-century views of the monastery show a ruined building extending eastwards from the northern end of the east range (fig. 72), and the marble slab may have belonged to that extension.[101]

96. Aubert, *L'architecture cistercienne,* 2:50.

97. See below, A. ARCHITECTURAL DATA, Wall 7; Barclay Lloyd, 'Masonry', 233–236, 247, 271–272, Type III.

98. Barclay Lloyd, 'Masonry', 231, 241, 244, 247; Barclay Lloyd, S. *Clemente,* 21–22, 175.

99. Pistilli considered this as evidence for earlier, medieval double-light windows, Pistilli, 'Considerazioni', 177, and Bertelli mentioned traces of one small, blocked medieval window, Bertelli, 'L'enciclopedia', 42. The original disposition of the wall at this point is not clear. The masonry may merely have been disturbed when the modern windows were inserted. We saw no trace of double-light openings.

100. Pistilli, 'Considerazioni', 177.

101. See below, B. EARLY ILLUSTRATIONS, *c.* 1600.

The portico leads into an area east of wall 8, with an arch across, wall 28, also built of *opus saracinescum* (Plan I, figs. 32 and 33). The northernmost pier is an extension of a pre-existing buttress built of twelfth-century *opus listatum* (Plan I). This would have created a groundfloor space which could be entered through three arches along the east and one on the north. In the canonry of S. Clemente there was in the twelfth-century north wing on the groundfloor a similar area entered through five arches of unequal span, three on the east and two on the north.[102]

Above this space, on the first floor (Plan II), walls 7 and 30 were most likely extended upwards in the Middle Ages, but their masonry at that level is not accessible. Similarly, a wall was probably built above the arch in wall 28—which crosses the portico at ground level (Plans I and II, wall 28)—but again, its masonry on the floor above is not visible. The thickness of the wall, however, suggests a medieval date. In that case, the twelfth-century windows in wall 8 (Plan II and fig. 41), would have been blocked at that time. Walls 7, 30, and 28 (Plan II and fig. 89) extended the space on the first floor east of the dormitory, and north of room X, perhaps forming one long room delimited by walls 7, 25, 8, and 30; or—if the upward extension of wall 28 were medieval—two rooms, Y and Z (fig. 89). It is possible that rooms Y and Z originally communicated with the dormitory (D) and room X, but they may also have formed an independent apartment reached by an external staircase at the northeastern corner of the monks' wing.[103]

Bertelli connected the portico and its upper floor with an inscription which announced that Iacobus, 'POENITENTIARIUS' and chaplain to Pope Honorius III (1216–1227), had built this house, 'HANC DOMUM' (perhaps a part of the monastic complex?), for the salvation of his soul and that of his nephew, also called Iacobus.[104] The inscription is now

102. Barclay Lloyd, *S. Clemente*, 159, 171, 188, Plan and Reconstruction IV, and figs. 31 and 101–103.

103. This is suggested by Pistilli, 'Considerazioni', 177.

104. The inscription reads: FRATER IACOBUS DOMINI HONORIJ PP. POENITENTIARIUS AC CAPEL-LANUS, HANC DOMUM FIERI FECIT, PRO ANIMAM SUAM, ET JACOBI NEPOTIS. In the early thirteenth century there was a Cardinal Giacomo de Pecorara (1231–44) who was a cistercian monk at Trois Fontaines in France, and he has been confused with the first Iacobus in this inscription. The chaplain and penitentiary of Pope Honorius III was instead a *magister* and Apostolic Legate in Ireland and Scotland. He was mentioned in the papal Register from 31 July 1220–

over a window in the north wall of the north range of the monastery
(Plan II, wall 29),[105] but this window is surrounded by a modern
version of *opus listatum,* and the brick voussoirs normally built over a
marble-framed window of its type in the Middle Ages have been omitted
(fig. 66). Moreover, in 1640 Jongelinus wrote: 'In certain cells at the
end of the dormitory, towards the city of Rome, an inscription in
lombard letters appears on the outside above a window of the said cells,
which have been destroyed.'[106] The location of the inscription may
have been its present position, but 'the end of the dormitory' would
more properly have been at the northern end of Wing M, perhaps
above the eastern portico. If so, rooms Y and Z northeast of the dormitory could have been the 'destroyed cells' mentioned by Jongelinus;
not long before Jongelinus wrote his account,[107] a ruined, roofless
building appears in that place—as we noted above—in Van Aelst and
Lauro's views of Tre Fontane made respectively in *c.* 1600 and in
1612–1630 (fig. 72). The roof covering that side of the building likely
needed repair at that time. It is possible that the inscription was moved
to its present position in the trappist renovations of the late nineteenth or twentieth century. While Pistilli dates the portico and its
upper storey to the end of the thirteenth century, by comparing the
groundfloor arches to others of that date,[108] a date in the first half of
the thirteenth century is just as plausible.

How high this extension was originally built is not clear. It has been
suggested that it was much lower than the dormitory, and that the
slope of its roof was at a significantly different angle.[109] According to

---

9 May 1226, and he died before 3 July 1240; as explained by Agostino Paravicini-Bagliani,
Cardinali di Curia e 'familiariae' cardinalizie dal 1227 al 1254, Italia Sacra: Studi e Documenti di
Storia Ecclesiastica, 18 and 19 (Rome: Editrice Antenore, 1972) 112–123, esp. 118–119, n. 2;
see also Giuseppe Ruotolo, *L'abbazia delle Tre Fontane* (Rome: Abbazia delle Tre Fontane, 1972)
86–91; and Pistilli, 'Considerazioni', 165 and notes 13–15. Evidently there was an abbot of
S. Anastasius at Tre Fontane called Iacobus from 1230–1244, perhaps the second Iacobus of
the inscription, Ruotolo, *L'abbazia,* 86–91.

105. Bertelli, 'L'enciclopedia', 41–42, and n. 6.

106. See below, C. DATES AND DOCUMENTS, 1216–1227.

107. For example, in Giacomo Lauro's *View of Tre Fontane,* 1612, published in I. (G.) Lauro,
Antiquae urbis splendor. (Rome: no typ., [drawn 1612], printed 1630) fol. 151 r), our fig. 72.

108. Pistilli, 'Considerazioni', 175–187.

109. Pistilli, 'Considerazioni', 177–178.

Pistilli, this roof would have joined our wall 8 approximately 3 m. below the present roof of the dormitory, that is, just below the frescoes discovered in the upper reaches of wall 8 in the 1960s.[110] There is, however, no real evidence for this assertion.

The uppermost reaches of wall 8 can be examined from a modern terrace on its eastern side, where the frescoes of the late thirteenth or early fourteenth-century scenes of an *Encyclopedia* or *Vita Umana* were discovered and subsequently removed from the wall (Plan III; figs. 49 and 50).[111] At its northern end a continuation of wall 30, with a setback of *c.* 25 cm. on the south, is built against wall 8. Moving southwards from wall 30 along wall 8, one finds first the modern door to the terrace and then two large nineteenth-century windows. At a distance of 10.30 m. from wall 30 there is a buttress, 1.80 m. wide, strengthening wall 8. On either side of the buttress there are traces—reaching to a height of 1.25 m. above the terrace floor—of a blocked medieval window. These windows were closed before the frescoes were painted over them. At a distance of 9.50 m. south of the buttress, and 21.60 m. from the extension of wall 30, there is a setback in wall 8, after which the wall continues in a narrower form, with two openings and another, narrow, buttress. Further south still wall 24 originally met wall 8. South of it there is a kind of roof-space. The masonry of this upper part of wall 8, from wall 30 to the setback, is twelfth-century *opus listatum* to a height of 1.80–2.27 m. above the modern terrace floor. Above that there is a band of thirteenth or fourteenth-century *opus saracinescum*.[112] This latter is clearly related to the *opus saracinescum* in the upper reaches of walls 9, 23, and 30; it obviously formed part of a campaign to raise the roof of the dormitory (Sections BB' and CC').

These features of the uppermost level of Wing M can be related to what stands below. Starting from the south, the 'roof-space' (Plan III) rises above the ribbed groin vault of the sacristy (SI) beneath (Plan II, Section CC'). Wall 24—which is 60 cm. wide at terrace level—rests on its counterpart—which is 85 cm. wide on the first floor. On the terrace the distance from the southern face of wall 24 to the setback in

---

110. Bertelli, 'L'enciclopedia', 24–49; Pistilli, 'Considerazioni', 178.

111. See also Barclay Lloyd, 'The medieval murals', 337–344.

112. See below, A. ARCHITECTURAL DATA, Wall 8.

wall 8 measures 12.90 m., while on the floor below the distance from the southernmost face of wall 24 to the northernmost face of wall 25, is 13.15 m. Given the irregular nature of the medieval walls, the difference is minimal. This means that the space from wall 24 to the setback in wall 8 at the uppermost level covers the room above the eastern end of the chapter room (X) (Plan II and fig. 89).

On the ground floor, the distance from the external wall of the chapter room, wall 25, to the arch in wall 28, is 14 m. (Plan I). This is the same as the distance at first floor level from the north face of wall 25 to the south face of wall 28 (Plan II), which is the length of room 'Y' east of the dormitory (fig. 89). On the terrace, this distance—14 m. from the setback in wall 8—is 7.60 m. from wall 30, which is the point at which Bertelli said the frescoes of the *'Enciclopedia'* began.[113] He mentioned that the mural decoration extended from a point 7.60 m. from the northern end of the terrace to the setback, which he variously placed 11.70, 13 or 14 m., further south.[114] Bertelli also noted that north of the point where the *'Enciclopedia'* cycle began there was a painted surface, but with a different design, including horizontal stripes of white and red, which seemed to have been done on the same sort of plaster and with the same colours as the *'Enciclopedia'* murals.[115] One can see the difference in a photograph taken by Bertelli at the time (our fig. 50). Behind the modern piers holding up the lean-to roof, one can see the buttress and the two nineteenth-century windows, with a pier between them. The pier has stripes painted at the top. On the left of the nearer window is a very narrow vertical strip of the same design, a wider vertical gap, and the beginning of the

113. Bertelli, 'L'enciclopedia', 28 and 43, n. 6.

114. Bertelli is inconsistent in the dimensions he gives for this wall. In his 1969 study he says, 'Fortunatamente, quanto ora resta è un ciclo in sé concluso. E' una fascia alta circa tre metri (2,93) e lunga *tredici*.' Bertelli, 'L'enciclopedia', 28. Cf. 'La zona affrescata ha inizio a m. 7,60 da Nord e finisce in corrispondenza dello spigolo per una lunghezza de *m. 11, 70.*' Bertelli, 'L'enciclopedia', 43, n. 6. Cf. '. . . sul muro del dormitorio, all'esterno, era una striscia affrescata alta circa m. 3, lunga *m. 14.* . . .', Carlo Bertelli, 'Secolo XIII—Affreschi, Roma, Abbazia delle Tre Fontane', in *Restauri della Soprintendenza alle Gallerie e alle opere d'arte medioevali e moderne per il Lazio.* (Rome: De Luca, 1972) 12. (I have italicized the relevant dimensions.)

115. 'Più a nord, dove sono aperti due finestroni ottocenteschi, si notano solamente strisce orizzontali bianche e rosse che sembrano dello stesso intonaco e degli stessi colori degli affreschi..', Bertelli, 'L'enciclopedia', 43, n. 6.

nine compartments of the medieval 'Enciclopedia' scenes. What is of interest here is the vertical gap, which looks like the scar of a wall which no longer exists, but which formerly abutted wall 8. The scar is smooth, indicating that wall 8 existed before the wall that made the scar. Since wall 8 was to a height of 1.80–2.27 m. above the terrace built in the twelfth century, this is certainly possible. Downstairs (Plan II) wall 28 stands at almost exactly this position, its southern face 7.40 m. from wall 30; the difference of c. 20 cm. can be accounted for by the setback in wall 30 at terrace level. A wall abutting wall 8 at this point on the terrace would have stood on top of wall 28. It would have formed part of room 'Z' beside the dormitory (fig. 89).

It seems, then, that the two different mural programmes, the gap between them, and the correspondence of the point where the change occurs, indicate a different structure from that proposed by Bertelli, who presumed that these murals were originally on an *external* wall of the monastery.[116] It seems more plausible that they were *inside* two rooms which flanked the dormitory: one delimited by walls 8, 30, 7, and 28 (fig. 89, room Z), decorated with red and white stripes; and the other surrounded by walls 8, 28, 7, and 25 (fig. 89, room Y), with the 'Enciclopedia' series. If so, the murals would have been painted after the walls of the dormitory had been raised and the windows flanking the buttress had been closed. The structural changes may have been made in the same, or in a separate, building phase from that which extended the space on the first floor over the arched portico beneath. As we pointed out above, the mural decoration has been dated to the late thirteenth or early fourteenth century. Bertelli noted that there were no traces of frescoes south of the setback in wall 8.[117] Yet elsewhere he suggested that the whole eastern external facade of the monks' wing was decorated with murals.[118] Probably only the two rooms east of the dormitory were painted in this way and their deco-

116. Bertelli, 'L'enciclopedia', 43, n. 6.

117. '. . . Più a Sud non rimane nulla, ma il modo in cui la decorazione conclude sullo spigolo del muro fa ritenere che, anche se questa parte fosse stata intonacata, non avrebbe ricevuto sicuramente la stessa decorazione', Bertelli, 'L'enciclopedia', 43, n. 6.

118. 'Gli affreschi . . . costituiscono la sezione mediana di una decorazione che in origine doveva estendersi per tutta la lunghezza della facciata', Bertelli, 'L'enciclopedia', 28.

ration may have been part of a more wide-ranging campaign which covered the dormitory and perhaps the sacristy lunettes with murals.

The function of the two decorated rooms east of the dormitory is not clear. Initially—perhaps in the period 1200–1250—they may have formed an extension to the dormitory space in Wing M. By the time the frescoes were painted in the late thirteenth or early fourteenth century, the smaller room on the north—(fig. 89, room Z), decorated with stripes of red and white—may have been the abbot's bedroom; the larger room—(fig. 89, room Y), with the *'Enciclopedia'* frescoes— his study. Either in the early thirteenth century, or approximately fifty years later, the abbot may have moved from the small cell beside the church and the night stairs to this more commodious apartment. At the same time he may have built himself a vaulted private chapel in what has become the modern sacristy. Both these structures were decorated with elegant frescoes in the late thirteenth or early fourteenth century.

Opus saracinescum crowns dormitory walls 8 and 9 and forms the triangular gable of wall 30 (fig. 38). The uppermost parts of wall 23 were also constructed in this masonry.[119] This indicates that the walls were raised just before the dormitory was given a new roof. In the gable of wall 30 there are three windows (fig. 38). Pistilli claimed that this wall rose in a stepped gable, and indeed Silvestre showed this in his print of *c.* 1641–46 (fig. 75). This is an attractive theory, but, since no trace of such a gable survives and other views of the monastery made both before and after 1641 do not include it, it is difficult to accept. Bertelli, in the 1960s, found mural decorations in the roof spaces of the dormitory gable, similar in style to those on the eastern face of wall 8 and dating from the end of the thirteenth or early fourteenth century.[120] Mihályi has suggested that they were painted *c.* 1306, when Abbot Leonardus was responsible for improvements in the monks' wing.[121] It is likely that they were contemporaneous with those in rooms Y and Z (fig. 89), which were covered with the same roof.

---

119. The masonry of the uppermost parts of wall 23 was accessible during Belardi's restoration, see Romanini, "'Ratio fecit diversum'", fig. 45.

120. Bertelli, 'L'enciclopedia', 26, 36–40.

121. Mihályi, 'I Cisterciensi a Roma', 175.

The three parts of Wing M built of *opus saracinescum* may or may not all date from the same building campaign. The *opus saracinescum* itself does not vary much.[122] A 5 x 5 modulus of this masonry in wall 2 of the sacristy measured 38, 39, 40, 40.5 cm., occasionally 42, 42.5 cm.[123] In wall 7 of the portico it was almost always 40, 41, 42 cm., but in wall 28 is was only 31, 35.5, 36 cm.[124] In wall 8 under the eaves' line of Wing M, the modulus was 38, 40 cm.[125] It looks as though the 'sacristy' and the raising of wall 8 have most in common and they may have been built at the same time. The masonry of the portico is similar to the masonry of the 'sacristy' and the upper part of wall 8, but different from that of wall 28. It is possible the portico was built in 1200–1250. The sacristy—or abbot's chapel—could have been erected in the late thirteenth century, contemporaneously with the raising of the dormitory roof. The mural decoration of the sacristy and the uppermost levels of Wing M may have formed part of the same campaign. It is also possible that the frescoes were not associated with any particular structural changes in the monastery. What is certainly true, however, is that by the late thirteenth or early fourteenth century, the monastery buildings had grown in size, and parts of the monks' wing were splendidly decorated.

The precise date when all this was done is unknown. On 6 May 1284 during the reign of Abbot Martinus, Ildebrandino il Rosso Aldobrandeschi made a will in which he left two hundred pounds to the monastery of S. Anastasius in Rome for the building of the place and for the provision of 'pittances' or tasty dishes for the brethren.[126] Ildebrandino died shortly afterwards, on 18 May 1284. It is possible that this bequest financed part of the abbey construction that dates from the late thirteenth century. This could have been the re-roofing

---

122. Pistilli noticed that the masonry of the sacristy was neater than that of the portico, and that there was a difference in the proportion of tufa and peperino, Pistilli, 'Considerazioni', 165 and 178–179.

123. See below, A. ARCHITECTURAL DATA, Wall 2.

124. See below, A. ARCHITECTURAL DATA, Walls 7 and 28.

125. See below, A. ARCHITECTURAL DATA, Wall 8.

126. Gaspero Ciacci, *Gli Aldobrandeschi nella storia e nella "Divina Commedia"* (Rome: Multigrafica Editirice, 1980) 2:261–266, doc. DCVII: 'Item iudicavit et reliquit monasterio Sancti Anastasii de Urbe ducentas libras usualis monete pro fabrica loci et pietantiis fratrum.' See Barclay Lloyd, 'The medieval murals', 331.

of the dormitory and/or the construction of the vaulted room S/SI. Abbot Leonardus also undertook work in the monks' wing in 1306, as is attested by an inscription formerly over the door of the chapter room. It seems likely that between 1284 and 1306, the abbots of S. Anastasius erected a private chapel and restructured two rooms north of the dormitory, which they provided with a new roof. All these parts of the buildings were decorated with a splendid array of murals, including a liturgical calendar and a row of saints, dated 1347.[127]

Extensive mural decoration was very unusual in a medieval cistercian monastery, although the rules on this matter seem in fact to have been relaxed in the late thirteenth century. Such mural decoration within conventual buildings is, however, known elsewhere in Rome. In the canonry of S. Clemente there are traces of murals in the upper reaches of what was originally a large room—probably a dormitory— which was extended and heightened in the second half of the thirteenth century.[128] There the walls were decorated with simulated masonry divided by painted columns and crowned with a painted acanthus frieze, while another acanthus frieze extended into the gables. The style was not as elegant as in the murals at Tre Fontane; and the work can be dated a little earlier, *c.* 1260–1280. Even so, it attests to a custom in late thirteenth-century Rome of decorating the interior of conventual buildings with murals,[129] as do murals found in the monastic buildings beside S. Saba. There, in the interior of a 'tower', was painted a series of *Occupations of the Months* in roundels over a depiction of striped curtaining.[130] Recently murals were discovered in the monastic quarters at SS. Quattro Coronati.[131] If murals were unusual in cistercian monasteries, they were evidently quite common in thirteenth-century roman monastic establishments.

---

127. Other murals of the late thirteenth and early fourteenth centuries are discussed in Barclay Lloyd, 'Medieval Murals', 287–348.

128. Barclay Lloyd, *S. Clemente*, 177–178, 192–193.

129. We do not agree with Pistilli that the restructuring at Tre Fontane changed the interior organization of the monastery, nor that the monks were moved to another part of the building, while their dormitory took on other functions, see Pistilli, 'Considerazioni', 187 and 192, n. 93.

130. Barclay Lloyd, 'The medieval murals', 343, fig. 40.

131. Unfortunately, I have not yet been able to view these works.

THE NORTH RANGE (WING R)

At Tre Fontane, the refectory range stands north of the cloister garth (Plans I, II and III, Wing R; Sections DD'; figs. 15, 16, 23, 24 and 51–58). The northern ambulatory of the cloister is medieval. It opens in six bays, separated by brickwork piers. In five of the bays three colonnettes sustain an arcade (figs. 15 and 23, on right), while in the sixth a large arch gives access to the cloister garden (Plan I). The cloister colonnade in the north range differs markedly from that in the east range—instead of ancient roman spoils being used, slender colonnettes and bases were made specifically for this side of the cloister in the Middle Ages. In place of capitals there are simple impost blocks, as in Wing M. The brickwork of the intervening piers has been marked with *falsa cortina* pointing and has a modulus normal in Rome in the twelfth century.[132] From this one may conclude that the refectory range was built in the twelfth century, but later than the east range, in a separate building campaign.

The cloister ambulatory in Wing R is narrower than that in Wing M: 4 m. (13.53 roman feet) as against 5.40–5.60 m. (18.27–18.94 roman feet). In the recent renovations, the original paving of the ambulatory was found 45 cm. below the present floor.[133] That the vaulting in the cloister is medieval can be seen from the imprint of woven matting on the vaults. At a later date, as in Wing M, piers were inserted to carry arches across the ambulatory from north to south (figs. 23 and 52). They were very irregularly placed (Plan I). The structure later required three buttresses to shore it up from the south (fig. 51). Possibly, this was done to secure the upper floor. The masonry of the upper levels of wall 26 is not open to view.

Wall 27 runs across Wing R from east to west and on the ground-floor its masonry is accessible. It is the medieval twelfth-century *opus listatum* so common at Tre Fontane.[134] The cloister walk now leads into a vaulted room, two interconnected vaulted rooms, the refectory, the kitchen, and a corridor (Plan I). Openings have been changed—the

132. See below, A. ARCHITECTURAL DATA, Wall 26.
133. See above, at the end of Chapter I.
134. See below, A. ARCHITECTURAL DATA, Wall 27.

entrance to the kitchen and refectory were originally further west.[135] The jambs of the door to the refectory incorporate a fine ancient relief of vine leaves (fig. 58).

The masonry of the corridor, the kitchen, and the western side of the refectory is not open to view. Wall 42 stands approximately 1.30 m. south of wall 29; this may indicate that they were built at different times.

In an open space north of wall 29 one can examine the masonry of walls 10 and 29—i.e. the east wall of the refectory and the northern limit of the vaulted rooms (Plan I; figs. 54 and 57). In wall 10 the masonry is medieval *opus listatum* to a height just above the present refectory windows, which are modern (fig. 57). In 1998–2000 Belardi covered this wall with plaster, so the medieval masonry can no longer be seen. Before that there were traces of two low, blocked medieval windows, one possibly a double-light opening, the other narrower.[136] Its masonry indicates that the north wall of the refectory was built in the late nineteenth century (fig. 56). It may stand above its medieval counterpart. The evidence shows that the refectory was built in this place in the twelfth century, but it was a low room, with small windows on either side. It stood at right angles to the cloister ambulatory opposite the church. This disposition was typical of cistercian monastic architecture after *c.* 1150.[137] Today the pointed vault and the north wall of the refectory are modern, making the room a fine, well-lit medieval reconstruction (fig. 55).[138] Few early views of Tre Fontane show it at all.[139] It was probably in ruins by the seventeenth century, or was too low to be seen from the artists' western viewpoint.

In wall 29 twelfth-century *opus listatum* masonry rises to *c.* 2.70 m. below the eaves' line of Wing R, where it changes to *opus saracinescum,* (Section DD', fig. 54). This means that this part of Wing R was double-storeyed in the twelfth century. Where there are now three modern

---

135. See below, A. ARCHITECTURAL DATA, Wall 27.

136. See below, A. ARCHITECTURAL DATA, Wall 10.

137. Peter Fergusson, 'The Twelfth-century Refectories at Rievaulx and Byland Abbeys', in *Cistercian Art and Architecture in the British Isles,* edd. C. Norton and D. Park (Cambridge: Cambridge University Press, 1986) 160–180.

138. This was pointed out by D'Onofrio and Pietrangeli, *Abbazie,* 188.

139. This was discussed in more detail in Chapter Five.

rooms on the groundfloor east of the refectory, there would then probably have been the calefactory, or warming room. Above it there may have been one or two rooms (Plans I and II). In this place medieval cistercian monasteries often had a room where the monks could rest after their regular blood-letting in the calefactory.[140] Perhaps the upper room, or rooms, communicated with the northern end of the dormitory through an opening in wall 9.[141]

The *opus saracinescum* in the upper reaches of wall 29 appears to indicate an upward extension of Wing R built in the thirteenth or early fourteenth century. Possibly a new roof was needed and the monks took advantage of the situation to raise the height of the existing room or rooms.

In wall 29 there are traces of rather narrow blocked medieval windows and on the upper floor a blocked doorway (fig. 54)[142] which may have opened on to a balcony.[143] There are also four windows, still in use, which look modern. The masonry around them is disturbed, showing they have been inserted into wall 29. Above three of them there is no low relieving arch of bricks, as in most medieval openings of this type in Rome.[144] Instead, above these windows there are a few rows of tufelli and bricks, which look like a modern imitation of the *opus listatum* so common at Tre Fontane. Over the third window from wall 9 there is a relieving arch, but it looks modern, with two rows of bricks—instead of the usual single row—to make up the voussoirs. Two of the openings are, however, framed with medieval pieces of marble, including the window second from wall 9, with the inscription naming Iacobus, the chaplain and penitentiary to Pope Honorius III (1216–1227), as the builder of HANC DOMUM (fig. 66).[145] Given the modern-appearing masonry above and around the window, it is possible that the inscription was moved here from another location.[146] Perhaps the inscription referred, as Bertelli thought it did, to the struc-

---

140. Aubert, *L'architecture cistercienne* 2:114–116.
141. If so, this has since been blocked.
142. See below, A. ARCHITECTURAL DATA, Wall 29.
143. The two doors on the groundfloor are modern.
144. For this type of window, Barclay Lloyd, *S. Clemente*, 27–28.
145. See below, C. DATES AND DOCUMENTS, 1216–1227.
146. As suggested above, 160–161.

ture added to Wing M in the thirteenth century.[147] Indeed, the rooms east of the refectory in Wing R pre-date the inscription as their masonry is twelfth-century *opus listatum,* except for the *opus saracinescum* upward extension of 2.70 m.

THE WEST RANGE (WING C)

A doorway at the western end of the north aisle of the church leads into the *conversi* passageway west of the cloister (Plan I). The southern limit of Wing C, wall 22, is part of the north aisle wall of the church and continues west into the narthex. The location of the *conversi* building and its relation to the west end of the church suggest that the monastery and the church were planned as interdependent spaces, even if parts of the complex were built in separate phases.[148] Wing C communicates with the west end of the nave and aisles. The narthex seems to have been added to both the church and the *conversi* building in a later campaign.

On the groundfloor of Wing C, the original masonry is accessible only in the *conversi* corridor—walls 13 and 14—and in walls 22 and 35. It is all medieval *opus listatum,* like that in the east range and in the church, except for the twelfth-century brickwork in wall 22 in the narthex.[149] On the first floor, the upper level of wall 22 is partly visible from the steps leading up to S. Maria Scala Coeli. It is *opus saracinescum* and can therefore be dated to the thirteenth or early fourteenth century.

147. Bertelli, 'L'enciclopedia', 41–42. On the other hand, Pistilli, in Pio F. Pistilli, 'L'architettura a Roma nella prima metà del Duecento', in *Roma nel Duecento,* ed. A. M. Romanini (Turin: Edizioni SEAT, 1991) fig. on 21 and Pistilli, 'Considerazioni', 163–192, sees the 'Palazzetto di "Frater Jacobus"' as merely the upper floor of Wing R, between Wing M and the refectory. He does not explain the layout of this addition, nor whether it communicated with the dormitory. In fact, all 'Frater Jacobus' would have done, was to raise wall 29 about 2.70 m.—and perhaps wall 27 as well—and add a new roof. Pistilli's interpretation of this as a 'Palazzetto' does not take into account its position nor the more normal function of a room on this level in a cistercian monastery.

148. Here we disagree again with Romanini's assertion that the church and monastery were not related, Romanini, 'La storia architettonica', 673.

149. See below, A. ARCHITECTURAL DATA, Walls 13, 14, 22 and 35.

If masonry is of limited help in analysing Wing C, the thickness and position of the walls is more useful. From Plan I it is clear that wall 14—between walls 22 and 35—stands a little further east than it does between walls 34 and 38. Between walls 35 and 34 rather clumsy efforts have been made to connect the two parts of wall 14. The rather narrow join is constructed of *opus listatum,* presumably of the twelfth century. Wall 15 also has a narrower portion between walls 34 and 35. The western side of wall 15 is faced with a modern imitation of *opus saracinescum* (fig. 59).[150]

Wing C seems originally to have been built in two blocks, with a central passageway between them and the *conversi* corridor to the east. The southern block was bounded by walls 14, 22, 15, and 35; the northern block by walls 14, 34, 15, and 38 (see Plans I and II). A passageway ran between walls 34 and 35; the *conversi* corridor between walls 13 and 14. Given the alignment of the northern and southern parts of wall 14, it seems likely that the groundfloor of the southern and northern blocks of Wing C were constructed in separate building phases. Probably the southern block was built before the northern one. They may have been joined when the refectory range (Wing R) was laid out, still in the twelfth century, but after the first phase of the east range had been built.

At groundfloor level, when one excludes narrow modern walls and partitions, one can clearly see in the two blocks of Wing C a system of square central piers supporting cross vaults—four piers and ten vaults in the southern block; three piers and eight vaults in the northern. While there is no clear evidence that this layout is medieval, it is quite possibly so, as this kind of modular planning was typical of cistercian architecture of the twelfth and thirteenth centuries.

In the *conversi* corridor, the opening into the cloister and the groin vault connected with it are not medieval, and a barrel vault of uncertain date covers the rest of the passageway.[151] It is clear that the *conversi* building was separated from the cloister. This separation of the monks and *conversi* in two separate wings, east and west of the cloister with a lane or passageway cutting off the lay brothers' quarters

---

150. According to Fra Corrado of the trappist community at Tre Fontane, this facade was restored in the 1950s.
151. See below, A. ARCHITECTURAL DATA, 4. *Vaults,* (c) OTHER VAULTS IN WING C.

—was another characteristic feature of medieval cistercian architecture. Often, too, the *conversi* wing was divided into two distinct blocks with a passageway between them. On the groundfloor, according to normal cistercian practice, the southern block would have housed the great cellar, the northern block the lay brothers' refectory.

The southern block of the upper floor of Wing C was probably built much later than the groundfloor, as the *opus saracinescum* visible in the upper reaches of wall 22 seems to testify. The major walls at this level (Plan II) are also comparatively thin, especially above the southern block of Wing C. One large room delimited by walls 35, 15, 22, and 14 seems to have stood above the southern block. Another large room, bounded by walls 14, 35, 15, and 38, appears to have been built above the northern block; it oversails the passageway between the two blocks. A first floor passageway directly above the *conversi* corridor ran along the east side of this part of Wing C. The date of this arrangement is unknown. Quite recently, arches in this stretch of wall 14 were opened to extend the rooms on that side of the building to wall 13, thereby giving them a view over the cloister.[152]

North of wall 38 there is a tower-like extension to Wing C (fig. 59), bordered by walls 38, 15, 33 and 14. Where this 'tower' joins wall 15, it juts out to the west (Plans I and II), but its walls are narrower than the ground-floor walls of the northern block of Wing C. It rises higher than the rest of the wing, in three storeys. At present its external facades are faced with the same modern version of *opus saracinescum* as in wall 15. A colonnaded portico, also modern, surrounds it on ground-floor level on the north and west.

Old photographs show that the 'tower' is undoubtedly modern; but that there was such a structure is attested by early seventeenth-century prints (compare figs. 71, 72, 75 and 76 with 83, 84 and 85). The modern 'tower' may even stand on the foundations of its medieval predecessor. Such 'towers' seem to have been a common feature of late medieval roman monastic architecture.[153]

152. This is based on information from members of the trappist community. It seems to have been done in the last twenty or so years.

153. Towers still stand amid the monastic buildings at SS. Giovanni e Paolo, SS. Quattro Coronati and S. Lorenzo fuori le Mura in Rome, see Krautheimer, *Rome,* 321–322; Barclay Lloyd, *S. Clemente,* 200; Barclay Lloyd, 'S. Lorenzo fuori le Mura', 99–102.

The *conversi* building frequently appeared in prints from the early seventeenth century onwards. In 1600 Giovanni Maggi (fig. 71) showed its roof-line at two different levels—the higher over the southern block, the lower over the northern block and the intervening passageway. At the northern end Maggi depicted a medieval tower, where the modern one now stands; it had no flanking porticoes. On the ground floor three doors led into the *conversi* building—that in the middle would have corresponded with the entrance to the intervening passageway; those on either side gave access to the northern and southern blocks. Lauro's print of 1612, published in 1630, clearly showed the *conversi* wing divided into two parts, but with a common roof line (fig. 72). There was an arched ground-floor entrance just north of the southern block and a tower at the northern end of the wing. Silvestre c. 1641 (fig. 75) indicated the tower, the northern block (divided into two floors by a horizontal line) stretching a short way beyond a wide middle doorway, and the southern block. De Rossi in 1652 (fig. 76) showed the tower and the wing divided into two blocks, with three doorways, the middle one just north of the southern block. In Vasi's view, published in 1753, there was no tower (fig. 77). Presumably it had fallen down or been demolished by the mid-eighteenth century.

The *conversi* wing was in the foreground of several nineteenth and early twentieth-century photographs. In two of these views there is no medieval tower at its northern end (figs. 84 and 85), although a small lean-to structure may have taken its place. A photograph, taken perhaps in 1945–1949 (fig. 86),[154] included part of the tower rebuilt.

These old photographs give an impression of the masonry of wall 15 before the modern facing was applied. In two taken before 1890 (figs. 83 and 84) the northern block appears to be built in layers—there is a dark band at the base; then a pale stripe; a higher dark layer; and a pale band. The southern block is less clear, but there does seem to be a dark layer at the base, topped by lighter masonry on the first floor. In the early twentieth century (fig. 85) the lower floor of the entire wing seems to be of a uniform colour—perhaps it was plastered over. The

---

154. The date of the photograph was given by Fra Corrado of the Trappist community at Tre Fontane.

evidence from these photographs seems to confirm the theory that the two floors of the southern block were built in separate building phases.

The ground floor of each block appears to have been built of the same masonry. Later, the southern block was raised. A new floor was also added over the northern block and the intervening passageway, perhaps in three stages—first, the walls were raised in the pale masonry; then a higher upward extension was built; finally, the northern block's roof was raised to equal the height of that over the southern block. A mid-twentieth century photograph (fig. 86) shows that the lowest level of the northern block was constructed of quite large blocks of tufa, perhaps with a row of bricks between them; this may be twelfth-century *opus listatum,* but the photograph is not very clear. Above there are small blocks of tufa, with mortar smeared over them; this could be a form of *opus saracinescum.* Over that there is a kind of rough and irregular *opus saracinescum.* It seems the groundfloor of both blocks was constructed in the twelfth century, but the upper floors were built later in more than one building campaign, perhaps in the thirteenth or fourteenth century. From the photographic evidence, there seem to have been three phases of construction in the upper floor of the northern block. The final equalizing of the roof-level evidently took place shortly after 1600, when Maggi's print was made.

THE GUEST HOUSE (WING O)

Northwest of Wing C is the present guest house, Wing O, a two-storeyed block (Plans I and II; figs. 60–63). On the groundfloor at its west end there is a large room, spanned by two arches; there may have been some smaller rooms east of that. On the upper floor there appears to have been one large room.

There are traces of medieval roundheaded slit windows on both floors (figs. 60–62).[155] An arched medieval door, supported on one side by a stout column, gave access to this wing from the north (fig. 63).

---

155. See below, A. ARCHITECTURAL DATA, Walls 16, 19 and 37.

The arch itself is made up of tufa or peperino voussoirs; the same material was used in the arches of the portico in Wing M. The walls of Wing O are comparatively thin, *c.* 60 cm. The masonry is all *opus saracinescum;* a 5 X 5 modulus of this masonry in wall 37 measured 42, 42.5, 43 cm. Sometimes the tufelli alternate with one or two rows of bricks,[156] a feature not found in the *opus saracinescum* in Wing M. The thickness of the walls and the masonry in the guest house point to a different building campaign, perhaps in the late thirteenth or fourteenth century.[157]

Sartorio thought this wing was the early abbot's residence.[158] It is more plausible that it was built as a guest house, with reception rooms and a dining room downstairs and a dormitory above. Possibly, however, it served from the fifteenth to the seventeenth centuries as a residence for commendatory abbots; in the twentieth century it functioned as a retreat house.

THE NARTHEX

West of the church and south of the *conversi* wing is the narthex (Plan I; figs. 4–6). This colonnaded entrance porch formed an appropriate entrance to the church. The narthex is like many built in Rome during the twelfth and thireenth centuries, such as those surviving at S. Giorgio in Velabro and S. Lorenzo fuori le Mura. Unlike the church, it does not have a cistercian ground plan.

The narthex must have been constructed after the church, for its southern pier is clearly built against the church's southwest corner (fig. 5).[159] It was also erected after the groundfloor of the southern block of Wing C, because its northern pier is built against wall 22.

The columns are roman spoils, the capitals medieval ionic. The pavement level of the narthex was lowered in the late nineteenth cen-

156. See below, A. ARCHITECTURAL DATA, Walls 16, 19, 36 and 37.
157. Pistilli, on the other hand, suggested that 'la foresteria', the guest house (Wing O), was built at the same time as the sacristy, *c.* 1240, Pistilli, 'Considerazioni', 174.
158. Sartorio, 'L'abbazia', 57–58.
159. This was pointed out by Pistilli, 'Considerazioni', 168–170.

tury, giving the western colonnade a strange appearance, with its columns raised on high stilobates.[160] The straight architrave rests on side brackets, which are roman spoils (fig. 6). Above the marble entablature there are flat relieving arches and a typical roman sawtooth cornice (figs. 4 and 5). The inscription alluding to Pope Innocent II dates from the early seventeenth century.[161] The masonry of the narthex piers seems to date from the twelfth century.[162] The brickwork bears traces of *falsa cortina* pointing, which differentiates it from the brickwork in the church. It was probably erected by a different group of masons. In its upper reaches the narthex seems to have been decorated with coloured ceramics, similar to those seen in medieval roman bell-towers. The roof of the narthex slopes down from the facade wall of the church to the colonnade. Sartorio pointed out that one of the wooden brackets supporting the roof had a gothic design carved on it.[163]

It is often assumed that the narthex at SS. Vincenzo e Anastasio was built early in the thirteenth century.[164] Its masonry, however, is of twelfth-century date. It is true that it abuts the twelfth-century church and the ground floor of Wing C. This indicates that the narthex was erected after these two structures, but probably still in the twelfth century.[165] It may have been built late in that century.

In the thirteenth century two tombs were built in the narthex (fig. 70).[166] The interior was also decorated with murals, probably in the late thirteenth or early fourteenth century. Of these paintings only the faded and fragmentary images of Saint Leonard and Saint James survive on the piers. Eclissi's drawings show lost scenes of the siege of Ansedonia, the abbey's possessions in the Maremma, several saints

---

160. In nineteenth-century representations, the colonnade looks rather low, e.g. in Letarouilly's view of 1853, our fig. 81.

161. See below, C. DATES AND DOCUMENTS, 1608.

162. See below, A. ARCHITECTURAL DATA, Walls 6 and 19.

163. Sartorio, 'L'abbazia', 61.

164. See, for example, Sartorio, 'L'abbazia', 61; and Pistelli, 'Considerazioni', 170.

165. In this we agree with Ingo Herklotz, 'Der middelalterliche Fassadenportikus der Lateransbasilika und seine Mosaiken', *Römisches Jahrbuch der Bibliotheca Hertziana* 25 (1989) 32–33, but we believe it was built, not *c*. 1140, but later in the twelfth century.

166. One was probably for Tomasia, wife of Guglielmo Aldobrandeschi, who was buried in 1272 or 1277. See below, C. DATES AND DOCUMENTS, 1272–77.

and clergymen, and narrative scenes depicting the lives of Saints Vincent and Anastasius.[167]

THE GATEHOUSE

At the entrance to the monastery was the gatehouse. This two-storeyed building consisted of only the central part of what now stands, bounded by walls 43, 44, 45 and 47 (Gatehouse, Plans A, B and C, and Section AA'; figs. 2 and 3). It can be seen in several early views (figs. 71, 72, 75, 76 and 77). Eclissi drew a plan and elevation of the building (figs. 73 and 74), and also made drawings of the murals in its western vault, which depict Christ blessing. In the lower lunettes, on the northeast and southwest, there were paintings of the siege of Ansedonia and the donation to the abbey of the lands in Maremma by Charlemagne and Pope Leo III. On the middle wall above the gateway was an image of the Madonna and Child flanked by Saints Benedict, Paul, Bernard, and Anastasius, as well as two kneeling cistercian monks.[168]

By 1818 the multiple-light opening in its upper floor had disappeared. An early photograph shows that the upper storey was in a ruinous state in the nineteenth century;[169] later views show a small, double-storeyed edifice beside it to the southwest (figs. 83–85).

The gatehouse may have been built over an older structure. Excavations evidently revealed part of a roman road beneath the arch and traces of an apsed building nearby.[170] Most of the gatehouse, however, dates from the twelfth and thirteenth centuries.

At present there are two bays, one on either side of the arched gateway, which preserves its late thirteenth or early fourteenth-century marble doorframe and threshold. Marble paving covers the floor of the passageway. Both compartments are vaulted. The bay closer to the

---

167. See the Eclissi drawings in the Vatican Library, BAV, Barb. Lat. 4402, fols. 42r (our fig. 70), 43r, 46r–51r. The subject matter of these drawings is discussed in Barclay Lloyd, 'Medieval Murals', 312–323.

168. The Eclissi drawings are in the Vatican Library, BAV, Barb. Lat. 4402, fols. 35r, 36r, 37r, and 40v–41r. For this program see Barclay Lloyd, 'Medieval Murals', 294–308.

169. Barclay Lloyd, 'Medieval Murals', 294 and fig. 10.

170. See below, C. DATES AND DOCUMENTS, 1938/39.

church is built of twelfth-century brickwork and *opus listatum,* which continues northwest into about half the other bay. From there *opus saracinescum* takes over, showing that that bay was extended and restructured in the thirteenth century.[171] It is in this bay that the frescoes were painted; they must therefore date from after 1200, possibly between 1200 and 1250, except for the *Madonna and Child,* which was executed *c.* 1270. The wall between the two bays does not bond with those on either side of the passageway; it is moreover built of brickwork with a low 5 X 5 modulus characteristic of roman masonry from the middle of the thirteenth century onwards.[172] The upper floor of the gatehouse has been rebuilt. Parts of the outer walls survive; they are constructed of *opus saracinescum,* indicating that the upper storey was probably also part of the thirteenth-century restructuring of the building. Wall 48, which now runs across it (Gatehouse, Plan C and Section), does not stand above wall 46, but over the vaulting in the northwestern bay.[173] The multi-light window is modern, made in imitation of the one shown in early prints.

In the medieval gatehouse, then, there are three phases of construction. The first, of the twelfth century, would have included the southeastern bay and part of the northwestern one. In the thirteenth century, perhaps in the pontificate of Honorius III (1216–1227), the building was extended to the northwest and an upper storey was constructed. The new northwestern bay was decorated with thirteenth-century murals. In the second half of the thirteenth century, *c.* 1270, a new gate with a marble frame was inserted and the fresco of the *Madonna and Child with Saints* and two Cistercians was painted over it.

CONCLUSION

The gatehouse provided a fitting entrance to the abbey. To gain access to the monastic precinct visitors had to pass through it and be greeted by the guest master. Pilgrims who were going to the shrines of Saint

---

171. See below, A. ARCHITECTURAL DATA, Walls 43, 44, 45, 46 and 47.
172. See below, A. ARCHITECTURAL DATA, Walls 46.
173. See below, A. ARCHITECTURAL DATA, Walls 48.

Paul or S. Maria Scala Coeli would have turned right; visitors to the abbey would have been taken to the guest house. There they would perhaps have had a meal in the refectory, the large room with transverse arches overhead, and they might have stayed the night in the dormitory above. Cistercian lay brothers would have entered the west range, Wing C, with its cellar, refectory and dormitory. They would have attended prayers in the western half of the church of S. Anastasius. Visiting monks would have been welcomed into the cloister, with its chapter room, refectory, warming room, dormitory and other communal spaces opening off it. They would have joined the community of S. Anastasius at Mass and in the offices in the church. They would have attended daily chapter and perhaps assisted in the daily labour in the fields nearby.

Cistercian visitors would have found their way easily around the abbey at Tre Fontane. The church was a small version of that built at Clairvaux, c. 1135–1145. The austere but beautiful building was illuminated with stepped and splayed windows and created a serene ambience for prayer and contemplation. The monastic structures around the cloister followed the sequence found in other houses of the Order. Blake has made a reconstruction drawing of the medieval monastic buildings beside a plan of the church (Isometric Reconstruction of the abbey of S. Anastasius *ad Aquas Salvias*). It shows how the layout of the early monks' building, along the east range, was later extended on the north of the cloister to incorporate the monks' refectory and warming room. The lay brothers on the west were separated from the monks' quarters by the normal corridor. In the thirteenth century that must have been helpful, since the lay brothers at S. Anastasius were accused at the General Chapter in 1260 and 1261 of being unruly.[174]

Over the years interesting additions were made to the buildings of S. Anastasius. Whereas the abbot had originally resided in a small cell to the south of the dormitory, a new residence seems to have been built for him in the first half of the thirteenth century, probably at the

---

174. *Statuta capitularum generalium Ordinis Cisterciensis*. 9 vols, ed. J. M. Canivez, Bibliothèque de la Révue d'Histoire Ecclésiastique, 9–16B (Louvain: Bureaux de la Révue d'Histoire Ecclésiastique, 1933–1941) vol. 2:466–467 (1260); 2:480 (1261); and James Donnelly, *The Decline of the Medieval Cistercian Laybrotherhood* (New York: Fordham University Press, 1949) 76.

southern end of the east range, perhaps by Iacobus. When a prison cell was needed, the old room previously occupied by the abbot was used for that purpose.

In the late thirteenth or early fourteenth century the abbots of Tre Fontane extended the monks' wing of the monastery. They built an abbot's chapel between the north transept, the sacristy, and the chapter room. This gothic rib-vaulted structure was ornamented with paintings of the *Nativity* and the *Coronation of the Virgin Mary* in lunettes above the entrance and the altar. Possibly at the same time a sophisticated cycle of images was painted in the abbot's residence at the northern end of the east range, and frescoes of birds amid acanthus tendrils against a red background adorned the monks' dormitory. The interior of the narthex was also covered with murals. For the fifteen monks recorded as being at Tre Fontane in 1320, the abbey must have been one of the most splendid monasteries in Rome.

VIII

A CHRONOLOGY OF
MEDIEVAL BUILDING PHASES

T HE MEDIEVAL CISTERCIAN ABBEY of SS. Vincenzo e
Anastasio grew, as we have seen, in several building campaigns
through the twelfth, thirteenth and early fourteenth centuries
(fig. 90). In some places it is possible to see from the architectural data
how one part of the complex succeeded another. There are, moreover, a number of documented references to the building activities of
individual patrons. In this chapter the phases of construction will be
arranged in a relative sequence and then related to documents and
inscriptions which mention the patrons.

1. TWELFTH-CENTURY PHASES

Building at Tre Fontane in the twelfth century seems to have fallen into
three main phases. Initially, part of the east range seems to have been
erected by the founder, Innocent II (130–1143). The first abbot, Pietro
Bernardo Paganelli, who became Pope Eugenius III (1145–1153),
probably began the church and extended the monastic buildings.
Other work done in the monastery and the narthex of the church may
have been financed by the abbey's income from the lands in the
Maremma, especially after 1153, when the General Chapter of the
Cistercian Order was asked to confirm these possessions.

The twelfth-century core of the east range, Wing M

The earliest part of the medieval complex was the twelfth-century
core of the east range (Plan I), delimited on the west by wall 9 and on

183

the east by walls 8, 25, 7, and 24, on the south by wall 23 and on its north by wall 30, or possibly wall 31. At least one major wall (Plan I, wall 4) rose above a thick wall belonging to a pre-existing building, which was paved in marble.[1] The monks' building included on the ground floor: the eastern cloister walk; the present sacristy vestibule, which in the twelfth century was probably the sacristy and housed the book cupboard, the *armarium;* the chapter room; the passageway beside it; the rooms at the northern end, which may have included the monks' room, the novitiate, and the latrine. The east range appears to have been built as a double-storeyed block.[2] Upstairs (Plan II) there was a dormitory —delimited by walls 30, 8, 23, and 9—and a smaller room to the east—surrounded by walls 8, 25, 7 and 24—which may have been an infirmary. Two staircases connected the ground and upper floors of this block.

Sometime in the twelfth century, piers were inserted in the cloister ambulatory to support diaphragm arches across it. No doubt their purpose was to secure that part of the building. One pier partly obstructs one of the chapter room windows and another stands in front of the original entrance to the old sacristy. The architect or master builder probably had to block these openings partially because he had to take into account the previously built system of cross vaults covering the cloister walk.[3]

Pope Innocent II (1130–1143), according to Arnold of Bonneval, after 'having constructed monastic buildings, restored the church, and assigned as income houses, fields and vineyards,' brought monks of Clairvaux to live at Aquas Salvias.[4] It seems 'the monastic buildings' Innocent erected comprised the twelfth-century core of the east range. This may then be dated *c.* 1140, when Pope Innocent II founded the cistercian monastery of S. Anastasius.[5] The plan of the east range is very 'cistercian' in layout, and it is possible that the pope's builders

1. Maria Letizia Mancinelli, Laura Saladino and Maria Carla Somma, 'Indagini all'interno della chiesa dei SS. Vincenzo e Anastasio', *Arte Medievale* 2 Serie, 8 (1994) 111–118.

2. In this my interpretation differs from that expressed in Angiola Maria Romanini, '"Ratio fecit diversum": la riscoperta delle Tre Fontane a Roma chiave di lettura dell'arte bernardina', *Arte Medievale* 2 Serie, 8.1 (1994) 37–42.

3. Again, my interpretation differs from that of Romanini, '"Ratio fecit diversum"', 38.

4. See below, C. DATES AND DOCUMENTS, *c.* 1140 (3).

5. See below, C. DATES AND DOCUMENTS, *c.* 1140.

were assisted by a member of the Order, and that the building was finished after the monks came to Rome. The church Innocent restored could have been any of the three already at the site—the martyrium of Saint Paul, the basilica of Saint John the Baptist, or the sanctuary of Saint Mary.[6]

The Church

The medieval church appears to have been built after the twelfth-century core of the east range. It is of an early cistercian type, with a long, narrow, and high nave flanked on either side by groin-vaulted aisles, a transept with a low arched crossing, four eastern chapels, and a rectangular chancel.[7] The proportions and the bonding of the upper walls show that building began in the north arm of the transept and presbytery. The south arm of the transept was added later.[8] Attempts to vault the transept and nave were only partly successful. It seems the pointed barrel vault over the south transept arm began to crack during construction and the nave vault fell down.[9] This church is a typical early cistercian building in its lay out, its proportions, its rectangular sanctuary, its transept chapels, its square piers, and its windows. Hahn suggested a date of 1140–1150.[10] One suspects that the planning was done by a cistercian architect or master builder. The drainage of water from the roof and the slope of the floor towards the cloister were typical of cistercian practice.[11] On the other hand,

---

6. These were mentioned in the sources from the early eighth century onwards, see below, e.g., C. DATES AND DOCUMENTS, 713 and 807.

7. It is possible that the chapels that open off the south transept were rebuilt in the twentieth century. Their arched entrances are clearly medieval, however, indicating that they were preceded by medieval counterparts.

8. This was pointed out by Roberta Caglianone and Alessandro Iazeolla, 'Prime osservazioni dal rilievo architettonico del complesso delle Tre Fontane', *Arte Medievale* 2 Serie, 8.1 (1994) 121–129; and Giovanni Belardi, 'Il restauro dell'abbazia delle Tre Fontane', *Arte Medievale* 2 Serie, 8.1 (1994) 80; Giovanni Belardi, 'Il restauro architettonico', in Giovanni Belardi, Fra Jacques Brière Liliana Pozzi *et al.*, *Abbazia delle Tre Fontane: il complesso, la storia, il restauro* (Rome: Edilerica s.r.l., 1995) 114.

9. Belardi, 'Il restauro', 83–85; Belardi, 'Il restauro architettonico', 127–133 and Romanini, '"Ratio fecit diversum"', 3–6, 27–28.

10. Hanno Hahn, *Die Frühe Kirchenbaukunst der Zisterzienser* (Berlin: Verlag Gebr. Mann, 1957) 171–173.

11. Belardi, 'Il restauro', 87–90; Belardi, 'Il restauro architettonico', 138–160.

the masonry, the semi-circular arches, brick pilasters, and brick and marble cornices were all characteristic of medieval roman construction. An unusual feature in Rome at this time were the tufa 'quoins' at the corners.

When the church was added on to the core of the east range, the cloister ambulatory in that wing was extended to the north aisle wall. At that time the small room P may have been added to the dormitory. This may have functioned originally as a separate cell for the abbot or the sacristan, but from at least the fifteenth century onwards it was a monastic prison.

The church was probably begun shortly after 1140 by the first abbot of S. Anastasius, Pietro Bernardo Paganelli, who continued it and provided financial backing when he became Pope Eugenius III in 1145. It is clear that he continued to care for the monks of the monastery after his accession to the papal throne: he granted the abbey a privilege of papal protection; while allowing the community to go to Nemi in the treacherous summer months, he established that S. Anastasius would be 'the head of the abbey', that is, its permanent home; he secured permission for the monks to retain their property in the Maremma; and he donated a book.[12] All this suggests that he retained an interest in the monastery at Tre Fontane. Pope Alexander III, on the other hand, still wrote in 1161 about the monastery of Saint Anastasius, the church of Saint John the Baptist, and the church of Saint Mary, the buildings recorded *ad Aquas Salvias* since the early eighth century.[13] He may have been repeating earlier references, or the new cistercian church may not yet have been completed in 1161. This new church probably took the place of the earlier basilica of Saint John the Baptist.

Pope Honorius III consecrated the cistercian church in 1221 under the patronage of the Mother of God.[14] The inscription recording the consecration lists numerous relics.[15] Along with fragments of the wood of the cross and of the manger, there was cloth associated with the Virgin Mary. In addition, there were relics of several saints: the

---

12. See below, C. DATES AND DOCUMENTS, *c.* 1140 (3), (5); 1140–1145; Feb. 15, 1145; 1145–1153 (1), (2); August 1152.

13. See below, C. DATES AND DOCUMENTS, 713 and 10 July 1161.

14. See below, C. DATES AND DOCUMENTS, 1 April 1221.

15. See below, C. DATES AND DOCUMENTS, 1 April 1221.

precursor, John the Baptist; the apostles Peter, Paul, Andrew, and Bartholomew; the martyrs Lawrence, Vincent, Anastasius, Clement, and Sebastian; Bishop Nicholas; and the female saints Cecilia and Anastasia. Although the church was under the patronage of Mary, the name given was usually that of the adjacent monastery, Saint Anastasius.[16] Saint Vincent's name was added later; perhaps when his relics came to Tre Fontane in 1225; or perhaps in 1294, after the Chapter General had approved the join celebration of the feast of Saints Vincent and Anastasius.[17]

That the church was consecrated in 1221 does not mean that it was built at that time. Consecration of medieval churches in Rome sometimes took place long after the church building was complete.[18] It was probably dedicated and in use long before that time. The church of Saint Anastasius was, in my opinion, begun by Abbot Paganelli (Pope Eugenius III) between *c.* 1140 and 1153, and completed shortly after 1161. A tentative date would be *c.* 1140–*c.* 1170.

The conversi building, Wing C

When the church was laid out, the *conversi* corridor may perhaps have been built along the western side of the cloister and, beside it, the cellar in the groundfloor of the southern block of Wing C. It was cistercian practice to separate the lay-brothers from the monks in this way. The southern block of the *conversi* building incorporates part of the north wall of the church. The upper floor of this block was built— or rebuilt—much later.

---

16. In Rome, monasteries adjacent to extra-mural shrines were often given names different from those of nearby churches, catacombs, or martyria. For example, at S. Lorenzo fuori le Mura, Pope Hilarus (461–468) established two monasteries named after Saint Stephen and Saint Cassian; *Le Liber Pontificalis,* ed. L. Duchesne (Paris: E. De Boccard, 1981) 1:245.

17. See below, C. DATES AND DOCUMENTS, 1225 and 1294.

18. At San Clemente the church appears to have been built *c.* 1099–*c.* 1118/19, but the only surviving record of a papal consecration dates from 1295. See Joan E. Barclay Lloyd, *The Medieval Church and Canonry of S. Clemente in Rome.* San Clemente Miscellany, 3 (Rome: San Clemente, 1989) 66 and 69–70. Similarly, the church of S. Maria in Trastevere, which was built by Pope Innocent II (1137–43), was consecrated officially by Pope Innocent III in 1215, see Dale Kinney, *S. Maria in Trastevere from its founding to 1215* (unpublished Ph. D. Thesis, Institute of Fine Arts: New York University, 1975) 335 ff.

The lay-brothers' refectory on the groundfloor of the northern block of Wing C may have been built in the twelfth century too, but it is not strictly aligned with the southern block, as can be seen in wall 14. This suggests that it may have been built a short time after the southern block. As in other cistercian monasteries, there appears to have been a passageway between the two blocks (Plan I, walls 34 and 35).

Although the ground floor of the *conversi* building appears to have been built in the twelfth century, its precise date remains unclear. It may have been built *c.* 1140–1175. Again, the plan reflects the work of a cistercian architect or master builder, but the techniques of construction are typically roman.

The North Range

The north range was also built in the twelfth century, but after the east range. The techniques of construction are somewhat different from those in Wing M and in the church, and this would suggest a separate building phase. Where the north range meets the *conversi* corridor there is a rather clumsy thickening of wall 14 which would suggest that Wing R was built after both blocks of Wing C had been laid out, but still in the twelfth century.

On the groundfloor, the medieval refectory and adjoining rooms open on to the northern cloister walk. The cloister portico has medieval colonnettes, which differ markedly from the pieces of reused roman columns in Wing M (figs. 21 and 23). The cloister walk in the north range may originaly have been built as a single-storey lean-to structure. Following cistercian custom after *c.* 1150, the refectory was built at right angles to the cloister. It seems to have been a low structure, lit by two windows on the east and on the west. Later it may well have fallen into ruin, to be reconstructed in the nineteenth century with a pointed barrel vault and large windows. There appear to have been one or two rooms above the eastern end of north range, between the refectory and the dormitory, where the calefactory and its upper room were usually situated. Access on the first floor may have been from the dormitory.

No evidence survives regarding the patron or date of the twelfth-century structures in the refectory range. The design is cistercian; the building techniques, where visible, are typical of roman work of the twelfth century. Possibly this part of the monastery was constructed between *c.* 1175 and *c.* 1200.

The Narthex

The narthex was added on to the church, as a clear fissure between its southern side and the church facade indicates (fig. 5). In form, the portico is typical of roman nartheces of the twelfth century (fig. 4). Four ancient columns sustain ancient ionic capitals, an architrave, low relieving arches, and a brick and marble cornice. On the northern end, the narthex abuts the *conversi* building. At the southern end there is an opening between two piers. The masonry of the piers is typical of twelfth-century construction in Rome.

The narthex was certainly erected after the church, but, because of the masonry techniques employed in it,[19] the date often assigned to it, *c.* 1221,[20] is not convincing. A date *c.* 1175–*c.* 1200 seems more likely. It may have been built at the same time as the north range.

The Gatehouse (Gatehouse, Plans and Section)

To judge from its masonry, the southeastern part of the present gatehouse was built in the twelfth century. There is no evidence of a patron or a precise date. It may have been built at any time after the establishment of the monastery *c.* 1140, and before *c.* 1200.

2. THIRTEENTH AND FOURTEENTH-CENTURY BUILDING PHASES

There were several building campaigns in the thirteenth and fourteenth centuries (fig. 90). At that time the monastic complex expanded

19. Masonry techniques in Rome changed after *c.* 1208, as pointed out in Joan E. Barclay Lloyd, 'Masonry techniques in medieval Rome'. *Papers of the British School at Rome* 53 (1985) 238–242.
20. See below, C. DATES AND DOCUMENTS, 1 April, 1221. This date was accepted by Pio F. Pistilli, 'Architettura a Roma nella prima metà del Duecento (1198–1254)'. *Roma nel Duecento.* ed. A. M. Romanini (Turin: SEAT, 1991) 49–51 and Pio F. Pistilli, 'Considerazioni sulla storia architettonica dell'abbazia romana delle Tre Fontane nel duecento'. *Arte Medievale* 2 serie, 6, 1 (1992) 168–170. Aristide Sartorio, 'L'abbazia cisterciense delle Tre Fontane'. *Nuova Antologia* 167, settembre (1913) 50–65, suggested the narthex was built in the thirteenth century.

outwards and upwards to increase the community's living space. These additions were constructed in brickwork typical of roman construction in the two periods—*c.* 1200–*c.* 1250; and *c.* 1250 to the early fourteenth century; and in *opus saracinescum,* used in Rome from *c.* 1200 to the late fourteenth century.[21] Because the evidence does not allow assigning precise dates, these building phases are placed in a sequence indicating how one succeeds the other. While precise dates are not possible, some written references mention work done in the thirteenth and early fourteenth centuries. Apart from the structural additions, large parts of the east range were decorated with elegant murals in a style datable to the late thirteenth, or early fourteenth century.

The east and north ranges, Wings M and R, in the thirteenth or fourteenth centuries

There were three areas in which the monks' building was extended in the thirteenth or fourteenth century.[22] An arched portico was built along the northeast of the wing, possibly with one or two rooms laid out above it. A new sacristy—or abbot's private chapel—was erected beside the church. The roof level of the dormitory was raised.

The portico was built north of wall 25 and east of wall 8, with three arches of unequal span on its eastern side and one at its northern end in wall 30 and another in wall 28 on the ground floor (figs. 34 and 35). Above it there were probably one or two rooms (fig. 89). The piers and arches were built of *opus saracinescum,* which was used in Rome throughout the thirteenth and fourteenth centuries. The southernmost pier is also faced with brickwork, which has a modulus typical of roman construction of the first half of the thirteenth century. For this reason this structure seems to date from that time, i.e. *c.* 1200–*c.* 1250. It may be related to the building mentioned in the IACOBUS inscription now immured over a window in wall 29 in the north range (fig. 66). The east range was further extended through the addition of wall 2, north of wall 23, and wall 24, east of wall 7, both built in *opus saraci-*

---

21. Barclay Lloyd, 'Masonry', 233, 238–239, 241–242, 271–272, 275–276.
22. This was pointed out by Pistelli, 'Considerazioni'.

nescum. The result was the enclosure of the present sacristy and the room above it; both formed one space, possibly the private chapel of the abbot (Section CC' and figs. 45–47). This was a high, elegant room covered with a ribbed groin vault (fig. 48) and decorated in the late thirteenth or early fourteenth century with murals (fig. 87), as one sees today following Belardi's most recent restoration campaign.

An inscription over the lintel of the doorway refers to 'I' and 'L', who had this work made, FEC. FIERI. H. OP : ET: I : ET : L (fig. 67). In spite of the inscription, it is not clear who these patrons were; nor is there a precise date.[23]

The masonry would suggest a date in the thirteenth or fourteenth century. The two murals may be dated from their style to the late thirteenth or early fourteenth century (fig. 87).[24] They were painted, however, after the sacristy/chapel was complete and they may have been done long after its construction.

The east range was extended upwards over the original dormitory, moreover, when walls 9, 30, 8, and 23 were raised. This campaign was evidently connected with re-roofing that part of the complex. The masonry is *opus saracinescum,* datable to the thirteenth or fourteenth century. New windows were opened in the northern wall of the dormitory (fig. 38). It is probable that the two rooms delimited by walls 7, 25, 8, 28 and 30' were also raised and covered by the same new roof.

The walls of the dormitory and of the two rooms on the northeast were decorated with murals, datable by their style to the late thirteenth or early fourteenth century (figs. 49 and 50).[25] Again, it is not

23. Pistilli's suggestion that 'I' and 'L' were members of the monastic community is convincing, but we do not necessarily accept his date *c.* 1240 for the inscription and this phase of the building, Pistilli, 'Considerazioni', 173–175. It is also possible that the work was done by Abbot Iohannes (1302–1304) and his successor, Abbot Leonardus (1306–1329), as pointed out above (Chapter Seven), and also in Barclay Lloyd, 'The medieval Murals in the Cistercian abbey of SS. Vincenzo e Anastasio *ad Aquas Salvias* at Tre Fontane, Rome in their architectural settings', *Papers of the British School at Rome* 65 (1997) 343–344. See below C. DATES AND DOCUMENTS, 13th century.

24. Carlo Bertelli, 'L'enciclopedia delle Tre Fontane'. *Paragone-Arte* 20. 235 (1969) 34–36; Melinda Mihályi, 'I Cistercensi a Roma e la decorazione pittorica dell'ala dei Monaci nell'abbazia delle Tre Fontane'. *Arte Medievale*, 2 Serie, 5, 1 (1991) 155–161.

25. Bertelli, 'L'enciclopedia', 26, 36–40; Mihályi, 'I Cistercensi a Roma', 161–175; Barclay Lloyd, 'The medieval murals', 323–344; Aavitsland, *Florilegium.*

certain that they were painted when the rooms were covered with the new roof—they could have been done at any time after the construction of the upward extension—but this does seem likely.

The three thirteenth or fourteenth-century additions to Wing M may have been constructed concurrently or they may each represent a separate building phase. A comparison of the measurements of the *opus saracinescum* suggests that the sacristy and re-roofing may have been contemporaneous, but the evidence is not conclusive. The extension with the arched portico seems to date from the first half of the thirteenth century. The sacristy and upward extension may have been built at the end of the thirteenth or early in the fourteenth century. They may have been financed by the bequest of Ildebrandino Aldobrandeschi in 1284.[26] The murals, too, may have formed part of this building campaign. An inscription which used to be over the chapter room door—referring to work done by Abbot Leonardus in 1306[27]—has been connected with the murals.[28] This may have been part of a long-term plan by Abbot Martinus and his successors to extend and decorate the monks' residence.[29] A further set of frescoes, depicting standing figures of saints, was painted in the cloister in 1347, as is indicated by an inscription on one of them.[30]

In the north range, wall 29 was also raised in *opus saracinescum* datable to the thirteenth or fourteenth century (fig. 54). This was probably part of a campaign to renew the roof. Apart from this upward extension, there is no clear evidence of any other changes to Wing R in the thirteenth century.

Epigraphic evidence records that Jacobus constructed a residence—HANC DOMUS—within the monastic complex in the early thirteenth century (fig. 66).[31] The inscription referring to the campaign is now on the lintel of a window in the upper floor of wall 29 in Wing R. It has been claimed that this small area formed a *palazzetto* built by

---

26. See below, C. DATES AND DOCUMENTS, 1284.
27. See below, C. DATES AND DOCUMENTS, 1306.
28. Mihályi, 'I Cistercensi a Roma', 175.
29. Barclay Lloyd, 'The medieval murals', 342–344.
30. Barclay Lloyd, 'The medieval murals', 334 and 344.
31. See below, C. DATES AND DOCUMENTS, 1216–27.

Jacobus,[32] yet the window bearing the inscription is not surmounted by the arc of brick voussoirs normally placed over windows of that type in medieval Rome.[33] Jongelinus in 1640, moreover, referred to the inscription as being above a window at the end of the dormitory in some cells which had been destroyed.[34] The 'cells' Jongelinus referred to may have been the rooms in the upper floor of Wing R, but in my opinion that is unlikely. Alternatively, the inscription may have been moved to its present position from Wing M when large windows were opened in wall 30 in the nineteenth century (fig. 38), and the 'cells' may have been at the northern end of east range, beside the dormitory, where some seventeenth-century prints show a dilapidated building (e.g. fig. 72). If the latter were the case, the portico on the west of Wing M and its upper room, or rooms, may have been the DOMUS built by Jacobus. The masonry of that extension is datable to the first half of the thirteenth century, which would agree well with a project by Jacobus, who was penitentiary to Honorius III (1216–1227), perhaps between 1222 and 1227.[35]

The upper floors of the conversi buildings, Wing C

The building phases of Wing C are not precisely dated, but the *opus saracinescum* masonry visible in the upper floor of the southern block points to a date after 1200, possibly in the late thirteenth or fourteenth century. Graphic sources illustrate that the *conversi* dormitory, bounded by walls 14, 35, 15, and 38, was built above the lay-brothers' refectory and the central passageway, while there was also an upper room over the cellar and the *conversi* corridor to the east. In 1600 the roof-level from wall 38 to wall 35 was lower than that over the southern block; later it was the same (compare figs. 71, 72, 75, and 76). Old photographs (figs. 83–86) show bands of masonry which comprise a base of twelfth-century *opus listatum,* and some rough forms of *opus saracinescum* which can be dated after 1200 and before 1350.

---

32. Pistilli, 'L'architettura', 53; Pistilli, 'Considerazioni', 170.
33. See below, A. ARCHITECTURAL DATA, wall 29.
34. See below, C. DATES AND DOCUMENTS, 1640.
35. See below, C. DATES AND DOCUMENTS, 13th century.

Early prints show a medieval tower at the northern end of the *conversi* building, which had disappeared by the middle of the eighteenth century (compare figs. 71, 72, 75 and 76 with 77, 84, and 85). A modern 'tower', built perhaps on the medieval foundations, has replaced it (fig. 59). It is not clear when the original tower was built. It was probably constructed in the late thirteenth or early fourteenth century.

The Guest house, Wing O

The guest house was built against the southern block of the *conversi* building (figs. 60–63). Its masonry is all *opus saracinescum* of a late kind, and sometimes includes a few rows of bricks. There is no precise evidence for its date, but from its position, its masonry, and its relatively thin walls, it would appear to have been built in the late thirteenth or in the fourteenth century.

The Gatehouse (Gatehouse, Plans and Section)

The gatehouse was partly built in the twelfth century. The rest of this small building—most of the northwestern bay—was added in the thirteenth century in *opus saracinescum*. This bay was covered with a vault which was decorated with murals that extended to the lunettes beneath it.[36] In a later phase, wall 46 was built across the inner passageway of the gatehouse to hold the medieval gate. This was constructed of brickwork with a low modulus, typical of roman construction after 1250. Graphic sources show that there was an upper floor, with a six-light opening on the northwest side; they also indicate that this had fallen into ruin by the nineteenth century (compare figs. 71, 72, 74, 75, and 76 with 83–85). The upper floor has been restored. Likely the gatehouse was probably extended towards the northwest and decorated with murals in the early thirteenth century, perhaps in the pontificate of Honorius III (1216–1227), and a new gate was inserted after 1250.

36. Barclay Lloyd, 'The medieval murals', 237–312.

From *c.* 1140 till the middle of the fourteenth century, numerous benefactors and patrons supported the building of the abbey. While some remain anonymous, others are recorded in documents and inscriptions. Pope Innocent II, who reigned effectively in Rome between 1138 and 1143, founded the cistercian monastery, providing monastic buildings and restoring one of the three existing churches at Aquas Salvias.[37] Pietro Bernardo Paganelli, as first abbot *c.* 1140–45 and as Pope Eugenius III from 1145 to 1153, probably continued building the monastery and began the church; he granted the abbey the privilege of papal protection, confirmed its possessions, and began negotiations to have the Cistercian General Chapter confirm its property.[38] Enough income to complete the twelfth-century building of the north range and the narthex was probably produced by the lands in the Maremma. In the reign of Pope Honorious III (1216–27) Iacobus provided a house, which was possibly a residence for the abbot.[39] Ildebrandino Aldobrandeschi left money for building at the abbey in 1284,[40] during the time of Abbot Martinus, who also provided a silver reliquary for the head of Saint Anastasius in 1283.[41] Abbot Martinus (1283–1302) was succeeded by Abbots Iohannis (1302–6) and Leonardus (1306–29),[42] possibly the persons referred to as 'I' and 'L' in the inscription over the doorway into the 'sacristy' or abbot's chapel.[43] In a painted inscription over the chapter house door Leonardus is recorded in 1306 as having had work done.[44] Finally, some paintings of saints in the cloister bear the date 1347, during the abbacy of Gervasius (1339–56).[45] Gradually, from the abbey's foundation until the early fourteenth

37. See below, C. DATES AND DOCUMENTS, 1130–1138; May 1138; 1139, *c.* 1140.

38. See below, C. DATES AND DOCUMENTS, 1145–1153; August 1152.

39. See below, C. DATES AND DOCUMENTS, 1216–1227.

40. See below, C. DATES AND DOCUMENTS, 6 May 1284.

41. See below, C. DATES AND DOCUMENTS, 1283.

42. The names and dates of the abbots mentioned here are taken from Don Gabriel, *L'Abbaye des Trois-Fontaines située aux Eaux-Salviennes près de Rome* (third edition: Landerau: P. B. Moulins, 1882) 27–33; and from Giuseppe Ruotolo, *L'Abbazia delle Tre Fontane* (Rome: Abbazia Tre Fontane, 1972) 171–192.

43. For the inscription, see C. DATES AND DOCUMENTS, 13th century. For a possible identification with Abbots Iohannis and Leonardus, see Barclay Lloyd, 'The medieval murals', 343–344.

44. C. DATES AND DOCUMENTS, 1306.

45. Barclay Lloyd, 'The medieval murals', 344.

century, its buildings grew upwards and outwards to accommodate the community of monks who established S. Anastasius *ad Aquas Salvias* as a place of continuous prayer which has lasted—with some interruptions in the nineteenth century, until today.

PART II:
DOCUMENTATION

A

ARCHITECTURAL DATA

MANY ORIGINAL PARTS OF the medieval cistercian monastery of S. Anastasius are still standing. This makes it possible to present an abundance of important architectural data in a schematic way. To facilitate the discussion, the major walls of the church and monastery have been numbered and written on the plans and sections of our survey (Plans I, II, and III; Sections AA', BB', CC' and DD', Gatehouse, Plan and Sections). They are described briefly below, with notes on their masonry[1] and on blocked or open medieval windows and doors.[2] After this, columns, bases, and capitals are listed unless they are post-medieval. The vaults are discussed[3] and so are the medieval staircases. Medieval murals survive in the narthex, in the 'Arch of Charlemagne', and in Wing M. Although these are not

1. The names of various types of masonry will follow those given in Joan E. Barclay Lloyd, 'Masonry techniques in medieval Rome, c. 1080–c. 1300'. *Papers of the British School at Rome 50* (1985) 225–277. For masonry at Tre Fontane, see also, Maria Avagnina, 'SS. Vincenzo e Anastasio alle Tre Fontane' in Maria Avagnina, Vittoria Garibaldi and Claudia Salterini, 'Strutture murarie degli edifici religiosi di Roma nel XII secolo'. *Rivista dell'Istituto Nazionale d'Archeologia e Storia dell'Arte 23–24* (1976–77) 173 ff., esp. 239–241; Maria Mancinelli, Laura Saladino and Maria Somma, 'Abbazia delle Tre Fontane. Analisi delle strutture murarie' in A. M. Romanini (ed.) *et al., 'Ratio fecit diversum'. San Bernardo e le arte. Arte Medievale 2* Serie, 8.1 vol. 1 (1994) 93–105; and Liliana Pozzi, 'Definizione delle tipologie di paramento murario'. in Giovanni Belardi, Jacques Brière OCSO, Liliana Pozzi *et al., Abbazia delle Tre Fontane: il complesso, la storia, il restauro.* (Rome: Edilerica, 1995) 161–164.

2. The names of types of windows and doorways will be those given in Joan E. Barclay Lloyd, *The medieval church and canonry of S. Clemente in Rome.* San Clemente Miscellany, 3 (Rome: San Clemente, 1989) 25–30.

3. For the types of medieval vaulting mentioned, Barclay Lloyd, *S. Clemente,* 22–24.

discussed extensively, some indication of their original location is given.[4]

THE WALLS OF THE CHURCH AND MONASTERY

Wall 1
(Plans I and II; figs. 10 and 11)

Wall 1 is the east wall of church. Its masonry is twelfth-century brick-work, with a 5 x 5 modulus of 27.5, 28, 29.3, 29 cm., with no *falsa cortina* pointing, built over a base about 1.13 m. high, of irregular stonework.[5] The corners are strengthened by squared blocks of tufa, 33.5, 33 and 29 cm. high and 47, 24, 37 cm. long. The wall opens in four windows: in the upper part one oculus with quatrefoil tracery; lower down one large roundheaded window, approximately 4.025 m. high and 2.45 m. wide; and flanked by one smaller roundheaded window, approximately 1.915 m. high and 1.31 m. wide, on either side.

Wall 2
(Plans I and II; Section CC', figs. 40, 45 and 47)

This is the east wall of the transept chapels, sacristy 'S', and infirmary chapel. The masonry of the southern chapels is not visible; that of the northern chapels is twelfth-century *opus listatum*,[6] ending in a vertical row of tufa 'quoins' similar to those at the corners of wall 1 (fig. 45). There is one large roundheaded splayed window in each of the chapels, except in that south of the chancel, where there is a large

---

4. A fuller discussion of the murals is given in Barclay Lloyd, 'The medieval murals in the Cistercian abbey of SS. Vincenzo e Anastasio *ad Aquas Salvias* in their architectural setting'. *Papers of the British School at Rome* 65 (1997) 287–348.

5. This stonework is reminiscent of the foundations of the twelfth-century church at S. Clemente, see Barclay Lloyd, *S. Clemente*, 16–17.

6. For this type of masonry and its twelfth-century date, Barclay Lloyd, 'Masonry,' 228, 239–241, 243–244, and 273–274.

modern oculus.[7] Above the northern chapels wall 2 continued to form part of the infirmary chapel, which opened to the east in two modern rectangular windows (Plan II and figs. 40 and 45).[8]

In the sacristy ('S' on Plan I) and in the vaulted room above it ('S1' on Plan II and figs. 45 and 46),[9] wall 2 is built of thirteenth or early fourteenth-century *opus saracinescum;*[10] the lengths of the tufelli: 21, 9.5, 15.5 cm.; height of tufelli: 6.5, 7, 7.5, 8 cm.; height of mortarbeds: 1.5, 2.5 cm. The mortar is grey with brown specks and is very crumbly. A 5 x 5 modulus measures 38, 39, 40, 40.5, 42, or 42.5 cm. Buttresses strengthen the north and south ends of this part of the wall. In the sacristy there is one large roundheaded window; in the room above there was a door leading to a modern balcony, since removed.

Wall 3
(Plans I, II and III; figs. 7, 10 and 11)

Built of twelfth-century brickwork with no *falsa cortina* pointing, wall 3 is the west wall of the chancel and transept chapels. A wide semi-circular arch with some voussoirs of re-used roman *bipedales* opens into the chancel, whose floor is raised four steps above that of the nave (fig. 10). A semi-circular arch, framed by brick voussoirs, opens into each transept chapel. Above the chancel arch a large roundheaded splayed window, approximately 2.49 m. wide, is flanked on either side by one smaller roundheaded splayed window, approximately 1.22 and 1.30 m. wide. These windows are surmounted by an oculus with quatrefoil tracery. Above the transept chapels (figs. 10 and 11) on either side of the chancel, there are two roundheaded splayed windows, approximately 1.30 m. wide, and with an opening 1.51 m. high on the inside, 1.82 m. high on the outside and voussoirs 21 or 22 cm. long.

---

7. Our fig. 11, taken in the late 1960's, still shows a roundheaded window in that chapel.

8. The recent renovations by Giovanni Belardi have isolated the infirmary chapel.

9. The floor/ceiling between 'S' and 'S1' (see our Section CC') was removed by Belardi in the recent renovations.

10. For this type of masonry and its date, Barclay Lloyd, 'Masonry,' 228, 238–239, 241–244 and 275–276.

Wall 4
(Plans I, II, III; Section AA'; figs. 9, 19, 25, 29, 30, and 43)

Wall 4 is the west wall of the transept and east wall of the cloister ambulatory in Wing M. During the recent excavations in the church, at the corner of the north transept and north aisle wall at a depth of 0.392 m., there was uncovered an earlier wall which was built of alternating rows of brick and tufa in a masonry typical of seventh-century construction in Rome.[11] This early wall was 1.22 m. wide. At its juncture with its foundation, at a depth of 1.04 m., a small fragment of marble paving was discovered. Clearly, the medieval wall was built over this earlier wall, which must have belonged to a marble-floored building of some importance.

In the southern arm of the transept, the medieval wall stands on a base of irregular stonework, 57–63 cm. high.[12] Above this, it is faced with twelfth-century brickwork with no *falsa cortina* pointing; the exterior is constructed of twelfth-century *opus listatum*. In the northern arm of the transept, wall 4 is built of twelfth-century *opus listatum,* inside and out (fig. 9). The piers of the nave crossing are faced with twelfth-century brickwork with no *falsa cortina* pointing. Across the aisles of the church there are semi-circular arches with brick voussoirs; the corners are strengthened with tufa 'quoins' similar to those in wall 1. Beside wall 4 in the north transept are the monks' night stairs. Where wall 4 crosses the transept it is narrower than it is in Wing M—0.85 as against 1.25 m. in the sacristy vestibule.

On the groundfloor of Wing M, wall 4 is built of twelfth-century *opus listatum*–one row of tufelli X two rows of bricks: height of tufelli 15, 7.6, 11.5 cm.; length of tufelli, 17.5, 25.5, 11 cm.; height of bricks, 4.5, 3.5, 2.5 cm.; length of bricks, 19.5, 21, 16 cm.; modulus of 1 row of tufelli and 2 rows of bricks, 22, 26.5, 24.5 cm.; grey mortar, with white and maroon specks. Around the door of the chapter room this masonry has clearly been neatly repointed (fig. 29). West of wall 4 there

---

11. Maria Letizia Mancinelli, Laura Saladino and Maria Carla Somma, 'Indagini all'interno della chiesa dei SS. Vincenzo e Anastasio'. *Arte Medievale,* serie 2, 8 (1994) 111–114.

12. This formed part of the medieval foundations, uncovered during the nineteenth-century repairs.

are piers which support arches and vaults across the cloister ambulatory (fig. 19). These piers do not bond with wall 4, and are covered with modern brick facing. The second, third, and fourth arches from the church are built of medieval masonry with voussoirs 45–46 cm. long (roman *sesquipedales*) with *falsa cortina* pointing between them.

In the chapter room (Plan I, CR), there are two triple-light windows in wall 4, each separated by two pairs of colonnettes (fig. 30). The windows are partly obscured by the piers built against the west face of wall 4. Inside the chapter room are the remains of a blocked arched opening, possibly the original doorway; its northern jamb is 52 cm. north of the present door; the springing of the arch is only 1.00 m. high, and the arch itself rises approximately 1.72 m. above the present pavement of the chapter room, which has been raised.[13]

North of and above the present door into the sacristy vestibule, and partly obscured by a pier built against wall 4, there are traces of a blocked medieval doorway: part of a stone lintel with a semi-circular relieving arch above it and a marble step beneath it (fig. 25). The door was 2.286 m., the step 24 cm. high.

At first floor level in the monastic 'prison' (Plan II, P), wall 4 is narrower than in the transept. It is built of twelfth-century *opus listatum*—one row of tufelli x two rows of bricks. In this part of the wall and surmounted by brick voussoirs is a small niche marked with *falsa cortina* pointing (fig. 43). North of 'P' on the first floor wall 4 does not continue, but a narrow wall, our wall 40, runs parallel to it.

Wall 5
(Plans I, II and III; figs. 4 and 9)

This is the façade wall of the church. At ground level it opens in three doorways: one into the nave; and one into each aisle. Above the narthex there are two tiers of windows: on the lower level are three large roundheaded windows, that in the centre being stepped above

---

13. There are no bases beneath the two columns in the chapter room; perhaps they are buried beneath the modern floor, which has been raised. It was common in Cistercian architecture to have the floor level of the chapter room below that of the cloister ambulatory.

the other two; on the upper level is a rose, flanked by two large round-headed openings (figs. 4 and 9). The wall is crowned by a typical medieval cornice of bricks and marble brackets. Inside the church the outline of the medieval vault is visible.[14] The facade wall stands on a foundation of irregular blocks of peperino.[15] Approximately 63 cm. above the foundations, the wall is built of twelfth-century brickwork, with no *falsa cortina* pointing and a 5 x 5 modulus of 28, 28.5, 29, 29.5 and 30 cm.[16]

Wall 6
(Plan I; figs. 4–6)

Wall 6 forms the entrance to the narthex. There is a pier built against the south wall of Wing C; four grey granite columns stand on bases and plinths, raised on blocks of stone 63 cm. high, and supporting medieval ionic capitals; and there is a brickwork corner pier (fig. 4). The columns support a marble entablature; the piers each support a medieval moulding and a piece of ancient roman architrave used as a bracket (fig. 6). Above the narthex entablature are a medieval mould-ing and a series of low relieving arches and small roundels, probably originally made to contain ceramic decoration. Above, there is a medieval cornice of sawtooth marble brackets and slanted bricks, and sawtooth arranged in the opposite direction. The roof of the narthex slopes down on to wall 6. The piers at either end of the porch colon-nade are built of twelfth-century brickwork, with a 5 x 5 modulus of 29, 30 cm., with plaster smeared over the bricks and with *falsa cortina* pointing.

14. Giovanni Belardi, 'Il restauro dell'abbazia delle Tre Fontane (seconda parte)'. *Arte Medievale,* serie 2, 8 (1994) 79–91 and Giovanni Belardi, 'Il restauro architettonico'. Giovanni Belardi, Jacques Brière, Liliana Pozzi et al., *Abbazia delle Tre Fontane: il complesso, la storia, il restauro.* (Rome: Edilerica, 1995), 127–133.

15. This is reminiscent of the foundations of the twelfth-century church of S. Clemente, described in Barclay Lloyd, 'Masonry,' 243 and 276, and Barclay Lloyd, *S. Clemente,* 16–17, type VI. That the foundations are visible is due to the lowering of the floor level in the narthex in the nineteenth or early twentieth century.

16. Barclay Lloyd, 'Masonry,' 233, 236–237, 267–271.

Wall 7
(Plans I and II; Section BB'; figs. 31, 34 and 35)

This is the eastern wall of Wing M. The masonry in the chapter room is twelfth-century *opus listatum*. Two tall roundheaded windows open in this wall; from outside it is clear that they are not original, since the masonry around them is much redone (fig. 31).[17]

North of the chapter room there are three piers which sustain arches of different span (figs. 34 and 35); buttresses strengthen the east wall of the chapter room and each of these piers. The pier north of the chapter room is faced on its west side with brickwork from the first half of the thirteenth century—short brick fragments, 7, 13, 15, 18.5 cm. long, 3.4, 4.2, 5 cm. high, and with a 5 X 5 modulus of 24.5, 25, 25.5, 26, 26.5 or 27 cm.[18] The rest of wall 7 north of the chapter room is built of thirteen or fourteenth-century *opus saracinescum*, with tufelli 8, 9, 10, 11, 13 cm. long, 4.5, 6.5, 6.1, 7.5, 8 cm. high, and a 5 x 5 modulus of 40, 41, 42 cm.[19] While the tufelli in the main parts of the wall are a yellowish colour, the voussoirs of the arches are of grey-greenish peperino, 33, 35 cm. long. Where the masonry of the wall changes beside the buttress, there is a clear fissure (fig. 31). This marks two separate building phases.

The upper part of the wall is plastered over. It opens in a row of modern rectangular windows (figs. 34 and 35).

Wall 8
(Plans I, II, III; Sections BB' and CC'; figs. 32, 41, 49 and 67)

Wall 8 stands approximately at the centre of Wing M. It runs from the north transept of the church, through the chapter room, over two

17. They are also much taller than most medieval windows, showing that the present fenestration is modern. Carlo Bertelli, 'L'enciclopedia delle Tre Fontane'. *Paragone-Arte* 20.235 (1969) 42, mentioned two double-light windows; they are visible in photographs taken at that time, e.g. in Cesare D'Onofrio and Carlo Pietrangeli, *Abbazie del Lazio* (Rome: Cassa di Risparmio, 1969) fig. 194, and they are much smaller than the present openings..

18. Barclay Lloyd, 'Masonry,' 233, 238, 271–272, for this type of brickwork. The 5 x 5 modulus is often 26 cm.

19. For this type of masonry and the date, Barclay Lloyd, 'Masonry,' 241–242, 275–27. At S. Clemente there are walls with *opus saracinescum* on one side, brickwork on the other, as in this case, see Barclay Lloyd, *S. Clemente*, 19, type XII, and 172, 173, 175.

columns, to near the northern edge of Wing M (Plan I). No masonry is visible in the sacristy area, where the lintel of the doorway bears an inscription, legible from the east: 'FEC FIERI H: OP:ET:I:ET:L' (fig. 67).[20] North of the chapter room, wall 8 is built of medieval *opus listatum,* much repointed around windows and doors (fig. 32); at the northernmost end, the masonry changes to nineteenth-century work with four rows of tufa blocks alternating with four rows of bricks in wall 32.

On the first floor wall 8 runs from the north transept wall of the church right across Wing M. A number of niches on its eastern side may mark the site of original openings. Towards the northern end there are also rectangular niches—75 cm. high, 37–47 cm. wide, and 33.5 cm. deep—on its western side. Some of these have traces of mural decoration (fig. 41).

In the uppermost reaches of Wing M, wall 8 flanks a terrace (Plan III, Sections, BB' and CC'). There were on its eastern face a number of late thirteenth or early fourteenth-century murals (figs. 49 and 50).[21] Against wall 8 at this level there is a buttress. From the terrace one can see that wall 8 was built of medieval *opus listatum* to a height of 1.80– 2.27 m. above the terrace floor and then continued in thirteenth or early fourteenth-century *opus saracinescum*—length of tufelli, 12, 16, 17 cm.; height of tufelli, 5.5, 6, 7 cm.; 5 x 5 modulus, 38, 40 cm. There are traces of two blocked medieval windows, one on either side of the buttress, approximately 55 cm. wide and more than 98 cm. high, and with voussoirs 25–28 cm. long. Their sills are not visible; the tops of their openings were 0.98 and 1.00 m. above the terrace floor. They

20. See below, C. DATES AND DOCUMENTS, 13th century.

21. Most of these have been taken off the wall. See Bertelli, 'L'enciclopedia', 25–49; Carlo Bertelli, 'Affreschi, miniature e oreficerie cistercensi in Toscana e in Lazio'. *I Cistercensi e il Lazio: Atti delle giornate di studio dell'Istituto dell'Arte dell'Università di Roma (Roma 17–21 maggio 1977).* (Rome: Multigrafica Editrice, 1978) 71–81, esp. 80; Anna Menichella, 'Il maestro delle Tre Fontane,' in: *Atti (della IV settimana) di Studi di Storia dell'Arte medioevale dell'Università di Roma 'La Sapienza' (18–24 maggio 1980).* (Rome: L'Erma di Bretschneider, 1983) 477–485; S. Lo Giudice, 'Gli affreschi enciclopedici dell'abbazia delle Tre Fontane,'. *Strenna dei Romanisti* 46 (1985) 353–368; with beautiful coloured reproductions, Melinda Mihályi, 'I Cistercensi a Roma e la decorazione pittorica dell'ala dei Monaci nell'abbazia delle Tre Fontane'. *Arte Medievale,* 2 serie, 5,1 (1991) 155–189 and Barclay Lloyd, 'The medieval murals', 323–344; and Kristin Bliksrud Aavitsland, *Florilegium. En undersökelse av billedspråket i Vita Humana-frisen, Abbazia delle Tre Fontane, Roma,* Acta Humaniora 134 (Oslo: Unipub, 2002).

opened within the *opus listatum* masonry and were obviously closed before the late medieval frescoes were painted along this wall.

Wall 9
(Plans I, II, III; Sections BB' and CC'; figs. 17, 24 and 39)

This is the western wall of Wing M, running from the north aisle wall of the church to beyond Wing R (figs. 18 and 39). After crossing Wing A, wall 9 becomes the inner cloister wall of Wing M; beyond that it crosses Wing R and extends to wall 32. At its lowest level north of Wing A wall 9 opens in the cloister arcade (figs. 17–22), divided into five large bays, separated by rectangular piers, built of twelfth-century brickwork with a 5 x 5 modulus of 28.5, 28, 27.6 cm., marked by *falsa cortina* pointing. Above the piers are semi-circular arches, open in the central bay (fig. 18), but merely relieving arches in the first, second, fourth and fifth bays from Wing A (figs. 17, 18, 20 and 24); *falsa cortina* pointing marks the mortar between the voussoirs, which are reused roman *sesquipedales,* approximately 45 cm. long. Above and between the arches there is twelfth-century brickwork, with a 5 x 5 modulus of 29, 30.5 cm. (figs. 20 and 24). In each large bay beneath the relieving arches the cloister colonnade opens in an arcade with four semi-circular arches (figs. 17–21). Each bay is divided by one row of columns, which stand on a ledge, 63 cm. high; the ledge, which has a marble top, is built of twelfth-century brickwork with a 5 x 5 modulus of 30 cm. and marked by *falsa cortina* pointing.

Above the relieving arches and beyond the cloister, wall 9 is built of twelfth-century *opus listatum,* up to a level close to the top of the highest row of windows, where it changes to *opus saracinescum,* of thirteenth or early fourteenth-century date (figs. 17, 18 and 39). At its northern extremity wall 9 is built of *opus listatum* only up to first floor level, where it changes to nineteenth-century tufa and brick masonry (fig. 39); the changes of masonry at this end show that in the Middle Ages wall 9 supported wall 30 by forming a sloping buttress, which was extended and strengthened in the nineteenth century.

At its southern end at first floor level (Plan II) there is a setback in wall 9. The wall, built of the same masonry, is narrower and lower at this point, where it forms part of the monastic 'prison', 'P' (fig. 17). In this part of wall 9 there are the remains of a medieval doorway,

0.75 m. wide and 1.56 m. high; the stone lintel is still in place. From the west one can see traces of medieval windows in wall 9 (figs. 17, 18 and 39). In the 'prison' there is a rectangular stone-framed window, of the type seen often in medieval roman monastic architecture.[22] At the level of the modern first floor window sills there are traces of five small rectangular openings, each with a marble lintel and a relieving arch of short voussoirs above; beyond Wing R at the same level there are the remains of one more blocked opening of this type (fig. 39). Higher up, between the two rows of modern windows overlooking the cloister, there are two blocked rectangular stone-framed windows of somewhat more than twice the size (fig. 18); beyond Wing R is another of these larger windows (fig. 39).[23] Other fenestration in this wall appears to be post-medieval.

Wall 10
(Plans I, II and III; figs. 55 and 57)

Wall 10 is the east wall of the refectory (fig. 57). From the exterior one could once see that it is built of medieval *opus listatum* to a height just above the refectory windows, which are modern; above that masonry is a narrow band of large tufa blocks, above which the wall is plastered over. In 1998–2000 this wall was covered with plaster, so that the masonry and blocked windows are no longer accessible. Approximately 2.00 m. north of the south window there was a blocked medieval opening, 1.14 m. wide and crowned by a flat arc of small voussoirs; about 30 cm. from wall 33, the north wall of the refectory, there was a similar blocked opening, 86 cm. wide, with brick voussoirs above. The medieval openings were perhaps rectangular stone-framed or double-light windows.

Wall 11
(Plans I, II and III)

Wall 11 is the west wall of the refectory. It is approximately the same width as wall 10, but completely covered with plaster (fig. 55). There are two modern windows, directly opposite those in wall 10.

22. Barclay Lloyd, *S. Clemente*, 27–28.
23. Immediately below there is a window which looks deceptively similar; since it does not have the usual arc of voussoirs above its lintel, it may be a more modern insertion.

Wall 12
(Plans I and II; Section BB'; figs. 8 and 16)

Wall 12 is the cloister facade of Wing C (figs. 8 and 16). Where it is not plastered over, it is clear that this wall is post-medieval, probably built in the twentieth-century.[24] The colonnettes in the cloister ambulatory copy those in Wing R.

Wall 13
(Plans I and II; Section BB')

Wall 13 is the east wall of the *conversi* passage in Wing C. It is built of twelfth-century *opus listatum*. It continues northwards beyond wall 27; this extension is narrower than the rest of wall 13 and is plastered over. In the first bay of the cloister walk in Wing R there are traces of a blocked medieval window 2.10 m. above floor level. In three bays on the east side of wall 13 towards the cloister there are traces of an earlier vaulting system. The entrance to the *conversi* corridor in the central bay is post-medieval.

Wall 14
(Plans I and II; Section BB'; figs. 8 and 16)

Wall 14 is the west wall of the *conversi* passage; beyond wall 35 it continues in a narrower form to wall 34; a thicker version of the same wall runs northwards to wall 38 and then a narrower part to wall 33. The varied thickness of the wall, its slant and the various changes are apparent on Plan I. They seem to indicate it was built in various phases. Masonry is only accessible in the *conversi* corridor. It is twelfth-century *opus listatum*, though parts have been much repointed in modern times. The barrel vaulting over the passage is of uncertain

24. Tomassetti in 1896 wrote that there were only two cloister ambulatories, Giuseppe Tomassetti, 'Della Campagna Romana'. *Archivio della Società Romana di Storia Patria* 19 (1896) 148; presumably they were the ones in Wings M and R. The ambulatory in Wing C must have been built after Tomassetti obtained his information. Sartorio in 1913 did not see it either and did not include it in his sketch plan of the abbey, Aristide Sartorio, 'L'abbazia cisterciense delle Tre Fontane'. *Nuova Antologia* 167, settembre (1913) 58 and fig. 2 (our fig. 82).

date, and the cross-vault in the centre is post-medieval. In it upper level, wall 14 opens in a row of modern rectangular windows (fig. 16).

Wall 15
(Plans I and II; Section BB'; fig. 59)

Wall 15 is the west wall of Wing C. The thickness of the wall changes less dramatically than wall 14, but there are some variations. North of Wing O, it is thicker on the west, perhaps because of a modern facing, and built of a kind of modern *opus saracinescum* (fig. 59).[25] Between walls 35 and 34, wall 15 is a little narrower than it is to both the south and the north. North of wall 38 there is a clear change in thickness, where this part of wall 15 appears to abut wall 38. This part of wall 15 rises above the rest (Plan III). On account of the twentieth-century refacing of its western side, it is not possible to see any traces there of the original masonry or apertures in this wall. Masonry is only accessible from the east side of the wall, between walls 34 and 35; this seems to be a modern version of medieval *opus listatum*.

Wall 16
(Plan I)

Wall 16 runs across the groundfloor of Wing O. Where its masonry is accessible, it is *opus saracinescum,* probably built in the late thirteenth or fourteenth century. The doorway seems to have been wider originally; another blocked doorway once opened at the northern end of this wall. A ledge and three pilasters now stand against wall 16.

Wall 17
(Plans I and II; fig. 60)

Wall 17 is the westernmost wall of Wing O (fig. 60). It is built of medieval *opus saracinescum*. At ground level there is a door; above are two medieval roundheaded splayed windows;[26] a third opening of that

---

25. Fra Corrado of the community at SS. Vincenzo e Anastasio told me that the wing was restored in the 1950's.

26. For this kind of opening, Barclay Lloyd, S. Clemente, 25–26.

type is on the floor above, as well as three stone-framed rectangular windows, of which the southernmost looks genuinely medieval.

Wall 18
(Plans I and II; Section AA'; fig. 13)

Wall 18 is the south transept wall of the church. It is built of twelfth-century *opus listatum* on the outside, twelfth-century brickwork with no *falsa cortina* pointing inside. The corners are reinforced with tufa 'quoins'. Below the roof there is the usual frieze of sawtooth, marble brackets and sawtooth in the opposite direction; the height of the frieze is c. 50 cm.[27] There are three roundheaded splayed windows, 1.10–1.31 m. wide, in the south wall of the transept; two are 5.40 m. above floor level, the third centred above them (fig. 13). The outline of the blocked 'death door' is visible from inside the transept (fig. 13).

Wall 19
(Plan I; figs. 5 and 9)

Wall 19 is the south aisle wall of the church. It is built of medieval *opus listatum;* the corner of wall 19 and wall 8 is reinforced with tufa quoins (fig. 9). In each bay of the aisle there is one roundheaded slit window; the aisle is covered with cross-vaults.

West of the church, after a clear fissure, wall 19 continues as part of the narthex, in two piers (fig. 5). The east pier is built of brickwork with some *falsa cortina* pointing and a 5 x 5 modulus of 25, 26.5, 27 and 28 cm. The L-shaped pier has roughly the same masonry, with a 5 x 5 modulus of 27, 28, and 29 cm. and some *falsa cortina* pointing.

Wall 20
(Plans I and II; Section AA'; figs. 7, 9 and 10)

Wall 20 is the south wall of the nave and continues into the transept and chancel. Along the nave, nine rectangular brick piers sustain semicircular arches with voussoirs of reused roman *sesquipedales* (fig. 7);

---

27. In December 1992 I was able to examine the wall and measure this from the scaffolding erected by Giovanni Belardi.

the pier at the entrance to the transept is longer than the others and supports a wide semi-circular arch, with voussoirs mostly of reused roman *bipedales,* across the transept (fig. 10). Wall 20 continues into the chancel to meet wall 1. Above the nave arcade are roundheaded splayed windows, one to every bay (figs. 7 and 9). The window openings are 53 cm. wide, the splayed surroundings 1.43 m. wide. The medieval marble window frames are still in place.[28] Outside, in the clerestory zone there are brick pilasters, 93 cm. wide, between the clerestory windows (Plan II).[29] In the interior of the church wall 20 curves inwards near its apex, part of the pointed vault that was originally built (fig. 9); later, the nave was covered with wooden beams. All parts of wall 20 which are accessible to view are built of medieval twelfth-century brickwork with no *falsa cortina* pointing. The bricks, all roman spoils, are 2,3 or 4.5 cm. high and 12, 16 or 17.5 cm. long; a 5 x 5 modulus consistently measures 29.5 cm.[30]

Wall 21
(Plans I and II; Section AA'; figs. 7, 8 and 9)

Wall 21 is the north nave wall of the church. It is similar to wall 20 (figs. 7, 8 and 9). The twelfth-century brickwork of the piers has a 5 x 5 modulus of 28, 28.5 cm. and no *falsa cortina* pointing.

Wall 22
(Plan I; figs. 8, 9, 37)

Wall 22 is the south aisle wall (figs. 8 and 9), which extends westwards as the southern limit of Wing C. In the church (fig. 9) it is built of twelfth-century *opus listatum,* with 'quoins' of tufa at the corner with wall 4. The *opus listatum* has two rows of bricks to one of tufa—height of tufa, 9, 12, 13, 14 cm.; length of tufa, 9, 11.5, 17, 20.5, 24 cm.; height

28. I was able to take these measurements in 1992. Architect Giovanni Belardi pointed out to me the marble frames, clearly made for the clerestory windows when the church was built. See Paola Rossi, 'Le transenne di fenestra alle Tre Fontane. Appunti per una ricerca'. *Arte Medievale,* serie 2, 8 (1994) 133–140.

29. I measured one of the pilasters in December 1992.

30. I was able to examine the brickwork of this clerestory wall and take measurements in December, 1992, during the restorations of Giovanni Belardi.

of bricks, 2.9, 3, 3.2, 4 cm.; length of bricks, 8, 13.5, 19.5, 20 cm.; modulus of two rows of bricks and one of tufa, 23, 24.5, 25 cm.; the mortar is grey, with specks of white and maroon. In each bay of the aisle is a roundheaded splayed window (fig. 8). Embedded in this wall below one of the windows is the dedicatory inscription of the medieval church (fig. 65).[31] Two doors open in wall 22. One leads from the easternmost bay of the aisle into the cloister ambulatory of Wing M (fig. 37); the masonry around the doorway has been repointed. The other door at the western end of the aisle opens into the *conversi* corridor in Wing C. Against wall 22 have been built post-medieval piers, which sustain modern vaulting over the south ambulatory of the cloister (fig. 88, with vaults still plastered), except for the easternmost bay, also part of the Wing M ambulatory, which has a medieval vault showing the imprint of woven matting.[32] In the narthex the masonry of wall 22 is accessible in some places—it is twelfth-century brickwork with no *falsa cortina* pointing, with a 5 x 5 modulus of 26.5, 27, 28.5, 29.5 and 30 cm.

Wall 23
(Plans I and II; Section AA'; figs. 8, 14, 42 and 43)

This is the north wall of the transept (fig. 14), which extends westwards, across the cloister ambulatory of Wing M, along the cloister colonnade in Wing A (fig. 8). In the northernmost chapel of the transept it is covered with plaster. West of the chapel is a doorway (fig. 14); another opens beside the western wall of the transept, wall 4. Just east of this second door is a cupboard in the sacristy vestibule, which looks as though it was formerly a third doorway in this wall. There are traces of a blocked niche, perhaps a *piscina,* in the present sacristy. From wall 4 to a point approximately 3 m. from wall 3, wall 23 in its upper part is built of medieval *opus listatum;* this masonry continues obliquely towards the eastern doorway lower down. The intervening space is built of twelfth-century brickwork with no *falsa cortina* pointing (visible in fig. 14).

---

31. See below, C. DATES AND DOCUMENTS, 1 April 1221.
32. For this type of vault, Barclay Lloyd, *S. Clemente,* 22–23.

West of the transept an arch across the cloister ambulatory of Wing M is supported by two piers covered with plaster. The westernmost pier abuts an L-shaped pier built of twelfth-century brickwork with *falsa cortina* pointing; it has a 5 x 5 modulus of 26, 27, 27.5, 28, 28.5, 29, 29.3 cm. The rest of wall 23 along the northern side of Wing A (fig. 8), is all modern, built in the twentieth century.

At first floor level wall 23 is the southern limit of the upper part of the 'sacristy', perhaps the abbot's chapel (Plan II, S1)—where a door once led into the infirmary chapel;[33] the north transept arm; the dormitory; and the prison, 'P'. East of wall 8 it is built of brickwork; west of wall 8 in medieval *opus listatum*. In the prison a semi-circular medieval arch, with voussoirs of roman *sesquipedales,* spans the distance between walls 4 and 9 (figs. 42 and 43). The door of 'P' was not original; an older door, fitted with a small opening served the prison from about the fifteenth century onwards (fig. 44).

Wall 24
(Plans I and II; figs. 26 and 47)

Wall 24 is the northern wall of the sacristy and its adjacent vestibule. Up to its junction with wall 7 it is built of medieval *opus listatum;* east of that it is built of thirteenth or early fourteenth-century *opus saracinescum* (fig. 47). The northeast end is strengthened by an external buttress. There are three small modern rectangular windows in this part of wall 24. In the sacristy vestibule there are two roundheaded niches (fig. 26).

Wall 25
(Plans I and II)

Wall 25 delimits the northern end of the chapter room and about half of its upward extension. On the goundfloor its masonry is accessible; it is medieval *opus listatum*.

33. Our survey (Plan II) shows this arrangement, which was changed in the 1998–2000 renovations by Belardi. The door was blocked up and the former infirmary chapel was made inaccessible.

Wall 26
(Plans I and II; Section DD'; figs. 15, 16, 23, 51)

Wall 26 is the cloister colonnade in Wing R and its upward extension. The colonnade has six bays, five with three colonnettes each (fig. 23); the fourth bay from Wing M is merely a large arched doorway. The piers between the colonnade on the groundfloor are built of twelfth-century brickwork, with a 5 x 5 modulus of 28–30 cm. and the mortar is marked with *falsa cortina* pointing (fig. 51), but the third pier from Wing M, which is faced with brickwork with a slightly lower modulus of 25, 26 and 27 cm. and no *falsa cortina* pointing, is perhaps the result of a medieval repair.

On the inside of the cloister colonnade piers are built against the original medieval ones; they are faced with modern brickwork (figs. 23 and 52). The vaults that cover the ambulatory are all medieval, bearing the imprint of woven matting.

Above the cloister colonnade, the masonry of this wall is medieval *opus listatum* (fig. 23). Above groundfloor level wall 26 is entirely plastered over and no masonry is open to view (figs. 15, 16 and 51). At its western end wall 26 is supported by three sloping buttresses (fig. 51).

Wall 27
(Plans I and II; Section DD'; figs. 52, 53 and 58)

Wall 27 is the north wall of the cloister ambulatory in Wing R and its upward extension. At groundfloor level (fig. 52) the masonry of this wall is accessible. Although repointed in its lower parts, it is all medieval *opus listatum*. On the first floor no masonry is accessible. Plan II shows that this wall changes its thickness at that level.

At groundfloor level some features are worthy of note. The jambs of the door into the refectory are made of a beautiful ancient roman marble vine frieze (fig. 58).[34] Traces of a blocked medieval opening, 1.99 cm. high and probably a doorway, are visible in the third bay west of Wing M close to the modern door leading into the rooms east of the refectory (fig. 53). Remains of another lower opening, only 1.12

---

34. An arch above the door continues the ancient design, but is modern.

cm. high, are apparent in the westernmost bay. Both openings were originally surmounted by a flat arch of bricks with *falsa cortina* pointing between the voussoirs.

Several early inscriptions and reliefs are embedded in the lower parts of wall 27. Among them are those found at S. Paolo alle Tre Fontane in the nineteenth century.[35]

Wall 28
(Plans I and II; figs. 32 and 33)

On groundfloor level wall 28 consists of a broad pier and a semi-circular arch near the northeast end of Wing M (figs. 32 and 33). At first floor level this continues as one of the thick, medieval walls running in an east-west direction. At groundfloor level, the wall is built of *opus saracinescum,* of the thirteenth or early fourteenth century—length of tufelli 8, 9, 13 cm., height of tufelli, 4.5, 6, 6.5 cm.; 5 x 5 modulus: 31, 35.5, 36 cm. The arch has voussoirs of tufa.

Wall 29
(Plans I and II; Section DD'; fig. 54)

Wall 29 is the northern limit of Wing R east of the refectory. Its masonry is visible from the north (fig. 54). It is medieval *opus listatum,* except for a band of *opus saracinescum* at the top (see Section DD').

Apart from the two modern doors leading into the rooms east of the refectory, there are traces of two medieval doorways, now blocked; one is 60 cm. west of wall 9 on the groundfloor; the other is above the first door east of the refectory on the first floor, where its marble threshold can clearly be seen (fig. 54). The windows on the first floor of this wall look modern, but have medieval marble frames. They do not have the usual relieving arches above them, except for one, which has an unmedieval-looking double row of voussoirs. Beside three of the present windows are traces of narrower blocked openings, filled with rows of tufelli; these may have been the original windows. The

---

35. They include those referring to Pope Sergius, and the cross with an inscription in Armenian, see below, C. DATES AND DOCUMENTS, 688–689 and 1305.

lintel of the present window second from wall 9 bears the inscription of Jacobus (fig. 66).[36] From the masonry around the window, especially above the inscription, it seems clear that this was not its original location; it was probably inserted here at a later date.

Wall 30
(Plans I and II; Section AA'; fig. 38)

Wall 30 is the very thick wall near the northern end of Wing M. Clearly the uppermost part connecting walls 8 and 7, which is plastered over internally, was built in a different phase. Externally the masonry of wall 30 west of wall 8 is visible in its upper reaches—it is medieval *opus listatum,* except for the uppermost portion, which is *opus saracinescum.* Windows and doors in the *opus listatum* part are all modern, including the new french windows installed by Belardi in 1998–2000, which open on a terrace north of the dormitory. In the higher reaches of the gable, where *opus saracinescum* takes over, there is one stone-framed blocked rectangular opening, which looks medieval. Another rectangular window, with a marble grill to the east of the central one at this level, may be medieval, but its marble frame has disappeared (fig. 38).[37] There are buttresses about halfway along this part of wall 30 and at the end of wall 9 (fig. 39).[38] East of wall 8 at groundfloor level stand a pier and a respond of medieval *opus listatum,* which support a semi-circular arch. The pier is connected by tufa-fill to a larger pier of *opus saracinescum,* which is part of the sequence of piers in wall 7.

Wall 31
(Plan I; Section AA')

This is an intermediate wall between walls 8 and 9 and north of wall 30. Its thickness may indicate a medieval date, but nothing can be seen of its masonry and all openings are modern.

---

36. See below, C. DATES AND DOCUMENTS, 1216–1227.

37. The disposition of these windows corresponds with the interior decoration observed by Bertelli in 1969, see Bertelli, 'L'enciclopedia', 26.

38. See above, Wall 9.

Wall 32
(Plans I; Section AA'; fig. 38)

Wall 32 is located at the northern limit of Wing M. It rises only one storey, forming a terrace between it and wall 30. It is built of several rows of large tufa blocks, alternating with four or five rows of bricks. This masonry was typical in Rome in the nineteenth century. The wall was probably built shortly after the Trappists took over the monastery in 1868.[39]

Wall 33
(Plans I, II and III; fig. 56)

Wall 33 is the northern end of Wings C and R, and the rooms between them, extending eastwards. It all appears to be modern. The north wall of the refectory is built of large blocks of tufa, interspersed with occasional pieces of marble. Like the rest of wall 33, it looks post-medieval. The windows are large and appear to be modern.

Wall 34
(Plans I and II)

Wall 34 stands approximately halfway along Wing C. Where the masonry of this wall is accessible on the groundfloor; it is all a modern version of the medieval *opus listatum,* which is so frequent in the church and monastery. It is possible, but not certain that this was the original masonry, which has merely been repointed. The thickness of the wall seems to indicate that it is a major one, and medieval in date.

Wall 35
(Plans I and II)

Wall 35 rises a short distance south of wall 34. A small section of masonry is accessible on the groundfloor. Low down this is a modern repointing of medieval *opus listatum,* but its upper rows could be medieval. It consists of one row of bricks to one of tufa; length of tufelli

---

39. See below, C. DATES AND DOCUMENTS, 1868.

10.4, 14, 19, 21, 22.5 cm., height of tufelli, 12, 13, 14 cm.; a modulus of one row of each material is 20, 22, 23 cm. The thickness of the wall suggests a medieval date.

Wall 36
(Plans I and II; figs. 61–63)

Wall 36 is the north wall of Wing O. Externally the masonry is visible; it is *opus saracinescum,* of medieval date, but much repointed in modern times. At the east end on the groundfloor is an arched doorway, supported by a column on the west (figs. 61 and 63). At the east the arch is set back into wall 15, where there is evidence of modern refacing.[40] The voussoirs of the arch are shaped blocks of peperino. Windows in wall 36 are mostly modern, but four roundheaded splayed openings between the ground and first floors look medieval (figs. 61 and 62). The marble-framed rectangular windows on the first floor look like modern imitations of medieval windows of that type.

Wall 37
(Plans I and II; fig. 60)

Wall 37 is the south wall of Wing O. It is built of medieval *opus saracinescum,* with much modern repointing—length of tufelli, 9, 11.5, 12.5, 15 cm.; height of tufelli 6.5, 7, 8.5 cm.; 5 x 5 modulus 42, 42.5, 43 cm. In one place the masonry consists of two rows of small tufelli alternating with one or two rows of bricks. Similar masonry occurs in an undated medieval tower, Tor Sanguigna, and in S. Nicola in Carcere.[41] It is probably of late thirteenth or fourteenth-century date. The windows and doors are almost all modern.

Wall 38
(Plans I and II)

Wall 38 stands at the north of Wing C. No masonry is accessible. The thickness of the wall suggests an early date.

---

40. See above, Wall 17.
41. Barclay Lloyd, 'Masonry,' 242 and 275.

Wall 39
(Plan I and Section AA')

Wall 39 stands east of wall 4 and north of wall 25 in Wing M. No masonry is visible, but the thickness of this wall suggests that it may be medieval in date.

Wall 40
(Plan II, Sections BB' and CC')

Wall 40 is rather narrow and crosses Wing M from south to north on the first floor, east of wall 9. It does not stand directly upon any of the walls running across Wing M on the ground floor. From its narrowness and its position, it would appear to be a post-medieval structure. No masonry is accessible.

Wall 41
(Plan I)

Wall 41 stands north of the staircase leading to the dormitory from the cloister. In its upper reaches it is constructed of *opus listatum*. It supports a bracket, which is connected to the cloister vaulting, where there are a few rows of brickwork marked with *falsa cortina* pointing. Lower down, for 3.42 m. from the west and to the height of 1.955 m. from the cloister floor, the masonry appears to be a modern imitation of medieval *opus listatum*. There is then a clear break, after which the modern masonry continues to a level of 1.985 m. above the cloister floor, as far as the highest step of the adjacent staircase. The masonry may have been changed considerably, when the modern stairs were erected.

Wall 42
(Plans I and II)

This is the northern limit of Wing R west of the refectory. It does not correspond with wall 29, which is the northern limit of Wing R east of the refectory. It is plastered over.

THE WALLS OF THE GATEHOUSE (GATEHOUSE, PLANS AND SECTION)

Three plans and a section illustrate the gatehouse, the so-called 'Arch of Charlemagne' (figs. 1–3). It is built on a northwest-southeast axis and evidently stands above an ancient roman road.[42] Only the central passageway, with its vaulted ceiling, is medieval. The rest is modern.

Wall 43
(Gatehouse, Plans A, B, C)

Wall 43 is the northeastern side of the passageway through the gate-house; it opens in two doorways on the groundfloor and a doorway and a window on the second floor (Plans A and C). Masonry is accessible at groundfloor level, where it has been changed and repointed several times. In the northwestern bay to about half the height of the door to the southeast it is built of brickwork with no *falsa cortina* pointing and a 5 x 5 modulus of 28, 30, 31 cm.; hence it probably dates from the twelfth century.[43] Above, the brickwork changes to twelfth-century *opus listatum;* northwest of the door there is thirteenth or fourteenth-century *opus saracinescum.* Southeast of the central door-way is a stretch of modern brickwork; the masonry of the southeast bay is medieval *opus listatum.*

Wall 44
(Gatehouse, Plans A, B and C)

Wall 44 is the southwest side of the passageway through the gate-house; it opens in a doorway in the northwest bay; there are also traces of two blocked rectangular windows, one in each bay. Most of this wall is built of medieval *opus listatum,* but southeast of the door in the northwest bay, and reaching about halfway up the door, there is a

---

42. An excavation beneath the passageway revealed roman paving stones of basalt; it is likely that this road was the same that led to the *memoria* of Saint Paul at Tre Fontane, see below, C. DATES AND DOCUMENTS, 1938/39.

43. For this type of masonry, Barclay Lloyd, 'Masonry,' 233, 267–269.

stretch built of the same kind of twelfth-century brickwork as that directly opposite in wall 43; opposite the stretch of *opus saracinescum* in wall 43, there is a stretch of that same thirteenth or fourteenth-century masonry.

Wall 45
(Gatehouse, Plans A, B, C and Section AA'; fig 2)

This is the northwest wall of the gatehouse (fig. 2). In the centre is the tall entrance archway, the arch semi-circular and outlined with brick voussoirs. On either side are what appear to be heavy buttresses, which slope upwards and inwards on either side of the arch. In the floor above there is a six-light opening, with five modern colonnettes. Southwest of the central arch, close to ground level, there is a rectangular niche, 1.82 cm. high and 81 cm. wide; it has a low relieving arch above it, with modern voussoirs. The footings of the wall appear to be built of *opus saracinescum*, above which is a kind of modern *opus listatum* of alternating rows of tufelli and bricks (one of each); the tufa blocks are 6.2–8.5 cm. high and 15, 18, 21 cm. long. At the springing of the arch there is a thin marble cornice; above this the groundfloor is built of *opus saracinescum*. The masonry of the upper floor is a modern imitation of the *opus saracinescum*. The wall upstairs is narrower than on the groundfloor (Gatehouse, Section).

Wall 46
(Gatehouse, Plans A and B)

This wall contained the arched doorway into the monastic complex. The medieval marble jambs, arch and threshold are still in place; they appear to date from the late thirteenth or fourteenth century. This inner wall does not bond with walls 43 and 44. It is built of late thirteenth or early fourteenth-century brickwork with a low 5 x 5 modulus of 23, 23.5, 24, 25 cm.[44] It is clear that this wall was built after the vault

---

44. For this type of masonry and its date, Barclay Lloyd, 'Masonry,' 233, 238–239, 272–273.

in the northwestern bay of the gatehouse had been constructed. The support for the northeastern corner of the vault is covered by wall 46.

Wall 47
(Gatehouse, Plans A, B, C and Section AA'; fig. 3)

Wall 47 is the southeast facade of the gatehouse, facing the church and monastery (fig. 3). There is a central arch on the groundfloor and a triple-light window, with modern colonnettes, in the upper floor. The masonry in the lower part of this wall is twelfth-century brick-work, with a 5 x 5 modulus of 26.5, 27, 27.5, 28, 28.5 and 29 cm.,[45] much refaced in modern times. The wall on the first floor is narrow and modern (see Gatehouse, Section).

Wall 48
(Gatehouse, Plans A and B)

Wall 48 on the southwestern side of the gatehouse is part of the present gatekeeper's residence and is entirely modern.

Wall 49
(Gatehouse, Plans A and B)

Wall 49 is the northeastern side of the gatehouse and supports the staircase to the upper floor and its northern end. It is probably modern; no masonry is visible.

Wall 50
(Gatehouse, Plan C and Section AA')

Wall 50 divides the upper floor of the gatehouse into two rooms. It does not stand above wall 46, as may be seen in the Section of the Gatehouse.

---

45. For this type of masonry and the date, Barclay Lloyd, 'Masonry,' 233–236, 267–269.

COLUMNS, CAPITALS AND BASES

The Narthex of The Church

Four columns stand in the narthex of the church (fig. 4). Their shafts, of grey granite, are all ancient roman spoils; they support medieval ionic capitals and stand on simple ancient or medieval bases. The bases stand 1.30 m. above the present floor of the narthex.[46]

Wing A

All the colonnettes, capitals and bases in the cloister colonnade of Wing A are modern copies of those in Wing R, which are medieval.

Wing C

All the colonnettes, capitals and bases in the cloister colonnade of Wing C are post-medieval copies of the medieval ones in Wing R.

Wing M

In the chapter room two columns sustain the vaulting. The shafts are ancient roman and are made of cipollino marble and grey granite; their capitals are ancient ionic; their bases, if there are any, are buried under the modern floor. Although the southern column is a replacement, it is made up of ancient spolia and stands in the same place as the medieval original.[47] In wall 4 of the chapter room there are two triple-light windows each with two pairs of medieval white marble colonnettes (fig. 30); these support medieval ionic capitals and impost

46. See above, Wall 5.
47. That the floor has probably been raised, see above, Wall 4. Romanini says the southern column was replaced in a recent restoration campaign, but gives no details of when that occurred, Angiola Maria Romanini, 'La storia architettonica dell'abbazia delle Tre Fontane a Rome. La fondazione cisterciense'. *Mélanges Anselme Dimier*, 3 (Arbois: 1982) 684, n. 82. D'Onofrio and Pietrangeli in 1969 saw only two piers here, one containing a column; they believed there were originally two columns, as at present (D'Onofrio and Pietrangeli, *Abbazie*, 188).

blocks; they stand on simple double bases cut in one piece with their plinths, which are embedded in the window sills—height of colonnettes, 72.5 cm., height of capitals, 7.5 cm., height of bases, 5 cm., height of bases and plinths 20 cm.

In the cloister colonnade in Wing M the columns are arranged in groups of three (figs. 20 and 21), in four of the five bays, but the central bay opens in a plain arched doorway. The shafts, which are all cut down ancient roman spoils, do not sustain capitals, but simple medieval 'impost blocks', 24 cm. high. At a corresponding height on the piers there are simple marble cornices.

Counting from the south, the columns, bases and plinths are:

1. the upper part of a pinkish white marble column, standing on an ornate ancient ionic base and separate plinth;

2. the upper part of a grey granite column, standing on a medieval 'attic' base attached to a plinth;

3. the upper part of a pavonazzetto column with spiral fluting, standing on a simple medieval base and an ornately carved ancient block used as a plinth;

4. the lower part of a pavonazzetto column with spiral fluting, standing on an ancient ionic base and separate plinth (fig. 22);

5. the lower part of a grey granite column standing on a simple medieval base and no plinth;

6. the lower part of a grey-white marble column standing on an ancient 'ionic' base and no plinth;

7. the upper part of a grey-white marble column, standing on a medieval 'attic' base and no plinth;

8. the upper half of a grey-white marble column, standing on a medieval 'attic' base carved in one piece with its plinth;

9. the upper part of a grey-white marble column with a simple medieval base and separate plinth;

10. the upper half of a rough white marble column, with the inscription 'SPIRALIO FONTIS', standing on a medieval base attached to its plinth;

11. the upper half of a white marble column, standing on a simple medieval base attached to a plinth, and part of a block with ornate ancient carving, similar to that in 3. above;

12. the upper part of a white marble column, standing on a medieval base and plinth.

There are two columns in Wing M, each of which supports a medieval staircase. One, in the sacristy vestibule, is part of an ancient roman shaft, 1.31 m. high, made of grey granite; it sustains a late antique composite capital and an impost block; no base is visible (fig. 27). A similar column, capital and impost block stand further north, beyond wall 39 (fig. 36).

Against wall 8 is the stump of an ancient shaft, sustaining a medieval impost block, like those in the cloister colonnade of Wing M. Its function is not clear.

Wing O

One column supports the western side of the arched doorway in wall 36 in Wing O (fig. 63). Its shaft, 1.32 m. high, is the lower part of an ancient roman column of grey marble; its capital is of medieval lotus design and is 30 cm. high; there is no base visible.

Wing R

There are five sets of three colonnettes in the north range of the cloister (fig. 23). These consist of unfluted medieval colonnettes, standing on medieval bases, plinths and impost blocks.

The Gatehouse

In the gatehouse all the colonnettes are modern.

VAULTS

Parts of the church and monastery buildings are vaulted. Some vaults appear to be medieval, some are modern, and some cannot be dated.

The Church

The aisles of the church are groin-vaulted. Their disposition would lead one to suppose that they are medieval, built at the same time as the surrounding structure. It seems that the builders covered the nave of the church with a pointed barrel vault, which later fell down. To accommodate the vault the upper parts of walls 20 and 21 curve towards the centre of the building (figs. 7 and 9). The nave is now covered with a wooden roof.

The choir, the transept arms and the transept chapels are covered with pointed barrel vaults (figs. 10, 12, 14). The vault over the south transept arm showed signs of damage, which seems to have occurred during or shortly after construction.[48]

The Cloister

The ambulatories around the cloister are all groin-vaulted. In *Wing A* the vaulting is all modern (fig. 88), except for that in the easternmost bay in the corner of Wing M, which is medieval and bears the imprint of woven matting.

In *Wing C* all the vaults are plastered over. In the second, third and fifth bays from the church, there are traces of an earlier vaulting system visible on the eastern face of wall 13. The present cloister vaults are modern, but may replace earlier ones of unknown date.

In *Wing M* all the cloister vaults are medieval, bearing traces of the imprint of woven matting (figs. 19, 23, 24 and 37). The piers that support the arches between them seem to have been constructed after wall 4; two piers partially block the chapter room windows (fig. 30). The piers and the arches may be later reinforcements.

In *Wing R* the cloister vaults are medieval (figs. 23 and 52); the imprint of matting is visible on them all. The system of piers and supporting arches in Wing R is irregular in plan and may be part of a later building phase.

---

48. This was pointed out to me by Giovanni Belardi in December, 1992. He has discussed the vaulting in Giovanni Belardi, 'Il restauro dell'abbazia delle Tre Fontane (seconda parte)'. *Arte Medievale* 2 serie, 8,1 (1994) 79–91 and Giovanni Belardi, 'Il restauro architettonico'. Giovanni Belardi, Fra Jacques de Brière, Liliana Pozzi, *et al., Abbazia delle Tre Fontane: il complesso, la storia, il restauro.* (Rome: Edilerica s.r.l., 1995) 97–160.

Other Vaults in Wing C

A barrel vault of unknown date covers the *conversi* passage in Wing C. About half way along it is a modern cross-vault.

In the groundfloor of Wing C there are two parallel rows of groin vaults. They are supported by walls 14 and 15, 22, 34, 35 and 38 and rectangular piers—sometimes joined to narrow modern partitions— down the centre of Wing C. The vaults are all plastered over, so it is not possible to date them. Nonetheless, such a system of parallel vaulted bays is typical of medieval Cistercian architecture.

Other Vaults in Wing M

In Wing M there are vaults in the chapter room, in the sacristy vestibule, above the sacristy and in the monastic 'prison'. In the chapter room, two columns now support a system of six cross-vaults. The vaults are mostly plastered over, but they still show the imprint of woven matting in some places, so they are undoubtedly medieval. Elsewhere in medieval roman monastic architecture a single central column supports a system of four cross-vaults in a similar fashion.[49]

In the sacristy vestibule the vaulting zig-zags across the room in an irregular way (Plan I). There are slight traces of the imprint of woven matting under a whitewashed plaster surface; they are medieval.

Above the sacristy there is a medieval ribbed groin vault (fig. 48) which dates to the late thirteenth or early fourteenth century. The former floor of this room was a late insertion, and the vault once covered the sacristy, as it was extended in the late thirteenth or early fourteenth century. Belardi restored this room to its medieval form.

North of the chapter room is a vaulted passage. It is not possible to date its groin vault, which is plastered over, but it may be medieval. At the northern end of Wing M is a large vaulted room with four groin

---

49. This was the case in the medieval canonry at S. Clemente, Barclay Lloyd, *S. Clemente*, 187, 198 and Plan and Reconstruction IV; there are remains of a similar room at S. Maria in Cosmedin, Barclay Lloyd, *S. Clemente*, 198; and one at the monastery of S. Lorenzo fuori le Mura, which Jeremy Blake and I surveyed in 1984: see Joan E. Barclay Lloyd, 'The architecture of the medieval monastery of S. Lorenzo fuori le Mura, Rome'. *Architectural Studies in Memory of Richard Krautheimer*. ed. Cecil L. Striker (Mainz: Verlag Philipp von Zabern, 1996) 100.

vaults sustained by a central pier. The vaults are modern. On the first floor of Wing M the monastic prison is covered with a cross vault, with traces of woven matting (fig. 43). It is probably of twelfth-century date.

Other Vaults in Wing R

In Wing R the pointed barrel vault over the refectory is modern (fig. 55). The three rooms east of the refectory are covered with cross vaults. In the two western rooms the vaults are plastered over, so it is not possible to ascertain whether they are medieval or not. The eastern room has a modern vault.

Vaults in The Gatehouse

The passageway of the gatehouse is covered with two cross-vaults, one on either side of the main doorway. There are medieval frescoes on the vault over the northwestern bay and its corresponding lunettes.

MEDIEVAL STAIRCASES

At the monastery of SS. Vincenzo e Anastasio there are remains of two medieval staircases, both in Wing M (shown schematically on Section AA'; see figs. 27, 28 and 36). The 'night stair' led from the dormitory to the north transept; in the second room north of the chapter room there remains the 'day stair', which led up to the first floor. In both cases the staircase is supported by a column with a late antique elementary composite capital, a semi-circular and a parabolic arch—with its voussoirs marked with *falsa cortina* pointing.

MEDIEVAL MURALS

There are fragmentary remains of medieval murals in three parts of the church and monastery of SS. Vincenzo e Anastasio—in the narthex; in the gatehouse; and in Wing M.

Murals in The Narthex

Only two fragments survive of the murals that once decorated the narthex.[50] On the southern face of the north pier there is a faded remnant of a painting of Saint Leonard, holding a chain against a greenish-turquoise background (fig. 6). On the south pier there is part of a nimbed figure, depicted against a green background; a painted inscription, 'IACOBUS', identifies him as Saint James.

Murals in The Gatehouse

All the frescoes are in the vault and its corresponding lunettes in the northwestern bay of the gatehouse.[51] In the vault, there was a bust of Christ Pantokrator in a central roundel, surrounded by four angels, the symbols of the Evangelists, and patterns, including animals, birds and flowers, circles and diamonds.[52] Now only part of the hand of Christ raised in blessing survives in the centre; in the southeast corner is the lion of Saint Mark; in the northeast corner there is a remnant of the bull of Saint Luke; on the north there is part of an angel; on the west there is part of another. In the remaining space there are circles, lozenges and other shapes, with birds, flowers, a lion and part of another lion depicted between them.

In the lunette on the southeastern wall there are fragments of a *Madonna and Child,* with partial remains of two standing figures and a small kneeling monk in white on the righthand side, and of standing

---

50. In 1630 Eclissi made copies of these murals, which are now in the Vatican Library, Barb. lat. 4402, fols. 42r–51r; see also Anonymous (i.e. A. Barbiero OCSO), *S. Paolo e le Tre Fontane.* (Rome: L'Abbazia 'Nullius' dei Santi Vincenzo e Anastasio alle Acque Salvie, 1938) Tavv. XVII, 121–125 and XVIII, 126–131, 134; see our fig. 70; the murals are discussed briefly in Barclay Lloyd, 'The medieval murals', 309–323; see below, B. EARLY ILLUSTRATIONS, 1630 (3), (4) AND (5).

51. These, too, were copied by Eclissi in 1630, Vatican Library, Barb. lat. 4402, fols. 35 r, 36 r, 37 r and 40 v–41 r. For a discussion of the gatehouse murals, Fernanda De Maffei, 'Riflessi dell'epopea carolingia nell'arte medievale: il ciclo di Ezechiele e non di Carlo a S. Maria in Cosmedin e l'arco di Carlo Magno a Roma'. in *Atti del Convegno Nazionale sul tema: la poesia epica e la sua formazione (1969).* (Rome: Accademia Nazionale dei Lincei, 1970) 351–386, esp. 368–378 and Carlo Bertelli, 'Affreschi', *I Cistercensi e il Lazio,* 71–81, esp. 74–80; and Antonio Iacobini, 'La pittura e le arti suntuarie'. in *Roma nel Duecento.* ed. A. M. Romanini (Rome: Edizioni SEAT, 1991) 267–271; see also Barclay Lloyd, 'The medieval murals', 287–312.

52. This is shown in an Eclissi drawing, BAV Barb. lat. 4402, fols. 40 v–41 r.

figures and part of a kneeling monk on the left.[53] In the northeastern lunette, which is divided into two registers, there survive, at the top on the right, part of a military camp; and at the bottom on the left, the dream of Charlemagne; the emperor and pope are enthroned in the centre and part of their camp is to be seen on the right.[54] The southwestern lunette is divided into three registers, with two fragmentary figures in the middle at the top; Pope Leo III and Charlemagne hold up their charter in the central band; and some of the lands in the Maremma donated to S. Anastasius are depicted at the bottom.[55]

Murals in The Monks' Wing

In the uppermost levels of the monks' wing, Wing M, there are traces of medieval murals. These have been described and discussed by Carlo Bertelli and others.[56] Since Bertelli wrote his study, some of the frescoes have been removed from the walls.

---

53. In Eclissi drawing, BAV Barb. lat. 4402, fol. 35 r; the names of the standing figures on the left are given as Saints Paul and Benedict; they hold a sword and a book respectively.

54. Eclissi shows this lunette in Barb. lat. 4402, fol. 36 r. In the upper register on the left Charlemagne is depicted with his army, a boat and a military camp, followed by an image of Pope Leo III, while inscriptions refer to Charlemagne, his army, Ansedonia, the people of Rome and Pope Leo III. In the lower register on the left an angel speaks to Charlemagne in a dream; there is an image of a military camp, with a saint and two men, possibly monks, behind the tents; in the centre Charlemagne and Pope Leo III are enthroned, the pope pointing to an inscription above his hand, ITE AD AQUAS SALVIAS, 'Go to Aquae Salviae'; there follows an image of a military camp where an angel appears to the pope in a dream and part of an inscription explains that the following morning the pope is to send to Aquae Salviae to bring (the head of Saint Anastasius).

55. Eclissi shows more details. At the top a monk hands over to Charlemagne the head of Saint Anastasius, identified by an inscription, CAP. SCI ANASTASII, while four figures kneel on the far right; in the middle register on the far left is a battle scene, where Pope Leo III, accompanied by three monks, holds up the head of Saint Anastasius, while a man, perhaps Charlemagne, rides forth on a horse, with two dead enemies at his feet, near a walled city, and another man tends a wounded soldier; this scene is followed on the same register by an image of a boat at sea, near a castle named 'GILGO' (sic!), the island of Giglio; then, accompanied by a cleric, Charlemagne and Pope Leo III hand their charter to the abbot, monks and *conversi* (labelled as such) of S. Anastasius; in the bottom register there are images of Ansedonia and the other *castra,* all labelled, which Charlemagne and Pope Leo III were believed to have given to the abbey.

56. Bertelli, 'L'enciclopedia', 25–49; Bertelli, 'Affreschi,' 71–81, esp. p. 80; Menichella, 'Il maestro delle Tre Fontane', 477–485; S. Lo Giudice, 'Gli affreschi', 353–368; Mihályi, 'I Cistercensi a Roma', 155–189; and Barclay Lloyd, 'The medieval murals', 323–344; Aavitsland, *Florilegium.*

In the roof-space of Wing M,[57] Bertelli found murals decorating the two triangular gables of the dormitory. On the south wall near the church (Plan III, wall 23), there was a richly painted acanthus ornament. On the opposite side (Plan III, wall 30), there were at that level three windows, the central one closed with an unusual marble grill;[58] above this was depicted a phoenix and the windows were flanked by two painted palm trees, with two large peacocks at their feet. Above the two side windows were two more peacocks and, on the right, traces of a painted band of palmettes;[59] at the apex of the triangular gable was a large bird with one wing outstretched. All this was set against a red background.

On the eastern side of the monks' building at this level (Plan III, Wing M) there is a modern terrace looking eastwards towards the countryside (fig. 49); a row of ten slender modern pillars hold up a lean-to roof along the west (Plan III, wall 8).[60] Along the top of the wall was a band of frescoes, most of which have since been removed, 2.93 m. high and approximately 13 m. long in 1969.[61] Below a vegetal frieze immediately beneath the roof, Bertelli found nine panels, each 1.30 m. wide and surrounded by a painted border with a pointed arch on top (fig. 50); between the 'arches' were shell-shaped canopies. The panels covered not only the wall itself, but also the buttress, which is 10.20 m. south of wall 30;[62] further south there is a setback, where the decoration ended.[63] The painted panels were surrounded by tendrils, leaves and flowers. Bertelli identified the subjects of the scenes as: *Adam and Eve at work, Balaam in the tree, The eagle putting its young to the test, A Fisherman with his rod, The Senses, The Ages of Man* (clearly visible in our fig. 50), *The fruit harvest, A putto with a cage* (an allegory of hope)

57. We were unable to go into the roof-space of Wing M.
58. This is visible on the exterior in our fig. 38.
59. In 1969 Bertelli believed this was an egg and dart frieze, but corrected this in 1972, after the mural had been cleaned, Bertelli, 'Affreschi,' 12.
60. Bertelli's measurements of this wall, mostly given in Bertelli, 'L'enciclopedia', note 6, 41–43, do not all correspond with ours.
61. Bertelli gives this length in the text, Bertelli, 'L'enciclopedia', 28, but only 11.70 m. in note 6, p. 43. In 1972 he referred to a band 3 m. high and 14 m. long, Bertelli, 'Affreschi,' 12. We measured a length of 14 m. for this part of wall 8.
62. This measurement agrees with ours.
63. Bertelli appears to locate the setback nearly 2 m. north of where we measured it.

and *A double cage*.[64] This was a sophisticated and unusual programme.[65] Its location in a Cistercian monastery, is equally uncommon.

In the sacristy (Plan II, 'S') there are two frescoes in the lunettes under the vault: *The Nativity* on the west, (Plan II, wall 8) (fig. 87); and *The Coronation of the Virgin Mary* on the east, wall 2. Each scene is painted in an oblong panel, surrounded by acanthus scrolls. These scenes, when studied by Bertelli, were in bad condition and had been much retouched.[66]

Bertelli believed that the murals in the roof-space above the dormitory, along the terrace and in the room now above the sacristy were all part of the same decorative campaign.[67] Those along wall 8 were rather less delicate than the others, but still in the same style. He found the closest comparisons for these works in the Cimabuesque decoration of the Sancta Sanctorum of *c.* 1281, in the apse mosaics of S. Maria Maggiore, made by Torriti in 1296, and in the vaults of the upper church of S. Francesco in Assisi, also attributed to Torriti; the fisherman on wall 8 reminded him of the one in Giotto's *Navicella*.[68] Bertelli attributed the frescoes at Tre Fontane to an unknown painter of Torriti's circle, in the late thirteenth century, perhaps before 1296; he situated them in Italian art between Cimabue and Giotto.[69] Mihályi, on the other hand, suggested a date early in the fourteenth century, seeing them perhaps as part of the work done by Abbot Leonardus.[70] A date in the last decades of the thirteenth or in the first decade of the fourteenth century would fit the style of the paintings.

64. Bertelli, 'L'enciclopedia', 30–34.

65. Bertelli, 'L'enciclopedia', 31. Mihályi prefers to call this a cycle of 'Human Life', Mihályi, 'I Cistercensi a Roma', 164. Some aspects of its iconography are treated in Carl Nordenfalk, 'Les cinq sens dans l'art du moyen âge'. *Revue de l'Art* 34 (1976) 17–28; Carl Nordenfalk, 'The Five Senses in Late Medieval and Renaissance Art'. *Journal of the Warburg and Courtauld Insitutes* 48 (1985) 1–22; and Gino Casagrande and Christopher Kleinhenz, 'Literary and philosophical perspectives on the wheel of the five senses in Longthorpe tower'. *Traditio* 41 (1985) 311–327; see also Aavitsland, *Florilegium*.

66. They are still *in situ* and have been restored. They are discussed by Bertelli, 'L'enciclopedia', 30–36.

67. Bertelli, 'L'enciclopedia', 36. Other scholars do not agree and would like to see two phases, the murals in the sacristy perhaps done at a different time, see Mihályi, 'I Cistercensi a Roma', 155–189, who sums up the state of the question.

68. Bertelli, 'L'enciclopedia', 36–38.

69. Bertelli, 'L'enciclopedia', 35–40.

70. Mihályi, 'I Cistercensi a Roma', 175; for Abbot Leonardus' work, see below, C. DATES AND DOCUMENTS, 1306.

B

EARLY ILLUSTRATIONS

A list of early illustrations of the abbey of S. Anastasius *ad Aquas Salvias*, given in chronological order.

1469	Pietro del Massaio, miniature of Rome. (Frutaz, *Piante*, 2: tav. 157; see also Schwager, 'Santa Maria Scala Coeli', 401–402, Tafel 84.2.)
1471	Copy of Pietro del Massaio's miniature of Rome (fig. 68). (Frutaz, *Piante*, 2: tav. 158; see also Schwager, 'Santa Maria Scala Coeli', 401–402.)
1450–1500	Pietro del Massaio, miniature of Rome. (Frutaz, *Piante*, 2: tav. 160; see also Schwager, 'Santa Maria Scala Coeli', 401–402.)
1474	Alessandro Strozzi, *Map of Rome,* detail (fig. 69). (Frutaz, *Piante*, 2: tav. 159; see also Schwager, 'Santa Maria Scala Coeli', 401–402.)
1561	Giovanni Dosio, *Map of Rome,* detail. (Frutaz, *Piante*, 2: tav. 229.)
1550–1567	Sallustio Peruzzi, plan of S. Maria Scala Coeli prior to the sixteenth-century rebuilding. (Uffizi A 694 r; see also Schwager, 'Santa Maria Scala Coeli', 401–402, Tafel 83.1.)
1600	Giovanni Maggi, *View of Tre Fontane,* engraving (fig. 71); the print is part of a series of the *Nine*

Churches of Rome, made for the Jubilee of 1600. (Baglione, Le nove chiese di Roma, 2, 200–201; see also D'Onofrio and Pietrangeli, Abbazie del Lazio, fig. 193.)

c. 1600   Nicholas Van Aelst, Santi Vincentio et Anastasio alle Tre Fontane o vero all'Aqua Salvia, view of the three churches, gatehouse and monastery. (Now in the British Museum, and illustrated in Clare Robertson, 'Il gran cardinale', 198, fig. 188.)

1612 (1630)   Giacomo Lauro, View of Tre Fontane (fig. 72) engraving, drawn in 1612, published in 1630. (Lauro, Antiquae urbis splendor, fol. 151r.; see also Mulazzani, L'abbazia, 19).

1630   Antonio Eclissi, 'Pianta dell'Arco avanti la Chiesa de' SS. Vincenzo et Anastasio' (fig. 73), 'Facciata dell'Arco' (fig. 74), Interior of the narthex of the church of SS. Vincenzo e Anastasio, entitled 'portico' (fig. 70), drawings, pen and brown wash, and copies of the frescoes in the 'Arch of Charlemagne' and the narthex, drawings, pen and wash in various colours. (BAV, Barb. lat. 4402, fols. 35r, 36v–51r, 58r; Waetzoldt, Die Kopien, 80, and Barclay Lloyd, 'Medieval Murals', figs. 12, 16, 19, 22–29).

1641–1646   Israel Silvestre, Le Tre Fontane (fig. 75) engraving, view of the monastery from the west. Mulazzani, L'abbazia, 15, gives an erroneous date of 1776; Pistilli, 'Considerazioni', 182, n. 79 and tav. 43, gives the correct date.

1652   Filippo De Rossi, View of Tre Fontane (fig. 76), print. (De Rossi, Ritratto, 122.)

1753   Giuseppe Vasi, View of Tre Fontane (fig. 77), engraving. (Vasi, Tesoro sacro e venerabile, tav. 43; see also Mulazzani, L'abbazia, 18.)

c. 1789   Seroux D'Agincourt, measured drawings of the church—plan, longitudinal and transverse sections (fig. 78), the facade and narthex, view of church from the south (fig. 79)—and a plan and interior views and details of the chapter room. (BAV, Vat. Lat. 13479, fols. 47, 178, 184, 185 and 186; the location of the drawings of the chapter room is unknown, but it and other Seroux D'Agincourt drawings are illustrated in Romanini, '"Ratio fecit diversum"' 1–78, figs. 61 and 117.)

1804   Anonymous, *Arch of Charlemagne at Tre Fontane*, engraving, published in Paris, of the gatehouse, with the church of SS. Vincenzo e Anastasio and part of the guest wing behind. (Civica Raccolta Bertarelli, Milan; illustrated in Mulazzani, *L'abbazia*, 21.)

1818   Luigi Rossini, *View of the remains of the Arch of Charlemagne*, engraving done c.1818. (Rossini, *I monumenti*, (no date, but some prints have date, '1818') tav. V.)

July 1820   Friedrich Woldemar Olivier, *View of Tre Fontane*, drawing, pen and wash (Graphische Sammlung, Kunstmuseum Dusseldorf, Inv. Nr. 19/973; reproduced in Schwager, 'Santa Maria Scala Coeli', Tafel 82.1.)

1825   Seroux D'Agincourt, prints of six architectural drawings of the church of SS. Vincenzo e Anastasio: a longitudinal elevation; a section along the same axis; and a plan of the church (fig. 80); a view of the facade; a detail of one bay in the nave arcade; and a detail of regular brickwork. (Seroux D'Agincourt, *Storia dell'Arte*, Tavv. XXV, 3, 4 and 5; LXIV, 16; LXV, 15; and LXXI, 21.)

1853	Paul Letarouilly, prints of architectural drawings (fig. 81): a *View of the three churches at Tre Fontane;* a section of S. Maria Scala Coeli; and a plan of each church. (Letarouilly, *Édifices*, 3: pl. 339.)
1870 (1)	John Henry Parker, *View of Tre Fontane,* photograph, east facade of the church of SS. Vincenzo e Anastasio, *conversi* and present guest wings of monastery. (Reproduced in D'Onofrio an Pietrangeli, *Abbazie*, 177.)
1870 (2)	Anonymous, *View of Gatehouse from the east,* early photograph, shows most of the upper floor in ruins. (Illustrated in Barclay Lloyd, 'Medieval Murals', fig. 10; copy in Rome, ICCD, E 70111.)
c. 1870 (1)	Anonymous, *View across the cloister from the south-west,* early photograph, of the west façade of the Monks' wing, and part of north wing. (Copy in Rome, ICCD, E 70113.)
c. 1870 (2)	Anonymous, *View of Tre Fontane* (fig. 83), early photograph, shows the three churches, the monastery and the gatehouse. (Illustrated in Mulazzani, *L'abbazia*, 25; copy in Rome, ICCD, E 70095.)
1870s	Anonymous, *Interior view of the cloister ambulatory in the Monks' wing,* early photograph. (Copy in Rome, ICCD, E 70112.)
1879	Anonymous, *View of Tre Fontane,* woodcut, possibly based on an early photograph. (Reproduced in Mulazzani, *L'abbazia*, 23.)
1880–1890	Anonymous, *View of Tre Fontane* (fig. 84), early photograph. (Copy in Rome, ICCD, E 70105.)
late 19th century (1)	Anonymous, *View across the cloister from the northwest,* early photograph. (Copy in Rome, ICCD, E 70102.)

late 19th century (2)	Anonymous, *View across cloister looking south-east,* early photograph, shows an arch at the southern end of the cloister ambulatory in the monks' wing, below the monastic 'prison' (Plan I, P). The photograph was taken before Wing A was constructed. (Copy in Rome, ICCD, E 70107.)
late 19th century (3)	Anonymous, *View across the cloister looking northeast,* early photograph, shows part of Wing M and R. (Copy in Rome, ICCD, E 70106.)
early 20th century	Anonymous, *View of Tre Fontane* (fig. 85), early photograph. (Copy in Rome, ICCD, E 70104; reproduced in Mulazzani, *L'abbazia,* 24.)
early 20th century	Anonymous, *View of avenue of eucalypts leading from the narthex of SS. Vincenzo e Anastasio to S. Paolo alle Tre Fontane,* early photograph. (Copy in Rome, ICCD, E 70109.)
early 20th century	Anonymous, *View of Tre Fontane from the northwest,* early photograph. (Copy in Rome, ICCD, E 70088.)
1913	Aristide Sartorio, *Plan of the Abbey at Tre Fontane,* (fig. 82) includes the church of SS. Vincenzo e Anastasio, the cloister, chapter room and refectory as in 1913. (Published in Sartorio, 'L'abbazia' 52, fig. 2.)
before 1938	Anonymous, *Plan and two sections of SS. Vincenzo e Anastasio alle Tre Fontane and the monastery* (fig. 1). (Published in Anonymous, *San Paolo e le Tre Fontane,* tav. XXII.)
c. 1945–1949	Anonymous, *View of the northern end of the Conversi wing* (fig. 86), early photograph, shows the 'tower' being reconstructed. (Copy in Rome, ICCD, E 70110.)
mid-20th century (?)	Anonymous, *View of reconstructed south cloister ambulatory,* (Plan I, Wing A), with walls and

vaults plastered and with wooden benches in place (fig. 88), early photograph. (Copy in Rome, ICCD, E 52648.)

c. 1960 (?)

Anonymous, *View of Tre Fontane from the northeast,* early photograph. (Copy in Rome, ICCD, E 70101.)

late 1960s

A collection of photographs of the Gatehouse and the Monks' Wing, including especially the late medieval murals found there, was made for Carlo Bertelli. (Now in the ICCD.)

c. 1994

Analytical drawings and colour photographs were made during Giovanni Belardi's restoration and the concurrent excavations (published in 'Ratio Fecit Diversum', Angiola Maria romanini, ed., *Arte Medievale,* II series, 8.1 [1994]; and Giovanni Belardi, Jacques Brière, *et al., Abbazie delle Tre Fontane* (Rome: edilerica s.r.l., 1995).

C

DATES AND DOCUMENTS

Dates of events important in the history
of the monastery and its churches.

Significant documents are summarised in English, with relevant excerpts in the original language in the footnotes. Inscriptions are given in the text.

AD 67   Saint Paul is martyred in Rome, along the via Ostia.[1]

c. 200   The 'tropaeum' of Saint Paul is described by the Presbyter Gaius along the Via Ostia.[2]

251–253   Pope Cornelius (251–53), at the request of the roman matron Lucina, takes the bodies of the Apostles Peter and Paul from the Catacombs. Saint Paul's body is buried by Lucina on her property on the Via Ostiense, near the place where he was beheaded.[3]

299   Saint Zeno and 10,203 soldiers are martyred *ad Aquas Salvias* by Diocletian and Maximian.[4]

1. Richard Krautheimer, *Corpus Basilicarum Christianarum Romae*. Monumenti di Antichità Cristiana, 2nd Series, 2 (Vatican City: Pontificio Istituto di Archeologia Cristiana-Institute of Fine Arts, New York University, 1977) 5:97, with further bibliographic details.

2. Eusebius, *Ecclesiastical History* trans. Roy J. Deferrari, Fathers of the Church, 19. (Washington, D.C.: Catholic University Press, 1965–69) Book 2:25,7; Krautheimer, *Corpus*, 5:97.

3. *Le Liber Pontificalis*. ed. L. Duchesne (Paris: E. De Boccard, 1981) 1:150: '[Cornelius] . . . rogatus a quodam matrona Lucina, corpora apostolorum beati Petri et Pauli de Catacumbas levavit noctu: primum quidem corpus beati Pauli accepto beata Lucina posuit in praedio suo, via Ostense, iuxta locum ubi decollatus est . . .'. This account was written in the early sixth century, presumably using older sources. Hans Lietzmann, *Petrus und Paulus in Rom* (Bonn: A. Marcus und E. Eber Verlag, 1915) 131–140, suggested 'Lucina' may be a later addition.

4. Cesare Baronio, *Annales Ecclesiastici*. (Lucca: Typ. Leonardi Venturi, 1738) 2:290.

5th century	Ps-Marcellus, in the *Acts of Peter and Paul,* gives the location of Saint Paul's execution *ad Aquas Salvias* near a pine tree.[5]
25 Jan 604	Pope Gregory the Great in a bull inscribed on marble at S. Paolo fuori le Mura cedes the *massa*[6] called *Aquas Salvias* to the basilica of S. Paolo fuori le Mura, on the grounds that the Apostle Paul received the palm of martyrdom there when he was beheaded. The property in the *massa* includes Cellavinaria, Antonianum, Villa Pertusa, Bifurcum, Priminianum, Cassianum, Silonis, Cornelia Tessellata, and Cornelianum; on this occasion the *massa* is separated from the *patrimonium Appiae.*[7]
627	Saint Anastasius, a persian monk, is martyred by Chosroes II.[8]

5. A reference to the Apostle's martyrdom at *Aquas Salvias* near a pine tree is in the greek *Acts of Peter and Paul* by Ps-Marcellus, which has been dated to the fifth century; see Constantin von Tischendorf, *Acta Petri et Pauli* (Leipzig: Hermann Mendelssohn, 1851) 35; and see Richard A. Lipsius, *Die apokryphen Apostelgeschichten.* (Brunswick: C. A. Schwetschke und Sohn, 1887) 2, Pt. 1: 284 ff., esp. 303; and Giovanni Battista De Rossi, 'Recenti scoperte nella chiesa alle Aque Salvie dedicata alla memoria del martirio dell'Apostolo Paolo'. *Bullettino di Archeologia Cristiana.* 7(1869) 83–92; Johann Peter Kirsch, 'Der Ort des Martyriums des Hl. Paulus'. *Römische Quartalschrift für christliche Altertumskunde und für Kirchengeschichte* 2(1888) 237; Anonymous (i.e. A. Barbiero, OSCO), *San Paolo e le Tre Fontane.* (Rome: Abbazia 'Nullius' dei Santi Vincenzo ed Anastasio alle Aque Salvie, 1938) 40–41.

6. 'Massa' was a term used from late antiquity until *c.* 1000 to designate a grouping of properties within the same geographical zone, belonging to a great landowner, see Pierre Toubert, *Les structures du Latium médiéval.* Bibliothèque Française d'Athènes et de Rome, 221 (Rome: École Française de Rome, 1973) 328, 455–456, esp. 455 and n. 2.

7. De Rossi, 'Recenti scoperte', 83–92: '. . . in qua palmam sumens martyrii capite est truncatus ut viveret utile iudicavimus eandem massam quae Aquas Salvias nuncupatur cum omnibus fundis suis id est Cellavinarius, Antoniano, Villa Pertusa, Bifurco, Priminiano, Cassiano, Silonis, Corneli Tessellata atque Corneliano cum omni iure instructo instrumento que suo et omnibus generaliter ad eam pertinentibus eius cum Christi gratia luminaribus deputare . . .'. See also Kirsch, 'Der Ort', 235; Giuseppe Tomassetti, 'Della Campagna Romana'. *Archivio della Società Romana di Storia Patria* 19 (1896) 138; Hartmann Grisar, 'Le iscrizioni cristiane di Roma negli inizii del Medio Evo, Num. 13, Anno 604, Tav. III, n. 2.'. in *Analecta Romana* 1 (Rome: Desclée Lefebvre e C., 1899) 157–160; Paul Fridolin Kehr, *Italia Pontificia.* (Berlin: Weidmann, 1906) 1:166, no. 3; Anonymous, *San Paolo e le Tre Fontane,* 39 and tav. XIII; no. 102; Luisa Chiumenti and Fernando Bilancia, *La Campagna Romana.* (Rome: Banco di Roma, 1977) 5:422. This is the earliest authentic source for the tradition that Saint Paul was beheaded at *Aquae Salviae.* The tradition was probably much older; cf. the previous entry for the fifth-century and bibliography quoted in the note there.

8. Baronio, *Annales,* 2:221–224. Sansterre gives the date 22 January 628 for the martyrdom of Saint Anastasius (Jean-Marie Sansterre, *Les moines grecs et orientaux à Rome aux epoques*

649   George, abbot of the 'monastery from Cilicia situated *in Aquas Salvias*', is present at a synod held in Rome, under Pope Martin I.[9] The earliest authentic record of a monastery *ad Aquas Salvias*,[10] this suggests that the monastic congregation came from Cilicia in Asia Minor. The monks no doubt used the eastern rite. References to the foundation of a monastery on the site in 625 by Pope Honorius I (625–638) remain unproven.[11]

c. 650   It is reported that in the southern part of the city along the Via Ostia lies the body of the Apostle Paul—at S. Paolo fuori le Mura; not far south of that is the monastery '*Aquae Salviae*', where there is the head of Saint Anastasius and the place where Saint Paul was beheaded.[12]

---

byzantine et carolingienne. Académie Royale de Belgique, Mémoires de la Classe des Lettres, 66 [Brussels: Palais des Académies, 1983] 15). He adds that the head of Saint Anastasius was taken to his monastery in Jerusalem and solemnly deposited there on 2 November, 631; by the time the *De locis sanctis martyris quae sunt in Romae* was written (650–682/3) the head of the martyr was in Rome. Sansterre believes the relic probably came to Rome at the latest under Pope Theodore (642–649), Sansterre, *Les moines grecs et orientaux*, 16. Tomassetti claims that the relics of Saint Anastasius came to *Aquae Salviae* in 628–649, Tomassetti, 'Della Campagna Romana,' 139.

9. Jean Dominique Mansi, *Sacrorum Conciliorum nove et amplissima collectio*. (reprinted Graz: Akademische Druck und Verlagsanstalt, 1960) 10:c. 903: 'Georgius abba presbyter venerabilis monasterii de Cilicia, qui ponitur in Aquas Salvias, quod in hac Romana civitate habitare dignoscitur . . .'. See Guy Ferrari, *Early Roman Monasteries*. Studi di Antichità Cristiana, 23 (Vatican City: Pontificio Istituto di Archeologia Cristiana, 1957) 33; and Sansterre, *Les moines grecs et orientaux*, 9–14.

10. Benedict of Soracte and, following him, some later authors believed the first monastery *ad Aquas Salvias* was established by Narses in 551–568, but there is no surviving primary source for this, see below, C. DATES AND DOCUMENTS, *c.* 1000.

11. This date and the name of this founding pope are given by Onofrio Panvinio, *De praecipuis Urbis Romae sanctioribusque basilicis, quas Septem Ecclesiae vulgo vocantur*. (Rome: Apud Haeredes Antonii Bladii, 1570) 85; Giovanni Severano, *Memorie sacre delle sette chiese di Roma*. (Rome: Giacomo Mascardi, 1630) 411, and many later authors.

12. *De locis sanctis martyrum*, Roberto Valentini and Giuseppe Zucchetti, *Codice topografico della Città di Roma*. Fonti per la Storia d'Italia, 88 (Rome: Tipografia del Senato, 1947) 2:109 'In parte australi civitatis juxta viam Ostiensem Paulus Apostolus corpore pausat . . . Inde haud procul in meridiem monasterium est Aquae Salviae, ubi caput sancti Anastasi est, et locus ubi decollatus est Paulus. . . .'. See Ferrari, *Early Roman Monasteries*, 33; Herman Geertman, *More Veterum. Il Liber Pontificalis e gli edifici ecclesiastici di Roma nella tarda antichità e nell'alto medioevo*. (Groningen: H. D. Tjeenk Willink, 1975) 200–202.

648–682   The twelfth gate, at the road called the Via Ostiense, is said to be called Porta San Paolo because the Apostle rests there in his church, i.e. S. Paolo fuori le Mura. The head of Saint Anastasius the martyr is '*in Aqua Salvia*'.[13]

688–689   Two fragmentary inscriptions, excavated in the church of S. Paolo alle Tre Fontane in 1867, refer to Pope Sergius, probably Sergius I (687–701):

+ AC PALMA POSITA EST TEMPORIB. DOM SERGI PAPA. ANNU SECUNDU and

. . . AS PAULI . . . Q

. . . SCA. I . PRISCA DUD . . .

. . . V CUNCTOS CONS . . .

. . . NISI IAM SERGIUS . . .

. . . P PP INC . . .

. . . FUFIN. . . .[14]

713   A syrian bishop at the time of Emperor Anastasius of Constantinople brings his daughter, who is possessed by an unclean spirit, to the sanctuary, *mansio*, of Mary the Mother of God at the site of the decapitation of Saint Paul in the place called

---

13. William of Malmesbury, *Gesta Regum Anglorum*, IV, 351:1: 'Duodecima porta et via Ostiensa dicitur, modo porta Sancti Pauli vocatur, quia iuxta eam requiescit in ecclesia sua . . . In Aqua Salvia est caput Anastasii martyris.' Valentini-Zucchetti, *Codice topografico*, 2:150; and William of Malmesbury, *Gesta Regum Anglorum: The History of the Kings of England*, edited and translated R. A. B. Mynors and completed by R. M. Thomson and M. Winterbottom, Oxford Medieval Texts (Oxford: Clarendon Press, 1998) 1:620. This part of William's history is based on a much earlier itinerary of Rome which is similar to the *De locis sanctis martyrum* and which has been dated to after 648 and before 682, from the saints' tombs mentioned in it. See also Tomassetti, 'Della Campagna Romana,' 139; and Ferrari, *Early Roman Monasteries*, 33.

14. De Rossi, 'Recenti scoperte', 83–92; Giovanni Battista De Rossi, 'Scoperte alle Acque Salvie'. *Bullettino di Archeologia Cristiana* serie 2, 2 (1871) 71–76; Kirsch, 'Der Ort', 239–241; Tomassetti, 'Della Campagna Romana,' 139; Anonymous, *San Paolo e le Tre Fontane*, 43–44; Sansterre, *Les moines grecs et orientaux*, 14; see also our entry below, C. DATES AND DOCUMENTS, 1867.

Aqua Salvia, where the relics of Saint Anastasius are kept. Since no woman may enter the monastery, the bishop goes to pray in the basilica of Saint John the Baptist, next to the monastery, where the relics of Saint Anastasius are brought out and prayers are offered for the deliverance of the girl.[15]

731   The Venerable Bede refers to Anastasius, the noble persian monk who suffered martyrdom for Christ. His relics were kept first in his own monastery and then brought to Rome, where they were venerated in the monastery of Saint Paul the Apostle, which is called *ad Aquas Salvias.*[16]

---

15. 'Miraculum S. Anastasii'. *Analecta Bollandiana* 11 (1892) 233–241: 'Factum est temporibus piissimi imperatoris Anastasii Constantinopolitani, in monasterio quod appellatur Aqua Salvia. . . . Surrexit vir venerabilis episcopus habens plurimam fidem in Christo et in sancto Anastasio martyre, et assumens filiam suam habens spiritum immundum, et venit in mansionem sanctae genitricis Mariae, ubi sanctus ac beatus Paulus apostolus decollatus est in loco qui appellatur Aqua Salvia, ubi requiescunt venerabiles reliquiae beati martyris Anastasii, et quia in ipso monasterio mulier non ingreditur, iuxta monasterium autem est basilica beati Iohannis Baptistae et praecursoris, intravit ipse episcopus et coepit ibi esse in orationem; et adsumens secum presbyterum et diaconum et postulans abbatem ipsius monasterii, ut reliquiae sancti martyris Anastasii adducerentur in basilica sancti Iohannis, et omnis congregatio genua flecterent pro puella ipsa et postularent D.N.I.C. et beatum martyrem Anastasium. . . . See Tomassetti, 'Della Campagna Romana', 140; Ferrari, *Early Roman Monasteries,* 33–34. There seem to be several copies of this story: it is included in three MSS in the Vatican Library: BAV, Vat. Lat. 1195, fols. 106r–109v, from the eleventh century; BAV, Vat. Lat. 1193, fols. 82r–86r, from the twelfth century; and BAV, Vat. Lat. 6075, fols. 53r–55v, copied in 1601 from a very old codex belonging to S. Cecilia in Trastevere.

16. Bede the Venerable, *Chronica,* MGH Auctorum Antiquissimorum, 13 (Berlin: Weidmann, 1894) 310–311: 'Anastasius Persa monachus nobile pro Christo martyrum patitur . . . reliquiae beati martyris Anastasii primo monasterium suum, deinde Romam advectae venerantur in monasterio beati Pauli apostoli, quod dicitur ad aquas Salvias.' See Ferrari, *Early Roman Monasteries,* 34. The Venerable Bede says he was responsible for a revised latin version of the Life and Passion of Saint Anastasius, which had been badly translated from Greek and even more badly emended by an unskilled person; *Bede's Ecclesiastical History of the English People.* ed. Bertram Colgrave and R. A. B. Mynors (Oxford: Clarendon Press, 1969) 568–571: '. . . librum vitae et passionis Sancti Anastasii male de Greco translatum et peius a quodam inperito emendatum, prout potui, ad sensum correxi.' While the editors suggest (p. 570, n. 1) that the Saint Anastasius in question might have been a greek friend of Saint Gregory who became patriarch of Antioch in 599 and was killed in 610, one wonders whether it may have been Saint Anastasius of Persia, the patron saint of the monastery *ad Aquas Salvias.* Bede's corrected life of Saint Anastasius has unfortunately not survived.

723 or 739	The lombard king Luitprand comes to the monastery of Saint Anastasius during one of his visits to Rome.[17]
c. 787	King Luitprand builds a shrine and a monastery of Saint Anastasius in Corte d'Olona in Lombardy, probably as a result of his visit to the monastery of that name in Rome.[18]
787	At the Second Council of Nicaea, during the iconoclast controversy, the priests Peter and Peter, representing Pope Hadrian the bishop of Rome, declared, 'This image of Saint Anastasius has until today been in his monastery in Rome with his precious head'.[19]
789–790	Pope Hadrian I rushes to the monastery of Saint Anastasius early in the morning when he hears that the basilica, the vestry *(vestario)*,[20] the hygumenarch's residence, and other buildings have been burnt from the foundations to the roof by a fire caused by the monks' negligence; at the time of the blaze the relics of Saint Anastasius were salvaged and left lying in the middle of a courtyard. The pope renovates and restores to a better state the basilica and the other buildings.[21]

17. This was recorded in an inscription, published by Baronio, *Annales,* 12:308–9; Ferrari, *Early Roman Monasteries,* 34.

18. Paulus Diaconus, *Historia Longobardorum.* 6:58, MGH, Scriptores rerum Longobardorum, (Hanover: Societas Aperiendis Rerum Germanicarum Medii Aevi, 1878) 185–186. See also Ferrari, *Early Roman Monasteries,* 34.

19. Giovanni Mansi, *Sacrorum Conciliorum . . . collectio,* 13:23; AA SS, Ianuarii, 2:422: 'Petrus et Petrus Deo amabiles presbiteri et vicarii Hadriani papae senioris Romae dixerunt: Haec imago sancti Anastasii usque in hodiernum diem est Romae in monasterio ipsius cum pretioso eius capite'. Also Ferrari, *Early Roman Monasteries,* 34; Carlo Bertelli, 'Caput Sancti Anastasii'. *Paragone-Arte* 21 (1970) 12–25.

20. An eleventh-century version of the *Liber Pontificalis* has '*baptisterio*' instead of '*vestario*' see *Le Liber Pontificalis,* 1:512; perhaps from this error, several authors refer to a baptistery on the site, e.g. Antonio Nibby, *Analisi storico-topografico-antiquaria della carta de'Dintorni di Roma.* (Rome: Tipografia del Senato, 1837) 3:274. It seems highly unlikely that there ever was a baptistery in the monastery.

21. *Le Liber Pontificalis,* 1:512–513: 'Basilicam vero monasterii beati Anastasii Christi martyris una cum vestario seu ygumenarchio ceterisque aedificiis per incuriam monachorum

8th century

The feast of Saints Valerius and Vincent is celebrated on the same day, 22 January, in Valencia, Spain, as the feast of Saint Anastasius is celebrated *ad Aquas Salvias* in Rome.[22]

800–801

Pope Leo III gives the monastery of Saint Anastasius an altar cloth with the patron saint's martyrdom depicted on it, and a silver lamp with an octagonal canister.[23]

(805 ?)

Pope Leo III and Charlemagne are said to have donated to the monastery twelve *castra* or *castella*,[24] islands and other property in the Maremma in Tuscany—Ansedonia, Orbitello, Caporbio, Giglio, Monte Argentario, Altrecorba, Aquapiteo, Monte Acuto, Cerpena, Massiliano, Sciapilascia and Monte Oreste. The deed of donation was recorded on a gilded bronze plaque and in a painted inscription in the narthex, both lost. The events were

---

nocturno silentio exusta a fundamenta usque ad summum tegnum conbusta sunt. Quo audito, misericordissimus praesul valde diluculo velociter, currens, repperuit eam adhuc ardentem et solummodo arca eiusdem martyris lympsani eruta in media corte iacente. Cetera vero sanctuaria seu ministeria, tam in ecclesia quam in vestario, ab ipso igne conflata sunt. Qui cum nimio merore cum suis ministerialibus certatim extinguens ignem, confestim nisibus totis a flammiferis ruinis eruta noviter in meliori statu praedictam ecclesiam cum vestario et ygumenarchio ceteraque aedificia renovavit ac restauravit. Et amplius in ea sanctuaria atque ministeria et ornatum maxime quem ibidem conbusta sunt contulit.' See Tomassetti, 'Della Campagna Romana,' 140; Ferrari, *Early Roman Monasteries*, 34 and 35; Geertman, *More Veterum*, 9. Some authors attribute this rebuilding to Leo III in 796, surely an incorrect assumption, but see Panvinio, *De Praecipuis Urbis . . . basilicis*, 85; Ottavio Panciroli, *I tesori nascosti nell'alma città di Roma*. (Rome: Luigi Zanetti, 1600) 802; Severano, *Memorie sacre*, 415; Augustin Lubin, *Abbatiarum Italiae brevis notitia*. (Rome: typis Jo: Jacobi Komarek Boëmi apud S. Angelum Custodem, 1693) 329.

22. Epternach codex of the *Martyrologium Hieronimianum*. edd. J. B. De Rossi and L. Duchesne, in *AA SS*, Novembris, 2:12: 'XI kl feb spania civi valentia sci valeri epi et vincenti diac . . . et rom ad aq salvi sci anastasi epi.' See also *AA SS*, Januarii, 2:393; Ferrari, *Early Roman Monasteries*, 35; Pierre Jounel, *Le culte des saints dans les basiliques du Latran et du Vatican au douzième siècle*, Collection de l'École Française de Rome, 26. (Rome: École Française de Rome, 1977), 45–46, 57–61, 216–217.

23. *Le Liber Pontificalis* 2:11: 'Immo et in monasterio sancti Anastasii fecit vestem cum chrisoclabo, eiusdem martyris passione depicta; et farum de argento cum canistro octogoni, pens. lib. XXV.' See also Ferrari, *Early Roman Monasteries*, 35; Geertman, *More Veterum*, 42.

24. The terms *castrum* and *castellum* were commonly used in medieval Latium from the tenth to the thirteenth centuries; they are defined in Toubert, *Les structures*, 314, n. 1.

depicted in the 'Arch of Charlemagne', the gate-way leading into the monastery. Thought by most modern authorities to be an eleventh or twelfth-century forgery, a copy of this deed was made in 1369 by Pope Urban V, and it, in turn, was copied in the sixteenth and seventeenth centuries. The donation was confirmed by Popes Alexander III in 1161, Lucius III in 1183, Clement III in 1188, Celestine III in 1191, and Alexander IV in 1255.[25] The 'ninth-century' donation is thought to be spurious, but is included here because many later authentic documents refer to it.

807   Pope Leo III gives a silver crown to the monastery of Saint Anastasius and a silver canister to the oratory of the Virgin Mary in the monastery of Aqua Salvia.[26]

835–836   Pope Gregory IV donates an altar cloth to the monastery of Saint Anastasius the martyr.[27]

847–855   Pope Leo IV, for the eternal redemption of his soul, gives the monastery of Saint Anastasius an

25. BAV, Vat. lat. 11897, fols. 48r–52v; BAV, Barb. lat. 3232, fols. 47r–50r.; BAV, Vat. lat. 5844, fols. 47r–51r; Panvinio, *De Praecipuis Urbis . . . basilicis,* 85–86; Gaspar Jongelinus, *Notitia Abbatiarum Ordinis Cisterciensis per orbem universum.* (Cologne: Apud Johannes Henningium bibliopolam, 1640) 7:8; Tomassetti, 'Della Campagna Romana,' 140–141. Among those who believe it is spurious are: Kehr, *Italia Pontificia,* 1:173, Gian Lodovico Bertolini, 'Su la figurazione geografica della badia alle Tre Fontane'. in *X Congresso internazionale di geografia, Roma (1913), Atti.* (Rome: Tipografia dell'Unione Editrice, 1915) 1–9; Fernanda De Maffei, 'Riflessi dell'epopea carolingia nell'arte medievale: il ciclo di Ezechiele e non di Carlo a S. Maria in Cosmedin e l'arco di Carlo Magno a Roma'. in *Atti del Convegno Nazionale sul tema: la poesia epica e la sua formazione (1969).* (Rome: Accademia Nazionale dei Lincei, 1970) 351–386; Anthony Luttrell, 'The Medieval Ager Cosanus'. in. M. Ascheri, ed., *Siena e Maremma nel medioevo* (Siena; Betti Editrice, 2001) 27–58, dates the forged document to 1140–1161; and Elizabeth Fentress and Chris Wickham, 'La valle dell'Albegna fra i secoli VII e XIV'. *Siena e Maremma,* 59–81.

26. Le *Liber Pontificalis,* 2:22 and 24: 'Verum etiam et in monasterio beati Anastasii martyris modo fecit coronam ex argento, pens. lib. VIII, unc. IIII semis.' and 'Immo et in oratorio sanctae Mariae qui ponitur in monasterio aque Salviae fecit canistrum ex argento, pens. lib. II.'. See Ferrari, *Early Roman Monasteries,* 35; Geertman, *More Veterum,* 50, 87, 89, 90, 115–119.

27. Le *Liber Pontificalis,* 2:79: 'Verum etiam et in monasterio beati Anastasii martyris eodem modo fecit vestem de stauraci cum periclisin de quadrapulo I'. Ferrari, *Early Roman Monasteries,* 35; Geertman, *More Veterum,* 75.

altar cloth, decorated with the story of the eagles, and two curtains.[28]

855–858   Pope Benedict III gives a silver lighting fixture to the monastery of Saint Anastasius, called *Aqua Salvia*.[29]

858–867   Pope Nicholas I donates to the basilica of Saint Anastasius four curtains to be hung around the altar.[30]

998   Saint Nilus, not wishing to stay in Rome, is taken to the monastery of Saint Anastasius, 'which was situated far from the crowd and had always been served by greek monks. . . .'[31]

c. 1000   Benedict of Soracte attributes the building of the church and monastery of Saint Paul the Apostle *ad Aquas Salvias* to Narses, who governed Italy from 551–68 and who died in Rome in 574. Benedict refers to the relics of Saint Anastasius venerated there.[32]

---

28. *Le Liber Pontificalis*, 2:109: 'Ipse vero a Deo protectus venerabilis et praeclarus pontifex fecit in monasterio sancti Anastasii, pro aeterna (sic) animae suae redemtionem, vestem siricam de fundato I, habentem istoriam aquilarum; similiter et vela de fundato II, compta in circuitu de blata.'. Ferrari, *Early Roman Monasteries*, 35.

29. *Le Liber Pontificalis*, 2:145: 'Optulit etiam in monasterio sancti Christi martyris Anastasii qui vocatur Aqua Salvia gabatham saxiscam ex argento purissimo I, pens. lib. numero IIII.' Ferrari, *Early Roman Monasteries*, 35.

30. *Le Liber Pontificalis*, 2:158: 'Fecit etiam in basilica beati Christi martyris Anastasii, in circuitu sacri altaris, cum periclisin de blatthin vela IIII.' Ferrari, *Early Roman Monasteries*, 35.

31. *Vita S. Nili Abbatis*, 13. 90; *AA SS*, Sept. 7:387: 'Recusante Sene commorationem in Urbe, protulerunt illi sanctum Anastasium, procul a turba positum et Graecanicae genti semper addictum. 'See Bernard Hamilton, *Monastic Reform, Catharism and the Eastern Churches in the Tenth Century* (London: Variorum Reprints, 1979) 7; Ferrari, *Early Roman Monasteries*, 36.

32. Benedict of Soracte, *Chronicon*. ed. G. Zucchetti (Rome: Tipografia del Senato, 1920) 32: 'Narsus vero patricius fecit ecclesia cum monasterium Beati Pauli apostoli qui dicitur ad aquas Salvias, reliquie beati Anastasii martyris adducte venerantur.' Giovanni Battista De Rossi, 'Oratorio e monasterio di S. Paolo apostolo alle Acque Salvie costruiti da Narsete patrizio'. See *Bullettino di Archeologia Cristiana* s. 4, 5 (1887) 79–81; Tomassetti, 'Della Campagna Romana,' 138; Chiumenti and Bilancia, *La Campagna Romana*, V, 422–3; and Ferrari, *Early Roman Monasteries*, 35, who is skeptical about this late attribution to Narses.

1059–1073	Suppus, archpriest of S. Anastasius, was the spiritual father of Pope Nicholas II.[33]
1081	Pope Gregory VII (1073–85), formerly papal provider *(provvisor apostolicus)* of the monastery of S. Paolo fuori le Mura, takes that monastery under his protection and confirms its privileges and possessions. Among its possessions is the monastery of Saint Anastasius, with all its property, including the lands belonging to the *massa* referred to in the bull of Pope Gregory the Great.[34] Gregory VII's bull also lists some of the property in the Maremma reputedly donated to S. Anastasius by Pope Leo III and Charlemagne,[35] but without referring to that donation. Later in the document there is mention of the church of the martyr Saint Phocas, which formerly belonged legally to S. Anastasius.[36]
late 11th century	A Lectionary with Collects survives from the benedictine monastery of S. Anastasius *ad Aquas*

33. *Le Liber Pontificalis*, 2:336: '. . . Suppus archipresbyter sancti Anastasii, qui erat spiritalis pater dict. Nicholay pontifici. . . .'

34. See above, C. DATES AND DOCUMENTS, Jan. 25, 604.

35. See above, C. DATES AND DOCUMENTS, (805?).

36. Cornelius Margarini, *Bullarium Casinense*. (Todi: Vincentij Galassij, 1670) 106–110: '. . . Monasterium quoque Christi martyris Anastasij, cum omnibus suis pertinentiis, casis, casalibus, vineis. Atque Cellam Vinariam, Antonianum, Villam Pertusam, Bifurcum, et Priminianum, Cassianum, Silonem, Cornelium Tesolatum atque Cornelianum, cum omne iure, instrumentoque suo, et cum omnibus ad eam generaliter pertinentibus . . . (a long list of other property follows) . . . Simulque Ansedoniam Civitatem, cum pertinentiis suis, et Portu suo. Montem, qui vocatur Argentarium, cum Lacu Catamare, ubi est Ecclesia S. Angeli. Et medietatem Castri Orbitelli, cum pertinentiis suis. Et Castrum, quod vocatur Elba, cum omnibus suis pertinentiis. Pari modo Lacum prope Montem Argentarium, cum Piscariis suis; ita ut medietas piscium, qui ibi capiuntur reddatur suprascripto Monasterio S. Pauli Apostolo. (i.e. S. Paolo fuori le Mura) . . . Ecclesiam Sancti Focae Martyris, quae iuris Sancti Anastasii olim fuit. . . .' Antonio Coppi, 'Documenti storici del Medio Evo . . .', *Dissertazioni della Pontificia Accademia Romana di Archeologia*. (9th Jan. 1862) 209; Ignazio Giorgi, 'Il regesto del monastero di S. Anastasio ad Aquas Salvias'. *Archivio della Società Romana di Storia Patria* 1 (1878) 55; Tomassetti, 'Della Campagna Romana,' 142; Basilio Trifone, 'Le carte del Monastero di San Paolo di Roma dal secolo XI al XV'. *Archivio della Società Romana di Storia Patria* 31 (1908) 278–285; PL, 148:cc. 722–728; Luttrell, 'Ager Cosanus' (above, n. 25), 33–35. Several authors give a date of 1073 or 1074 for this document, e.g. Coppi, 'Documenti . . .', 209 and Tomassetti, 'Della Campagna Romana,' 142.

Salvias. For 22 January it gives Saint Vincent (deacon), martyred in Saragossa in 304/305 and Saint Anastasius, martyred in Persia in 627.[37]

1130–1138	In the papal schism of 13/14 February 1130–25 January 1138, Bernard of Clairvaux supports Innocent II against Anacletus II.[38]
1130	A Bull of Anacletus II of 27 March 1130 confirms the possessions of the monastery of S. Paolo fuori le Mura, including the church of Saint Anastasius *ad Aquas Salvias,* with the church of Saint Nicholas, other churches and property—farmland, vineyards, gardens, watermills and fishponds—in the *massa* called Nemi, along with the *castella* belonging to the church of Saint Anastasius.[39]
25 Jan 1138	Anacletus II dies.[40]
May 1138	Saint Bernard of Clairvaux records that the followers of Anacletus II (Pierleone) have sworn allegiance and fealty to Innocent II; and that the followers of anti-pope Victor IV have also promised him their obedience.[41]

37. Rome, Vallicelliana Library, MS C62; Jounel, *Le culte des saints,* 45–46, 57–61, 216–217.

38. Elphège Vacandard, *Vie de Saint Bernard.* (Paris: Librairie Victor Lecoffre, 1895); Pier Fausto Palumbo, *Lo Scismo del MCXXX.* Miscellanea della R. Deputazione Romana di Storia Patria, 13 (Rome: Presso la R. Deputazione alla Biblioteca Vallicelliana, 1942) esp.10; Mary Stroll, *The Jewish Pope: Ideology and Politics in the Papal Schism.* (Leiden: E. J. Brill, 1987).

39. PL 179: 692–695: 'Simili modo concedimus, et confirmamus eidem venerabili monasterio S. Pauli apostoli ecclesiam sancti Anastasii de fundo ad Aquas Salvias, cum ecclesia sancti Nicolai, et aliis ecclesiis, quae sunt in massa, quae dicitur Nemus; necnon et eamdem massam, cum terris, vineis, hortis, canapinis, aquaemolis, piscariis, et cum omnibus ad eam generaliter pertininentibus; simulque castella ad eamdem sancti Anastasii ecclesiam pertinentia . . . .'. See. Tomassetti, 'Della Campagna Romana,' 142; Philippe Jaffé and Samuel Lowenfeld, *Regesta Pontificium Romanorum.* (rpt Graz: Akademische Druck und Verlagsanstalt, 1959) 1:913, no. 8373; Ildefonso Schuster, *La basilica e il monastero di S. Paolo fuori le Mura.* (Turin: Società Editrice Internazionale, 1934) 94–95; Anonymous, *San Paolo e le Tre Fontane,* 109; Palumbo, *Lo Scismo,* 651; Luttrell, 'Ager Cosanus' (above n. 25), 35, 37.

40. Jaffé-Lowenfeld, *Regesta,* 1:919; Palumbo, *Lo Scismo,* 679.

41. Epistola 317; *Sancti Bernardi Opera.* edd. Jean Leclercq and H. M. Rochais (Rome: Editiones Cistercienses, 1977) 1:297: 'In octavis pentecostes ipsa die filii Petri Leonis omnes simul humiliaverunt se ad pedes domini papae et facti sunt homines eius ligii, iuraverunt ei ligiam

1139   Abbot Adenolfo of Farfa and Pope Innocent II have cistercian monks under Pietro Bernardo Paganelli come to Farfa, where they are to live at the summer residence, San Salvatore. This episode is referred to in letters from Pietro Bernardo Paganelli to Innocent II and to Saint Bernard of Clairvaux.[42]

To the pope Paganelli writes that he and his small community have left the joys of Clairvaux to go to San Salvatore,[43] only to find that they can no longer rely on the pope's promise.[44] To Saint Bernard he relates that the pope will no longer keep his promise to them and complete the work, but that the lord abbot of Farfa has received them with great joy and cannot do enough for them.[45]

c. 1140[46]   Pope Innocent II establishes a cistercian monastery of S. Anastasius *ad Aquas Salvias*. References to this foundation are given in the sources listed below:

(1) Replying to a request from Pope Innocent II to send monks to found a new monastery in Rome,

---

fidelitatem. Clerici quoque, qui in schismate erant, simul cum idolo [Victore IV antipapa], quod erexerunt, humiliantes se ad pedes domini papae, obedientiam ei iuxta morem promiserunt. . . .' Also quoted in Jaffé-Lowenfeld, *Regesta*, 1:880, no. 7900.

42. Epp 343 and 344; PL 182: 547–549.

43. Charles Mc Clendon, *The Imperial Abbey of Farfa*. Yale Publications in the History of Art, 36. (New Haven and London: Yale University Press, 1987) 13–14. McClendon, however, refers to 'Bernard of Pisa' later becoming 'Abbot of Scandriglia'; surely not the same man.

44. Ep 343, a letter from Pietro Bernardo Paganelli to Pope Innocent II; PL 182: 547: '. . . Factum ut imperasti: venimus ad monasterium Sancti-Salvatoris sicut mandaveris in litteris tuis servo tuo, patri nostro. Ubi est ergo nunc exspectatio mea, et tua promissio?'

45. Ep 344, from Pietro Bernardo Paganelli to Bernard of Clairvaux; PL 182: 549: '. . . Nam dominus papa, cujus litteris evocati sumus, promissionem quam de ejusdem loci confirmatione fecerat, opere non complevit, sicut et praesens tempus probat. Dominus Fars ad introitum nostrum gavisus est gaudio magno, et in toto corde suo pueros vestros recepit, ita ut, si fieri posset, oculos suos eruisset, et dedisset nobis. In hoc solum reprehensibilis est, et corrigendus est a vobis, quod omnia faciat vehementer, et ultra promissionem suam et nostram voluntatem.'

46. We prefer this date to 1137 or 1138, given in some authors, e.g. Anonymous, *San Paolo e le Tre Fontane*, 112.

Saint Bernard of Clairvaux claims it would be difficult because there are not as many monks available as usual; nonetheless he promises to recall some from elsewhere and to send them to Rome, as he wishes to obey the pope's commands in all things.[47]

(2) Pope Innocent does not wait for Saint Bernard's offer to materialize. According to Geoffrey of Auxerre, the abbot of Farfa summoned a group of brothers from Clairvaux and was going to build them a monastery; but the pope of Rome stopped the abbot by taking them for himself and establishing them in another place, i.e. at S. Anastasius *ad Aquas Salvias*.[48]

(3) Arnold of Bonneval gives a fuller account of Pope Innocent II's foundation of the cistercian monastery *ad Aquas Salvias*. When the pope returned to Rome, he reports, he began to restore the ruins of the Church, to bring back exiles, and to reorganize the church farms. He established the monastery in honour of the martyr Saint Anastasius *ad Aquas Salvias*. Formerly there had been a monastery there, but now there was only a church and no one lived there. Therefore, after constructing monastic buildings and restoring the church, and after assigning houses, fields, and vineyards for the upkeep of the new foundation, the lord pope requested and obtained that an abbot and a community of cistercian monks be sent to him from

---

47. Ep. 184; *Sancti Bernardi Opera*, 7: 4: 'Verum quod vobis de mittendis ad vos fratribus placet difficile adimplebitur, praesertim cum non sit copia personarum quae esse solebat . . . Curamus tamen undecumque evocare, quos vobis mittamus, cupientes per omnia vestris oboedire mandatis. . . .' Also in Angel Manrique, *Annales Cistercienses*. (Paris: G. Borsat and Laurentius Anissan, 1642) 1:391–392.

48. Geoffrey of Auxerre (Gaufredus Antissiodorensis), in *Vita Sancti Doctoris*, 3. 6, quoted in Manrique, *Annales,* 1: 392: 'Abbas Farfensis conventum fratrum a Claravalle vocaverat, Monasterium eis aedificaturus. Sed Romanus impedivit Antistes, et sibi tollens eos, in loco altero ordinavit'. See also *Sancti Bernardi Vita Prima*, lib. 3, auctore Gaudredo; PL 185: 317.

Clairvaux. Therefore Bernardo Paganelli, formerly second in command *(vice dominus)* of the Church in Pisa, was sent with some brother monks to serve the Lord in that place according to the Rule of Saint Benedict. Soon this foundation made progress and, when men 'from that locality', i.e. Rome and its environs, joined them, their number increased.[49]

(4) The new foundation is numbered as the thirty-fourth daughter house of Clairvaux.[50]

(5) Pietro Bernardo Paganelli of Pisa corresponds with Pope Innocent II and Saint Bernard about his move from Clairvaux to Farfa and thence to Rome.[51]

1140–1145

Saint Bernard writes to the monks of S. Anastasius in reply to a letter from Abbot Pietro Bernardo Paganelli. He cannot come to Rome to see them, but he encourages them in their cistercian way of life, especially in seeking unity in spirit and the bond of peace with humble charity, the seal of perfection. He stresses humility above all and peace, that they may have the indwelling of the Holy Spirit. He is aware that they live in an unhealthy region *('Scio . . . quod in regione habitatis infirma . . .')* and that some labour with many infirmities

---

49. Ernaldus Carnotensis, *Sancti Bernardi abbatis Vita,* 1.2.7, quoted in Manrique, *Annales,* 1: 91; *Sancti Bernardi Vita Prima,* lib. 2, auctore Ernaldo; PL 185: 296–297: 'Monasterium etiam apud Aquas-Salvias, in sancti Anastasii Martyris honore constituit; quod quidem ibi prius fuerat, sed hoc tempore sola ecclesia, deerat habitator. Constructis itaque coenobialibus mansionibus, et reformata Ecclesia, assignatis etiam ad alimonias domibus, agris, et vineis, a Clara-Valle abbatem et conventum fratrum sibi mitti dominus Papa petiit et obtinuit. Mittitur ergo Bernardus, Pisanae olim ecclesiae vice-dominus, et religiosi cum eo fratres, qui secundum beati Benedicti Regulam in eodem loco Domino deservirent. Cito profecit illa plantatio, et associatis sibi viris indigenis servorum Dei multiplicatus est numerus . . .'.

50. Leopold Janauschek, *Originum Cisterciensium.* (Vienna: Alfred Hoelder, 1877) 1:289, 307.

51. Epp. 343 and 344; PL 182: 547–549; and Bernard, Ep. 184.4; *Sancti Bernardi Opera,* 8:181–310, 311–547.

('. . . *et multis aliqui ex vobis laborant infirmitatibus
. . .'*). He sympathizes with their bodily weakness, but fears much more their vulnerability of
soul. Therefore he is not in favour of their seeking
medical advice or taking medicines for their bodily
ailments. Instead he recommends the potion of
humility and patience, and says they should cry
out to the Lord with all their heart, 'Heal my soul,
Lord, for I have sinned against thee' (Psalm 41:4b).[52]

15 Feb 1145	Abbot Pietro Bernardo Paganelli of S. Anastasius is elected pope, and takes the name Eugenius III (1145–53).
1147	Pope Eugenius III attends the Cistercian Chapter at Cîteaux, not asserting his papal authority, but sitting among the abbots like one of their number.[53]
c. 1149	Saint Bernard of Clairvaux writes his *De considera-tione* for Pope Eugenius III.[54]
1145–1153	(1) Pope Eugenius III grants to the monastery of S. Anastasius a privilege of papal protection. He stipulates that this monastery should be the head of the abbey *(caput abbatiae)*; the monks must live there in winter, but in summer they may go to Nemi. He confirms the possessions of the monastery, naming one called S. Donatus.[55]
	(2) Pope Eugenius gives the monks a book of the Homilies of Origen. This, with a dedicatory

52. Ep. 345; *Sancti Bernardi Opera*, 8:286–288; PL 182: 550–551.

53. 'S. *Bernardi Vita Prima*, lib. IV, auctore Gaufredo; PL 185:344: 'Igitur . . . eodem anno apud Cistercium iuxta morem, abbatibus congregatis, praedictus papa venerabilis adfuit, non tam auctoritate apostolica praesidens, quam fraterna charitate residens inter eos, quasi unus ex eis.' Cf. *Statuta* 1:37.

54. *Sancti Bernardi Opera* 3:393–493; PL 182:727–808.

55. P. F. Kehr, *Italia Pontificia* (Berlin: Weidmann, 1906) 1:174, no. 4; Alessandro Calandro, 'Nemi e i cistercensi delle Tre Fontane', *Castelli Romani* 29 (1984) 50–54.

inscription, was later found in the choir of S. Anastasius.[56]

1 Aug 1152   Pope Eugenius III confirms the *Carta Caritatis.*[57]

5 Aug 1152   Pope Eugenius III writes to the abbots at the Cistercian Chapter from Segni, explaining that he would like to be with them, but the duties of his office prevent it; he admonishes them to consider the virtues of their founding fathers and to imitate them.[58]

August 1152   Pope Eugenius III writes to the abbots at the Cistercian Chapter for a dispensation to enable the monastery of S. Anastasius *ad Aquas Salvias* near Rome to retain a certain *castrum* and some other possessions belonging to it by ancient law. Although the rigour of the Order would not allow this, the harshness of the site demands it, for without these possessions, the service of God cannot be maintained. Earlier, in the reign of Pope Innocent II, he himself, not fully knowing the malice of his people, had wished to give up those possessions, without realizing how difficult it would be to provide for the monastery without them. Pope Innocent II, having weighed the gravity of the case, had not wished to give his consent to Abbot Paganelli in this matter and had determined that the possessions should be retained until they could be exchanged for others more fitting for S. Anastasius. Now Pope Eugenius III can see that the posses-

---

56. G. Jongelinus, *Notitia Abbatiarum* (Cologne, 1640) 7:7: 'In S. Anastasij choro reperitur liber vetustate et antiquitate venerandus, donatus Monachis S. Anastasij per B. Eugenium Papam Tertium, et primum huius loci Abbatem, estq.: manuscriptus in membranis, continens Homelias Adamantij Origenis. In eiusdem libri primo folio, hae leguntur litterae Longobardae HUNC LIBRUM DEDIT DOMINUS PAPA EUGENIUS FRATRIBUS SANCTI ANASTASIJ'.

57. Jaffé-Lowenfeld, *Regesta,* 2:80, no. 9600; Manrique, *Annales* 2:205; PL 180:1541; *Statuta* 1:39–41.

58. *Statuta,* 1:39–41; Jaffé-Lowenfeld, *Regesta,* 2:80, no. 9603; PL 182:476.

sions cannot be given up without great danger. They can neither be exchanged for others nor sold, even if a buyer could be found. He therefore asks the Chapter to temper the rigour of the Order in this case and to rid themselves of any scandal or murmuring about it. He judges it more honest for the brothers of the monastery to support themselves with their own possessions than to have to beg from others.[59]

1153

(1) Hugo, Cardinal Bishop of Ostia, writes to Gozoinus, Abbot of Cîteaux, Bernard, Abbot of Clairvaux, and all the other abbots at the Cistercian Chapter, to announce the death of Pope Eugenius III. He asks the Chapter to grant the petitions which he is sending regarding the houses of S. Anastasius, Fossanova and Casamari.[60]

---

59. Samuel Lowenfeld, 'Documenta quaedam historiam monasterii S. Anastasii ad Aquas Salvias illustrantia', *Archivio della Società Romana di Storia Patria* 4 (1881) 400–403, esp. 402: 'Hec ideo diximus filii dilectissimi ut circa ecclesiam S. Anastasii pro commonitione nostra dispensatione utamini et quoniam ad huc retinet castrum quoddam et alias quasdam possessiones ad ejus jus antiquitus pertinentes, aliquorum ex vobis animi non turbentur. Licet enim id ordinis rigor inhibeat, loci tamen necessitas retineri compellit, dum nec aliis possessionibus ecclesia ipsa ita potuit ampliari, ut suppetat fratribus inhibi commorantibus unde sine istis possessionibus in dei valeant servitis sustentari . . . Quocirca necessitates loci nostroque consilio utiliori sicut arbitramur inspecto, rigorem ordinis in hac parte circa ipsam ecclesiam temperate, ac de medio vestram omne scandalum super his et murmur auferte. Non siquidem honestius judicamus, ut fratres eiusdem ecclesiae de propris possessionibus aliorum studio conquisitis in divinis obsequiis sustentur, quam sub incerta multotiens impetrandi fiducia aliena compellantur suffragia mendicare, dicente beato Gregorio, turpe fore religiosis viris oblata etiam libenter accipere, nedum quod non oblata cum exactione debeant postulare'. See Jaffé-Lowenfeld, *Regesta*, 2:81, no. 9604; Kehr, *Italia Pontificia*, 1:173, n. 3; Canivez, *Statuta*, 1:42–45; Giuseppe Ruotolo, *L'abbazia delle Tre Fontane*. (Rome: Abbazia delle Tre Fontane, 1972) 15. The letter is in Paris, Bibliothèque Nationale, MS nouv. acq. latin 1402, which also contains a copy of occasional statutes (1160–1161) of the Cistercian General Chapter, published by Chrysogonus Waddell, *Twelfth-Century Statutes from the Cistercian General Chapter*, Studia et Documenta, 12 (Brecht: Cîteaux: Commentarii Cistercienses, 2002) 703–708.

60. Paris, Bibliothèque Nationale, MS 1402, fol. 2r; Lowenfeld, 'Documenta', 403; PL 182: 694; Canivez, *Statuta*, 1:49–51; Waddell, *Twelfth-Century Statutes*, 703: '. . . pater, inquam, noster ac defensor, felicis memoriae papa Eugenius, trabea carne exutus, VIIIᵃ idibus iulii immactatus (immaculatus?) migravit ad Christum . . . Praeterea vos obnoxie rogamus quatinus, si parvitas nostra quidquam in oculis vestris potest, petitiones quas latores praesentium pro domo Sancti Anastasii et pro domo Novaefossae et pro domo de Casamarii vobis facient, benigne et efficaciter exaudiatis. . . .'

(2) Pope Anastasius IV requests the abbots assembled at the Cistercian Chapter to temper the rigour of their Rule to allow the monastery of S. Anastasius to retain its possessions.[61]

20 Aug 1153   Saint Bernard of Clairvaux dies.

1153–1154   (1) Abbot Gozoinus and the Cistercian Chapter write to Pope Anastasius IV, requesting he confirm the donation made by Innocent II, already confirmed by Pope Eugenius III, of the house of Saint Anastasius in Rome to Clairvaux and their Order for the cure of souls and religious discipline, and to grant a dispensation so that the monastery may retain its possessions.[62]

(2) Abbot Gozoinus and the chapter write to the prior, Benedict, and the community of S. Anastasius. Their abbot, Everard, has explained the state of their house and all their discomforts. He has shown the members of the Chapter the letters of Popes Eugenius and Anastasius regarding this matter. Gozoinus sympathizes with their plight. Out of reverence for Pope Innocent II, who gave the land, and Eugenius III, who worked strenuously in and was taken from the monastery, he does not wish to oppose their requested dispensation. He has written to the pope (Anastasius IV) about it, leaving it to his authority to grant the dispensation for them to keep their possessions with-

---

61. Paris, Bibliothèque Nationale, MS 1402, fol. 2v; Jaffé-Lowenfeld, *Regesta*, 2:93, no. 9798; Kehr, *Italia Pontificia*, 1:174, no. 5; Waddell, *Twelfth-Century Statutes*, 703.

62. Paris, Bibliothèque Nationale, MS 1402, fols. 2v–3r; Lowenfeld, 'Documenta', 403; Waddell, *Twelfth-Century Statutes*, 703: '. . . supplicamus vestrae beatitudini ut domum ipsam secundum domini Innocentii donationem et domini Eugenii confirmationem Clarevallis ecclesiae et ordini nostro in his quae ad animarum curam et disciplinam religionis pertinent confirmetis. De facienda autem dispensatione, ut possessiones suas retineant, in bene placito vestro et in vestra reliquimus potestate, ut vestra auctoritas et dispenset et facta confirmet dispensationem.'

out any scruple. Thus the care of their souls and the protection of discipline is to be confirmed by the pope.[63]

(3) There is a lawsuit between Carantius, bursar of S. Anastasius *ad Aquas Salvias,* and Cecilia, abbess of S. Maria in Tempulo.[64]

1154–1159	Pope Hadrian IV confirms the papal privilege of the monastery of S. Anastasius.[65]
1157–1162	Frasterius, abbot of Clairvaux (1157–1162), writes to the community of S. Anastasius *ad Aquas Salvias* about moving the monastery from its unhealthy site to a more salubrious place.[66]
1161	During a great schism in the Church, the community of S. Anastasius is evicted by Frederick Barbarossa and anti-pope Victor.[67] The abbot of S. Paolo fuori le Mura claims the monastery of S. Anastasius for himself through the schismatic

63. Paris, Bibliothèque Nationale, MS 1402, fol. 3; Lowenfeld, 'Documenta', 403–404; Canivez, *Statuta,* 1:52; Waddell, *Twelfth-Century Statutes,* 703: 'Frater Gozoinus Cisterciensis et humilis conventus abbatum in capitulo congregatorum dilectis fratribus Benedicto priori et conventui salutem in domino. Venerabilis frater noster Everardus abbas vester statum domus vestrae et omnes incommoditates nobis diligenter exposuit. Sed et litteras patris nostri beate memoriae Eugenii et domini qui nunc est Anastasii nobis ostendit, ad idem negotium pertinentes. Compatimur vestrae necessitati nec revelationem vestram ullomodo nobis credimus praesumendam, tum propter devotionem domini Innocentii, qui locum dedit tum propter singularem reverentiam domini Eugenii qui in eo strenue conversatus et ex eo assumptus est. Attamen veriti sumus necessarie licet dispensationi manum nostrae confirmationis apponere, ne presumptionem redolere aliquibus videatur. Scripsimus autem ad dominum papam, ipsius arbitrio et potestati dispensationem hanc relinquentes, ut quod ipse inde fecerit et apud nos et apud vos ratum deinceps sine aliquo scrupulo teneatur de his possessionibus quas in praesenti habetis, ita ut cura animarum et disciplinae custodia nobis ab eodem summo pontifice confirmetur'.

64. Kehr, *Italia Pontificia,* 1:122 and 174, nos. 7, 8 and 9.

65. Kehr, *Italia Pontificia,* 1:174, no. 10.

66. Paris, Bibliothèque Nationale, MS 1402, fols. 1–3; Lowenfeld, 'Documenta', 399; Waddell, *Twelfth-Century Statutes,* 703.

67. The entire Cistercian Order resolved at its General Chapter to support Pope Alexander III against anti-pope Victor and Frederick Barbarossa, see Canivez, *Statuta,* 1:73; Waddell, *Twelfth-Century Statutes,* 646 and 707.

king. It is restored to the Cistercians by Pope Alexander III.[68]

10 July 1161

Pope Alexander III takes under his protection the monastery of Saint Anastasius, the church of Saint John the Baptist, and the church of Our Lady located next to the monastery (Monasterium sancti Anastasij, ecclesiam sancti Johannis Baptiste et ecclesiam beate Marie sitas juxta Idem Monasterium . . .). As in the privileges of Popes Eugenius III and Anastasius IV, he stipulates that S. Anastasius should be the head of the abbey and that the monks should stay there in winter, but may go to Nemi for the summer months on account of the inclement air (propter intemperiem Aeris'). He confirms the monastery's possessions, including the property in the Maremma in Tuscany, and the summer residence in Nemi.[69]

1179–1181

There is litigation between Paul, bursar of the monastery of S. Anastasius, and Peter, bursar of S. Maria in Aquiro, concerning some property at Monte Genzano.[70]

April 1183

Pope Lucius III confirms the privilege of papal protection and the possessions of the monastery of S. Anastasius.[71]

---

68. Le Liber Pontificalis 2:450: 'Istius tempore maximum scisma fuit, et evectus fuit conventus sancti Anastasii, et abbas Sancti Pauli eundem locum sibi per regem scismaticum vindicavit; qui locus per eundem Alexandrum est restitutus. . . .' See also Kehr, Italia Pontificia, 1:175, no. 14; Schuster, La basilica, 99; and Tholomei Lucensis Annales, ed. B. Schmeidler, MGH, Scriptores Rerum Germanicarum, Nova Series, 8 (Berlin: Weidmann, 1930) 64: 'Anno Domini MCLXIII [sic]. Videns Alexander furorem Romani populi et scisma in orbe favoremque Frederici ad predictos scismaticos, contra ipsum in Galliam se transfert. Tunc ratione dicti scismatis conventus monasterii Sancti Anastasii cum suo abbate de Urbe eiectus est.'

69. BAV, Vat. lat. 5844, fols. 1 and 2; BAV, Bar. lat. 3232, fols. 1r–3r; Giorgi, 'Il regesto', 59–60; Kehr, Italia Pontificia, 1:175, no. 11; Luttrell, 'Ager Cosanus', Siena e Maremma, 27–58.

70. Kehr, Italia Pontificia, 1:175, nos. 12 and 13.

71. Tomassetti, 'Della Campagna Romana,' 143–144; Kehr, Italia Pontificia, 1:175, no. 15.

1188	Pope Clement III confirms the privilege of papal protection and the possessions of the monastery of S. Anastasius.[72]
July 1191	Pope Celestine III confirms the privilege of papal protection and the possessions of the monastery of S. Anastasius.[73]
1191	The monastery of S. Anastasius acquires a daughter house at S. Maria di Casanova at Civitella Casanova.[74]
late 12th century	A cistercian calendar includes for 22 January *(XI. Kal. februarii)* Saint Vincent priest and martyr in Valencia, Spain, and Saint Anastasius monk and martyr in Rome *ad Aquas Salvias.* Saint Anastius, monk and martyr, after many torments, suffered imprisonment, blows and chains in Palestine from the Persians and, in the end, was beheaded with seventy others.[75]
1208	The monastery of S. Anastasius acquires a daughter house at S. Maria d'Arabona.[76]
1211	The monastery of S. Anastasius acquires a daughter house at S. Maria de Caritate.[77]

72. Kehr, *Italia Pontificia*, 2:288–291; cf. Luttrell, 'Ager Cosanus', *Siena et Maremma*, 43–44.

73. Kehr, *Italia Pontificia*, 1:176, no. 16; Luttrell, 'Ager Cosanus', *Siena et Maremma*, 38.

74. Ruotolo, *L'abbazia*, 99–100; cf. Cesare D'Onofrio and Carlo Pietrangeli, *Abbazie del Lazio.* (Rome: Cassa di Risparmio, 1969) 180, giving a date of 1195.

75. Philippe Guignard, *Les monuments primitifs de la règle Cistercienne . . .*, Analecta Divionensia, 10 (Dijon: Imprimerie Darantière, 1878) 311: 'In hispaniis. civitate valentia . . . sancti vincentii levite et martyris . . . Rome ad aquas salvias, sancti anasthasii monachi et martyris: qui post plurima tormenta, carceris, verberum. et vinculorum que in palestine perpessus fuerat a persis . . . ad ultimum decollatus est, cum aliis septuaginta . . .'. Bibliothèque de Dijon, MS 82, *Kalendarium*. xi: kl. Februarii.

76. BAV, Barb. lat. 3232, fols. 3v–8r; Ruotolo, *L'abbazia*, 100–103; cf. Balduino Bedini, *Breve prospetto delle abbazie cisterciensi d'Italia.* (Casamari: Tipografia di Casamari, 1966) 31, who gives the date 1209 for this.

77. Ruotolo, *L'abbazia*, 103.

1212	The Cistercian General Chapter orders the abbot of S. Anastasius to recall some monks sent to S. Benedetto de Silva, which later appears as one of the daughter houses of the roman monastery.[78]
1216	The Aldobrandeschi control the monastery's lands in the Maremma, while still recognizing the monks' overlordship of the region.[79]
1216–1227	Iacobus, *poenitentiarius* and chaplain to Pope Honorius III for the salvation of his soul and that of his nephew Iacobus builds 'this house' *(hanc domum),* meaning part of the monastic buildings?

> FRATER IACOBUS DOMINI HONORIJ PP. POENITEN-
> TIARIUS AC CAPELLANUS, HANC DOMUM FIERI FECIT,
> PRO ANIMAM SUAM, ET JACOBI NEPOTIS'.[80]

The inscription was recorded in 1640 by Jongelinus, who located it over a window in one of the cells which had been destroyed, at the end of the dormitory towards the city of Rome.[81]

---

78. Canivez, *Statuta,* 1:397; Ruotolo, *L'abbazia,* 103–106; Luttrell, 'Ager Cosanus', 38–39, 43–46. See below, C. DATES AND DOCUMENTS, 1250.

79. Fentress and Wickham, 'La valle dell'Albegna', *Siena et Maremma,* 59–81; Luttrell, 'Ager Cosanus', *Ibid.,* 27–58.

80. This inscription is now on the lintel of a window on the first floor of our wall 29 in our Wing R, see our fig. 66. There was in the early thirteenth century a Cardinal Giacomo de Pecorara (1231–1244), who was a cistercian monk at Trois Fontaines in France, who has been confused with the first Iacobus in this inscription. The chaplain and penitentiary of Pope Honorius III was instead a *magister* and Apostolic Legate in Ireland and Scotland; he was mentioned in the papal Register from 31 July 1220–29 till May 1226, and he died before 3 July 1240, as explained by Agostino Paravicini-Bagliani, *Cardinali di Curia e 'familiariae' cardinalizie dal 1227 al 1254.* Italia Sacra: Studi e Documenti di Storia Ecclesiastica, 18 and 19 (Rome: Antenore, 1972) 112–123, esp. 118–119, n.2; see also Ruotolo, *L'abbazia,* 86–91; and Pistilli, 'Considerazioni', 165 and nn. 13–15. There was evidently an abbot of S. Anastasius at Tre Fontane called Iacobus from 1230–1244, perhaps the second Iacobus of the inscription, Ruotolo, *L'abbazia,* 86–91.

81. Jongelinus, *Notitia Abbatiarum,* 7:7: 'In quibusdam cellis ad finem dormitorij, versus Urbem, supra unam fenestram dictarum cellarum destructarum, extra haec apparet inscriptio litteris Longobardicis.'

1 April 1221   Pope Honorius III, assisted by seven cardinals, dedicates the church of the monastery of S. Anastasius to the Mother of God, and consecrates seven altars, in which relics are placed; the pope grants indulgences. This takes place when Nicholas is abbot. The inscription was formerly located to the right of the altar, and is now in the north aisle (our fig. 65):

IN NOMINE DOMINI. ANNO MILLESIMO BISQUE CENTENO, UNO QUATERQUE QUINO QUO CHRISTUS VENIT,[82] MUNDUMQUE REDEMIT ACTU DIVINO, KALENDIS APRILIS, HONORIUS FELIX, MONOS DIA SACER HANC AULAM SACRAVIT, PAPAQUE DICAVIT DIVINIS ACER. SEPTEM CARDINALES COLLATERALES INTERFUERUNT, AD MATRIS DEI HONOREM EI TUNC ADSTITERUNT: PRAESUL SABINIENSIS, TUSCULA-NENSIS, HI BONITATE, PONTIFICALI HONORI TALI FULGEAT DIGNITATE: POST PRAENESTINENSIS, ARCHI-NARBONENSIS ET DUO FRATRES SIBI DEVOTI, SUBDITIT TOTI, EPISCOPI VATES, ALTER FLORENTINUS CULTUS DIVINUS, ACTU SERENO: SPERNIT AMOREM MUNDI, HONOREM, ARESCENTE FOENO: SEPTEM ARIS CONSE-CRATIS, AC RELIQUIIS DITATIS SANCTORUM BASILICA HAC COLLOCAT, UT SMARAGDUS REDOLEAT SAT PLUSQUAM NARDUS SPONSA THEOS UNICA. HAC ALTARE CRUCIS LIGNUM, ET VOLUMEN CARNIS DIGNUM, UTERO CUM PRODIIT, HIC VELAMEN ET PRAESEPE, PALLIUM ET LAPIS, SAEPE TUMULI QUI SUBIIT HIC EST VESTIS MATRIS DEI, ATQUE PRAECUR-SORIS ET ZACHARIAE FILII; PETRUS; PAULUS ET ANDREAS, QUEM OCCIDIT TUNC AEGEAS, BARTHOLO-MAEUS EXIMIUS PARTES CORPORUM DEDERUNT, QUO NEC TENTAE TUNC FUERUNT DENTES CAEPHAS

---

82. Forcella interpreted this date erroneously as 1244, see Vincenzo Forcella, *Iscrizioni delle chiese e d'altri edifici di Roma dal secolo XI fino ai giorni nostri* (Rome: Ludovico Cecchini, 1878) 12:322.

PRINCIPIS. OPULENTUM DECORATUR, HOC EXIMII
DILATUR MERITORUM ADIPES: HIC LAURENTIUS
CONSISTIT, CUI VINCENTIUS ADSISTIT DE COMMUNI
MARTYRIO, ANASTASIUS ET CLEMENS QUEM AFRIDI-
ANUS DEMENS CONSUMPSIT SUPPLICIO. NICOLAUS
PRAESUL DIGNUS, SEBASTIANUS BENIGNUS, DECORA
CAECILIA, ANASTASIA VIRGO PIA, A VERA PLAENA
SOPHIA REDOLET UT LILIA; ISTUD FATETUR QUISQUIS
GRADIETUR, AD HANC AULAM DEI SEPTEM ANNIS ET
SEPTEM CARINAE REMISSIONIS CONFERRI CRIMINIS
SOLUTIONISQUE DATUR EI FERIA QUINTA CUM
CELEBRATUR ANTE PALMARUM DIEM HABEBATUR
PAPA JUBENTE HOC RECORDETUR ET MEMORETUR
QUOLIBET MENSE REMISSIO DATUR ET CONDONATUR
TEMPORE ISTO. CREDAT FIDELIS, FIAT INDE FELIX
PETENTE CHRISTO. MERUIT ABBAS HOC NICOLAUS,
UT SIBI SEMPER INSIT LAUS OPERE TALI: CUNCTI
DEVOTI SIBI FUERUNT ET PRECES DIGNAS ADMINIS-
TRAVERUNT HOMINI QUALI HAEC RELIQUIAE SANC-
TORUM HIC DEGENTIUM BINORUM, PAENITENDI
SPACIUM NOBIS ATQUE MONACHORUM PRECEDENT
ET ANGELORUM IN COELIS CONSORTIUM.[83]

1225 The relics of Saint Vincent arrive at the monastery from Spain.[84]

1234 The abbey of S. Anastasius acquires the daughter house of S. Agostino di Montalto, in the diocese of Castro.[85]

---

83. Transcription taken from Gabriel d'Aiguebelle, *L'Abbaye des Trois-Fontaines située aux Eaux-Salviennes près de Rome*. 3rd ed. (Landerau: P. B. Moulins, 1882), 23–25.

84. Gabriel, *L'Abbaye*, 13; Ferrari, *Early Roman Monasteries*, 45. These authors give no references to primary sources, but cf. Panvinio, *De Praecipuis Urbis . . . basilicis*, 88 and Panciroli, *I tesori nascosti*, 2nd ed., 1625, 658, which refer to the relics of Saint Vincent; see also AA SS, Januarii, II, p. 399. A reliquary was made for them in 1577, see below, C. DATES AND DOCUMENTS, 1577.

85. Bedini, *Breve prospetto*, 31; Ruotolo, *L'abbazia*, 106–107; see below, C. DATES AND DOCUMENTS, 1250.

1236	The abbey of S. Anastasius is ordered by the Cistercian General Chapter to reform the monastery of S. Giusto di Tuscania and to secure its possessions.[86]
13 Aug 1237	The abbey of S. Anastasius acquires the daughter house of S. Maria di Palazzuolo.[87]
July 1243	Pope Innocent IV decrees the union of the monasteries of S. Maria de Insula Pontiana and S. Anastasius.[88]
13th century	An inscription now in the sacristy refers to work done by 'I' and 'L', 'FEC. FIERI. H : OP : ET : I : ET : L' ; our fig. 67.[89]
1250	The monastery of S. Anastasius is recorded as having daughter houses at S. Benedetto de Silva and S. Agostino di Montalto.[90]
13 Jan 1255	Pope Alexander IV in his bull, *Congrua nos,* reconfirms the papal privileges of his predecessors, Eugenius III, Anastasius IV, Hadrian IV, Alexander III, Lucius III, Celestine III, and Innocent III. As Pope Eugenius III had stipulated, S. Anastasius is to be 'head of the abbey', the monks staying there in winter, but spending summers at Nemi. He confirms the possessions of the monastery—the monastery of S. Anastasius itself and the churches of Saint John the Baptist and S. Maria located next to the same monastery, and other property including that donated by Leo III and Charlemagne in the Maremma in Tuscany.[91]

86. Canivez, *Statuta,* 2:162; Ruotolo, *L'abbazia,* 107–108.

87. BAV, Vat. lat. 7951, fols. 51r–52v; cf. Ferdinando Ughelli, *Italia Sacra,* 2nd ed. (repr. Venice: Arnoldo Forni, 1984) 1:cc. 259–261; *Statuta,* 2:171; Bedini, *Breve prospetto,* 31; Ruotolo, *L'abbazia,* 108–110.

88. Giorgi, 'Il regesto', 60; Ruotolo, *L'abbazia,* 110–113.

89. Bertelli, 'L'enciclopedia', 46, n. 26; Pistilli, 'Considerazioni', 174.

90. Kehr, *Italia Pontificia,* 2:219–220; Luttrell, 'Ager Cosanus', 45, with a date of 1234.

91. BAV, Barb. lat. 3232, fols. 35v–42r; Ughelli, *Italia Sacra,* 1:cc. 53–55: 'Monasterium B. Anastasii martyris quod apud Aquas Salvias positum est, et perpetuis temporibus caput

18 Feb 1255	The monastery of S. Anastasius acquires the daughter house of S. Giusto di Tuscania.[92]
1267	An inscription found at the church of S. Paolo alle Tre Fontane attests the existence of an armenian monastery there.[93]
1269	The property in the Maremma—Ansedonia, Monte Argentaria *et al.*—is leased to Aldobrandino of the Aldobrandeschi family, Count of Tuscia, by the monastery of S. Anastasius. Rent for the property is to be paid yearly on the feast of Saint Anastasius, 22 January.[94]
1272/77	*Domina Thoma comitissa*—Tomasia, wife of Guglielmo Aldobrandeschi—is buried in a raised tomb, *(sepulchrum alte elevatum)* in the narthex.[95]
1283	A silver reliquary is commissioned by Abbot Martinus to contain the head of Saint Anastasius.[96] Evidently, it had represented on it the twelve tuscan *castra* said to have been donated by Leo III and Charlemagne.[97]

Abbatiae vestrae consistat, ut illuc in Hyeme, propter intemperiem autem aeris in loco, qui dicitur Nemo, aestivo tempore commoremini. . . .' Gabriel, *L'Abbaye*, 114–120; Giorgi, 'Il regesto', 61; Ruotolo, *L'abbazia*, 137–152; Luttrell, 'Ager Cosanus', *Siena e Maremma*, 27–58, with a date of 1256 for this document.

92. BAV, Barb. lat. 3232, fols. 50r–55v; Giorgi, 'Il regesto', 60; Kehr, *Italia Pontificia*, 2:198–199.

93. De Rossi, 'Recenti scoperte', 87–90.

94. BAV, Barb. lat. 3232, fol. 21r; Ruotolo, *L'abbazia*, 152–154; Luttrell, 'Ager Cosanus', *Siena et Maremma*, 39; Fentress and Wickham, 'La Valle dell'Albegna', *Siena et Maremma*, 71–74.

95. Jongelinus, *Notitia Abbatiarum*, 7:6, with a date of 1277; Forcella, *Iscrizioni*, 12:323, with a date of 1277; Ingo Herklotz, 'Sepulcra' e 'Monumenta' del medioevo. Studi sull'arte sepolcrale in Italia. (Rome: Rari Nantes, 1985) 162–163, nn. 63 and 64, with a date of 1272 and identification of the deceased as Tomasia, wife of Guglielmo Aldobrandeschi; Luttrell, 'Ager Cosanus', *Siena et Maremma*, 42, who follows Herklotz.

96. Jongelinus, *Notitia Abbatiarum*, 7:8, quoting Panvinio, *De Praecipuis Urbis . . . basilicis*, 85.: 'Caput porro eiusdem S. Anastasij, adhuc argentea theca pie conservatur: cui in haec inscriptio: DOMINUS ABBAS MARTINUS FECIT FIERI HOC OPUS, SUB ANNUM M.CCLXXXIII'.

97. Panvinio, *De Praecipuis Urbis . . . basilicis*, 85; Jongelinus, *Notitia Abbatiarum*, 7:5; Gabriel, *L'Abbaye*, 11; Luttrell, 'Ager Cosanus', 42. On the threshold of a door in a house very

6 May 1284	In his will Ildebrandino il Rosso Aldobrandeschi, Conte de Pitigliano, leaves money to the monastery of Saint Anastasius in Rome for building and for providing tasty dishes, 'pitances', for the brethren.[98]
18 May 1284	Ildebrandino il Rosso Aldobrandeschi died.[99]
11 March 1286	The contract made with the Count of Tuscia is extended to his daughter, Domina Margarita Comitissa in Tuscia.[100]
1289	Pope Nicholas IV grants protection to the monastery of S. Anastasius.[101]
1290	Pope Nicholas IV grants an indulgence of one year and forty days to those who pray at the church of the monastery of Saint Anastasius *de Urbe* on the feasts of the Blessed Virgin Mary, Saints Vincent and Anastasius, Saint Paul and his Conversion, and the Nativity of Saint John the Baptist.[102]
1294	The Cistercian Chapter agrees to the celebration of the joint feast of Saints Vincent and Anastasius in Rome.[103]

---

near the monastery in the late nineteenth century Tomassetti noted the inscription : 'ANO DNI M CC LXXXVII. ABBS M . . .', which he believed referred to Abbot Martin, who had made the silver reliquary in 1283, Tomassetti, 'Della Campagna Romana,' 146. It is not possible to say where this inscription came from and it does not seem to have survived.

98. Gaspero Ciacci, *Gli Aldobrandeschi nella storia e nella 'Divina Commedia'* (Rome: Multigrafica Editrice, 1980) 2:261–266, doc. DCVII: '. . . iudicavit et reliquit monasterio Sancti Anastasii de Urbe ducentas libras usualis monete pro fabrica loci et pietantiis fratrum. . . .' The reference to the monastery of Saint Anastasius is on p. 263. The grant is one of several to religious houses in Orvieto, Grosseto, and other places.

99. Ciacci, *Gli Aldobrandeschi,* 1:241.

100. BAV, Barb. lat. 3232, fols. 17v–24v; Ciacci, *Gli Aldobrandeschi,* 2:273, doc. DCXVI; see above C. DATES AND DOCUMENTS 1269 for the earlier contract.

101. Ernest Langlois, *Les Registres de Nicholas IV,* Bibliothèque des Écoles d'Athènes et de Rome, 2e serie, 1 (Paris: Ernest Thorin Editeur, 1886) 1:320, no. 1708.

102. Langlois, *Les Registres de Nicholas IV,* 1:320, no. 1709.

103. *Statuta,* 3:276, no. 68.

1302	Pope Boniface VIII declares that Countess Margarita has forfeited the property in the Maremma because she has alienated part of it and now belongs to the party of Guido di Santa Fiore, a public enemy of the Roman Church, whom she has married.[104]
1303	Abbot Leonardus of S. Anastasius leases to Benedetto Caetani Ansedonia and other places in the Maremma in Tuscany.[105]
1305	An armenian inscription on a cross erected by a certain Moses at the church of S. Paolo alle Tre Fontane refers to an armenian monastery and to two armenian monks, Vartan and Gregory, the latter being the sacristan of the church of the decapitation of Saint Paul.[106]
1306	A faded inscription over the door of the Chapter Room (. . . *supra portam Capituli huius Coenobii, haec legitur attrita inscriptio*) refers to work done by Abbot Leonardus in 1306:

> DOMINUS LEONARDUS ABBA FECIT FIERI HOC OPUS, ANNO DOMINI M. CCC VI.[107]

c. 1320	The Catalogue of Turin lists an abbot and fifteen monks at the monastery of S. Anastasius.[108]
11 May 1358	Bernard, abbot of S. Anastasius, renews the contract with Niccolo and Gentile Ildebrandino for the lands in the Maremma.[109]
1364	Indulgences are granted at S. Anastasius *prope Urbem* and at S. Maria Scala Coeli.[110]

---

104. Giorgi, 'Il regesto', 63.

105. Ruotolo, *L'abbazia*, 174–175; Luttrell, 'Ager Cosanus', *Siena et Maremma*, 27–58.

106. De Rossi, 'Recenti scoperte', 87–90.

107. Jongelinus, *Notitia Abbatiarum*, 7:7; cf. Ruotolo, *L'abbazia*, 175.

108. Valentini-Zucchetti, *Codice topografico*, 3:312: 'Monasterium Sancti Anastasii habet abbatem et monachos .XV.'

109. Giorgi, 'Il regesto', 63; Luttrell, 'Ager Cosanus', *Siena e Maremma*, 46.

110. BAV, Reg. lat., 520, fol. 7, referred to by Christian Hülsen, *Le chiese di Roma nel Medio Evo* (Florence: Leo S. Olschki Editore, 1927) 143–144.

1369	Pope Urban V has a copy made of the donation of Pope Leo III and Charlemagne and inscribed on bronze; this is later transcribed in the sixteenth and seventeenth centuries.[111]
1362–1370 or 1370–1378	'Great indulgences' are given at S. Maria Scala Coeli, where one thousand ten martyrs are buried. The church is described as being on one side of the 'great church'.[112]
20 June 1372	Giovanni, abbot of S. Anastasius, cedes to Angeluccio, Pietro, Domenico, and Vanuccio of Leonessa all the property owned by the monastery in the territory of Leonessa; from this transaction the monastery receives a piece of land and four hundred golden florins— money needed to pay its debts.[113]
31 May 1373	The communes of Nemi and Genzano become vassals of the monastery of S. Anastasius.[114]
1375	Indulgences are granted on the day of the consecration of the church of S. Anastasius.[115]
28 May 1378	Tommaso de Marganis, abbot of S. Anastasius, leases property belonging to the monastery in the Rione Campitelli to Cecco Cole Alessio.[116]

111. BAV, Barb. lat. 3232, fols. 46r–50r ; BAV, Vat. lat. 11897, fols. 48r–52v; Giorgi, 'Il regesto', 63.

112. *Memoriale de mirabilibus et indulgentiis quae in urbe romana existunt,* written under Urban V (1362–70) or Gregory XI (1370–78), published in Valentini-Zucchetti, *Codice topografico,* 4:88: 'Item ad unum latus ecclesiae maiori est ecclesia Sanctae Mariae de Scala Dei ubi sunt magnae indulgentiae et MX martires sepulti subtus altare, quorum ossa videntur ibidem. . . .' See also Klaus Schwager, 'Santa Maria Scala Coeli in Tre Fontane'. in *Praestant interna: Festschrift für Ulrich Hausmann.* ed. B. von Freytag gen. Löringhoff et al. (Tübingen: Ernst Wasmuth, 1982) 398, n. 25.

113. BAV, Barb. lat. 3232, fols. 59v–66r; Giorgi, 'Il regesto', 63.

114. Giorgi, 'Il regesto', 64; Ruotolo, *L'abbazia,* 181–183; Calandro, 'Nemi e i cistercensi', 50–54.

115. BAV, Vat. lat. 4265, fol. 11; referred to by Hülsen, *Chiese,* 143: 'Item in e. s. A. sex milia annorum conceduntur, in consecratione ecclesiae s. Anastasii est vera peccatorum remissio.'

116. BAV, Barb. lat. 3232, fols. 91v–95r; Giorgi, 'Il regesto', 63.

Dec 1387	Antipope Clement VII cedes Nemi and Genazzano to Giordano Orsini, Lord of Marino, and his family to the third generation.[117]
1 Aug 1389	Some people from Nemi are excused payment of dues to the abbot of S. Anastasius *ad Aquam Salviam prope Urbem,* on account of the harshness of the times.[118]
14 June 1408	The relics of Saint Anastasius are found in two reliquaries—one gilded and decorated with enamels, the other made of crystal and gilded silver—in the sacristy of S. Maria in Trastevere, where they were placed by the Cardinal of S. Angelo in Pescheria; they are returned to the abbot of S. Anastasius.[119]
March 1412	Pope John XXIII grants an indulgence to pious visitors to S. Maria Scala Coeli.[120]
1419	The system of commendatory abbots begins.[121]
August 1420	Mabilia, daughter of Pietro Nannoli, sells a house to the abbot of S. Anastasius.[122]

117. Calandro, 'Nemi e i cistercensi', 54.

118. BAV, Vat. lat. 7930, fols. 151r–152v, a document from the archive of S. Angelo in Pescheria.

119. *Il Diario di Antonio Pietro dello Schiavo, 19 ottobre 1404–25 settembre 1417.* ed. L. A. Muratori, Rerum Italicarum Scriptores, 24 (Bologna: Nicola Zanichelli, 1917) pt. 5, fasc. 153–4: p. 32: 'Item in reversione venimus per regionem Transtiberim. Tunc in dicta regione invenimus pulzantes omnes campanas Sancte Marie de dicta regione . . . domini Capidolii cum dicto populo iverunt ad sacristiam supradicte ecclesie, et ibi in dicta sacristia . . . in dicta cassa invenerunt pulcerrimum tabernachulum deauratum cum smaltis, in quis tabernachulo stabat caput sancti Anastaxii martiris, et unum alium tabernachulum parvum de cristaldo circhuitum de argento deaurato valde pulcerrimum cum cellabro supradicti capitis . . . Quare erant in dicta sacristia supradicte reliquie, quia dominus cardinalis de Sancto Angelo posuerat . . . Item supradicte reliquie fuerunt restitute coram omni populo domino abbati Sancti Anastaxii, et factum sibi mandatum per supradictos dominos, quod deberet eas bene custodire. . . .' See also Severano, *Memorie sacre,* 415.

120. Archivio Segreto Vaticano, Reg. Lateranense, vol 158, fols. 159r–160r; Schwager, 'Santa Maria Scala Coeli', 400 and n. 37.

121. Jongelinus, *Notitia Abbatiarum,* 7:11–12; Tomassetti, 'Della Campagna Romana,' 146, where the date 1418 is given.

122. Giorgi, 'Il regesto', 63.

1423	Nemi is ceded to Antonio, Prospero, and Odoardo Colonna.[123]
12 Aug 1452	Some of the property in Tuscany is ceded to Siena by the commendatory abbot, Angelus.[124]
1518–1523	The monastery is given a new Rule and submitted to the tuscan branch of the Cistercian Congregation in Italy. Relations between the community and their commendatory abbot are clarified.[125]
1519	Pope Leo X's Bull, *Cathedram militantis Ecclesiae*, continues the system of commendatory abbots. The pope also discusses the problem of malaria and allows the monks to go to a healthier place from mid-June till the end of September.[126]
1560	Panvinio describes the church of S. Maria Scala Coeli as a round building with four chapels or apses, having two altars at either end of an ancient chapel.[127] To the north there is an altar and in the east is the main altar, in an apse decorated with mosaics. There are four columns supporting the ciborium: two of alabaster, one of granite, and one of marble. Beneath it is the cemetery or oratory of Saint Zeno and other martyrs; in this is the altar in which are located the martyrs' relics. This is where Saint Bernard saw the souls going up a ladder from purgatory to heaven while he was celebrating Mass.
	Panvinio describes the church of Saint Paul at Tre Fontane as having two chapels on different

---

123. Calandro, 'Nemi e i cistercensi', 54.

124. Giorgi, 'Il regesto', 67; Gabriel, *L'Abbaye*, 13; Kehr, *Italia Pontificia*, 1:171.

125. Gabriel, *L'Abbaye*, 121–127.

126. Gabriel, *L'Abbaye*, 121–127; Tomassetti, 'Della Campagna Romana,' 146.

127. 'Aedicula rotunda est et habet quattuor capellas sive absidas cum duabus aris hinc inde in antica capella', Onofrio Panvinio, *Schedae de ecclesiis urbis Romae c. 1560*. BAV, Vat.lat. 6780, 31v.

levels—the higher one, all covered with murals, has a fountain, a marble pulpit decorated with mosaic, and an altar; the lower chapel has no murals, but there are two fountains and two altars, one in an apse encrusted with marble inlay; there is a small courtyard in front of the two chapels.[128]

1570   In his book, published in 1570, Panvinio says the cemetery of Saint Zeno is under the church of S. Maria Scala Coeli, which he describes as a round sanctuary. Over the altar there is a marble canopy supported by four precious columns and under it are the bodies of the holy martyrs. In the apse of the oratory there are traces of mosaics of the Virgin Mary and Saint Zeno. It was in this chapel that Saint Bernard had his vision.[129] Panvinio describes the sanctuary of Saint Paul at Tre Fontane as having three chapels, each lower than the other, with three fountains.[130]

1577   Commendatory Abbot Alessandro Farnese has two magnificent reliquaries made, one for the head of Saint Vincent, the other for that of Saint Zeno.[131]

128. Panvinio, Schedae, 31v; Kirsch, 'Der Ort', 244–245; Anonymous, San Paolo e le Tre Fontane, 47–48: 'S. Pauli ad Tres Fontes. Prima cappella altior tota picta, habet fontem pulpito marmoreo tessellato ornatum. Super fontem et (ac) pulpitum ad quod per gradus ascenditur est altare. Prope fontis ostium est lapis litteris arabicis vel indianis. [This may have been armenian, since other inscriptions in that language and script were found at Tre Fontane in 1867; Anonymous, San Paolo e le Tre Fontane, 48, n. 56.] 'Est tota picta. Secunda aedicula inferior est divisa; habet duos fontes, in altera parte cum alio altari super tertium fontem, in alia parte cappellae sive aediculae est absis cum altare. Absis incrustata marmore. Est vestibulum ante ambas aediculas parvum, inferior cappella non est picta.'

129. Panvinio, De Praecipuis Urbis . . . basilicis, 88–89: '. . . sub sacello rotundo . . . quod S. Mariae Scala coeli . . . dicitur . . . Ubi est altare cum operculo marmoreo quattuor pretiosis columnis sustentato, sub quo iacent corpora sanctorum martyrum. In oratorij absida musivea, extant signa, beatae virginis Mariae, et sancti Zenonis. . . .'

130. Panvinio, De Praecipuis Urbis . . . basilicis, 90: 'Ibi aedificata sunt tria sacella, alterum altero depressus, cum tribus fontibus. . . .'

131. Jongelinus, Notitia Abbatiarum, 7:5.

1582	The church of S. Maria Scala Coeli at Tre Fontane, but not the crypt, is blown down by the wind in a storm.[132]
7 April 1582	Bishop Giovanni Antonio Odescalchi reports the foundation ceremony for the new church of S. Maria Scala Coeli to Guglielmo Gonzaga of Mantua.[133]
1582–1584	Commendatory Abbot Alexander Farnese begins to have the church of S. Maria Scala Coeli rebuilt by Giacomo della Porta[134] in honour of Our Lady, and the crypt restored in honour of Saint Zeno and his companions. The work is completed by Alexander's successors as commendatory abbot, the two Aldrobrandini cardinals, Ippolito and Pietro.[135] An inscription, formerly in the lantern of the dome referred to Alessandro Farnese and gave the date 1583: ALEXANDER CARDINALIS FARNESIUS S.R.E. VICECAN. FECIT MDLXXXIII.[136] Mosaics by

132. Panciroli, *I tesori nascosti*, 574.: '. . . l'anno 1582 essendo dalla furia de venti battuta a terra questa Capella, restando però salva quella parte da basso, dove fin'al hoggi si vedono l'ossa de quelli benedetti martiri. . . .' According to Schwager and Robertson, the church was struck by lightning; see Schwager, 'S. Maria Scala Coeli', 406 and Clare Robertson, *'Il gran cardinale': Alessandro Farnese, Patron of the Arts* (New Haven and London: Yale University Press, 1992) 199.

133. Archivio di Stato di Mantua, Archivio Gonzaga, Ser. E XXV 3, Busta 928, 4 f., quoted in Schwager, 'Santa Maria Scala Coeli', 406. 'Venerdì N[ostro] S[ignore] andò alle Sette Chiese, et il S[ignor] Card[ina]le Farnese fu alla sua Abbatia delle Tre Fontane con una gran Com[m]itiva di Prelati, dove fece cantare la messa solenne, et finita che fu S[ua] S[ignoria] Ill[ustrissi]ma con bellis[im]a ceremonia gettò nei fondam[en]ti della Chiesa, che deve fare novam[en]te; la prima pietra perche le venti grandi[s]mi che regnorono le giorni passati have[v]ano come si scrisse rovinato la Chiesa vecchia . . .'.

134. The architect is often given as Vignola, but this is impossible because Vignola died in 1573. See Schwager, 'Santa Maria Scala Coeli', 406–408 and 412; see also Giuseppe Vasi, *Roma del Settecento*, ed. M. Vasi and G. Matthiae (Rome: Editrice Golem, 1970) 330–331.

135. Ippolito was commendatory abbot from May 1589–January 1592; Pietro from March 1592–February 1621, Schwager, 'Santa Maria Scala Coeli', 407; see Panciroli, *I tesori nascosti*, 574; Fioravante Martinelli, *Roma ex ethnica sacra sanctorum Petri et Pauli apostolica praedictione profuso sanguine*. (Rome: Typis Romanis Ignatij de Lazaris, 1653) 145–146.

136. D'Onofrio-Pietrangeli, *Abbazie*, 189, also quoted by Robertson, *'Il gran cardinale'*, 265, n. 250.

Giovanni de' Vecchi adorn the apse which stands over the crypt; they show the Virgin and Child being crowned by angels, in the presence of Saints Anastasius, Bernard, Zeno, and Vincent, and patrons Pietro Cardinal Aldobrandini and Pope Clement VIII.[137]

29 Jan 1584   The new church of S. Maria Scala Coeli is consecrated by Cardinal Giulio Antonio Santoro.[138]

1592   Giovanni de' Vecchi paints an altarpiece showing Saint Bernard's vision of souls ascending to heaven while he said Mass, for S. Maria Scala Coeli.[139]

1593   Commendatory Abbot Pietro Cardinal Aldobrandini donates a silver reliquary containing the head of Saint Felix, pope and martyr.[140]

1599   Commendatory Abbot Pietro Cardinal Aldobrandini has the church of Saint Paul rebuilt by Giacomo della Porta.

1600   Panciroli describes the site of Tre Fontane as 'very far from the city of Rome and with bad air and marshes'. He refers to the new church of S. Paolo alle Tre Fontane, rebuilt from the foundations by Pietro Cardinal Aldobrandini in one year, with fine proportions and beautifully adorned; outside the Cardinal laid out a spacious piazza to accommodate pilgrims visiting this one of the nine pilgrimage churches of Rome.[141]

---

137. Robertson, 'Il gran cardinale', 200, who pointed out that this was only a small part of a larger programme for the decoration of S. Maria Scala Coeli devised for Alessandro Farnese. Robertson also published a letter from the Jesuit Simone Bartolo to Alessandro's heirs, in which he tried to persuade them to complete the programme, but to no avail, see Robertson, 'Il gran cardinale', 200 and 314–315, document 138.

138. Schwager, 'Santa Maria Scala Coeli', 407.

139. Robertson, 'Il gran cardinale', 200. This is probably the one pictured in the upper left-hand corner of Giovanni Maggi's 1600 print, our fig. 71.

140. Jongelinus, *Notitia Abbatiarum*, 7:5.

141. Panciroli, *I tesori nascosti*, 650–652.

1608	Flavio Mathei, who counted Pope Innocent II among his ancestors, is buried in the nave of SS. Vincenzo e Anastasius. His epitaph, which also bears his arms, speaks of him as the restorer of this monastery of Saints Vincent e Anastasius ad Aquas Salvias: . . . REPARATORIS MONASTERII HUJUS SANCTORUM VINCENTII ET ANASTASII AD AQUAS SALVIAS. . . .[142]

The arms of Flavio Mathei are also to be found at the end of an inscription on the architrave of the narthex.

INNOCENTIO II PONTIFICI MAXIMO EX FAMILIA ANICIA, PAPIA ET PAPARESCA NUNC MATHEIA, SANCTI BERNARDI OPERA SUBLATO ANACLETI SCHISMATE, EIDEM AC SUIS CISTERCENSIBUS HOC A SE RESTAURA-TUM MONASTERIUM DONO DEDIT ANNO DOMINI MCXL.[143]

1625	Regular abbots are restored.
1640–1670	Ferdinando Ughelli, author of *Italia Sacra*, is abbot of SS. Vincenzo e Anastasio alle Tre Fontane.[144]
1806	The roman government takes over the abbey.
1810	A french imperial emissary goes through the accounts of the monastery; the silver reliquaries disappear. Subsequently the site is abandoned.
1812	The monastery is suppressed.[145]
March 1813	The library from the suppressed monastery at Tre Fontane is taken to the Vatican Library, which keeps fifteen books and eight manuscripts.[146] Sixty-five other items are taken to the Biblioteca

---

142. Gabriel, *L'Abbaye*, 44; Forcella, *Iscrizioni*, 12:323.
143. Gabriel, *L'Abbaye*, 44.
144. For his epitaph, Forcella, *Iscrizioni*, 12:324.
145. Kehr, *Italia Pontificia*, 1:171.
146. BAV, Vat. lat. 10362, fols. 553–556.

Casanatense. The rest remain in the hands of Cavaliere di Forlía.[147]

1826[148] Pope Leo XII gives the monastery to the Franciscan Friars Minor of the Observance. They do not live at Tre Fontane, but a lay brother takes visitors round during the day and retires to S. Sebastiano on the Via Appia at night.[149]

1867 The Count of Maumigny gives money to restore the church of Saint Paul at Tre Fontane on the eighteenth centenary of the apostle's martyrdom. Excavations carried out in the church of S. Paolo reveal parts of a colonnaded portico and a mosaic pavement,[150] fragments of marble plaques, and some inscriptions, two of them naming Pope Sergius, probably Sergius I (687–701).[151]

21 April 1868 By the papal bull *Extra Urbis portam,* Pope Pius IX gives the monastery to the Trappists, who are to restore the buildings.[152]

1869 The Archbishop of Melbourne, James Alipius Goold, when he goes to Rome to attend the First Vatican Council, takes eucalyptus seeds donated by Ferdinand von Mueller from Australia to the monastery at Tre Fontane.[153]

---

147. BAV, Vat. lat. 10362, fols. 697–700.

148. Nibby, *Analisi,* 3:275, gives the date 1825 for this; he also refers to restorations by Pope Leo XII.

149. Gabriel, *L'Abbaye,* 129; Nino Savarese, *Ricordo delle Tre Fontane e dell'Abbazia dei cistercensi della stretta osservanza Trappista.* (Rome: Edizioni dell'Esposizione, 1938) 50; Alessandro Calandro, 'Arrivo dei Trappisti alle Tre Fontane nel 1868'. *L'Urbe* N.S. 36.5 (1973) 36.

150. This was not the mosaic of the *Four Seasons* now in the church of S. Paolo alle Tre Fontane, which came from Ostia Antica.

151. De Rossi, 'Recenti scoperte', 83–92; De Rossi, 'Scoperte alle Acque Salvie'. *Bullettino di Archeologia Cristiana.* series 2, 2 (1871) 71–76; Gabriel, *L'Abbaye,* 239–241; Anonymous, *San Paolo e le Tre Fontane,* 42–44.

152. Gabriel, *L'Abbaye,* 56 and 128–131.

153. Luigi Torelli, *L'eucalyptus e l'Agro Romano* (Rome: Tipografia del Senato, 1878) 16; Ferdinand von Mueller, *Eucalyptographia. A Descriptive Atlas of the Eucalypts of Australia and the*

1870	The Italian Government takes over much of the monastery's land to construct housing.[154]
1873	The monastic community becomes a Società Agricola, to cultivate eucalyptus.[155]
1875	Torelli reports that eucalyptus plants are flourishing at Tre Fontane.[156]
1878	Vincenzo Forcella reports that Father Giuseppe Franchino has raised the floor of the church of SS. Vincenzo e Anastasio and paved it with marble. Perhaps the marble paving Forcella refers to was in the chancel; elsewhere—in the transepts, the nave and the narthex—the floor is not marble, and on the south it seems to have been lowered in the nineteenth century.[157]

After the 1878 work, the church was no longer damp and had been cleaned; an iron grill had been put up across the nave and aisles, and the three existing altars had been repaired.[158]

Adjoining Islands (Melbourne-London: George Robertson, 1880) article: 'Eucalyptus globulus'; J. S. Duke, 'Von Mueller and the Eucalypts. Reclamation in Italy'. *The Argus* (Melbourne), Saturday 22 August 1931; Joan E. Barclay Lloyd, 'SS. Vincenzo e Anastasio alle Tre Fontane near Rome : The Australian connection', *Tjurunga: An Australasian Benedictine Review* 46 (1994) 57–70.

154. Savarese, *Ricordo*, 53.

155. Angelo Celli, *Storia della malaria* (Città di Castello: Società Anonima Tipografia 'Leonardo da Vinci', 1925) 424; Robert F. Zacharin, *Emigrant eucalypts.* (Melbourne: Melbourne University Press, 1978) 71.

156. Torelli, *L'eucalyptus*, 16.

157. The changes to the slope of the floor have been clarified by Giovanni Belardi, 'Considerazioni sui restauri in atto nell'abbazia delle Tre Fontane a Roma', *Arte Medievale* 2 serie, 7 (1993) 229–230; *idem.*, 'Il restauro dell'abbazia delle Tre Fontane (seconda parte)', *Arte Medievale* 2 serie, 8,1 (1994) 79–91; *idem.*, 'Il restauro architettonico'; Giovanni Belardi, Fra Jacques de Brière, Liliana Pozzi *et al.*, *Abbazia delle Tre Fontane: il complesso, la storia, il restauro* 9 Rome: Edilerca s.r.l., 1995) 99–160. See also the important data uncovered in the recent excavations under the floor, published in Maria Letizia Mancinelli, Laura Saladino and Maria Carla Somma, 'Indagini all'interno della chiesa dei SS. Vincenzo e Anastasio', *Arte Medievale* 2 serie, 8,1 (1994) 107–120.

158. Forcella, *Iscrizioni*, 12:319.

1938/39	Excavations under the 'Arch of Charlemagne', the gatehouse, reveal part of an ancient roman road as well as a large apse of peperino and two roman sarcophagi nearby.[159]
1942	Abbey land is expropriated for the 1942 Exhibition, EUR.[160]
1947–1948	The suburb of Valle Gaia is built close to Tre Fontane, to house twenty-five thousand people.[161]
1950s	The church is restored.[162] The *conversi* wing of the monastery is restored and restructured.[163]
1960s	Frescoes are discovered and removed from some walls in the monks' wing.[164]
1992–1994	The church of SS. Vincenzo e Anastasio is restored by the Soprintendenza dei Monumenti di Roma, under the direction of Architetto Giovanni Belardi.[165] Excavations are undertaken.[166]
1998–2000	Giovanni Belardi restores the monastery. The floor inserted between the 'sacristy', and the vaulted room above it (see our Plans I and II, and Section CC', at S and S1) is removed to renew the medieval interior. The door in the east wall of that room and its adjacent balcony are removed. The infirmary chapel above the north transept chapels is closed off. The chapter room, cloister walks and the *conversi* corridor are paved with terracotta tiles. In doing this the original floor of the cloister is found

159. Chiumenti and Bilancia, *La Campagna romana,* 5:421, 431–2, n. 3.

160. Chiumenti and Bilancia, *La Campagna romana,* 5:421.

161. Chiumenti and Bilancia, *La Campagna romana,* 5:421, n. 2.

162. Belardi, 'Il restauro architettonico', 99–160 and 165–179.

163. Information kindly given by Fra Corrado Marchesan, OCSO, a member of the trappist community at Tre Fontane.

164. Bertelli, 'L'enciclopedia'.

165. Giovanni Belardi, 'Considerazioni sui restauri', 229–230; Belardi, 'Il restauro', 79–91; Belardi, 'Il restauro architettonico', 99–160.

166. Mancinelli, Saladino, and Somma, 'Indagini' 107–120.

45 cm. below the present level. All post-medieval walls forming cells within the dormitory of the east range (between walls 23, 40, 30 and 8) are removed (our Plan I still shows them). The small medieval blocked windows along the east wall of the dormitory are reopened. Cells west of the dormitory (i.e. wall 40) are renewed. French windows are fitted in the north wall of the dormitory. The terrace east of uppermost reaches of the monks' wing is renewed and repaved. The dormitory roof is restored and strengthened with a few metal girders. The room above the refectory is transformed into a novitiate. The exterior of the east wall of the refectory (wall 10) is plastered. Modern amenities are provided throughout the complex. The churches of S. Maria Scala Coeli and S. Paolo alle Tre Fontane are restored.[167] In this restoration the three fountains in S. Paolo alle Tre Fontane are repaired.

167. Abbot Giacomo de Brière and Fra Ansgar Christensen supplied this information. In November 2002 I checked this at Tre Fontane, and discussed the restoration with Architect Giovanni Belardi.

GLOSSARY

Architrave	'A lintel in stone or timber carried from the top of one column or pier to another.' (Krautheimer, *Early Christian*, 541)
Arcosolium	A tomb with an arch above it.
Barrel vault	'A half-cylindrical vault, as in a continuous arch.' (Krautheimer, *Early Christian*, 541)
Bipedales	Bricks two roman feet long (29.56 cm. X 2 = 59.12, or c. 60 cm.).
Castellum	Literally a 'castle' or 'fort', a term used in medieval Italy to denote a town.
Castra	Literally a 'fortified place', a term used in medieval Italy to denote a town.
Chancel	The sanctuary of a church.
Chapter room	A room used for daily meetings in a monastery.
Cornice	A moulded projection which crowns or finishes the part of a building to which it is affixed.
Crossing	'The space occupied by the intersection of the nave and transepts.' (Krautheimer, *Early Christian*, 542)
Cross vault	'A vault formed by the intersection at right angles of two barrel vaults (see above).' (*Illustrated Dictionary*, 149)
Dorter	The dormitory in a monastery.
Entablature	'The superstructure carried by columns, usually divided into three parts: architrave, frieze, and cornice.' (Krautheimer, *Early Christian*, 542)

Extrados	'The exterior curve or boundary of the visible face of an arch' or vault. (*Illustrated Dictionary*, 206)
Falsa Cortina	A finishing of the mortar, often with a thin line made by a trowel (also called *stillatura*).
Hygumenarch	The head, or abbot, of a byzantine-rite monastery.
Lavra	'A cluster of cells or caves laid out for hermit monks, having in common a centre containing a church and sometimes a refectory.' (Krautheimer, *Early Christian*, 543)
Lintel	'A horizontal structural member (such as a beam) over an opening which carries the weight of the wall above it; often of stone or wood.' (*Illustrated Dictionary*, 330)
Modulus	A contant proportion or measurement, e.g. in masonry, of five rows of bricks and the mortar laid horizontally between them.
Mortarbeds	The mortar between courses of bricks or stone.
Narthex	'Architecturally the transverse vestibule of a church . . . preceding the facade.' (Krautheimer, *Early Christian*, 543)
Oculus	A circular window.
Opus caementicium	Masonry composed of pieces of stone arranged roughly in rows and held in place by mortar.
Opus listatum / listata	Masonry composed of one or more courses of bricks and small blocks of stone.
Opus mixtum	Sometimes an alternative term for *Opus listatum / listata*.
Opus saracinescum	Masonry composed of regular rows of small blocks of tufa (see below).
Pavonazzetto	A type of marble, in colour creamy white streaked with purple.
Peperino	A type of tufa (see below).
Pointing	A way of finishing mortar.
Quatrefoil	Tracery divided in a four-lobed pattern.

Quoins	Stones used to reinforce an external corner or edge of a wall.
Relieving arch	An arch built into a wall to discharge the load on a wall.
Sawtooth	Bricks laid at an angle, similar to the cutting edge of a saw.
Sesquipedales	Bricks one-and-a-half Roman feet long (29.56 cm. X 1.5 = 44.34 cm., or c. 45 cm.)
Splayed windows	Windows with a narrow arched opening, surrounded by an arch with a larger radius on the exterior on both sides.
Spoils / Spolia	Reused architectural material, such as capitals, columns, bases and bricks.
Springing	'The point where an arch rises from its supports.' (*Illustrated Dictionary*, 501)
Transenna	A marble plaque, often used to enclose a shrine or altar.
Transept	'The transverse part of a church, crossing the main axis at a right angle.' (*Illustrated Dictionary*, 545)
Tufa	The local volcanic stone around Rome.
Tufelli	Small blocks of tufa (see above).
Voussoir	'A brick or wedge-shaped stone which forms one of the units of an arch.' (Krautheimer, *Early Christian*, 545)

BIBLIOGRAPHY

I. PRIMARY SOURCES

Manuscripts

Bibliothèque Nationale, Paris

    MS 1402: Documents pertaining to the monastery of S. Anastasius.

Biblioteca Vallicelliana, Rome

    MS C62: Lectionary with Collects from the monastery of S. Anastasius, late eleventh century.

Biblioteca Vaticana Apostolica

    Barb. lat. 3232: Documents pertaining to S. Anastastius.

    Barb. lat. 4402, fols. 35r.–51r.: A. Eclissi, drawings, 1630.

    Vat. lat. 1193, fols. 82r.–86r.: Miracle of Saint Anastasius, twelfth century.

    Vat. lat. 1195, fols. 106r.–109v: Miracle of Saint Anastasius, eleventh century.

    Vat. lat. 4267, fol. 11: Liber indulgentiarum.

    Vat. lat. 5844, fols. 47r.–51r.: Documents pertaining to the monastery of S. Anastasius.

    Vat. lat. 6075, 53r.–55v.: Miracle of Saint Anastasius, copied in 1601 from a very old codex belonging to S. Cecilia in Trastevere.

    Vat. lat. 6780, 31v: Panvinio, Onofrio. *Schedae de ecclesiis urbis Romae.* c. 1560.

    Vat. Lat. 7930, fols. 151r.–152v., Archive of S. Angelo in Pescheria: Document pertaining to the monastery of S. Anastasius.

    Vat. lat. 11897, 48r–52v., Documents pertaining to S. Anastasius.

    Vat. lat. 13479, fols. 47, 178, 184, 185 and 186: Seroux d'Agincourt, Sketchbook.

285

Printed Works

Acta Sanctorum. I. Bollandus *et al.,* edd. Antwerp: Apud Ioannem Meursum, 1693 ff.

Anonymous. *Le cose maravigliose dell'alma città di Roma.* Venice: Girolamo Francini,1588.

Baglione, Giovanni. *Le Nove Chiese di Roma.* Parole e Forme 2. Fonti per la Storia dell'Arte e dell'Architettura 2. L. Barroero *et al.,* eds. Rome: Archivio Guido Izzi, 1990.

Baronio, Cesare. *Annales Ecclesiastici.* Lucca: Typ. Leonardi Venturi, 1738 ff.

Bede the Venerable. *Chronica, MGH* ed., Auctorum Antiquissimorum 13. Berlin: Weidmann, 1894.

Bede's Ecclesiastical History of the English People. B. Colgrave and R. A. B. Mynors, edd. Oxford: Clarendon Press, 1969.

Benedict of Soracte. *Chronicon.* Fonti per la storia d'Italia, pubblicati dal Reale Istituto Storico Italiano per il Medio Evo 55. Giuseppe Zucchetti, ed. Rome: Tipografia del Senato, 1920.

Bernardo di Chiaravalle, *Sermoni sul Cantico dei Cantici.* ed. and trans. Domenico Turco. Trani: Vivere In, 1982.

Eusebius, *Ecclesiastical History.* Fathers of the Church, 19. Trans. Roy J. Deferrari. Washington, DC: Catholic University Press, 1965–69.

Forcella, Vincenzo. *Iscrizioni delle chiese e d'altri edifici di Roma dal secolo XI fino ai giorni nostri.* vol. 12, Rome: Ludovico Cecchini, 1878.

Fra Mariano da Firenze, *Itinerarium Urbis Romae (1518).* Studi di Antichità Cristiana, 2. E. Bulletti, OFM, ed. Rome: Pontificio Istituto di Archeologia Cristiana, 1931.

Giorgi, Ignazio. 'Il regesto del monastero di S. Anastasio ad Aquas Salvias'. *Archivio della Società Romana di Storia Patria* 1(1878) 49–78

Guignard, Philippe. *Les monuments primitifs de la règle cistercienne.* Analecta Divionensia, 10. Dijon: Imprimerie Darantière, 1878.

Il Diario di Antonio di Pietro dello Schiavo, 19 ottobre 1404–25 settembre 1417. Rerum Italicarum Scriptores, 24. L. A. Muratori, ed. Bologna: Nicola Zanicheli, 1917, pt. 5, fasc. 153–154.

Jaffé, Philippe and Samuel Lowenfeld, *et al., Regesta Pontificum Romanorum.* 2 vols., Leipzig: Veit et Comp. 1885 and 1888, rpt Graz: Akademische Druck und Verlagsanstalt, 1959.

Janauschek, Leopold. *Originum Cisterciensium.* 1, Vienna: Alfred Hoelder, 1877.

Jongelinus, Gaspar. *Notitia Abbatiarum Ordinis Cisterciensis per orbem universum, lib X.* vol. 7. Cologne: Apud Joannes Henningium bibliopolam, 1640.

Kehr, Paul Fridolin. *Italia Pontificia.* vols. 1 and 2, Berlin: Weidmann, 1906.

Langlois, Ernest. *Les Registres de Nicholas IV.* vol. 1, Bibliothèque des Écoles Françaises d'Athènes et de Rome, 2e ser., I. Paris: Ernest Thorin Editeur, 1886.

Lauro, Iacobus (Giacomo). *Antiquae urbis splendor.* Rome: no typ., [drawn 1612] printed 1630

Leclercq, Jean, H. M Rochais, C. H. Talbot, *Sancti Bernardi Opera.* 8 volumes. Rome: Editiones cistercienses 1957–1977.

Le Liber Pontificalis. vols. 1 and 2, L. Duchesne, ed. Paris: E. De Boccard, 1886–92; vol. 3, with additions and corrections by C. Vogel, Paris: E. De Boccard, 1957 (3 vols. reprinted 1981).

Les Ecclesiastica Offficia Cisterciens du XIIème Siècle. Danièle Choisselet and Placide Vernet, edd. Le Documentation Cistercienne, 22. Reiningue: Abbaye d'Oelenberg, 1989.

Lowenfeld, Samuel. 'Documenta quaedam historiam monasterii S. Anastasii ad Aquas Salvias illustrantia'. *Archivio della Società Romana di Storia Patria* 4 (1881) 399–404.

Lubin, Augustin. *Abbatiarum Italiae brevis notitia.* Rome: Jo: Jacobi Komarek Boëmi apud S. Angelum Custodem, 1693.

Manrique, Angel. *Annales Cistercienses.* vols. 1 and 2. Paris: G. Borsat and Laurentius Anissan, 1642

Mansi, Jean Dominique. *Sacrorum Conciliorum nove et amplissima collectio.* rpt Graz: Akademische Druck und Verlagsanstalt, 1960.

Margarini, Cornelius. *Bullarium Casinense.* Todi: Ex typ. Vincentij Galassij, 1670.

Marillier, J. *Chartes et Documents concernant l'Abbaye de Cîteaux.* Bibliotheca Cisterciensis, 1. Rome: Editiones Cistercienses, 1961.

Martène, Edmond and Urbain Durand. *Voyage littéraire de deux bénédictins de la Congrégation de Saint Maur.* Paris, 1767.

Martinelli, Fioravante. *Roma ex ethnica sacra sanctorum Petri et Pauli apostolica praedicatione profuso sanguine.* Rome: Typis Romanis Ignatij de Lazaris, 1653.

Martyrologium Hieronimianum. Giovanni Battista De Rossi-L. Duchesne, eds. AA SS, Novembris, 2: 12 and Januarii, 2: 393.

Meglinger, J. *Iter cisterciense.* PL 185:1598-1609.

Migne, J. P. *Patrologia cursus completus . . . series Latina.* Paris: Garnier, 1844–1905, vols. 148, 179, 182, 185.

'Miraculum S. Anastasii martyris'. *Analecta Bollandiana* 11 (1892) 233–241.

Padredio, Carlo. *Misure delle sette e nove chiese.* Rome: Per il Tizzoni, 1677.

Panciroli, Ottavio. *I tesori nascosti nell'alma città di Roma.* Rome: Luigi Zanetti, 1600.

——. *I tesori nascosti nell'alma città di Roma.* Rome: Luigi Zanetti, 2nd ed. 1625.

Panvinio, Onofrio. *De praecipuis Urbis Romae sanctioribusque basilicis, quas Septem Ecclesiae vulgo vocantur.* Rome: Apud Haeredes Antonii Bladii, 1570.

Paulus Diaconus. *Historia Longobardorum.* ed. MGH. Scriptores rerum Longobardorum. Hanover: Societas Aperiendis Rerum Germanicarum Medii Aevi, 1878. Pp. 185–186.

Sancti Bernardi Opera. vol. 7, *Epistolae: I, Corpus Epistolarum 181–310; II, Epistolae extra Corpus, 311–547.* J. Leclercq and H. Rochais, eds. Rome: Editiones Cistercienses, 1977.

Serrano, M. A. *De septem urbis ecclesiis una cum earum reliquijs, stationibus et indulgentijs.* Rome: Apud Haeredes Antonii Bladii, 1575.

Severano, Giovanni. *Memorie sacre delle sette chiese di Roma.* Rome: Per Giacomo Mascardi, 1630.

St. Bernard's Apologia to Abbot William. trans. Michael Casey OCSO, Bernard of Clairvaux: Treatises, I, Cistercian Fathers Series 1. Cistercian Publications: Spencer, MA. 1970. Rpt *Cistercians and Cluniacs.* Apologia to Abbot William. Kalamazoo: Cistercian Publications.

Statuta capitularum generalium Ordinis Cisterciensis. 9 vols., Bibliothèque de la Révue d'Histoire Ecclésiastique, 9–14 B. Joseph Marie Canivez, ed. Louvain: Bureaux de la Révue d'Histoire Eccléstiastique, 1933–1941.

Tholomei Lucensis Annales. MGH SS. Rerum Germanicarum Nova Series, 8. B. Schmeidler, ed. Berlin: Weidmann, 1930.

Trifone, Basilio. 'Le carte del Monastero di San Paolo di Roma dal secolo XI al XV'. *Archivio della Società Romana di Storia Patria* 31 (1908) 267–313, esp. 278–285.

Ughelli, Ferdinando. *Italia Sacra.* 2nd ed. vol. 1 Venice: Apud Sebatianum Coleti. 1717. Rpt Arnoldo Forni, 1984.

Valentini, Roberto and Giuseppe Zucchetti, *Codice topografico della Città di Roma.* 4 vols., Fonti per la Storia d'Italia, pubblicati dal R. Istituto Storico Italiano per il Medio Evo, 81, 88, 90 and 91. Rome: Tipografia del Senato, 1940–53.

Vasi, Giuseppe. *Delle magnificenze di Roma antica e moderna.* vol. 3, Roma: Nella stamperia di Apollo, Presso gli eredi Barbiellini, 1753.

————. *Tesoro sacro e venerabile, cioè le basiliche e chiese antiche di Roma*. Rome: M. Pagliarini, 1778.

Vitalis, Orderic, *The Ecclesiastical History of Orderic Vitalis*. 6 volumes. ed. and trans. Marjorie Chibnall, Oxford: Clarendon Press, 1969–1980.

Waddell, Chrysogonus. *Narrative and Legislative Texts from Early Cîteaux*. Studia et Documenta, 9. Brecht: Cîteaux: Commentarii Cistercienses. 1999.

————. *Cistercian Lay Brothers. Twelfth-Century Usages with Related Texts*. Studia et Documenta, 10. Brecht: Cîteaux: Commentarii Cistercienses, 2000.

————. *Twelfth-Century Statutes from the Cistercian General Chapter*. Studia et Documenta 12. Brecht: Cîteaux: Commentarii Cistercienses, 2002.

William of Malmesbury. *Gesta Regum Anglorum: The History of the English Kings*. R. A. B. Mynors, ed. and trans., completed by R. M. Thomson and M. Winterbottom. Oxford Medieval Texts. Oxford: Clarendon Press, 1998.

II. Secondary Sources

Aavitsland, Kristin Bliksrud. *Florilegium. En undersøkelse av billedspråket i Vita Humana-frisen, Abbazia delle Tre Fontane, Roma*. Acta Humaniora 134. Oslo: Unipub, 2002.

Amore, Agostino. *I martiri di Roma*. Rome: Edizioni Antonianum, 1975.

Anonymous (A. Barbiero OCSO). *S. Paolo e le Tre Fontane. XXII secoli di storia messi in luce da un monaco cisterciense (Trappista)*. Rome: L'Abbazia 'Nullius' dei Santi Vincenzo ed Anastasio alle Acque Salvie, 1938.

Anonymous. *Tre Fontane*. Rome: Abbazia delle Tre Fontane, 1967.

Antonelli, Ferdinando. 'I primi monasteri di monaci orientali in Roma'. *Rivista di Archeologia Cristiana 5* (1928) 105–122.

Armellini, Mariano and Carlo Cecchelli. *Le chiese di Roma dal secolo IV al XIX*. vol. 2, Rome: Edizioni R.O.R.E di Nicolo Ruffolo, 1942.

Arte D'Occidente: temi e metodi: studi in onore di Angiola Maria Romanini. Antonio Cadei *et al.* Edd. Rome: Sintesi informazione, 1999.

Aubert, Marcel. *L'architecture cistercienne en France*. 2nd ed. 2 vols. Paris: Vanoest, 1947.

————. 'Existe-t-il une architecture cistercienne?' *Cahiers de Civilisation Médiévale* 1 (1958) 153–158.

Avagnina, Maria E., Vittoria Garibaldi and Claudia Salterini. 'Strutture murarie degli edifici religiosi di Roma nel XII secolo'. *Rivista dell'Istituto Nazionale d'Archeologia e Storia dell'Arte* 23–24 (1976–77) 173–255.

Barclay Lloyd, Joan E. 'Masonry techniques in medieval Rome *c.* 1080–*c.* 1300', *Papers of the British School at Rome* 53 (1985) 225–277.

––––––. *The Medieval Church and Canonry of S. Clemente in Rome.* San Clemente Miscellany 3. Rome: San Clemente, 1989.

––––––. 'SS. Vincenzo e Anastasio alle Tre Fontane near Rome: the Australian connection'. *Tjurunga: An Australasian Benedictine Review* 46 (1994) 57–70.

––––––. 'The Architecture of the Medieval Monastery at S. Lorenzo fuori le Mura, Rome'. *Architectural Studies in Memory of Richard Krautheimer.* ed. Cecil L. Striker. Mainz: Philipp von Zabern, 1996. Pp. 99–102.

––––––. 'The medieval murals in the Cistercian abbey of SS. Vincenzo e Anastasio *ad Aquas Salvias* at Tre Fontane in their architectural setting'. *Papers of the British School at Rome* 65 (1997) 287–348.

Barclay Lloyd, Joan E. and Karin Bull-Simonsen Einaudi. *S. Cosma e Damiano in Mica Aurea: Architettura, stora e storiografia di un monastero romano soppresso.* Miscellanea della Società Romana di Storia Patria XXXVIII. Rome: Società Romana di Storia Patria, 1998.

Barnes, Carl F. 'Le "Problème" Villard de Honnecourt'. *Les Bâtieeurs des Cathedrales Gothiques.* Roland Recht, ed. Strasbourg: Les Musées de la Ville de Strasbourg, 1989. Pp. 209–223.

Bedini, Balduino D. *Breve prospetto delle abbazie cisterciensi d'Italia.* Casamari: Tipografia di Casamari, 1966.

Belardi, Giovanni. 'Considerazioni sui restauri in atto nell'abbazia delle Tre Fontane a Roma'. *Arte Medievale* 2 serie, 7 (1993) 229–230.

––––––. 'Il restauro dell'abbazia delle Tre Fontane (seconda parte)'. *Arte Medievale* 2 serie, 8, 1 (1994) 79–91.

––––––. Fra Jacques Brière, Liliana Pozzi, *et al. Abbazia delle Tre Fontane: il complesso, la storia, il restauro.* Rome: Edilerica s.r.l., 1995.

––––––. 'Il restauro architettonico'. Giovanni Belardi, Fra Jacques Brière, Liliana Pozzi, *et al. Abbazia delle Tre Fontane: il complesso, la storia, il restauro.* Rome: Edilerica s.r.l., 1995. Pp. 98–160.

Bell, David N. 'The Siting and Size of Cistercian Infirmaries in England and Wales'. *Studies in Cistercian Art and Architecture, 5.* Cistercian Studies Series 167. Meredith Parsons Lillich, ed. Kalamazoo: Cistercian Publications, 1998. Pp. 211–237.

Bellini, Federico. 'Un'Opera di Giacomo della Porta: La Ricostruzione dell'Oratio di S. Maria de Scala Coeli nell'Abbazia delle Tre Fontane'. *Quaderni dell'Istituto di Storia dell'Architettura*, NS 14 (1989) 31–42.

Bertelli, Carlo. 'L'enciclopedia delle Tre Fontane'. *Paragone-Arte* 20.235 (1969) 24–49.

———. 'Caput Sancti Anastasii'. *Paragone-Arte* 21.247 (1970) 12–25.

———. 'Secolo XIII—Affreschi, Roma, Abbazia delle Tre Fontane'. *Restauri della Soprintendenza alle Gallerie e alle opere d'arte medioevali e moderne per il Lazio*. Rome: De Luca Editore, 1972. Pp. 10–13.

———. 'Affreschi, miniature e oreficerie cistercensi in Toscana e il Lazio'. *I Cistercensi e il Lazio*. Rome: Multigrafica Editrice, 1978. Pp. 71–81.

Bertolini, Gian L. 'Su la figurazione geografica della badia alle Tre Fontane'. *X Congresso internazionale di geografia, Roma (1913), Atti*. Rome: Tipografia dell'Unione Editrice, 1915. Pp. 1–13.

Bourgeois, Pierre. *Abbaye Notre Dame de Fontenay: Monument du Patrimoine mondial–Architecture et Histoire*. 2 vols. Bégrolles en Mauge: Abbaye de Bellefontaine, 2000.

Branner, Robert. 'Villard de Honnecourt, Reims, and the Origins of Gothic Architectural Drawing'. *The Engineering of Medieval Cathedrals*. Studies in the History of Civil Engineering, 1. Lynn T. Courtenay, ed. Aldershot: Ashgate, 1997. Pp. 63–80.

Braunfels, Wolfgang. *Monasteries of Western Europe*. London: Thames and Hudson, 1972. esp. pp. 67–110.

Bredero, Adriaan H. *Bernard of Clairvaux: Between Cult and Culture*. Edinburgh: T. and T. Clark-Grand Rapids: Eerdmans, 1996.

Brezzi, Paolo. 'San Bernardo a Roma'. *Studi Romani* 1.4 (=36) (1953) 496–509.

Brière, Jacques. 'La storia dell'Ordine Cistercense'. Giovanni Belardi, Fra Jacques Brière, Liliana Pozzi, *et al. Abbazia delle Tre Fontane: il complesso, la storia, il restauro*. Rome: Edilerica s.r.l., 1995. Pp. 79–95.

Broccoli, Umberto. *L'Abbazia delle Tre Fontane. Fasi paleocristiane e altomedioevali del Complesso'ad Aquas Salvias' in Roma*. Trani: Vivere In, 1980.

Brooke, Christopher. 'Saint Bernard, the patrons and monastic planning'. *Cistercian Art and Architecture in the British Isles*. Christopher Norton and David Park, edd. Cambridge: Cambridge University Press, 1986. Pp. 11–23.

———. *The Age of the Cloister: The Story of Monastic Life in the Middle Ages*. Mahweh, New Jersey: HiddenSpring/Paulist Press, 2003.

Bruzelius, Caroline. 'Cistercian High Gothic: The Abbey Church of Long-pont and the Architecture of the Cistercians in the Early Thirteenth century'. *Analecta Cisterciensia* 35 (1979) 1–204.

———. 'The twelfth-century church at Ourscamp'. *Speculum* 56, 4 (1981) 28–40.

Bucher, François. 'Cistercian architectural purism'. *Comparative Studies in Society and History* 3 (1960–61) 89–105.

Burton, Janet. 'The Cistercian Adventure'. *The Cistercian Abbeys of Britain: Far from the Concourse of Men.* David Robinson, ed. London: B. T. Batsford-Kalamazoo: Cistercian Publications, 1998. Pp. 7–33.

Cadei, Antonio. 'Chiaravalle di Fiastra'. *Storia dell'Arte* 34 (1978) 247–288.

———. 'Architettura monastica'. *Atti del Congresso Internazionale de Studi sull'alto medioevo.* 2, Spoleto, 1987. Pp. 795–813.

Caetani Lovatelli, Ersilia. 'L'antica abbazia di S. Paolo alle Tre Fontane'. *Nuova Antologia* 172, luglio-agosto (1914) 3–15.

Caglianone, Roberta and Alessandro Iazeolla. 'Prime osservazioni dal rilievo architettonico del complesso delle Tre Fontane'. *Arte Medievale* 2 serie, 8, 1 (1994) 121–132.

Calandro, Alessandro. 'Arrivo dei Trappisti alle Tre Fontane nel 1868'. *L' Urbe* N. S. 36.5 (1973) 34–38.

———. 'Un bagno penale alle Tre Fontane'. *L'Urbe* N.S. 37.1 (1974) 27–29.

———. 'Inizi di bonifica alle Tre Fontane'. *L' Urbe* N.S. 37.3-4 (1974) 41–43.

———. 'Nemi e i cistercensi delle Tre Fontane'. *Castelli Romani* 29 (1984) 50–54.

Cali, Francois. *L'Ordre Cistercien.* Paris: B. Arthaud, 1972.

Capocci, V. 'Sulla tradizione del martirio di S. Paolo alle Acque Salvie'. *Atti dell VIII Congresso Internazionale di Studi Bizantini.* 2, 1953. Pp. 18–19.

Carly, Carolyn M. 'The Role of Gunzo's Dream in the Building of Cluny III', *Gesta* 27 (1988) 113–123.

Casagrande, Gino and Christopher Kleinhenz. 'Literary and philosophical perspectives on the wheel of the five senses in Longthorpe tower'. *Traditio* 41 (1985) 311–327.

Cassidy-Welch, Megan. *Monastic Spaces and their Meanings: Thirteenth-century English Cistercian Monasteries.* Turnhout: Brepols, 2001.

Celli, Angelo. *Storia della Malaria.* Città di Castello: Società Anonima Tipografia 'Leonardo da Vinci', 1925.

Chiaravalle: Arte e storia di un'abbazia cistercense, Paolo Tomea ed. Milan: Electa, 1992.

Chiumenti, Luisa and Fernando Bilancia. *La Campagna Romana* vol. 5. Rome: Banco di Roma, 1977.

Ciacci, Gaspero. *Gli Aldobrandeschi nella storia e nella 'Divina Commedia'.* 2 vols. Rome: Multigrafica Editrice, 1980.

The Cistercian Abbeys of Britain: Far from the Concourse of Men. David Robinson, ed. London: B. T. Batsford-Kalamazoo: Cistercian Publications, 1998.

Cistercian Art and Architecture in the British Isles. Christopher Norton and David Park, edd. Cambridge: Cambridge University Press, 1986.

Cistercian Ideals and Reality. Cistercian Studies Series 60. John R. Sommerfeldt, ed. Kalamazoo: Cistercian Publications, 1978.

Claussen, Peter Cornelius. *Magistri doctissimi Romani.* Stuttgart: Franz Steiner Verlag, 1987.

———. 'Renovatio Romae. Erneuerungsphasen römischer Architektur im 11. und 12. Jahrhundert'. *Rom in hohen Mittelalter.* B. Schimmelpfennig and L. Schmugge, eds. Sigmaringen: Jan Thorbecke Verlag, 1992. Pp. 87–125.

———. *Die Kirchen der Stadt Rom im Mittelalter, 1050–1300, A-F.* Stuttgart: Franz Steiner Verlag, 2002.

Coccia, Stefano, *et al.* 'Abbazia di Fossanova: Indagini archeologiche nel refettorio'. *Archeologia Medievale* 24 (1997) 55–86.

Coldstream, Nicola. *Medieval Craftsmen: Masons and Scuptors.* London: British Museum Press-Toronto: University of Toronto Press, 1991.

———. 'The Mark of Eternity: The Cistercians as Builders'. *The Cistercian Abbeys of Britain: Far from the Concourse of Men.* David Robinson, ed. London: B. T. Batsford-Kalamazoo:Cistercian Publications, 1998. Pp. 35–61.

Conant, Kenneth. 'Medieval Academy Excavations at Cluny, IX: Systematic Dimensions in the Buildings'. *Speculum* 38 (1963) 1–45.

———. *Carolingian and Romanesque Architecture.* The Pelican History of Art, Harmondsworth: Penguin Books, 1966.

Coppack, Glyn. *The White Monks: The Cistercians in Britain 1128–1540.* Stroud: Tempus, 1998.

Coppi, Antonio. 'Documenti storici del Medio Evo . . . communicati all'Accademia di Archeologia'. *Dissertazioni della Pontificia Accademia Romana di Archeologia* (9th Jan., 1862) 209.

Courtois, René. 'La première église cistercienne (XIIe siècle) de l'abbaye de Vauclair (Aisne)'. *Archéologie Mediévale* 2 (1972) 103–135.

Crecimbeni, Giovanni M. *L'istoria della Basilica diaconale, collegiata e parrocchiale di S. Maria in Cosmedin.* Rome: Antonio de' Rossi, 1715.

D'Agincourt, Seroux. *Storia dell'Arte.* vol. 2, Milan: Per Ranieri Fanfani, 1825.

Datseris, Giorgio. *L'Abbazia delle Tre Fontane in Roma: Guida.* Rome-Trani: Vivere In, 1989.

De Maffei, Fernanda. 'Riflessi dell'epopea carolingia nell'arte medievale: il ciclo di Ezechiele e non di Carlo a S. Maria in Cosmedin e l'arco di Carlo Magno a Roma'. *Atti del Convegno Nazionale sul tema: la poesia epica e la sua formazione (1969).* Rome: Accademia Nazionale dei Lincei, 1970, 351–386.

Deroin, Jean Paul. 'Le choix de la pierre dans l'architecture cistercienne au XIIe siècle'. *Carrieres et Constructions en France et dans les Pays Limitrophes.* 7 Colloque. 115 Congrès National. Paris: Editions du CTHS, 1991. Pp. 21–39.

De Rossi, Filippo. *Ritratto di Roma moderna.* Rome: Apresso Filippo de Rossi, 1652.

De Rossi, Giovanni Battista. 'Recenti scoperte nella chiesa alle Acque Salvie dedicata alla memoria del martirio dell'Apostolo Paolo. *Bullettino di Archeologia Cristiana* 7 (1869) 83–92.

————. 'Scoperte alle Acque Salvie'. *Bullettino di Archeologia Cristiana* 2 serie, 2 (1871) 71–76.

————. *Piante iconografiche e prospettiche di Roma anteriore al secolo XVI.* Roma: Tip. de Salviucci, 1879.

————. 'Oratorio e monasterio di S. Paolo apostolo alle Acque Salvie costruiti da Narsete patrizio'. *Bullettino di Archeologia Cristiana* 4 serie, 5 (1887) 79–81.

Dimier, Anselme. *L'art cistercien: France.* 3rd ed. La Nuit des Temps, 16. Paris: Zodiaque, 1982.

————. *Les Moines bâtisseurs.* Paris: Fayard, 1964. [translated Gilchrist Lavigne: *Stones Laid Before the Lord.* Kalamazoo: Cistercian Publications, 1999.]

————. *Recueil de Plans d'Églises cisterciennes.* 3 vols. Paris: Vincent Fréal, 1949–1967.

Dizionario degli Istituti di Perfezione. G. Pelliccia and G. Rocca, eds. Rome: Edizioni Paoline, 8 vols., 1974 ff., esp. vol. 2, 1975, *cc.* 1034–1098

D'Onofrio, Cesare and Carlo Pietrangeli. *Abbazie del Lazio.* Rome: Cassa di Risparmio, 1969.

Donnelly, James S. *The Decline of the Medieval Cistercian Laybrotherhood.* Fordham University Studies, History Series 3. New York: Fordham University Press, 1949.

Duby, Georges. *Saint Bernard, l'art cistercien*. Les grands batisseurs, 1. Paris: Arts et Metiers Graphiques, 1976.

The Engineering of Medieval Cathedrals. Studies in the History of Civil Engineering, 1. Lynn T. Courtenay, ed. Aldershot: Ashgate, 1997.

Esquieu, Yves. *L'abbaye du Thoronet*. Ouest France: Ministère de la Culture, 1985.

Esser, Karl Heinz. 'Les fouilles à Himmerod et le plan Bernardin'. *Mélanges Saint Bernard*. (XXIV Congrès de l'Association Bourguignonne des Sociétés Savantes). Dijon: Association des Amis de Saint Bernard, 1953. Pp. 311–315.

———. 'Über den Kirchenbau des Hl. Bernhard von Clairvaux'. *Archiv für Mittelrheinische Kirchengeschichte* 5 (1953) 195–222.

Farina, Federico. *L'Abbazia di Casamari nella storia dell'architettura e della spiritualità cistercense*. Casamari: Edizioni Casamari, 1990.

Fentress, Elizabeth and Chris Wickham. 'La valle dell'Albegna fra i secoli VII e XIV'. *Siena e Maremma nel medioevo*. M. Ascheri, ed. Siena: Betti Editrice, 2001. Pp. 59–81.

Fergusson, Peter. 'The first architecture of the Cistercians in England and the work of Abbot Adam of Meaux'. *Journal of the British Archaeological Association* 136 (1983) 74–86.

———. *Architecture of Solitude: Cistercian Abbeys in Twelfth-century England*. Princeton: Princeton University Press, 1984.

———. 'The twelfth-century refectories at Rievaulx and Byland Abbeys'. *Cistercian Art and Architecture in the British Isles*. Christopher Norton and David Park, edd. Cambridge: Cambridge University Press, 1986 160–180.

———. '"Porta Patens Esto": Notes on Early Cistercian Gatehouses in the north of England'. *Medieval Architecture and its Intellectual Context. Studies in Honour of Peter Kidson*. London: The Hambledon Press, 1990 47–59.

———. 'Programmatic Factors in the East Extension of Clairvaux'. *Arte Medievale*, new series 8,1 (1994) 87–102.

Fergusson, Peter and Stuart Harrison. *Rievaulx Abbey: Community, Architecture, Memory*. New Haven-London: Yale University Press, 1999.

Fernie, Eric. 'Historical Metrology and Architectural History'. *Art History* 1.4 (1978) 387–399.

———. 'A Beginner's Guide to the Study of Architectural Proportions and Systems of Length'. *Medieval Architecture and Its Intellectual Context:*

Studies in Honour of Peter Kidson. Eric Fernie and Paul Crossley, edd. London-Ronceverte: Hambledon Press, 1990. Pp. 229–237.

———. 'The Ground Plan of Norwich Cathedral and the Square Root of Two'. *The Engineering of Medieval Cathedrals*. Studies in the History of Civil Engineering, 1. Lynn T. Courtenay, ed. Aldershot: Ashgate, 1997. Pp. 107–116.

Ferrari, Guy. *Early Roman Monasteries*. Studi di Antichità Cristiana, 23. Vatican City: Pontificio Istituto di Archeologia Cristiana, 1957.

Fraccaro Longhi, Lelia. *L'architettura delle chiese cistercensi italiane*. Milan: Casa Editrice Ceschina, 1958.

France, James. 'The Cellarer's Domain'. *Studies in Cistercian Art and Architecture* 5. Cistercian Studies Series 169. Meredith Parsons Lillich, ed. Kalamazoo: Cistercian Publications, 1998. Pp. 1–39.

Frothingham, Arthur L. *The Monuments of Christian Rome*. New York: Macmillan, 1908.

Frutaz, Amato P. *Le Piante di Roma*. 3 vols., Rome: Istituto di Studi Romani, 1962.

Gabriel d'Aiguebelle OCSO. *L'Abbaye des Trois-Fontaines située aux Eaux-Salviennes près de Rome*. 3rd ed., Landerau: P. B. Moulins, 1882.

Gandolfo, Francesco. 'Aggiormento scientifico e bibliografia'. Guglielmo Matthiae. *Pittura romana del medioevo*. vol. 2. Rome: Fratelli Palombi Editori, 1988. Pp. 283–284.

Gardner, Julian, 'An introduction to the iconography of the medieval italian City Gate'. *Dumbarton Oaks Papers* 41 (1987) 199–213.

Geertman, Herman. *More Veterum. Il Liber Pontificalis e gli edifici ecclesiastici di Roma nella tarda antichità e nell'alto medioevo*. Groningen: H. D. Tjeenk Willink, 1975.

Gilyard-Beer, R. 'Fountains Abbey: the early Buildings, 1132–50'. *Archaeological Journal* 125 (1968) 313–319.

Gimple, Jean. *The Cathedral Builders*. Salisbury: Michael Russell, 1983.

Giovenale, Giovanni Battista. 'Il chiostro medioevale di San Paolo fuori le Mura'. *Bullettino della Commissione Archeologica Comunale di Roma*. 45 (1917) 125–167, esp. 148–151.

Glass, Dorothy F. *Studies on Cosmatesque pavements*. International Series, 82. Oxford: B. A. R., 1980.

Gobry, Ivan. *Les Moines en Occident*. 5: Le Siècle de Saint Bernard. Paris: François-Xavier de Guilbert, 1997.

Goodrich, W. Eugene. '*Caritas* and Cistercian Uniformity: An Ideological Connection?' *Cistercian Studies Quarterly* 20 (1985) 31–43.

Gras, Pierre. 'Vues et plans de l'ancien Cîteaux'. *Mélanges à la Mémoire du Père Anselme Dimier,* 6. Benoît Chauvin, ed. Arbois, 1982–1987. Pp. 549–575.

Grisar, Hartmann. 'Le iscrizioni cristiane di Roma negli inizii del Medio Evo, Num. 13, Anno 604, Tav. III, n. 2'. *Analecta Romana.* 1, Rome: Desclée Lefebvre e C'e., 1899. 157–160.

Guidobaldi, Federigo, Claudia Barsanti and Alessandra Guiglia Guidobaldi. *San Clemente: la scultura del VI secolo.* San Clemente Miscellany, IV.2. Rome: San Clemente, 1992.

Gullota, Giuseppe. 'Un antico ed unico documento sul monastero di S. Maria e S. Nicola in Acqua Salvia'. *Archivio della Società Romana di Storia Patria.* 66 (1943) 185–195.

Gusmao, Artur. *A real abadia de Alcobaça, estudo histórico-arqueológico.* Lisbon: Editora Ulisseia, 1948.

Hahn, Hanno. *Die frühe Kirchenbaukunst der Zisterzienser.* Berlin: Verlag Gebr. Mann, 1957.

Halsey, Richard, 'The earliest architecture of the Cistercians in England'. *Cistercian art and architecture in the British Isles.* Christopher Norton and David Park, eds. Cambridge: Cambridge University Press, 1986. Pp. 65–85.

Hamilton, Bernard. *Monastic Reform, Catharism and the Eastern Churches in the Tenth Century.* London: Variorum Reprints, 1979.

Herklotz, Ingo. 'Sepulcra' e 'Monumenta' del medioevo. Studi sull'arte sepolcrale in Italia.* Rome: Edizioni Rari Nantes, 2nd ed. 1990.

———. 'Der mittelalterliche Fassadenportikus der Lateranbasilika und seine Mosaiken'. *Römisches Jahrbuch der Bibliotheca Hertziana.* 25 (1989) 23–95.

Hervé, Lucien. *Architecture of Truth: The Cistercian Abbey of Le Thoronet.* London-New York: Phaidon, 2001.

Hill, Bennett D. *English Cistercian monasteries and their patrons in the twelfth century.* Urbana, Chicago and London: University of Illinois Press, 1968.

Hiscock, Nigel. *The Wise Master Builder: Platonic Geometry in Plans of Medieval Abbeys and Cathedrals.* Aldershot: Ashgate, 2000.

Holdsworth, Christopher J. 'The blessings of work: the Cistercian view'. *Sanctity and Secularity: the Church and the World.* Studies in Church History, 10. Derek Baker, ed. Oxford: Basil Blackwell, 1973.

———. 'The Chronology and Character of Early Cistercian Legislation on Art and Architecture'. *Cistercian Art and Architecture in the British Isles.* Christopher Norton-David Park, eds. Cambridge: Cambridge University Press, 1986. Pp. 40–55.

Horn, Walter and Ernest Born. *The Plan of St. Gall.* 3 vols., Berkeley, Los Angeles and London: University of California Press, 1979.

Hülsen, Christian. *Le chiese di Roma nel Medio Evo.* Florence: Leo S. Olschki Editore, 1927.

Iacobini, Antonio. 'La Pittura e le arti suntuarie: da Innocenzo III a Innocenzo IV (1198–1254). *Roma nel Duecento.* Angiola Maria Romanini, ed. Rome: SEAT, 1991. Pp. 237–319.

I Cistercensi ed il Lazio: Atti delle giornate di studio dell'Istituto dell'Arte dell'Università di Roma (Roma 17–21 maggio 1977). Rome: Multigrafica Editrice, 1978.

Illustrated Dictionary of Historic Architecture. Cyril M. Harris, ed. New York: Dover Publications, Inc., 1977.

Jansen, Virgin. 'Architecture and Community in Medieval Monastic Dormitories'. *Studies in Medieval Cistercian Art and Architecture 5,* Cistercian Studies Series 167. Meredith Parsons Lillich, ed. Kalamazoo: Cistercian Publications, 1998. Pp. 59–94.

Jounel, Pierre, *Le culte des saints dans les basiliques du Latran et du Vatican au douzième siècle.* Collection de l'École Française de Rome, 26. Rome: École Française de Rome, 1977.

Kimpel, Dieter. 'Les méthodes de production des cathédrales', *Les Bâtisseurs des Cathédrales Gothiques.* Roland Recht, ed. Strasbourg: Le Musées de la Ville de Strasbourg, 1989. Pp. 91–101.

Kinder, Terryl N. *Architecture of the Cistercian Abbey of Pontigny, The Twelfth-century Church.* unpublished Ph. D. thesis, Indiana University, 1982.

———. *Cistercian Europe. Architecture of Contemplation.* Grand Rapids: Wm. B. Eerdmans-Kalamazoo: Cistercian Publications, 2002.

———. *L'Europe cistercienne.* Paris: Zodiaque, 1997.

———. 'A Note on the Plan of the First Church at Pontigny'. *Mélanges à la memoire du Père Anselme Dimier.* Pupillin, Arbois: B. Chauvin, 1982–87, vol. 6. Pp. 601–608.

———. 'Some Observations on the Origins of Pontigny and its First Church'. *Cîteaux, Commentarii Cistercienses* 31 (1980) 9–19.

King, Archdale. *Cîteaux and her Elder Daughters.* London: Burns and Oats, 1954.

Kinney, Dale. *S. Maria in Trastevere from its founding to 1215.* unpublished Ph. D. thesis, Institute of Fine Arts: New York University, 1975.

———. 'Spolia from the Baths of Caracalla'. *The Art Bulletin* 68.3 (1986) 379–397.

Kirsch, Johann Peter. 'Der Ort des Martyriums des Hl. Paulus'. *Römische Quartalschrift für christliche Altertumskunde und für Kirchengeschichte 2* (1888) 233–247.

Krautheimer, Richard. *Corpus Basilicarum Christianarum Romae.* 5 vols. Monumenti di Antichità Cristiana, 2 Serie, 2. Vatican City: Pontificia Istituto di Archeologia Cristiana-Institute of Fine Arts, New York University, 1937–1977.

———. 'Sancta Maria Rotunda,' Krautheimer, Richard. *Studies in Early Christian, Medieval and Renaissance Art.* New York: New York University Press, 1969. Pp. 107–114.

———. *Rome: Profile of a City, 312–1308.* Princeton: Princeton University Press, 1980.

———. *Early Christian and Byzantine Architecture.* The Pelican History of Art. Harmondsworth: Penguin Books, 1979.

Lambert, Elie. 'Remarques sur les plans d'églises dits cisterciens'. *Deutsch-Französische kunsthistoriker-Tagung. L'architecture monastique. Actes et travaux des historiens d'art (1951).* Mainz, 1951. Pp. 7–12.

Lawrence, Clifford H. *Medieval Monasticism.* London: Longman, 1984.

Leclercq, Jean. *Saint Bernard, mystique.* Bruges: Desclée de Brouwer, 1948.

———. *A Second Look at Bernard of Clairvaux.* Cistercian Studies Series, 105. Kalamazoo: Cistercian Publications, 1990.

Lekai, Louis J. *The Cistercians: Ideals and Reality.* Kent, Ohio: The Kent State University Press, 1977.

Les Bâtisseurs des Cathédrals Gothiques. Roland Recht, ed. Strasbourg: Les Musées de la Ville de Strasbourg, 1989.

Letarouilly, Paul. *Édifices de Rome moderne.* vol. 3. Liège: D'Avanzo et C'e, 1853.

Lietzmann, Hans. *Petrus und Paulus in Rom.* Bonn: A. Marcus und E. Eber Verlag, 1915.

Lillich, Meredith Parsons. 'Cleanliness with Godliness: A Discussion of Medieval Monastic Plumbing'. *Mélanges à la Mémoire du Anselme Dimier,* 3. Benoît Chauvin, ed. Arbois, 1982. Pp. 123–148.

Lipsius, Richard A. *Die apokryphen Apostelgeschichten.* Brunswick: C. A. Schwetschke und Sohn, 1887.

Lo Iudice, S. 'Gli affreschi enciclopedici dell'abbazia delle Tre Fontane'. *Strenna dei Romanisti 46* (1985) 353–368.

Luttrell, Anthony. 'The Medieval Ager Cosanus'. *Siena e Maremma nel medioevo.* M. Ascheri, ed. Siena: Betti Editrice, 2001. Pp. 27–58.

Lyman, Thomas W. 'Opus ad triangulum versus opus ad quadratum in medieval five-aisled churches'. *Artistes, Artisans et Production artistique au moyen âge*, 2. Xavier Barral I Altet, ed. Paris: Picard, 1987. Pp. 203–219.

Maggi, Luca. *Giacomo della Porta: II S. Paolo alle Tre Fontane.* Storia Architettura Saggi, II. Rome: Bonsignore Editore, 1996.

Malmstrom, Ronald. *S. Maria in Aracoeli in Rome.* Ph. D. thesis, Institute of Fine Arts: New York University, 1973.

Malone, Carolyn and Walter Horn. 'Layout of the Cistercian Monastery in the twelfth and thirteenth centuries'. Walter Horn and Ernest Born, *The Plan of St. Gall*, 2. Berkeley, Los Angeles , London: University of California Press, 1979. Pp. 315–319; 349–356.

Mancinelli, Maria Letizia, Laura Saladino and Maria Carla Somma. 'Abbazia delle Tre Fontane. Analisi delle strutture murarie'. *Arte Medievale* 2 serie, 8, 1 (1994) 93–105.

———. 'Indagini all'interno della chiesa dei SS. Vincenzo e Anastasio'. *Arte Medievale* 2 serie, 8, 1 (1994) 107–120.

Martindale, Andrew. *The Rise of the Architect in the Middle Ages and Early Renaissance.* London: Thames and Hudson, 1972.

Matthiae, Guglielmo. *Pittura romana del medioevo.* 2 vols. Rome: Fratelli Palombi Editori, 1987–88.

McClendon, Charles. *The Imperial Abbey of Farfa.* Yale Publications in the History of Art, 36. New Haven and London: Yale University Press, 1987.

Menichella, Anna. 'Il maestro delle Tre Fontane'. *Atti (della IV settimana) di studi di storia dell'arte medioevale dell'Università di Roma 'La Sapienza' (18–24 maggio 1980).* Roma: L'Erma di Bretschneider, 1983. Pp. 477–485.

Mihályi, Melinda. 'I Cistercensi a Roma e la decorazione pittorica dell'ala dei Monaci nell'abbazia delle Tre Fontane'. *Arte Medievale* 2 serie, 5, 1 (1991) 155–189.

———. 'Appunti sul tema iconografico della cavea cum ave incluse'. *Arte d'Occidente: temi e metodi: studi in onore di Angiola Maria Romanini*, 2. Antonio Cadei *et al.* edd. Rome: Sintesi informazione, 1999. Pp. 891–900.

Monasticon Italiae I: Roma e Lazio. F. Caraffa, ed. Cesena: Badia di S. Maria del Monte, 1981.

Morgan, Nigel J. 'The Scala Coeli Indulgence and the Royal Chapels'. *The Reign of Henry VII.* Proceedings of the Harlaxton Symposium. Stamford: Paul Watkins, 1995. Pp. 82–103.

Mothes, Oskar. *Die Baukunst des Mittelalters in Italien.* Jena: H. Costgenoble, 1884.

Mulazzani, Germano. *L'abbazia delle Tre Fontane*. Milan: Tranchida Editori, 1988.

Münz, Sigmund. *Tre Fontane. Ein Trappistenkloster in der römischen Campagna*. Frankfort: Rütter und Löning, 1889.

Musso, Jean-Michel. 'L'Abbaye de Clairvaux'. *Forme et sens. La Formation et la Dimension Religieuse du Patrimoine cultural*. Actes du colloque École du Louvre, 1997. Pp. 48–51.

Negri, Daniele. *Abbazie cistercensi in Italia*. Pistoia: Libreria Editrice Tellini, 1981.

Newman, Martha. *The Boundaries of Charity: Cistercian Culture and Ecclesiastical Reform, 1098–1180*. Standford, California: Stanford University Press, 1996.

The New Monastery: Texts and Studies on the Earliest Cistercians. Cistercian Fathers Series 60. E. Rozanne Elder, ed. Kalamazoo: Cistercian Publications, 1998.

Nibby, Antonio. *Analisi storico-topografico-antiquaria della carta de' Dintorni di Roma*. vol. 3. Roma: Tipografia del Senato, 1837.

Nordenfalk, Carl. 'Les cinq sens dans l'art du moyen âge'. *Revue de l'Art* 34 (1976) 17–28.

―――. 'The five senses in late medieval and Renaissance art', *Journal of the Warburg and Courtauld Institutes* 48 (1985) 1–22.

Norton, Christopher. 'Table of Cistercian legislation on art and architecture'. *Cistercian Art and Architecture in the British Isles*. Christopher Norton-David Park, edd. Cambridge: Cambridge University Press, 1986. Pp. 315–393.

Ousterhout, Robert. *Master Builders of Byzantium*. Princeton: Princeton University Press, 1999.

Palumbo, Pier Fausto. *Lo Scismo del MCXXX*. Miscellanea della R. Deputazione Romana di Storia Patria, 13. Rome: Presso la R. Deputazione alla Biblioteca Vallicelliana, 1942.

Panagopoulos, Beata K. *Cistercian and Mendicant Monasteries in medieval Greece*. Chicago and London: The University of Chicago Press, 1979.

Paravicini-Bagliani, Agostino. *Cardinali di Curia e 'familiariae' cardinalizie dal 1277 al 1254*. 2 vols. Italia Sacra: Studi e Documenti di storia Ecclesiastica, 18 and 19. Rome: Antenore, 1972.

Park, David. 'Cistercian Wall Painting and Panel Painting'. *Cistercian Art and Architecture in the British Isles*. Christopher Norton and David Park, eds. Cambridge: Cambridge University Press, 1986. Pp. 181–201.

Pietrangeli, Carlo. *S. Maria Maggiore.* Florence: Nardini, 1988.

Pistilli, Pio F. 'Santa Maria di Tiglietto: prima fondazione cistercense in Italia (1120)'. *Arte Medievale* 2 serie, 4,1 (1990) 117–149.

———. 'Architettura a Roma nella prima metà del Duecento (1198–1254)'. *Roma nel Duecento.* Angiola Maria Romanini, ed. Torino: Edizioni Seat, 1991. Pp. 1–71.

———. 'Considerazioni sulla storia architettonica dell'abbazia romana delle Tre Fontane nel duecento'. *Arte Medievale* 2 serie, 6, 1 (1992) 163–192.

Plouvier, Martine. 'L'Abbaye de Cîteaux'. *Congrès Archéologique de France* 152 (1994) 65–99.

———. 'L'Abbaye Médiévale: Histoire et Analyse Critique'. *Pour une Histoire monumentale de l'Abbaye de Cîteaux 1098–1998.* Studia et Documenta 8. Martine Plouvier and Alain Saint-Denis, edd. Cîteaux: Commentarii Cistercienses, 1998. Pp. 122–152.

Plouvier, Martine and F. Placide Vernet. 'Plans et vues de l'abbaye de Citeaux'. *Pour une Histoire monumentale de l'Abbaye de Cîteaux 1098–1998.* Studia et Documenta 8. Martine Plouvier and Alain Saint-Denis, edd. Cîteaux: Commentarii Cistercienses, 1998. Pp. 380–396.

Pozzi, Liliana. 'Definizione delle tipologie di paramento murario'. Giovanni Belardi, Fra Jacques Brière, Liliana Pozzi, *et al. Abbazia delle Tre Fontane: il complesso, la storia, il restauro.* Rome: Edilerica s.r.l., 1995. Pp. 161–164.

Priester, Ann E. *The Belltowers of Medieval Rome and the Architecture of Renovatio.* Unpublished dissertation, Princeton University, 1990.

———. 'The Belltowers and Building Workshops in Medieval Rome'. *Journal of the Society of Architectural Historians* 52 (1993) 199–220.

Quattrone, Stefania. 'L'evoluzione storico-architettonica del complesso monumentale "oggi detto le Tre Fontane allora ad Aquas Salvias"'. Giovanni Belardi, Fra Jacques Brière, Liliana Pozzi, *et al. Abbazia delle Tre Fontane: il complesso, la storia, il restauro.* Rome: Edilerica s.r.l., 1995. Pp. 13–77.

Reekmans, Louis. 'L'implantation monumentale chrétienne dans la zone suburbaine de Rome du IV e au IX e siècle'. *Rivista di Archeologia Cristiana* 44 (1968) 173–207, esp. 184–194.

———. 'L'implantation monumentale chrétienne dans le paysage urbain de Rome de 300 à 850'. *Actes du XIe Congrès international d'archéologie chrétienne, 2.* Vatican City: Pontificio Istituto di Archeologia Cristiana, 1989. Pp. 861–915.

Righetti Tosti-Croce, Marina. *Architettura per il lavoro: dal caso cistercense a un caso cistercense: Charavalle di Fiastra.* Rome: Viella, 1993.

————. 'Tra spolia e modelli altomedioevali: note su alcuni episodi di scultura cistercense'. *Arte d'Occidente: temi e metodi: studi in onore di Angiola Maria Romanini*, 1. Antonio Cadei *et al.* edd. Rome: Sintesi informazione, 1999. Pp. 381–389.

Robertson, Clare. *'Il gran cardinale': Alessandro Farnese, Patron of the Arts.* New Haven and London: Yale University Press, 1992.

Rochet, Anne Claire. 'The Refectory Wing of the Cistercian Abbey of Vaux-de-Cernay'. *Studies in Cistercian Art and Architecture, 5.* Cistercian Studies Series, 167. Meredith Parsons Lillich, ed., Kalamazoo: Cistercian Publications, 1998. Pp. 187–210.

Roehl, Ricard. 'Plan and reality in a medieval monastic economy: the Cistercians'. *Studies in Medieval and Renaissance History* 9 (1972) 82–113.

Roma del Settecento. M. Vasi and G. Matthiae, eds. Roma: Editrice Golem, 1970.

Roma nel Duecento. Angiola Maria Romanini, ed. Torino: Edizioni Seat, 1991.

Romanini, Angiola Maria. 'Le abbazie fondate da San Bernardo in Italia e l'architettura cistercense "primitiva"'. *Studi su S. Bernardo di Chiaravalle.* Bibliotheca Cisterciensis, 6. Rome: Certosa di Firenze, 1975. Pp. 281–305.

————. Review of W. Krönig, *Altenberg und die Baukunst der Zisterzienser.* Altenberg: Altenberg Dom-Verein und V. Bergish Gladbach, 1973. Pp. 128, con 94 tavv. *Studi Medievali* 19 (1978) 266–277.

————. 'La storia architettonica dell'abbazia delle Tre Fontane a Roma. La fondazione cisterciense'. *Mélanges à la Memoire du Anselme Dimier. 3.* B. Chauvin, ed. Pupillon, Arbois, 1982. Pp. 653–695.

————. '"Ratio fecit diversum": la riscoperta delle Tre Fontane a Roma chiave di lettura dell'arte bernardina'. *Arte Medievale* 2 serie 8, 1 (1994) 1–78.

————. (ed.) *et.al., 'Ratio fecit diversum': San Bernardo e le arte. Atti del congresso internationale, Roma, 27–29 maggio 1991.* Arte Medievale, Serie 2, 8, 1 (1994–appeared 1995) 1–140.

Rossi, Paola. 'Le transenne di finestra alle Tre Fontane. Appunti per una ricerca'. *Arte Medievale* 2 serie, 8, 1 (1994) 133–140.

Rossi, Paola and Maria Cristina Rossini. 'Breve nota sulle problematiche relative agli arredi liturgici nella chiesa abbaziale delle Tre Fontane a Roma'. *Arte d'Occidente: temi e metodi: studi in onore di Angiola Maria Romanini*, 1. Antonio Cadei *et al.* edd. Rome: Sintesi informazione, 1999. Pp. 405–423.

Rossini, Luigi. *I monumenti più interessanti di Roma.* Rome: L. Rossini for Scudellari, no date, but drawings *c.* 1818.

Rudolph, Conrad. 'The 'Principal Founders' and the early artistic legislation of Cîteaux'. *Studies in Cistercian Art and Architecture, 3.* Cistercian Studies Series: 89. Meredith Parsons Lillich, ed. Kalamazoo: Cistercian Publications, 1987. Pp. 1–33.

―――. 'Bernard of Clairvaux's Apologia as a Description of Cluny and the Controversy over Monastic Art'. *Gesta* 27 (1988) 125–132.

―――. *The 'Things of greater importance': Bernard of Clairvaux's Apologia and the Medieval Attitude toward Art.* Philadelphia: University of Pennsylvania Press, 1990.

Ruotolo, Giuseppe. *L'abbazia delle Tre Fontane.* Rome: Abbazia delle Tre Fontane, 1972.

Sahas, Daniel. *Icon and Logos: Sources in eighth-century Iconoclasm.* Toronto Medieval Texts and Translations, 4. Toronto: University of Toronto Press, 1986.

Sansterre, Jean-Marie. *Les moines grecs et orientaux à Rome aux epoques byzantine et carolingienne.* Académie Royale de Belgique, Mémoires de la Classe des Lettres, 66. Brussels: Palais des Académies, 1983.

Sartorio, Aristide. 'L'abbazia cisterciense delle Tre Fontane'. *Nuova Antologia* 167 (settembre 1913) 50–65. (Reprinted in Anonymous (i.e. A. Barbiero, OSCO), *S. Paolo e le Tre Fontane. XXII secoli di storia messi in luce da un monaco cisterciense (Trappista).* Rome: L'Abbazia 'Nullius' dei Santi Vincenzo ed Anastasio alle Acque Salvie, 1938. Pp. 113–121).

Savarese, Nino. *Ricordo delle Tre Fontane e dell'Abbazia dei cistercensi della stretta osservanza Trappista.* Roma: Edizioni dell'Esposizione, 1938.

Schaeffer, Jean Owens. 'The Earliest Churches of the Cistercian Order'. *Studies in Cistercian Art and Architecture, 1.* Cistercian Studies Series 66. Meredith P. Lillich, ed. Kalamazoo: Cistercian Publications, 1982. Pp. 1–12.

Schuster, Ildefonso. *La basilica e il monastero di S. Paolo fuori le Mura.* Turin: Società Editrice Internazionale, 1934.

Schwager, Kurt. 'Santa Maria Scala Coeli in Tre Fontane'. *Praestant interna: Festschrift für Ulrich Hausmann.* Bettina von Freytag gen. Löringhoff-Dietrich Mannsperger-Friedhelm Prayton, eds. Tubingen: Ernst Wasmuth, 1982. Pp. 394–417.

Shelby, Lon R. 'The Geometrical Knowledge of the Medieval Master Masons'. *Speculum* 47 (1972) 395–421; rpt in *The Engineering of Medieval Cathedrals.* Studies in the History of Civil Engineering, 1. Lynn T. Courtenay, ed. Aldershot: Ashgate, 1997. Pp. 27–53.

―――― and Robert Mark. 'Late Gothic Structural Designs in the "Instructions" of Lorenz Lechler'. *The Engineering of Medieval Cathedrals.* Studies in the History of Civil Engineering, 1. Lynn T. Courtenay, ed. Aldershot: Ashgate, 1997. Pp. 87–105.

Southern, Richard W. *Western Society and the Church in the Middle Ages.* Harmonsworth: Pelican, 1970.

Stalley, Roger. 'The Architecture of the Cistercian Churches of Ireland, 1142–1272'. *Cistercian Art and Architecture in the British Isles.* Christopher Norton and David Park, edd. Cambridge: Cambridge University Press, 1986. Pp. 117–124.

———. *The Cistercian Monasteries of Ireland.* London and New Haven: Yale University Press, 1987.

Steinke, Katharina B. *Die mittelalterliche Vatikanpaläste und ihre Kapellen.* Studi e Documenti per la Storia del Palazzo Apostolico Vaticano, 5. Vatican City: Biblioteca Apostolica Vaticana, 1984.

Stoddard, Whitney S. *Art and Architecture of Medieval France.* New York: Icon Editions, Harper and Row, 1972.

Stroll, Mary. *The Jewish Pope: Ideology and Politics in the Papal Schism.* Leiden: E. J. Brill, 1987.

Studies in Cistercian Art and Architecture 1, Cistercian Studies Series, 66. Meredith L. Lillich ed. Kalamazoo: Cistercian Publications, 1982.

Studies in Cistercian Art and Architecture 2, Cistercian Studies Series, 69. Meredith Parsons Lillich, ed. Kalamazoo: Cistercian Publications, 1984.

Studies in Cistercian Art and Architecture, 5. Cistercian Studies Series 167. Meredith Parsons Lillich, ed. Kalamazoo: Cistercian Publications, 1998.

Suckale, Robert. 'La Théorie de l'architecture au temps des Cathédrales'. *Les Bâtisseurs de Cathédrales Gothiques.* Roland Recht, ed. Strasbourg: Les Musées de la Ville de Strasbourg, 1989. Pp. 41–50.

Tempesta, Claudia. 'Il restauro degli affreschi: resoconti e progetti'. Giovanni Belardi, Fra Jacques Brière, Liliana Pozzi, *et al. Abbazia delle Tre Fontane: il complesso, la storia, il restauro.* Rome: Edilerica s.r.l., 1995. Pp. 185–212.

Tobin, Stephen. *The Cistercians: Monks and Monasteries of Europe.* London: Herbert Press, 1995.

Tomassetti, Giuseppe. 'Della Campagna Romana'. *Archivio della Società Romana di Storia Patria* 19 (1896) 135–150.

Torelli, Luigi. *L'eucalyptus e l'Agro Romano.* Roma: Tipografia del Senato, 1878.

Toubert, Pierre. *Les structures du Latium médiéval.* 2 vols., Bibliothèque Française d'Athènes et de Rome, 221. Rome: École Française de Rome, 1973.

Urban, Günther. 'Die Kirchenbaukunst des Quattrocento in Rom'. *Römisches Jahrbuch für Kunstgeschichte* 9 / 10 (1961 / 2) 73–287.

Vacandard, Elphège. *Vie de Saint Bernard.* 2 vols., Paris: Librairie Victor Lecoffre, 1895.

Valenzano, Giovanna, Giuliana Guerrini and Antonella Gigli. *Chiaravalle della Colomba: Il Complesso medievale.* Piacenza: Tip. Le.Co., 1994.

Vanderkerchove, Christian. 'L'iconographie mediévale de la Construction'. *Les Bâtisseurs de Cathédrales Gothiques.* Roland Recht, ed. Strasbourg: Les Musées de la Ville de Strasbourg, 1989. Pp. 61–80.

Van der Meer, Frédéric. *Atlas de l'Ordre Cistercien.* Paris-Brussels: Editions Sequoia, 1965.

Visser, Margaret. *The Geometry of Love: Space, Time, Mystery, and Meaning in an Ordinary Church.* Toronto: Harper Flamingo Canada, 2000.

Viti, Goffredo. *Architettura cistercense: Fontenay e le abbazie in Italia dal 1120 al 1160.* Casamari: Edizioni Casamari, 1995.

———. 'San Bernardo e le Arti'. *San Bernardo e I Cisterciensi in Umbria.* Geoffredo Viti, ed. Florence: Certosa di Firenze, 1995. Pp. 135–153.

Von Linden, Franz-Karl. *Abbayes cisterciennes en Europe.* Turnhout: Brepols, 1999.

Von Mueller, Ferdinand *Eucalpytographia. A descriptive atlas of the eucalypts of Australia and the adjoining islands.* Melbourne and London: George Robertson, 1880.

Von Tischendorf, Constantin. *Acta Petri et Pauli.* Leipzig: Hermann Mendelssohn, 1851.

Waetzoldt, Stephan. *Die Kopien des 17. Jahrhunderts nach Mosaiken und Wandmalereien in Rom.* Römische Forschungen der Bibliotheca Hertziana, 18. Vienna-Munich: Schroll-Verlag, 1964.

Wagner-Rieger, Renate. *Die italienische Baukunst zu Beginn der Gotik.* 2 vols. Graz-Köln: Verlag Hermann Böhlaus, 1956–1957.

Walsh, David A. 'Measurement and Proportion at Bordesley Abbey'. *Gesta* 19.2 (1980) 109–113.

———. 'An Architectural Study of the Church'. *Bordesley Abbey, 2.* British Series, 3. S. M. Hirst and S. M. Wright, edd. Oxford: British Archaeological Reports, 1983. Pp. 222–225.

———. 'Regionalism and Localism in Early Cistercian Architecture in England'. *Arte Medievale* 1 (1994) 103–112.

Wiemer, Wolfgang. 'Die computergestüzte Proportionsanalyse am Beispiel von Planaufnahmen und Entwürfen von Kirchgrundrissen'. *Architectura* 28.2 (1998) 107–155.

Zacharin, Robert F. *Emigrant eucalypts*. Melbourne: Melbourne University Press, 1978.

INDEX

CISTERCIAN PUBLICATIONS

Texts and Studies in the Monastic Tradition

TEXTS IN ENGLISH TRANSLATION

THE CISTERCIAN MONASTIC TRADITION

Aelred of Rievaulx

- Dialogue on the Soul
- The Historical Works
- Liturgical Sermons, I
- The Lives of the Northern Saints
- Spiritual Friendship
- Treatises I: Jesus at the Age of Twelve; Rule for a Recluse; Pastoral Prayer
- Walter Daniel: The Life of Aelred of Rievaulx

Bernard of Clairvaux

- Apologia to Abbot William (Cistercians and Cluniacs)
- Five Books on Consideration: Advice to a Pope
- Homilies in Praise of the Blessed Virgin Mary
- In Praise of the New Knighthood
- Letters
- Life and Death of Saint Malachy the Irishman
- On Baptism and the Office of Bishops
- On Grace and Free Choice
- On Loving God
- Parables and Sentences
- Sermons for the Summer Season
- Sermons on Conversion
- Sermons on the Song of Songs, I–IV
- The Steps of Humility and Pride

Gertude the Great of Helfta

- Spiritual Exercises
- The Herald of God's Loving-Kindness, Books 1 and 2
- The Herald of God's Loving-Kindness, Book 3

William of Saint Thierry

- The Enigma of Faith
- Exposition on the Epistle to the Romans
- Exposition on the Song of Songs
- The Golden Epistle
- The Mirror of Faith
- The Nature and Dignity of Love
- On Contemplating God, Prayer, Meditations

Gilbert of Hoyland

- Sermons on the Song of Songs, I–III
- Treatises, Sermons, and Epistles

John of Ford

- Sermons on the Final Verses of the Song of Songs, I–VII

Other Cistercian Writers

- Adam of Perseigne, Letters, I
- Alan of Lille: The Art of Preaching
- Amadeus of Lausanne: Homilies in Praise of Blessed Mary
- Baldwin of Ford: Commendation of Faith
- Geoffrey of Auxerre: On the Apocalypse
- Guerric of Igny: Liturgical Sermones, I–II
- Helinand of Froidmont: Verses on Death
- Idung of Prüfening: Cistercians and Cluniacs. The Case of Cîteaux
- In The School of Love. An Anthology of Early Cistercian Texts
- Isaac of Stella: Sermons on the Christian Year, I–[II]
- The Letters of Armand-Jean de Rancé, Abbot of la Trappe
- The Life of Beatrice of Nazareth
- Mary Most Holy: Meditating with the Early Cistercians
- Ogier of Locedio: Homilies [on Mary and the Last Supper]
- Serlo of Wilton & Serlo of Savigny: Seven Unpublished Works (Latin-English)
- Sky-blue the Sapphire, Crimson the Rose: The Spirituality of John of Ford
- Stephen of Lexington: Letters from Ireland
- Stephen of Sawley: Treatises
- Three Treatises on Man: A Cistercian Anthropology / Bernard McGinn

EARLY AND EASTERN MONASTICISM

- Besa: The Life of Shenoute of Atripe
- Cyril of Scythopolis: The Lives of the Monks of Palestine
- Dorotheos of Gaza: Discourses and Sayings
- Evagrius Ponticus: Praktikos and Chapters on Prayer
- Handmaids of the Lord: Lives of Holy Women in Late Antiquity and the Early Middle Ages / Joan Petersen
- Harlots of the Desert. A Study of Repentance / Benedicta Ward
- Isaiah of Scete: Ascetic Discourses

Cistercian Art, Architecture, and Music

- Cistercian Abbeys of Britain [illustrated]
- Cistercian Europe / Terryl N. Kinder
- Cistercians in Medieval Art / James France
- SS. Vincenzo e Anastasio at Tre Fontane Near Rome / J. Barclay Lloyd
- Studies in Medieval Art and Architecture, II–VI / Meredith P. Lillich, ed.
- Treasures Old and New. Nine Centuries on Cistercian Music [CD, cassette]
- Cistercian Chants for the Feast of the Visitation [CD]

Monastic Heritage

- Community and Abbot in the Rule of St Benedict, I–II / Adalbert de Vogüé
- Distant Echoes: Medieval Religious Women, I / Shank, Nichols, edd.
- The Freedom of Obedience / A Carthusian
- Halfway to Heaven [The Carthusian Tradition] / Robin Lockhart
- The Hermit Monks of Grandmont / Carole A. Hutchison
- A Life Pleasing to God: Saint Basil's Monastic Rules / Augustine Holmes
- Manjava Skete [Ruthenian tradition] / Sophia Seynk
- Monastic Practices / Charles Cummings
- Peace Weavers. Medieval Religious Women, II / Shank, Nichols, edd.
- Reading Saint Benedict / Adalbert de Vogüé
- The Rule of St Benedict. A Doctrinal and Spiritual Commentary / Adalbert de Vogüé
- Stones Laid Before the Lord [Monastic Architecture] / Anselme Dimier
- What Nuns Read [Libraries of Medieval English Nunneries] / D. N. Bell

Monastic Liturgy

- From Advent to Pentecost / A Carthusian
- The Hymn Collection from the Abbey of the Paraclete, 2 volumes
- The Molesme Summer Season Breviary, 4 volumes
- The Old French Ordinary and Breviary of the Abbey of the Paraclete, 5 volumes
- The Paraclete Statutes: Institutiones nostrae
- The Twelfth Century Cistercian Hymnal, 2 volumes
- The Twelfth Century Cistercian Psalter [NYP]
- Two Early Cistercian Libelli Missarum

MODERN MONASTICISM
Thomas Merton

- Cassian and the Fathers: Initiation into the Monastic Tradition
- The Climate of Monastic Prayer
- The Legacy of Thomas Merton
- The Message of Thomas Merton
- The Monastic Journey of Thomas Merton
- Thomas Merton Monk
- Thomas Merton on Saint Bernard
- Thomas Merton: Prophet of Renewal / John Eudes Bamberger
- Toward An Integrated Humanity [Essays on Thomas Merton]

Contemporary Monastics

- Centered on Christ. A Guide to Monastic Profession / Augustine Roberts
- Inside the Psalms. Reflections for Novices / Maureen McCabe
- Passing from Self to God. A Cistercian Retreat / Robert Thomas
- Pathway of Peace. Cistercian Wisdom according to Saint Bernard / Charles Dumont
- Poor Therefore Rich / A Carthusian
- The Way of Silent Love / A Carthusian

CHRISTIAN SPIRITUALITY PAST AND PRESENT

Past

- A Cloud of Witnesses. The Development of Christian Doctrine [to 500] / D. N. Bell
- Eros and Allegory: Medieval Exegesis of the Song of Songs / Denys Turner
- High King of Heaven. Aspects of Early English Spirituality / Benedicta Ward
- In the Unity of the Holy Spirit. Conference on the Rule of Benedict

- The Life of St Mary Magdalene and of Her Sister St Martha [Magdalene legend]
- The Luminous Eye. The Spiritual World Vision of St Ephrem / Sebastian Brock
- Many Mansions. Medieval Theological Development East and West / D. N. Bell
- The Name of Jesus / Irénée Hausherr
- Penthos. The Doctrine of Compunction in the Christian East / Irénée Hausherr

CISTERCIAN PUBLICATIONS Titles Listing

EDITORIAL OFFICES

Cistercian Publications • WMU Station
1903 West Michigan Avenue
Kalamazoo, MI 49008-5415   USA
tel 269 387 8920   fax 269 387 8390
e-mail cistpub@wmich.edu

CUSTOMER SERVICE—NORTH AMERICA: USA AND CANADA

Cistercian Publications at Liturgical Press
Saint John's Abbey
Collegeville, MN 56321-7500 USA
tel 800 436 8431   fax 320 363 3299
e-mail sales@litpress.org

CUSTOMER SERVICE—EUROPE: UK, IRELAND, AND EUROPE

Cistercian Publications at Columba Book Service
55A Spruce Avenue
Stillorgan Industrial Park
Blackrock, Co. Dublin, Ireland
tel 353 1 294 2560   fax 353 1 294 2564
e-mail sales@columba.ie

WEBSITE
www.cistercianpublications.org

Cistercian Publications is a non-profit corporation.

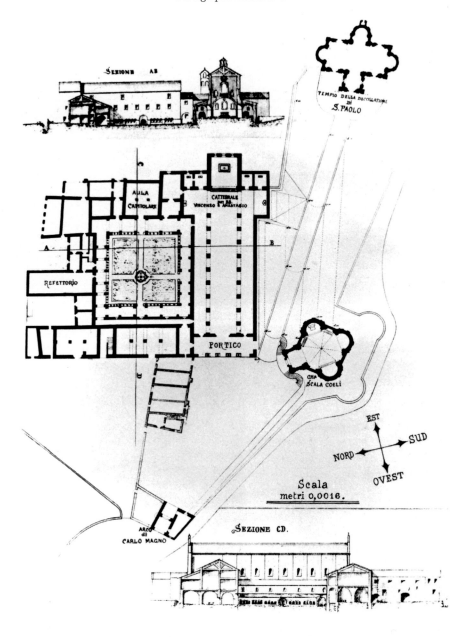

1. Site Plan of Tre Fontane, with two sections of the Church of SS. Vincenzo e Anastasio and the adjacent monastery (Anonymous, reproduced in Anonymous, San Paolo e le Tre Fontane (Rome: L'abbazia 'Nullius', 1938) Tav. XXII, N. 140)

2. (above) SS. Vincenzo e Anastasio alle Tre Fontane, Gatehouse, view from northwest (photo: Barclay Lloyd)

3. (left) SS. Vincenzo e Anastasio alle Tre Fontane, 'Arch of Charlemagne', the Gatehouse, view from southeast (photo: Barclay Lloyd)

4. Church of SS. Vincenzo e Anastasio alle Tre Fontane, facade and narthex (photo: Barclay Lloyd)

5. Church of SS. Vincenzo e Anastasio alle Tre Fontane, narthex,
south side (photo: Barclay Lloyd)

6. Church of SS. Vincenzo e Anastasio
alle Tre Fontane, narthex, northern
end, bracket and fragment of fresco
(photo: ICCD: E 52663)

7. Church of SS. Vincenzo e Anastasio alle Tre Fontane, interior of nave looking east (photo: ICCD: E 52630)

8. SS. Vincenzo e Anastasio alle Tre Fontane, view across cloister towards church, show-ing exterior of nave, north aisle, Wing A and part of Wing C (photo: ICCD: F 19709)

9. Church of SS. Vincenzo e Anastasio alle Tre Fontane, interior of nave and aisles, look-ing west (photo: ICCD: E 61232)

10. Church of SS. Vincenzo e Anastasio alle Tre Fontane, interior of chancel and part of southern arm of transept (photo: ICCD: E 52631)

11. Church of SS. Vincenzo e Anastasio alle Tre Fontane, exterior view from east (photo: ICCD: E 92665)

12. (left) Church of SS. Vincenzo e Anastasio alle Tre Fontane, interior of transept-chapel (photo: ICCD: E 52633')

13. Church of SS. Vincenzo e Anastasio alle Tre Fontane, south arm of transept, interior (photo: ICCD: E 52634)

14. Church of SS. Vincenzo e Anastasio alle Tre Fontane, crossing and north arm of transept, interior (photo: ICCD: E 52632)

15. Monastery of SS. Vincenzo e Anastasio alle Tre Fontane, view north across cloister towards Wing R (photo: Barclay Lloyd)

16. Monastery of SS. Vincenzo e Anastasio alle Tre Fontane, Wings C and R, viewed from cloister garth (photo: Barclay Lloyd)

17. Church and monastery of SS. Vincenzo e Anastasio alle Tre Fontane, view of north clerestory wall, Wing A and part of Wing M (photo: ICCD: F 13710)

18. Monastery of SS. Vincenzo e Anastasio alle Tre Fontane, Wings M and R, viewed from cloister garth (photo: Barclay Lloyd)

19. Monastery of SS. Vincenzo e Anastasio alle Tre Fontane, Wing M, cloister ambulatory, looking south (photo: ICCD: E 52642)

20. Monastery of SS. Vincenzo e Anastasio alle Tre Fontane, Wing M, part of cloister colonnade, view from garth (photo: Barclay Lloyd)

21. Monastery of SS. Vincenzo e Anastasio alle Tre Fontane, Wing M, one bay of cloister colonnade, from ambulatory (photo: Barclay Lloyd)

22. Monastery of SS. Vincenzo e Anastasio alle Tre Fontane, Wing M, cloister colonnade, cut-down spiral-fluted ancient roman shaft, ancient base and medieval impost block (photo: Barclay Lloyd)

23. Monastery of SS. Vincenzo e Anastasio alle Tre Fontane, Wings M and R, cloister colonnades (photo: ICCD: F 19716)

24. Monastery of SS. Vincenzo e Anastasio alle Tre Fontane, Wings M and R, northeast corner of cloister (photo: ICCD: F 19713)

25. Monastery of SS. Vincenzo e Anastasio alle Tre Fontane, doorway to sacristy vestibule (photo: Barclay Lloyd)

26. (above) SS. Vincenzo e Anastasio alle Tre Fontane, sacristy vestibule, interior (photo: Barclay Lloyd)

27. (left) Monastery of SS. Vincenzo e Anastasio alle Tre Fontane, Wing M, sacristy vestibule, interior—column, capital and semi-circular arch (photo: Barclay Lloyd)

28. Monastery of SS. Vincenzo e Anastasio alle Tre Fontane, Wing M, sacristy vestibule, interior — column, capital and parabolic arch (photo: Barclay Lloyd)

29. Monastery of SS. Vincenzo e Anastasio alle Tre Fontane, door to chapter room (photo: Barclay Lloyd)

30. Monastery of SS. Vincenzo e Anastasio alle Tre Fontane, Wing M, chapter room window from cloister colonnade (photo: Barclay Lloyd)

31. Monastery of SS. Vincenzo e Anastasio alle Tre Fontane, northeast corner of chapter room, adjoining portico (photo: Barclay Lloyd)

32. Monastery of SS. Vincenzo e Anastasio alle Tre Fontane, Wing M, eastern portico, interior (photo: Barclay Lloyd)

33. Monastery of SS. Vincenzo e Anastasio alle Tre Fontane, Wing M, eastern portico, interior, looking north (photo: Barclay Lloyd)

34. Monastery of SS. Vincenzo e Anastasio alle Tre Fontane, Wing M, view from south-east (photo: Barclay Lloyd)

35. Monastery of SS. Vincenzo e Anastasio alle Tre Fontane, view of Wing M from north-east (photo: Barclay Lloyd)

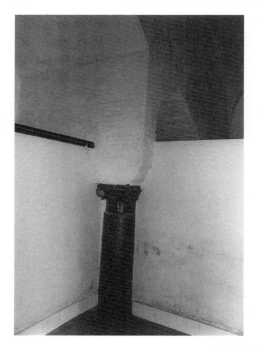

36. Monastery of SS. Vincenzo e Anastasio alle Tre Fontane, Wing M, remnant of north staircase column, capital and parts of semi-circular and parabolic arches (photo: Barclay Lloyd)

37. Church and monastery of SS. Vincenzo e Anastasio alle Tre Fontane, present door to church from Wing M (photo: Barclay Lloyd)

38. Monastery of SS. Vincenzo e Anastasio alle Tre Fontane, Wing M, north facade (photo: Barclay Lloyd)

39. (left) Monastery of SS. Vincenzo e Anastasio alle Tre Fontane, Wing M, northwest corner (photo: Barclay Lloyd)

40. (below) Church and monastery of SS. Vincenzo e Anastasio alle Tre Fontane, view from east (photo: Barclay Lloyd)

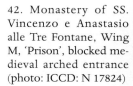

41. Monastery of SS. Vincenzo e Anastasio alle Tre Fontane, Wing M, first floor cell, with blocked medieval window (photo: Barclay Lloyd)

42. Monastery of SS. Vincenzo e Anastasio alle Tre Fontane, Wing M, 'Prison', blocked medieval arched entrance (photo: ICCD: N 17824)

43. Monastery of SS. Vincenzo e Anastasio alle Tre Fontane, Wing M, 'Prison', interior, showing blocked medieval arched entrance, vault and niche (photo: ICCD: N 17825)

44. Monastery of SS. Vincenzo e Anastasio alle Tre Fontane, wooden door to 'Prison', fifteenth-century (?), removed c. 1969 (photo: ICCD: N 17770)

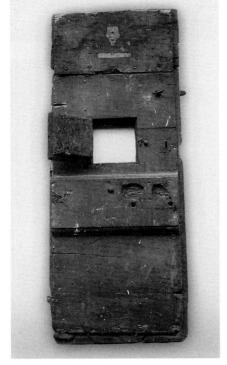

45. (above) Church and monastery of SS. Vincenzo e Anastasio alle Tre Fontane, view of north transept arm, sacristy and chapter room from east (photo: Barclay Lloyd)

46. (left) SS. Vincenzo e Anastasio alle Tre Fontane, sacristy from east (photo: Barclay Lloyd)

47. (left) SS. Vincenzo e Anastasio alle Tre Fontane, sacristy from north (photo: Barclay Lloyd)

48. (below) Monastery of SS. Vincenzo e Anastasio alle Tre Fontane, Wing M, ribbed vault above sacristy (photo: ICCD: F 19641)

49. Monastery of SS. Vincenzo e Anastasio alle Tre Fontane, Wing M, upper terrace (photo: ICCD: F 19702)

50. Monastery of SS. Vincenzo e Anastasio alle Tre Fontane, Wing M, terrace, with medieval murals *in situ,* c.1969 (photo: ICCD: F 21563)

51. Monastery of SS. Vincenzo e Anastasio alle Tre Fontane, Wing R, south wall (photo: Barclay Lloyd)

52. Monastery of SS. Vincenzo e Anastasio alle Tre Fontane, Wing R, cloister ambulatory (photo: Barclay Lloyd)

53. Monastery of SS. Vincenzo e Anastasio alle Tre Fontane, Wing R, room east of refectory, doorway (photo: Barclay Lloyd)

54. Monastery of SS. Vincenzo e Anastasio alle Tre Fontane, Wing R, rooms east of refectory, viewed from north (photo: Barclay Lloyd)

55. Monastery of SS. Vincenzo e Anastasio alle Tre Fontane, Wing R, refectory, interior (photo: Barclay Lloyd)

56. (left) Monastery of SS. Vincenzo e Anastasio alle Tre Fontane, Wing R, refectory, north wall (photo: Barclay Lloyd)

57. (below) Monastery of SS. Vincenzo e Anastasio alle Tre Fontane, Wing R, refectory, east wall (photo: Barclay Lloyd)

58. Monastery of SS. Vincenzo e Anastasio alle Tre Fontane, Wing R, refectory doorway (photo: ICCD: E 52652)

59. (left) Monastery of SS. Vincenzo e Anastasio alle Tre Fontane, Wing C, from northwest (photo: Barclay Lloyd)

60. (below) Monastery of SS. Vincenzo e Anastasio alle Tre Fontane, Wing O, from west (photo: Barclay Lloyd)

61. (above) Monastery of SS. Vincenzo e Anastasio alle Tre Fontane, Wing O, north wall (photo: Barclay Lloyd)

62. (right) Monastery of SS. Vincenzo e Anastasio alle Tre Fontane, Wing O, north wall, windows (photo: Barclay Lloyd)

63. Monastery of SS. Vincenzo e Anastasio alle Tre Fontane, Wing O, north wall, medieval doorway (photo: Barclay Lloyd)

64. *Icon of Saint Anastasius,* fifteenth-century copy, SS. Vincenzo e Anastasio alle Tre Fontane (photo: ICCD: F 88729)

65. Church of SS. Vincenzo e Anastasio alle Tre Fontane, north aisle, dedicatory inscription (photo: ICCD: E 52636)

66. (left) Monastery of SS. Vincenzo e Anastasio alle Tre Fontane, Wing R, rooms east of refectory, second window from Wing M on first floor, with medieval inscription on lintel (photo: ICCD: E 67930)

67. (below) Church and monastery of SS. Vincenzo e Anastasio alle Tre Fontane, Sacristy, inscription on lintel (photo: ICCD: F 19642)

68. Pietro Del Massaio, *Miniature of Rome,* detail, 1471. From Amato P. Frutaz, *Le piante di Roma.* Rome: Istituto di Studi Romani, 1962. 2: tav. 158, Pianta LXXXVIII.

69. Alessandro Strozzi, *Map of Rome,* detail, 1474. From Frutaz, *Le piante di Roma,* 2: tav. 159, Pianta LXXXIX.

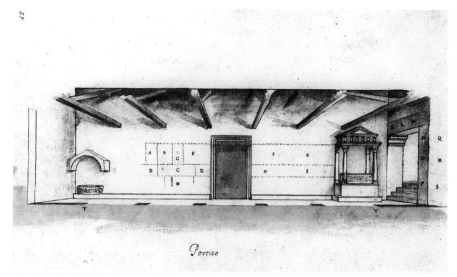

70. Antonio Eclissi, *Interior of the narthex of the church of SS. Vincenzo e Anastasio,* 1630. Biblioteca Apostolica Vaticana, Barb. Lat. 4402, fol. 42r (photo: Biblioteca Apostolica Vaticana)

71. Giovanni Maggi, *View of Tre Fontane,* 1600 (photo: Civica Raccolta delle Stampe Achille Bertarelli, Castello Sforzesco, Milan)

72. Giacomo Lauro, *View of Tre Fontane,* 1612 (published 1630). Iacobus Lauro, *Antiquae urbis splendor,* Rome: no typ. 1612 (1630), fol. 151 r (photo: Bibliotheca Hertziana, Rome).

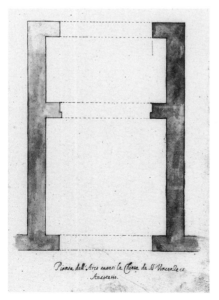

73. Antonio Eclissi, *Plan of Gatehouse,* 1630. Biblioteca Apostolica Vaticana, Barb. Lat. 4402, fol. 58r (photo: Biblioteca Apostolica Vaticana)

74. Antonio Eclissi, *West facade of Gatehouse,* 1630. Biblioteca Apostolica Vaticana, Barb. Lat. 4402, fol. 39r (photo: Biblioteca Apostolica Vaticana)

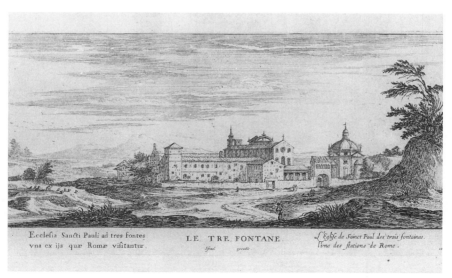

75. Israel Silvestre, *View of Tre Fontane,* 1641-46 (photo: Bibliotheca Hertziana, Rome)

A la Tefta di S. Paolo.
B la Chiefa delle tre Fontane.
C la Chiefa de' SS. Vincenzo, & Anaftafio.
D la Chiefa di Santa Maria *Scala Cæli.*
E la Chiefa di S. Maria Annuntiata.
1. 2. 3. forgenti d'acque nella decollatione.

76. Filippo De Rossi, *View of Tre Fontane,* 1652. Filippo De Rossi, *Ritratto di Roma moderna.* Rome: F. De Rossi. 1652. p. 122 (photo: Bibliotheca Hertziana, Rome)

77. Giuseppe Vasi, *View of Tre Fontane.* Giuseppe Vasi, *Tesoro sacro e venerabile...di Roma.*
Rome: M. Pagliarini. 1753, tav. 43 (photo: Bibliotheca Herziana, Rome)

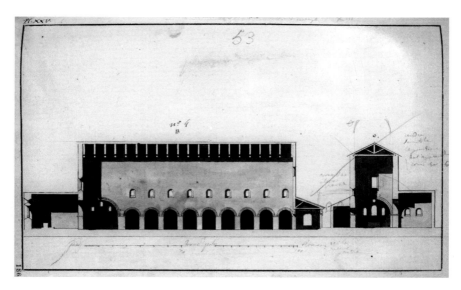

78. Seroux D'Agincourt, *Church of SS. Vincenzo e Anastasio, longitudinal and transverse
sections,* pen and wash, c.1798. Biblioteca Apostolica Vaticana, Vat. Lat. 13479, fol. 186r
(photo: Biblioteca Apostolica Vaticana)

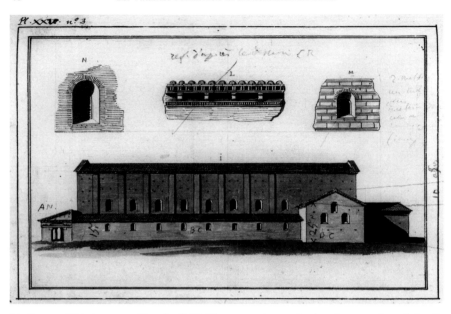

79. Seroux D'Agincourt, *Church of SS. Vincenzo e Anastasio,view from south, and details of windows and cornice,* pen and wash, c.1798. Biblioteca Apostolica Vaticana, Vat. Lat. 13479, fol. 185r (photo: Biblioteca Apostolica Vaticana)

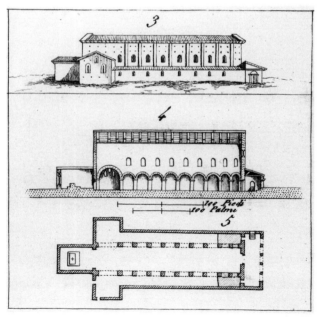

80. Seroux D'Agincourt, *Church of SS. Vincenzo e Anastasio, elevation, section and plan,* print. Seroux d'Agincourt, *Storia dell'Arte.* Milan: Per Ranieri Fanfani, 1825. 2: Tav. XXV, 3, 4 and 5 (photo: Bibliotheca Hertziana, Rome)

81. Paul Letarouilly, *View of the three churches at Tre Fontane, a plan of each church and a
section of S. Maria Scala Coeli.* Paul Letarouilly, *Édifices de Rome moderne.* Liège: D'Avanzo
et C'e.,1853. 3: pl. 339 (photo: Bibliotheca Hertziana, Rome)

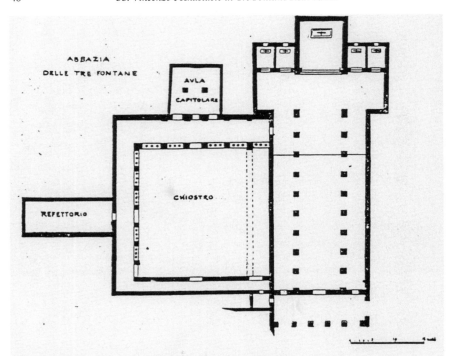

82. Aristide Sartorio, *Plan of the Abbey at Tre Fontane,* print, 1913. Aristide Sartorio, 'L'abbazia cisterciense delle Tre Fontane', *Nuova Antologia* 167 (settembre 1913) 52, fig. 2.

83. Anonymous, *View of Tre Fontane,* photograph, c.1870 (photo: ICCD: E 70095)

84. Anonymous, *View of Tre Fontane,* photograph, 1880-90 (photo: ICCD: E 70105)

85. Anonymous, *View of Tre Fontane,* photograph, early twentieth century (photo: ICCD: E 70104)

86. Anonymous, *View of northern end of 'conversi' wing,* photograph, c.1945-49 (photo: ICCD: E 70110)

87. Monastery of SS. Vincenzo e Anastasio alle Tre Fontane, Wing M, lunette above sacristy, *Nativity* (photo: ICCD: E 69590)

88. SS. Vincenzo e Anastasio alle Tre Fontane, Collation or Mandatum cloister, mid-twentieth century (?), from east (photo: ICCD: E 52648)

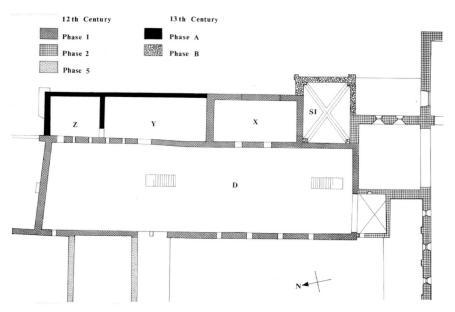

89. Monastery of SS. Vincenzo e Anastasio, first floor of Wing M, reconstruction plan (drawing: Barclay Lloyd)

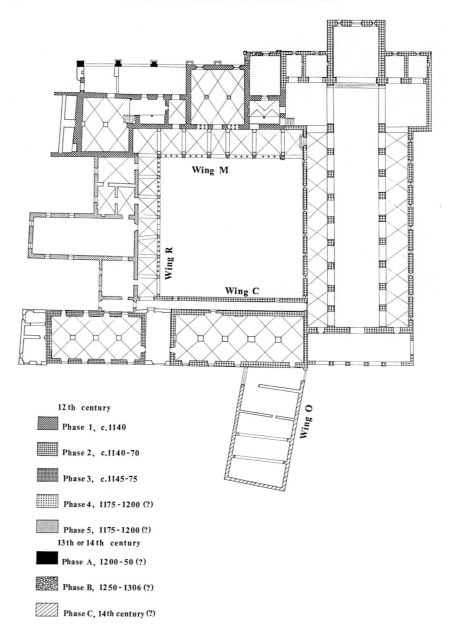

Wing M

Wing R

Wing C

Wing O

12th century

Phase 1, c.1140

Phase 2, c.1140-70

Phase 3, c.1145-75

Phase 4, 1175-1200 (?)

Phase 5, 1175-1200 (?)

13th or 14th century

Phase A, 1200-50 (?)

Phase B, 1250-1306 (?)

Phase C, 14th century (?)

90. Plan and reconstruction of the church and abbey of S. Anastasius *ad Aquas Salvias* in the twelfth and thirteenth centuries, (Jeremy M. Blake and Joan E. Barclay Lloyd)

91. Rome, S. Maria in Trastevere, 1130-1143, interior as of 1825, engraving Antonio Sarti (photo: Bibliotheca Hertziana, Rome)

92. Fontenay, analytical reconstruction (after Viollet le Duc, Frédéric Van der Meer, *Atlas de l'Ordre Cistercien* (Paris-Brussels: Editions Sequoia, 1965) Fig. 7)

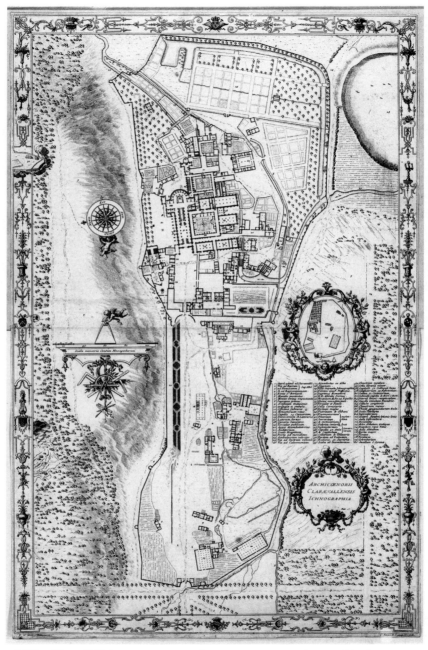

93. Milley, Plan of Clairvaux, engraving by C. Lucas, 1708 (Photo: Bibliothèque Nationale de France, Paris C 11787)

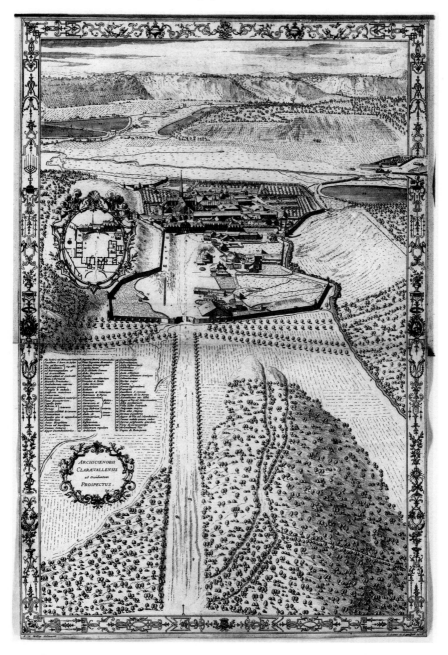

94. Milley, View of Clairvaux, engraving by C. Lucas, 1708 (Photo: Bibliothèque Nationale de France, Paris C 11785)

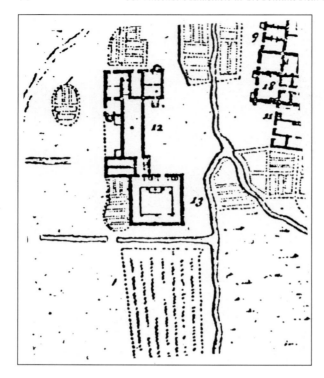

95. (left) Milley, Plan of Clairvaux, engraving by C. Lucas, 1708, detail: the old monastery (after Milley, Plan of Clairvaux. Photo: Bibliothèque Nationale de France, Paris C 11787)

96. (below) Milley, View of Clairvaux, engraving by C. Lucas, 1708, detail: the old monastery (after Milley, View of Clairvaux.(Photo: Bibliothèque Nationale de France, Paris C 11785)'

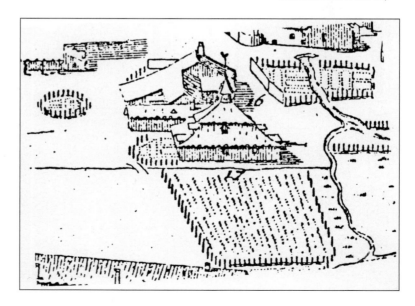

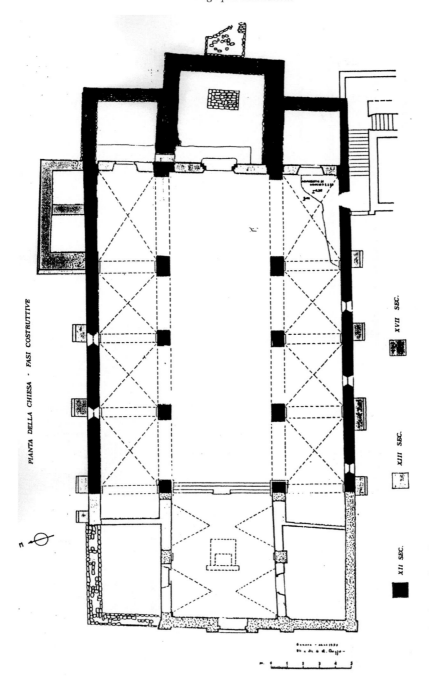

97. Tiglietto, plan of church (after Pio F. Pistilli. 'Santa Maria di Tiglietto: prima fondazione cistercense in Italia (1120)'. *Arte Medievale* 2 serie, 4,1 (1990) Tav. 2)

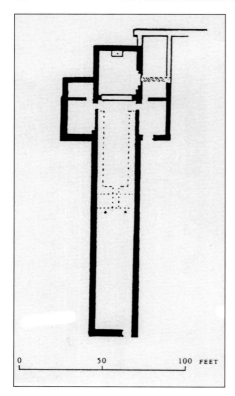

98. Waverley, plan of church. Peter Fergusson, *Architecture of Solitude.* Princeton: Princeton University Press, 1984, fig. 3.

99. Clairvaux, plan of church, after c.1135. Frédéric Van der Meer. *Atlas de l'Ordre Cistercien.* Paris-Brussels: Editions Sequoia, 1965, fig. 13

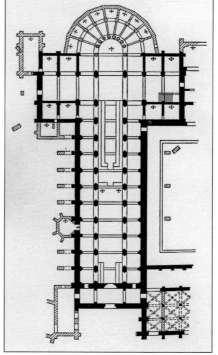

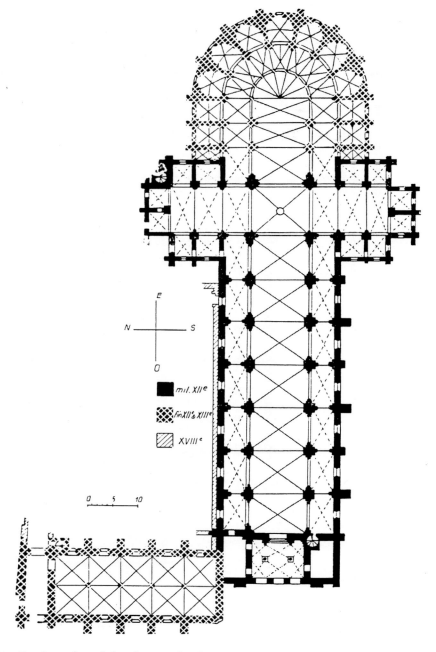

100. Pontigny, plan of church. Marcel Aubert. *L'architecture cistercienne en France.* Paris: Vanoest, 1947. 1: Fig. 89.

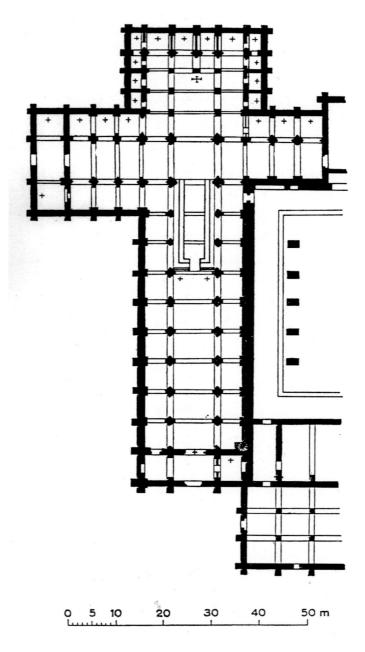

0   5 10   20   30   40   50 m

101. Cîteaux II (1193), plan of church. Frédéric Van der Meer. *Atlas de l'Ordre Cistercien.*
Paris-Brussels: Editions Sequoia, 1965, fig. 9

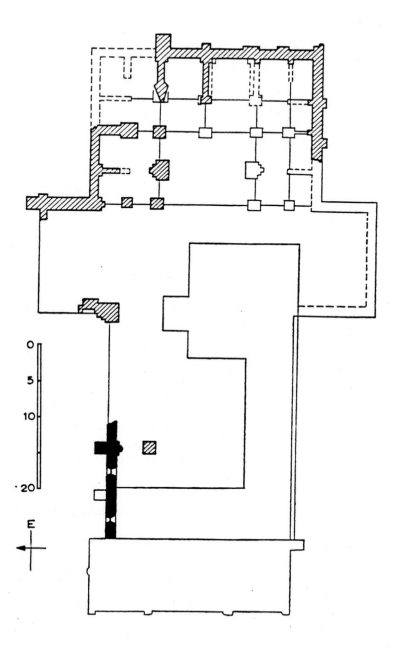

102. Morimond, plan of church, after Henri-Paul Eydoux, 1958, Frédéric Van der Meer. *Atlas de l'Ordre Cistercien.* Paris-Brussels: Editions Sequoia, 1965, fig. 8

103. Le Thoronet, plan of church and monastery. Anselme Dimier, *L'art cistercien: France*, 3rd ed. La Nuit des Temps, 16. Paris: Zodiaque, 1982, p. 191

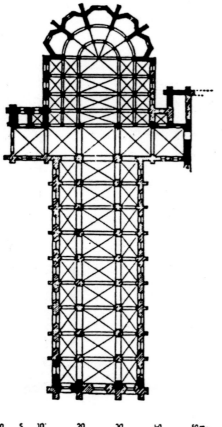

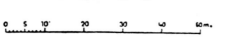

104. Ourscamp, plan of church. Anselme Dimier. *L'art cistercien: France*. 3rd ed. La Nuit des Temps, 16. Paris: Zodiaque, 1982, p. 48

105. Alcobaça, plan of east end of church (after Camilo de Paiva Soares. Artur Gusmao. *A real aba-dia de Alcobaça, estudo histórico-ar-queológico*. Lisbon: Editora Ulisseia, 1948, p. 77)

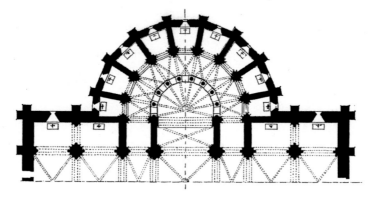

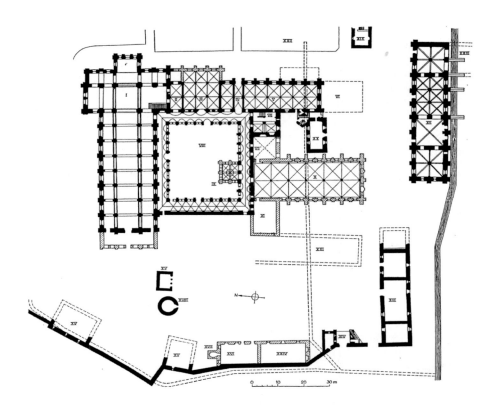

106. Fontenay, plan of church and monastery: I: Church; II: Sacristy; III: Chapter Room; IV: Corridor; V: Monks' Room; VI: Fish-pond; VII: Calefactory; VIII: Cloister; IX: Lavabo; X: Refectory: XI: Kitchen; XII: Forge; XIII: Guest House; XIV: Gatehouse; XV: Outbuildings; XVI: Bakery; XVII: Oven; XVIII: Dovecote; XIX: Infirmary; XX: Prison; XXI: Cellar; XXII: Herbarium; XXIII: Mill; XXIV: Public Chapel (after René Aynard, Frédéric Van der Meer, *Atlas de l'Ordre Cistercien.* Paris-Brussels: Editions Sequoia, 1965, fig. 6).